The Rise of Neoliberalism in Advanced Capitalist Economies

Also by M.C. Howard and J.E. King

THE POLITICAL ECONOMY OF MARX

A HISTORY OF MARXIAN ECONOMICS, VOLUMES I AND II

THE ECONOMICS OF MARX (*eds*)

Books by M.C. Howard

CLASSICAL AND MARXIAN POLITICAL ECONOMY (*ed.*)

MODERN THEORIES OF INCOME DISTRIBUTION

PROFITS IN ECONOMIC THEORY

Books by J.E. King

RELATIVE INCOME SHARES

TEN PER CENT AND NO SURRENDER: The Preston Strike 1853–4

ECONOMIC EXILES

LABOUR ECONOMICS

A HISTORY OF POST KEYNESIAN ECONOMICS SINCE 1936

The Rise of Neoliberalism in Advanced Capitalist Economies

A Materialist Analysis

M.C. Howard
Department of Economics, University of Waterloo, Canada

J.E. King
Department of Economics and Finance, La Trobe University, Australia

palgrave
macmillan

First published 2008 by
PALGRAVE MACMILLAN
Houndmills, Basingstoke, Hampshire RG21 6XS and
175 Fifth Avenue, New York, N.Y. 10010
Companies and representatives throughout the world

PALGRAVE MACMILLAN is the global academic imprint of the Palgrave Macmillan division of St. Martin's Press, LLC and of Palgrave Macmillan Ltd. Macmillan® is a registered trademark in the United States, United Kingdom and other countries. Palgrave is a registered trademark in the European Union and other countries.

ISBN-13: 978–0–230–53703–3 hardback
ISBN-10: 0–230–53703–0 hardback

This book is printed on paper suitable for recycling and made from fully managed and sustained forest sources. Logging, pulping and manufacturing processes are expected to conform to the environmental regulations of the country of origin.

A catalogue record for this book is available from the British Library.

Library of Congress Cataloging-in-Publication Data
Howard, Michael Charles, 1945–
The rise of neoliberalism in advanced capitalist economies:a materialist analysis/M.C. Howard, J.E. King.
p. cm.
Includes bibliographical references and index.
ISBN 0–230–53703–0 (alk. paper)
1. Neoliberalism. 2. Capitalism. 3. Economics—History.
I. King, J. E. (John Edward) II. Title.
HB95.H69 2007
330.12′2—dc22 2007050060

10 9 8 7 6 5 4 3 2 1
17 16 15 14 13 12 11 10 09 08

Printed and bound in Great Britain by
CPI Antony Rowe, Chippenham and Eastbourne

Contents

Preface

The argument made in this book concerning the causes of neoliberalism in advanced capitalism appeared first in an article with the same title, which was published in *International Papers in Political Economy* in 2002. The argument has now been considerably refined and significantly buttressed but it remains the same argument: the most persuasive account of neoliberalism in advanced capitalist economies is provided by historical materialism.

In writing both the article and this book, we have accumulated a large number of debts to people who provided us with comments on what we wrote, and to organisations who supplied funding and facilities to support the writing. We thank Richard Bodell, Tom Bramble, Jim and Tiina Brox, Christina Fader, John Henry, Ed Kaptein, Ramesh Kumar, Euclid Tsakalotos and Mary Ann Vaughan for comments. We also thank the Social Science and Humanities Research Council of Canada for providing a research grant aiding the completion of the book, and The Netherlands Institute for Advanced Study in the Humanities and Social Sciences for accepting Michael Howard as Fellow in Residence for the academic year of 2004/5, during which many of the chapters were written.

The argument as a whole, and several components of the argument, were presented to various audiences at conferences and universities in Australia, Cuba, several European countries, the United States and the United Kingdom during the past 7 years, and we are grateful to the participants for their observations and criticisms. Very great thanks are also due to Donna Schultz of the Department of Economics at the University of Waterloo, who provided extensive secretarial services and always with great efficiency and good humour.

Michael Howard
John King

Introduction

I.1 What is neoliberalism?

According to Perry Anderson,

> ... the novelty of the present situation stands out in historical view. It can be put like this. For the first time since the Reformation, there are no longer any significant oppositions – that is, systematic rival outlooks – within the thought-world of the West; and scarcely any on a world scale either, if we discount religious doctrines as largely inoperative archaisms, as the experiences of Poland or Iran indicate we may. Whatever limitations persist to its practice, neo-liberalism as a set of principles rules undivided across the globe: the most successful ideology in world history.[1]

The ideology is that all, or virtually all, economic and social problems have a market solution, or a solution in which market processes will figure prominently. Proponents of neoliberalism do not always regard markets as perfect, but they negate their recognition of market failure by arguing that state failure is typically far worse. The practice is the continuing application of this doctrine to an ever expanding area of life in the real world, through the privatisation of state companies and public services, loosened regulation of private economic activity, the elimination of 'dependency cultures' through the reform of welfare programmes and taxation systems, and the introduction of market-mimicking arrangements to those areas where genuine markets are inappropriate.

Neoliberalism is still an ongoing process, not a fully realised state of affairs anywhere in the world. And it takes a variety of forms in different types of economy. In this book we focus solely on the advanced capitalist economies of the West and say virtually nothing about those of the poor South or the transitional East.[2] This reflects our view that neoliberalism works out very differently in advanced capitalism than it does elsewhere. And it is crucial to understand neoliberalism in the West because it has been a phenomenon generated internally, rather than having been imposed from outside as has frequently been the case for the less-developed economies. Thus from our materialist perspective if the poorer nations were to become really rich in the near future (which is in fact very unlikely) there are good reasons for believing that the present set of advanced capitalist economies show to them 'the image of their own future'.[3]

I.2 Neoliberalism, classical liberalism and the postwar 'mixed economy'

One theme which runs throughout this book is that neoliberalism in the advanced capitalist economies is an outcome of developments in the twentieth century, not a return to the practices of the nineteenth. In short, neoliberalism is not a rebirth of classical liberalism but is a genuine successor to the 'mixed economy' that prevailed for over 30 years after World War Two, even though we will also argue below that it does represent a discontinuity in postwar history.

Classical liberalism is the more comprehensive set of ideas. At its core are principles of individualism, voluntary contracting, small government and the rule of law, with an emphasis on the importance of civil rights rather than democratic or social rights.[4] In contrast, neoliberalism is a considerably more specialised set of ideas, proclaiming the efficiency of markets over other mechanisms of coordination and disciplining.

Classical liberal states were strong but small. By historical standards, they had immense power, but they treated their public responsibilities restrictively, expenditures were modest, and the administrative reach of these states was still significantly limited.[5] In advanced capitalism today, states are very different and are likely to stay that way. They, too, are strong states, but they are considerably larger, raising between a third and two-thirds of GDP in taxation,[6] which is used to finance a huge range of services, and states in advanced capitalism administratively penetrate their societies to an unprecedented degree. Neoliberalism is unlikely to change this dramatically, because most of what is provided by states has pronounced public-good features and is crucial to the operation of modern capitalist economies. And mass democracy, itself functional to advanced capitalism,[7] provides majoritarian political support for this to continue.

Unlike classical liberalism, neoliberalism recognises that political agencies must frequently act as financiers, supervisors and regulators of markets and marketisation. Thus neoliberalism does not entail a massively reduced 'weight' for states or a reduction in their core powers. What is emphasised by neoliberals is that state activity must be significantly restructured and redirected. Political authorities will continue to raise substantial amounts in taxation and to finance, and supervise and regulate a very broad range of goods and services. But the goods and services will be provided more by private corporations, and, if provision remains public, will be delivered through markets or market-mimicking mechanisms.

This will entail *inter alia* many of the traditional professions dissolving into more complex sets of roles, where tasks are reassigned to the appropriate skill level in a new structure of occupations. Modern information technology facilitates this to an extraordinary degree. For example, paramedics and paralegals joined to appropriately programmed computers can frequently yield much more accurate medical diagnoses and forecasts of legal judgement than can the current vintage of fully trained medical doctors and lawyers. Likewise with professors. University lectures and student assignments can be communicated worldwide from a few locations, and market provision of many services is already well advanced. A similar process of deprofessionalisation is presently transforming state bureaucracies, and is poised to do so to an even greater extent. Thus, even for services that continue to be provided by the public sector, not only will they be allocated in a market-like fashion, but those who do the allocating will also be more suited to function in such markets. So the professions which constituted much of the civil society of classical liberalism will be hardly recognisable, and any professional autonomy they exercised will significantly diminish as market dependence extends its sway.[8]

This reconstruction of state services and the professions associated with them will make the public sector more closely resemble the private sector in advanced capitalism. Those aspects of welfare states most at variance with market dependence will contract and those contributing to the productivity of the workforce will expand. At the same time the services themselves will change to conform to consumer requirements for customised products. Affluence makes a 'one size fits all' practice increasingly anachronistic in health care, education and social security. Here, as in consumer markets more generally, preferences for differentiated products can be expected to strengthen.

Market mechanisms and the personnel appropriate to market contexts, along with a greater variety of services, will therefore increase. But it is wholly inaccurate to characterise these processes as a triumph of 'free markets'. There are no significant examples of legitimate free markets left in advanced capitalist economies. All markets are now substantially regulated, and a trend towards more markets will be accompanied by yet more regulation,[9] designed to counter information asymmetries, control fraud and limit negative spillover effects. It is not that these problems were absent from the era of classical liberalism, but the enhanced complexity of most goods and services and of social interdependencies, coupled with enlarged state capacities and resources, means both that there are many more powerful interests demanding regulations and that it is much more economical to supply them. However, unlike much of the past, regulations in the neoliberal age are orientated towards promoting and managing markets, rather than containing or eliminating them.[10]

Thus, both in terms of the delivery of public goods and the regulation of the private sector, neoliberal changes are not a return to classical liberalism. Rather, as we argue throughout this book, neoliberalism is a liberalisation undertaken on the basis of changes brought about by economic development during the twentieth century and by the 'age of extremes', where wars and depressions accentuated and accelerated the development of regulation, welfare policies and democratic rights.[11] The central point is that neoliberalism is a result not of an autonomous 'change of heart', or of an increased or decreased 'enlightenment' among those who wield political power, but of material development: the increasing sophistication of the productive forces and the economic requirements for their continued development.

Nonetheless, we do not view neoliberalism in advanced capitalism as simply a continuation of the liberalising trend evident since the end of the Second World War. It is true that, with the return of peace between the capitalist great powers, markets massively expanded, as did international trade. Restrictions on financial transactions were also progressively relaxed.[12] During the same period the chief political competitors to liberalism moved closer to their opponent: social democratic parties continued to make their peace with capitalism,[13] and most conservatives accommodated themselves to mass democracy and the welfare state.[14]

However, it is also true that an important discontinuity occurred with neoliberalism. Prior to the 1970s, liberalisation took place within structures and cultures that exhibited a strong Keynesian character. As we argue in Chapters 2, 3, 4, 5 and 7, politics appeared to be dominant over economics, organised labour was powerful and state activism was sufficiently popular to counter market dependency when it threatened the social rights of citizenship. Expenditures on social programmes as a percentage of national income rose in advanced capitalism throughout the postwar period, and extensive regulation embraced virtually all sectors of all economies. Both tendencies were regarded as countering markets as much as supporting them. Most advanced economies also included a large publicly owned sector providing infrastructural goods and services, substantial financial repression remained present everywhere, and leading economists of every school believed there to be a long-term market-elimination tendency in capitalist development. All this facilitated institutional variation between different capitalist economies, and there was a significant degree of autonomy in national economic policies. 'Command', 'Voice' and 'Planning' were substituted for markets on an extensive scale.[15] Modern economies were 'mixed economies', with the strictly capitalist parts sometimes appearing to have a subordinate role in the mix. And all this was widely viewed as stable because it was efficient, popular and easily justified in ways that brought conciliation of all significant interests.[16]

Virtually all of this has now disappeared, and what remains of the parts inhibiting markets and market dependency seems vulnerable to elimination. A new conception of the state, and many other non-market organisations, has emerged in which their most important task is seen to be the support and extension of markets, including in their own activities. And today there is considerably less diversity between advanced capitalist economies, since a great deal of convergence to a neoliberal standard has already occurred. These changes began in the 1970s, and widened and deepened in subsequent decades. Thus, in our view, neoliberalism is distinct from earlier postwar liberalisation, and we believe it is important to explain why it began in the 1970s and not before (or later).

I.3 Neoliberalism, globalisation and the politics of the 'New Right'

Globalisation and the politics of the 'New Right' play a subsidiary role in the story we have to tell. For us the current phase of globalisation is a consequence of the same materialist forces that underpin neoliberalism and is best viewed as one dimension of this phenomenon.[17] The chief reason why globalisation may appear to be more significant is that the process of extending neoliberalism in international relations has strong positive feedback effects. The material causes promoting neoliberalism also promote globalisation, but globalisation reacts back and reinforces the process of marketisation.[18] So it sometimes makes sense to see the proximate causes of particular neoliberal measures in globalisation.

Nor is neoliberalism synonymous with the rise of the New Right, important though the Thatcher and Reagan governments were in promoting neoliberal measures. Many centre-left parties have actually carried out neoliberal programmes too,[19] and intellectuals identified with the Left have been prominent in constructing neoliberal ideology.[20] As the passage from Perry Anderson that opens this chapter indicates, neoliberalism is today very much consensus politics in the advanced capitalist economies.

More generally, all the changes in economic and political relations that characterise neoliberalism, including the development of globalisation and 'new right politics', the privatisation and deregulation of economic activity, the decline of unions and transformation of 'Left' political parties and the restructuring of welfare programmes and taxation systems, form a loop of causation in which each component tends to reinforce the others. The key question for understanding neoliberalism as a whole, then, is what determines the loop itself. In other words, the really important problem is to explain why the loop of institutional interdependencies takes a neoliberal form rather than a form of another kind. Our answer is materialist, and is outlined in Section I.5 below.

I.4 Why neoliberalism matters

This is one reason why neoliberalism is important: it describes an unusual political situation in which there has been a convergence of centre-left and centre-right political parties to a new principle of governance. Both socialist hostility to markets and conservative unease about market excess have largely evaporated, or have been revalued. And this is so despite the fact that these traditional positions were well-founded. Socialists have correctly recognised markets as countering their aspiration for communal control of all social processes, so that they can be consciously fashioned to achieve genuinely human objectives, and as promoting inequality in income and wealth.[21] Conservatives have regarded markets with suspicion, again correctly, for their socially atomising effects, and the egalitarian and vulgarising consequences that they induce in culture, and as a result have seen the need for political management to restrict their domain.[22] Thus, whether considering contemporary politics in advanced capitalism or the intellectual traditions from which they have emerged, neoliberalism matters a great deal.

From a managerial perspective, the extent to which markets prevail, and the conditions under which they operate, is important because they are a system of coordination which can malfunction. Orthodox neoclassical economics is famous (or infamous) for demonstrating the efficiency properties of markets. But it has also shown how the 'invisible hand' can fail.[23] This analysis has been supplemented and eclipsed by Keynesian[24] and Post Keynesian theory.[25] All these systems of thought point to the potential fragility of finance organised on a neoliberal basis. Finance is not like other goods and services, as we explain at several points in this book.[26] Its capacity for generating crises that affect all other sectors of the economy is second to none. In our view, if neoliberalism in advanced capitalism suffers a reversal in the near future the most likely cause will be a financial crisis.[27]

I.5 How we explain neoliberalism

Our explanation of neoliberalism in advanced capitalism is based on historical materialism. It recognises that there are multiple causes, but also that they form a hierarchy of importance. The most fundamental are the developmental requirements of the productive forces, which include science and technology, and the least significant emanate from ideologies. Although this materialist stance originated with liberal theorists in the eighteenth century, it became associated with Marxism in the nineteenth. And that is the tradition in which we locate ourselves. We hasten to add, however, that we use the ideas of Marx rather than seeking to be faithful to them.[28] Some themes which are undoubtedly important in Marxism, such as class struggle, do not figure prominently, and other important ideas, such as those concerning human freedom, do not make an appearance. Moreover, some considerations raised by critics of Marx, especially by Max Weber and the significance he gave to war and geopolitics, are central to our argument. So the historical materialism we employ is a mongrel breed, and we feel no need to make apologies for this.

A materialist explanation of neoliberalism is usually associated with the ideologists of business and the 'information age', where the neoliberal expansion of markets is seen to be rooted in innovative new technologies. Virtually every magazine devoted to business issues is full of this, and we accept much of what is said as correct. It is, for example, obvious how the internet has expanded markets, both globally and within advanced capitalist economies. But our materialism is not actually a form of technological determinism (as we explain in Section 1.1 of

Chapter 1). Nor, insofar as it does consider technology, does it focus wholly on the new technologies of the information age. Furthermore, it explicitly recognises the effects that economic and political factors have had in bringing about the neoliberal age.

However, we do regard the existing explanations of neoliberalism cast in terms of economic and political factors as flawed. Most particularly, what has become the orthodoxy of the Left is deficient. The emphasis here is placed upon the decline in profitability that engulfed advanced capitalism in the late 1960s. This, it is claimed, activated property owners to pressure and support state policies seeking to break the power of the organised working class, and restore the profitability of capital through neoliberal reforms.[29] Again we can accept the facts upon which this account is based, but the interpretation fits Britain and New Zealand far better than Western and Central Europe or the United States.[30] And it fails to explain why the working class was defeated so easily, and remained defeated in the ensuing decades. Nor is it explained why the instruments of defeat were neoliberal policies rather than a resort to extra-economic disciplinary measures. Finally, the abandonment of Social Democratic principles in favour of neoliberalism by the political parties of the Left throughout advanced capitalism hardly fits with this class struggle perspective.[31]

Geopolitical explanation of neoliberalism emphasising the dominant role played by the United States in advanced capitalism, and the moves it made from the 1970s to restructure its hegemony through neoliberal measures, are on much firmer ground.[32] This theme plays a central role in our historical account of the onset of neoliberalism in Chapter 7. Nonetheless, we would again stress the limitations of this position if it is regarded as locating the principal cause of neoliberalism. Despite the immense influence exercised by the United States in the postwar years, it too was affected by materialist forces that it could not control, and it is these forces that prompted the restructuring of US hegemony.

The weakest explanations of neoliberalism are those concentrating on the role of ideas.[33] We do not dispute that people face choices and make decisions, and that actions involve ideas. But recognising these elementary facts says nothing about the origin of ideas, or their truth, or their motivations and consequences. For us, the kind of ideas that are relevant for explaining neoliberalism are actually more determined than determining, and their effects are frequently unintended rather than intended, as we explain at various points in this book.[34] We devote the whole of Part II to examining the ideas of leading economists and show that no principal school of thought actually anticipated neoliberalism.[35] Instead they all emphasised the importance of tendencies towards the elimination of markets: put simply, they were all wrong. This would seem to be as close as it is possible to get to a definitive refutation of claims stressing the causal role of economic ideas in bringing neoliberalism to advanced capitalism.

I.6 What we argue

The two chapters of Part I argue that historical materialism is the best available theory for understanding the broad contours of economic development. Historical materialism has long been regarded as the intellectually strongest dimension of Marxian analysis, even by critics who have shown serious deficiencies in the original specification. We seek to reformulate the theory to avoid most of the problems, and we maintain that those which remain diminish with economic development itself. In other words, the applicability of the theory improves as growth in productive power actually takes place. This makes historical materialism especially relevant for comprehending neoliberalism in the advanced capitalist countries.

Neoliberalism is also significant in intellectual history because it constitutes a refutation of much social and economic thought in the twentieth century. As we show in Part II, Marxian, Keynesian, institutional and neoclassical economists all believed that there was a trend towards the elimination of markets. Weberian analysts of increasing bureaucratisation have also been confounded, along with Parsonion advocates of the 'logic of industrialism' and 'new class theorists' such as James Burnham. Even Frederick von Hayek, who became identified with neoliberalism in the 1970s, had previously believed that markets were being rolled back by increasingly powerful states on a 'road to serfdom'. Neoliberalism in reverse, in fact.

There is no disguising that this failure constitutes a serious indictment of several leading schools of economics and political economy. Nonetheless, those who mistakenly believed in market elimination had good reasons for arguing as they did, as we show in Chapter 5. There actually were strong forces operating in capitalism during the nineteenth and much of the twentieth centuries that worked to reduce the significance of markets. The key point is, however, that there were also forces promoting markets, and these ultimately dominated, as we document in Chapter 6. From this perspective, the weaknesses of those economists whom we discuss in Part II were partial, in that they focussed on only one set of influences and neglected the other.

Chapter 7 then asks why these market-promoting forces triumphed when they did and not before (or later). It examines the history of the postwar years and explains how market-promoting influences were confined by the effects of two World Wars, the intervening Great Depression and the Cold War which followed. These great events restrained neoliberalism but became progressively weaker as a consequence of economic development, and were finally broken by the restructuring of American hegemony in the face of the multiple crises that characterised the world economy during the 1970s. Our argument here is consistent with the materialist theory outlined in Part I, and represents a further indictment of the economists discussed in Part II, who either failed to appreciate the enduring effects of depression and war or misdiagnosed them. Material forces always act as determinants of economic relations, political structures and social consciousness in a constrained fashion, where the two principal constraints stem from human needs for security and group identity. This points exactly to the importance of the counteracting forces associated with the 'short twentieth century' or 'age of extremes'.[36] Depression and war brought a significant expansion, or preservation, of collectivist institutions, and it was only with their receding impact, coupled with significant changes in productive and military technologies, that the constraining forces ceased to be so binding.

Our materialist explanation of neoliberalism therefore takes three forms. First, in Chapters 1 and 2 we outline historical materialism as a theory of economic systems in general and a theory of capitalist economic systems in particular. In this theory, economic development is explained in terms of a set of forces that have operated throughout human history, and the rise of neoliberal capitalism is shown to be the result of the specific character taken by these materialist forces in the period preceding it. The central claim is that neoliberal capitalism is more suited to fostering further development of productive power in advanced capitalism than are alternative institutional structures. Second, in Chapters 3–6 our focus changes to intellectual history, and we provide a materialist account of the development of neoliberalism by critically examining the ideas of economists and illuminating their mistakes in claiming that there was a tendency for advanced capitalist economies to experience market elimination – the exact opposite of what occurred with the onset of neoliberalism. Third, in Chapter 7 we provide a historical account of the onset of neoliberalism in advanced capitalism which stresses the importance of the contradictions inherent in the institutions prevalent in the postwar era, and the crises these contradictions spawned in the 1970s. All three forms of explanation are consistent with each other and represent but different perspectives on the same materialist causes of neoliberalism in advanced capitalism.

Chapter 8, the final chapter of the book, probes the question of what might reverse neoliberalism. We endeavour to be cautious in the light of the previous forecasting errors of so many eminent economists. But our materialist theory does provide some clues as to what is likely to reverse neoliberalism in the future. We explain why the most immediate threat to neoliberalism stems from financial crises, and government attempts to contain them. The deregulation of finance is the weakest link in all of neoliberalism, and any serious crisis here will certainly engender a partial reversal. But there are other factors that could have more pronounced and comprehensive effects over the longer term, including changes in the bias of technical change, environmental deterioration as a result of global warming, new imperial wars, and political opposition induced by the distributional consequences of neoliberalism.

Part I

Historical Materialism: A Theory of Economic Systems

1
A General Theory of Economic Systems

1.1 The nature of historical materialism

Our explanation of neoliberalism in advanced capitalism is cast in terms of historical materialism, and the explanation takes place at three different levels of generality. In this chapter, we make a case for historical materialism being applicable to all of human history, followed in the next chapter with the case for historical materialism limited to the capitalist era. Then, in the remainder of the book, and especially in Chapters 5–8, there follows the application of historical materialism to advanced capitalism at the end of the twentieth century and the beginning of the twenty-first century. The aim is to strengthen our argument sequentially, by lowering the level of abstraction in two stages. We claim that there are good arguments in favour of historical materialism as a general theory of economic systems, but they are strengthened if their explanatory range is confined to capitalist economic systems, and further strengthened if limited to contemporary advanced capitalism.

Historical materialism, of course, is associated with Marxism, and especially with the view that all political and cultural phenomena can be reduced to 'the economic' or to 'the technological' and, moreover, that the inevitable culmination of the historical process will be socialism. As a consequence it has been subject to ridicule and abuse as well as to serious criticism, and this has brought successive reformulations of the theory. We will deal with the criticism at many points and begin here, in the opening section of this chapter, with a commentary on some of the misunderstandings that have brought dismissals of the theory. This will clarify what we believe historical materialism can best be presented as.

The theory originated not with Karl Marx but with thinkers of the French and Scottish Enlightenment in the eighteenth century, and was especially prominent in the work of Adam Smith.[1] Thus many of its themes were originated by liberal theorists who have had a huge influence quite independently of Marxism. What Marx contributed was a rigorous reconstruction of the theory and a deepening of its explanatory power. But some of the claims made by Marx proved to be exaggerated, or valid only for special cases, and the refinement of historical materialism continued after his death. Significant modifications were made in the early twentieth century in order to incorporate complexities connected with interstate warfare between the great powers.[2] And the experience of these conflicts has motivated various Darwinian renovations of historical materialism, which have reduced some of the explanatory ambitions of the theory while strengthening it against criticisms that would otherwise be very damaging.[3] This, in turn, has facilitated more recognition of themes associated with the sociology of Max Weber, who stressed the importance that humans always attach to cultural identity and the pervasiveness of conflict between organised political entities, both of which phenomena he believed to be irreducible to economics and technology.[4] Finally, during the last few decades, the heavy artillery of analytical philosophy has been deployed to provide further conceptual refinement of historical materialism.[5]

To characterise historical materialism as a form of technological determinism or as economic determinism suggests a simplicity that the theory lacks. It does claim that the character of the 'productive forces' explains the character of the economic, political and cultural systems. But, as we will explain, some exceptions can be recognised, and the productive forces are not synonymous with either technology or 'the economic'. Moreover, the type of explanation envisaged is not only consistent with causal reciprocity, but also requires it. Historical materialism proposes a causal primacy for the productive forces because it envisages that they determine the prevailing type of economic system in a *functional* manner. The economic system is as it is in virtue of its capacity to best develop the productive forces in their current form. A similar *functional* causation is claimed by historical materialism to characterise the relation of the economic system and the political sphere. The polity has the character it has because it best consolidates the economic system when it has this character. Thus causation is envisaged as a qualitative hierarchy in which the interaction of technology, economy, politics and culture is actually mandated rather than prohibited. And no claim as to the quantitative significance of the different causal flows has to be defended because none need be made. Moreover, claiming primacy for the productive forces does not negate human activism and choice, or presume a perfectly malleable human nature. Quite the reverse, in fact. Historical materialism recognises that it is always humans who produce and innovate, that they do so intentionally and often rationally, and always as beings with natures that are rooted in biology as well as having characters that invariably take particular cultural forms.

Instead of describing historical materialism as a form of technological determinism, the theory is more appropriately regarded as an account of the systematic interactions that take place between technologies, economies, polities and cultures. But, this said, it is not a genuinely pluralist theory, in which these different parts of social life are treated as having their own causal autonomy, and where no particular parts are regarded as always exercising primacy over others. Such a pluralism appears more fertile than historical materialism because it seems to allow greater explanatory flexibility in dealing with the complexities of the historical process. However, this appearance is misleading. Any theory which genuinely seeks to rival historical materialism does not have any legitimate explanatory flexibility at all, because it has to specify the systematic relationships which exist between the different components of the systems it treats, and, then, on this basis, provide an account of socioeconomic systems different from that of historical materialism. It cannot just observe particular events and use whatever permutation of causal imputations appears to fit best, as many narrative historians seem to do. Sociological stories asserting that in some circumstance 'this' was most important, and in another circumstance 'that' was predominant, without specifying systematically what governs the causal weight of 'this' and 'that', should not be taken much more seriously. Genuinely alternative theories must either dispute the very possibility of social science, on the ground that the type of regularities presumed by historical materialism do not exist in the social world,[6] or else provide a different account of what these regularities are.[7]

It is well to be aware, though, that the centrality of functional causation lends a paradoxical quality to historical materialism. It implies that there is no contradiction in acknowledging that 'everything can influence everything else' while simultaneously accepting that the causation running from the productive forces is unambiguously primary. Moreover, functional causation in historical materialism implies that this is the case because the productive forces are the ultimate determinants of the causal weight of everything else. Thus pointing to circumstances in which, say, it can be agreed that religion is a powerful and all-pervasive influence on everything does not in itself represent a falsification of historical materialism. The doctrine can legitimately claim that, given the character of human nature and the prevailing circumstances, it is the condition of the productive forces that requires religious organisations to play a dominant role because this is the best way of preserving whatever productive power has been developed.[8] (Whether or not this is empirically true, of course, is a different matter. At this point we are concerned only to explain the logical structure of historical materialism.)

Nonetheless, a critic might respond by arguing that the very acceptance of any causal significance for entities that are not part of the productive forces indicates that historical materialism is internally contradictory. Surely, if the forces of production are primary as historical materialism claims, they alone should be causal. Or, at least, they ought to be classified as 'overwhelmingly most important' in some well-defined quantitative sense. The mistake in such a critique is twofold. First, there is the failure to recognise that the nature of functional causation allows assigning a causal primacy that is not quantitative. Second, there is the failure to recognise that the statement 'the productive forces are primary' is a shortened form of the statement, 'the productive forces are primary subject to various constraints, some of which stem ultimately from human nature'. Recognising the constraint posed by human nature allows those phenomena stressed by pluralists to carry a degree of causal weight in historical materialism because human nature includes the capacity for violence and the need to find meaning in life, along with the drive to overcome scarcity. Thus where historical materialism differs from any genuine historiographical pluralism is not in denying that human conflicts and legitimations are causally important, but in adding the claim that they are important because they are required for the development of the productive forces in conditions where human beings are as they are (rather than how we might wish them to be, or how they believe themselves to be).

However, historical materialism is not just a theory of the type of interactions that occur between material and social phenomena; it is also a theory of historical directionality. Although reversals and stasis are accepted as possibilities in particular cases, historical materialism claims that overall productive power does tend to increase through time. And it also claims that associated with this increase the areas of the world in which 'law and order' prevail expand, that interactions between people become more extensive and that human cultural heterogeneity declines. Behind all these trends is the transhistorical tendency for labour productivity to rise as a result of the predominance of economic needs, or of other needs that bring about the same outcome less directly. Marxists have also typically believed that the culmination of this process would be socialism, and on this they appear to have been hugely mistaken. Historical materialism certainly allows for the possibility that the Marxists could, ultimately, turn out to be correct, but, in our view, the material and social conditions required to make this so are unlikely to occur. Today, those interested in promoting socialism often do so on grounds quite independent of historical materialism, and the theory itself strongly suggests they will fail.[9]

It is also important to recognise that historical materialism is not intended to be a theory of everything.[10] It views technologies, social formations and historical processes from a particular perspective, and many phenomena are outside its field of vision. The concern is with 'big structures, large processes and huge comparisons'[11] and much less with any specific sequences of occurrences. Above all, the focus is on how economic systems rise and fall accordingly as they foster or fetter the development of human productive power. The mechanisms through which this is said to occur leave space for many particular chronologies of events, as we will explain in Section 1.7 below. Moreover, while historical materialism claims that the developmental requirements of the productive forces are primary in determining the type of economic system that prevails, and the type of economic system is primary in determining political and cultural forms, these claims do not rule out autonomous developments in political and cultural phenomena. Historical materialism only requires that they be those that best promote the productive forces or, if they are not, that they will be subject to mechanisms of change that will make them functional for doing so. In other words, there is no requirement that political and cultural characteristics in any society be directly caused by, or 'reflect', technological or economic relations. Rather, historical materialism needs to claim only that there will be mechanisms present that 'select' political and cultural forms to ensure they are appropriate for the development of the productive forces. And, in the case where political and cultural characteristics have no influence on the productive forces or on the economic system, historical materialism does not comment on what forms they might take.

The very ambitiousness of the theory makes its justification (and also its criticism) a particularly difficult task. Historical materialism seeks to provide an account of some important features of the historical process as a whole and, since there is only one such process, there are special obstacles in the way of assessing the causal importance of particular variables. Moreover, historical materialists maintain that the chief characteristics of the historical process – the increase in productive power, the enlargement of pacified areas of the world, the expansion of human interactions, the decline in cultural heterogeneity – are inevitable, so that alternative trajectories of development have to be shown to be impossible, no matter how seemingly likely they appear to have been.[12] As a result of these two problems – justifying causal importance and causal necessity – reliance is often placed on the properties of human nature: the needs, capacities, potentials and vulnerabilities of the human species, and what they make imperative and what they preclude in various material environments. There is no need to apologise for this, because there is no other way of arguing for (or against) the theory once the implications of the empirical data are exhausted. Nonetheless, it is the case that arguments cast in terms of human nature have an especially speculative character.[13] It follows that evaluations of historical materialism must be tentative, because decisive arguments are not available and are unlikely ever to be available. (The same judgement, of course, applies to any other theories of the same breadth.)

Nonetheless, the case for historical materialism does not rest solely on what we say about human nature and the environment in which it operates. In addition, there is an appeal to those mechanisms that 'select' the economic system which best develops the productive forces, and which 'selects' the political forms that best support the economic system, and so on. These mechanisms may be assessed quite independently of what we say about human nature. It may be agreed that what we say about them in Section 1.7 is correct without any commitment to what we say about human nature. And the converse holds too. So our argument in favour of historical materialism is of two types. They do not contradict each other, but they do not logically entail each other either.

Finally, the propositions of historical materialism outlined below differ from those elucidated in most scholarly works on the subject.[14] Nearly all authorities treat the theory as one claiming there to be a particular sequence of historical stages, through which all societies must pass, and for which there is a definite termination. By contrast, the historical materialism that we defend in this chapter places no limit on stages of development, rejects the idea that all societies will have the same trajectory, and is reticent to pronounce any 'end of history', or even suggest a convergence of all societies to the same condition. Instead, historical materialism is seen as a theory of world history, in which the societies that constitute it are affected differently according to whatever selection mechanisms they are subject. In some societies, the selection mechanisms have operated powerfully and brought sustained productive development. This is most obviously true in the case of capitalism, as we argue at length in Chapter 2. In other societies, selection mechanisms have usually operated more weakly in developing the productive forces and, in some, it has only been encounters with more productively developed societies, and more effective military powers, that have brought about a conformity with the propositions of historical materialism. But historical materialism contends that some selection mechanisms have always been in operation somewhere in all of world history, and that they strengthen and widen in influence under capitalism.

1.2 The propositions of historical materialism

In what has become the canonical statement of historical materialism, Marx wrote:

> In the social production of their existence, men inevitably enter into definite relations, which are independent of their will, namely relations of production appropriate to a given stage in the development of their material forces of production. The totality of these relations of production constitutes the economic structure of society, the real foundation, on which arises a legal and political superstructure and to which correspond definite forms of social consciousness.... At a certain stage of development, the material productive forces of society come into conflict with the existing relations of production or — this merely expresses the same thing in legal terms — with the property relations within the framework of which they have operated hitherto. From forms of development of the productive forces these relations turn into their fetters. Then begins an era of social revolution. The changes in the economic foundation lead sooner or later to the transformation of the whole immense superstructure.... In studying such transformations it is always necessary to distinguish between the material transformation of the economic conditions of production ... and the legal, political, religious, artistic or philosophic — in short, ideological forms in which men become conscious of this conflict and fight it out.[15]

In this chapter and the next, we will depart from some of the assertions made in this passage. As it stands, Marx's famous statement is insufficiently cognizant of the importance of evolutionary ideas, and geopolitical selection mechanisms, that came to prominence in the twentieth century. However, our position is that the basic concepts and ideas in this passage need to be reinterpreted rather than rejected outright.

The productive forces consist of means of production and labour power. The means of production include natural resources and geographic spaces; tools, machines and buildings; and energy, transportation and communication infrastructures. Labour power is taken to mean the productive abilities of people who produce, including their strength, skills and productive knowledge. Thus scientific learning which is useful in production counts as a productive force.[16] The level of development of the productive forces as a whole can be measured by an index of labour productivity, assuming that they are being operated in relationships that constitute 'best practice' combinations. These constitute the *material* relations of production as distinct from the *social* relations of production, but both reflect the fact that labour productivity is raised as a result of the division of labour and cooperation.

The social relations of production are the relations of effective control, or powers, that people have over the productive forces, including the productive abilities of labour.[17] The prefix 'social' refers precisely to the controls that people exercise over each other in production (sometimes through controls over non-human things), and these controls function to facilitate the development of the productive forces by providing incentives (positive and negative) to motivate producers to be productive. 'Economic system' and 'economic structure' are synonyms for the social relations of production. And they are often referred to by what is believed to be their central components, such as wage labour in the case of capitalism or serfdom in the case of feudalism or slavery in the case of slave systems.

The superstructure consists of all those institutions which are crucial to the functioning of the economic system; in particular, these institutions specify ownership rights over the productive forces, which typically constitute analogues of the powers that define the social relations of production. The superstructure is managed by political authorities to consolidate, or stabilise, or legitimise, the productive relations.[18] And the world has always exhibited multiple political authorities because, to date, the limitations of productive power have made a single jurisdiction for all humanity impossible or inefficient. Thus superstructural institutions and relations of production have always had a particular territorial dimension in their definition (even if, prior to modern states, it was not always precisely defined).

'Social consciousness' is a set of ideas and beliefs, rather than a set of institutions. Thus it is not part of the superstructure, although it is closely related to it. These ideas and beliefs are treated as distinct from those of genuine science (even if they are influenced by science) and consist of the understandings that people have as to how economic systems and superstructures actually work. Historical materialists evince no exclusive commitment to human rationality. Indeed, they claim that social consciousness will normally be riddled with errors and biases, which stem from misperceptions of the operation of socioeconomic systems and also from being misperceived differently from different social positions. Furthermore, historical materialists also claim that some of this false consciousness will take an ideological form in the sense of being theoretical constructions specifying the right and proper way the world should work. But, in all cases, the falsity of false consciousness is not judged by any failure to achieve practical objectives. Its falsity is assessed in terms of genuine knowledge. To call false consciousness 'ideological' is to add that the falsity is also endowed with both theoretical elaboration and normative content, so that it justifies particular social conditions in a way that can be shown by social science to be erroneous. Thus ideologies may provide important legitimation for superstructural institutions,[19] but, since people's actions are conditioned by the ideas they have, this implies that their behaviour will typically fall short of being fully rational because their beliefs are not fully rational.[20]

The productive forces are sometimes referred to as *material* forces of production, which denotes that they are to be conceived in their technical or engineering dimensions alone, in abstraction from any social qualities. Since the productive forces include knowledge about production, to call something material is not to contrast it with something mental. In this context, the antonym of material is *social*, so that the forces of production are clearly distinct from the relations of production, the superstructure and social consciousness, as befits a theory which argues that the ultimate explanation of these relations, institutions and ideas lies in the material conditions of life.[21] The relations of production are social in being non-material relations between people that stem from the powers that people have with regard to each other in the operation of the productive forces. These powers are to be thought of as conceptually distinct from their sources, which may well include the institutions of the superstructure.

As we have already mentioned in Section 1.1, historical materialism is also dependent on assumptions about human nature. But in our presentation of the theory, they are conventional rather than idiosyncratic.[22] Thus it is assumed that *ceteris paribus* most people prefer 'more' to 'less' of outputs which are positively valued, and that they will seek to avoid unpleasant tasks, including most forms of labour, and thus need to be motivated by incentives. It is also assumed that people have the capacity to coordinate with others, and will behave in a more orderly manner, and be less opportunistic, if they regard what they do as legitimate and also as a basis for providing meaning to their lives. Furthermore, it is assumed that productive activity is always a cooperative activity because of the enhanced productivity associated with the division of labour, and that the type of order prevailing, along with the meaning assigned to phenomena, always has a social dimension. Thus, while there obviously exist individual people, they are invariably 'grouped' individuals and therefore of a particular social type. Their characteristics – goals, capacities, beliefs and commitments – will be infused with particular attributes arising from the groups of which they are part. 'Self interest' will necessarily involve a defence and promotion of 'the group' because it constitutes a huge part of what people are and is infused with emotion, and perhaps even sacrilised, in that life can hardly be envisaged without it. Not surprisingly, different groups are highly susceptible to conflict. Categorisation in terms of 'insiders' and 'outsiders' tends to be normal, and outsiders tend to be viewed with suspicion and hostility because they represent different principles of coordination, security and meaning, so threatening material interests, the existing institutions affording protection and prevailing emotional commitments. It follows that the development of the productive forces may well involve destructive antagonisms, and progress can take a 'one step backwards, two steps forward' pattern as wars and revolutions destroy old forms of production and create new possibilities. These, in turn, often require new groupings of people and, as a consequence, new divisions.

If these elementary claims are forgotten, much in the picture presented by historical materialism will appear to be in contradiction to its own propositions. In particular, inefficiency and waste in economic and political systems will appear to be pervasive and the result of ghastly mistakes that could have been easily overcome by a more judicious employment of reason and a few doses of moral elevation. Historical materialists certainly do not argue that all events have been unavoidable, but they do believe that the chief causes of human misery and violence, along with the apparent mindlessness that has accompanied them, have not been remediable, given the nature of humans and their environment.[23]

There are six principal propositions of historical materialism.[24] We first outline them briefly and then examine them critically at greater length in the remainder of this section and in the following sections of this chapter. The *development thesis* states that the productive forces have a natural tendency to develop. The *compatibility thesis* maintains that no set of production relations is best suited to all levels of development in the productive forces. The *fettering thesis* adds that, when production relations do inhibit the further development of the productive forces, there will be pressures to change in order to break the fettering, and those pressures will tend to generate crises of various kinds. The *primacy thesis* claims that any compatibility between the productive forces and production relations is achieved by functional adaptation of the productive relations to the development requirements of the productive forces. The *superstructural thesis* declares that the superstructure is as it is because of its capacity to consolidate the productive relations and will change in accordance with this functional requirement. The *uniqueness thesis* avows that all the correspondences in the five preceding theses are unique, so that for any level of the productive forces there is one, and only one, type of production relations that is compatible with the productive forces and one, and only one, type of superstructure that is most suitable to consolidate the production relations.

At this point it is appropriate to ask three questions. To what entities do the concepts and theses of historical materialism apply? What kinds of change do they envisage occurring? What is meant by 'best' in relation to the relations of production being 'best' to develop the productive forces and superstructures being 'best' to consolidate productive relations? For example, in relation to the first question, to what economic systems do the production relations refer: to household, local, regional, national, or continental economies, or the world economy as a whole, or to all forms of economy? The answer hinges on matters which we deal with in Section 1.7, namely the causal mechanisms that select the production relations and superstructures. Historical materialists claim that some set of selection mechanisms will be in operation for all the changes to those entities which can be sensibly described by its concepts. But historical materialists also recognise that the mechanisms operative in any time and place and their range, strength and speed of operation are themselves historically variable, generally increasing in strength along with the productive forces.

This is why we can argue that, while historical materialism is a general theory of economic systems, its accuracy improves when applied solely to capitalism and especially to advanced capitalism. More selection mechanisms operate in accordance with the propositions of historical materialism, and they each operate more strongly and quickly in doing so, while countervailing forces are reduced in power. As a consequence, historical materialism applies increasingly more comprehensively through time. Thus, in this chapter, which deals with historical materialism as a general theory, we argue that its propositions are most persuasive in characterising the historical process as a whole, and that many particular economic systems and their superstructures may be imperfectly portrayed by historical materialism. However, as we also argue in subsequent chapters, with economic development, and especially with the development of capitalism, the propositions of historical materialism more accurately describe a wider array of particular economic systems and their superstructures, as well as the whole historical process. And this becomes even more true in the present era of advanced capitalism.

As to the kind of changes envisaged by the theses of historical materialism, the answer is very broad. They can be reformist or revolutionary changes, type-preserving changes (where the social form remains unchanged) or type-altering changes (where the social form does change), carried out in a peaceful manner or through violence. It is to be expected that changes will be the more peaceful the easier it is to reach enforceable agreements between those affected, while the harder it is to formulate such agreements the more likely it is that force will be employed.[25] This means that, in general, large and type-altering changes will tend to be more violent, and smaller and type-preserving changes more peaceful.

The most obvious way of interpreting what is meant by 'best' in the case of economic systems being best for developing the productive forces, and the superstructure being best to stabilise the economic system, is in the traditional economistic sense of being those which are maximal subject to the prevailing constraints. But such an optimising interpretation would be difficult to justify, because many of the changes considered by historical materialism occur in circumstances of more or less radical uncertainty, where even the estimates of the probable consequences of any action are insecure. People can only act in the light of what they believe to be feasible alternatives, and the results of their actions, whether intended or unintended, will reflect these limitations. Similarly, all strategies of change involve costs, including the costs of prevailing over whatever opposition is provoked in the process, so that the 'best' outcome believed to be available may give way to one which is merely 'satisfactory' and not obviously inferior to feasible alternatives. Furthermore, as already mentioned earlier in this section the claims of historical materialism as to the errors and biases in social consciousness are, if true, further reinforcement for the conclusion that outcomes will fall short of being fully optimal.[26]

1.3 The connections between the productive forces, the productive relations and the superstructure

Before examining the six theses of historical materialism which we outlined in the previous section, it is appropriate to explain more fully what constitutes the productive forces and indicate how they affect the productive relations and agencies of the superstructure. This will show historical materialism to be a more reasonable doctrine than it is commonly supposed to be, because the productive forces cover a broad array of entities, and their connections to the relations of production and superstructure are multiple. The theory is still properly classified as non-pluralist, but these terms do not imply quite the restrictiveness that they are often thought to do.

The physical and mental capabilities of agricultural and manufacturing activities are obvious constituents of the productive forces. So too are the means of transportation and communication. Perhaps less evidently, the productive forces also embrace the technologies of data storage, data processing and data retrieval, along with those of surveillance and monitoring. Furthermore, the productive forces include the productively relevant knowledge and skills of labour, and the processes through which they are learnt. All of these different elements affect the level of aggregate productive power, and all have been the focus of innovative activity to raise productivity beyond the level already attained.

The structure of roles which constitutes the economic system is affected by the productive forces in four principal ways. First, the most elementary influence of the productive forces is on the type of human cooperation that is feasible, because the extent and complexity of cooperation, whether voluntary or coerced, depends so heavily on technologies of transportation, surveillance and monitoring. Second, the productive forces determine the relative efficiency of different types of economic relationships, such as self-provisioning and natural economy, hierarchy and command, or markets of various sorts. For any particular technology, material production can often be carried out in different constellations of economic roles. But they will typically have different costs associated with achieving the same level of output, or the same level of costs will be associated with different levels of output. Then, to say that the productive forces determine the relations of production is to say that they determine which set of roles is most efficient. Providing there is a mechanism that 'selects' this set of roles (in the sense discussed in Section 1.7 below) the productive forces can be said to determine which economic system prevails. And changes in the productive forces can induce a substitution of one type of economic organisation for another because of an alteration in the constellation of economic roles with which it is most efficient to produce.

Third, by determining the overall level of productivity, the productive forces determine the average standard of living and, via the effect on the economic system just discussed, also how the incomes are distributed. Both factors influence what people regard as their needs and, therefore, the composition of outputs produced. Since different outputs involve different processes of production and different economic roles, this is another way in which the productive forces are connected to the economic system. Important sociological characteristics may be involved here, including the degree of communal or privatised consumption and the demand for standardised or customised productions. The supply of various kinds of labour and other inputs may also be affected, because income levels affect the willingness to bear risks and thereby the disposition to specialise in particular economic activities.

Fourth, because the productive forces include the productively relevant knowledge and skills of labour, along with the technologies that inculcate the knowledge and skills, they help determine the type of people involved in the economic system. What is entailed here is far more than the occupational mix; it relates to the character of individuals, including their degree of self-control and time discipline, as well as their capacities to communicate and cooperate with others. All these characteristics will, in turn, affect the kind of production relations that are most productive, and also the type of consumption that will predominate.[27]

The fourfold connections between the productive forces and productive relations also have importance in understanding the superstructure. As defined in the previous section, the superstructure includes the set of rights that function to stabilise the powers which define the roles of the economic system. But rights always have to be enforced by political agencies. These can be organised in various ways, parallel to economic systems, so that the forms of the state and the legal system are hugely affected by the productive forces in ways analogous to those by which the productive forces affect the economic system. Thus the forces of production will have an effect on the superstructure through their determination of what forms are feasible, which are the most efficient, income levels and income distribution, and via the type of people who embody productively relevant knowledge.

We now turn to examine the six theses of historical materialism outlined at the end of Section 1.2.

1.4 The development thesis

The development thesis states that the forces of production have a *natural* tendency to develop, one that does not stem solely from the incentives inherent in the production relations. Or, expressed alternatively, the development thesis suggests that economic systems will typically promote the development of the productive forces because without such a bias no system would prove sustainable in normal circumstances. Sets of production relations that brought about a systematic regression in productive power, or stagnation, would engender or encounter forces promoting change, and these would typically prove irresistible in the long run.

The long run may prove to be very long indeed, especially the further back in history are the cases of apparent stagnation and reversal considered. For example, American and Australasian aboriginals before European colonisation may well have experienced stasis for centuries, if not millennia. Colonisation, of course, eliminated or marginalised these less productive forms, but it had to await the development of relatively sophisticated transportation technology and weaponry. Another obvious example is the 'Dark Ages' after the collapse of the Roman Empire in the West. Here, there were other mechanisms generating endogenous processes of change, and leading to recovery and a return to economic growth, but they, too, took many centuries to have their effects.[28] Thus the development thesis is best interpreted as a 'tendency law' when applied to individual economic systems, where apparent exceptions in particular places and times may occur. However, as productive power rises, and especially with the onset of capitalism, the mechanisms selecting the economic systems that are most suited to develop the productive forces do increase in scope and strength so that even the apparent exceptions become less evident.[29] And throughout human history, development tendencies have never been completely crushed or blocked. There have always been some areas where productive power rose through time.

G.A. Cohen's description of the transhistorical human nature underpinning the development thesis has proved to be especially influential. He regards human beings as naturally having intelligence, being somewhat rational and living in circumstances of scarcity, so that they possess both the motivation and the capacities to do what is necessary to improve the productive forces.[30] However, as Cohen himself recognises, there are three grounds for doubting that this is sufficiently powerful to justify the development thesis. First, human nature is a broader set of capacities, needs, potentials and vulnerabilities, some of which may counter, and perhaps override, those operating in favour of productive improvement. Second, intelligence, rationality and scarcity can underpin predacity as well as production, and this might annul any tendency to develop the productive forces. Third, since the effects of human nature are always mediated by economic, political and cultural relations, it is conceivable that these might block the natural inclinations of humans to develop the productive forces. We consider each of these problems in turn.

As we have already stressed in Section 1.2, historical materialists acknowledge that there is much more to human nature than rationality and intelligence, because economic systems are recognised as being in need of superstructures and as affecting social consciousness. Thus historical materialists can admit the human requirement for legitimacy and for meaning without compromising their claims. And the enforcement of property rights obviously involves coercion, while it is known that social change sometimes takes place via the use of force, so that the human capacity for violence is also no embarrassment to historical materialism. Moreover, there is a plausible argument as to why the motivations for improving productive power springing from human nature will normally prove to be dominant over contrary tendencies. Physical nature has intrinsic properties that are immune to alteration by the human imagination, and for humans to survive they must adjust to this nature in ways that allow its manipulation. It is quite the reverse with regard to the imposition of meaning on the human condition. The only source for this imputation is the human imagination, so that cultural systems have many more degrees of freedom than do material systems.[31] Thus it is reasonable to expect over the long run that the need for meaning will adjust to productive requirements more completely than productive requirements adjust to particular conceptions of identity. The same cannot be said so easily for matters of security because they, like production, must involve the manipulation of an independently existing nature for defence to be successful against hostile others. But, that said, it is also true that security can be achieved through balances of power and human agreement in a way that has no counterpart in human relations with the natural world and its threats. So, again, there are more degrees of freedom in achieving security than there are in overcoming scarcity, and, therefore, over the long run, it is easier for security needs to adjust to production needs than vice versa.

To recognise that 'rationality, intelligence and scarcity' itself can underpin predacity as well as production raises different issues. In itself, the existence of predation is not a problem for historical materialism. The theory specifies that the task of the superstructural agencies is to enforce property rights, both inside their jurisdictions and against external predators. Thus simply devoting resources to the activities of coercion, as opposed to production, cannot be regarded as a refutation of historical materialism. Moreover, this activity can actually encourage the development of productivity, since weaponry and military activities rest upon much the same knowledge as do the means of production and skills of producers.[32] But, nonetheless, there could be a problem in the extreme case. In principle, predacity and the requirements of protection might become so absorbing of resources as to threaten human survival, let alone productive capacity.

However, in practice these activities seem rarely, if ever, to have been sustained at a level sufficient for this extreme possibility to emerge. And, indeed, there is a good reason why they have generally been moderate (relative to production) in their absorption of resources and human life. Overwhelmingly, in history the 'rate of return' to production, or to 'production, exploitation and defence', has been higher than the 'rate of return' to 'predacity and militarism' for the majority of people, including power holders. Ruling groups, especially, have typically faced both alternatives in regard to the territories they actually rule, and other territories that they may be able to conquer. The majority of rulers have chosen the former strategy over the latter most of the time and have done so because it promises to be more successful in adding to their power and wealth.[33] Where they have not done so, and instead engaged in conquest, they have sometimes contributed to a powerful selection mechanism buttressing historical materialism (as we outline in Section 1.7 below).

Nevertheless, matters of security might be thought to lessen the validity of historical materialism for a quite different reason. They can exhibit bootstrap characteristics, where expectations become self-fulfilling so that they lack any anchor in material reality, and thereby seemingly set up a rival logic of development to that of the productive forces stressed by historical materialism.[34] For example, taking precautions to ensure effective defence in the case of attack may cause others to feel threatened, because military power used for defence can also be employed aggressively. Others will then undertake defensive countermeasures that can justify the acts which induced them in the first place. Likewise, conceptions of identity may also follow a bootstrap logic, in which friend–enemy distinctions become more sharply drawn as a result of militarism and, in turn, add reinforcement to arms races. Consequently, a self-sustaining loop can emerge, where resources are increasingly diverted away from production into accumulating the means of violence and into programmes aimed at cementing the solidarity of the community. This appears to be a problem for historical materialism precisely because it can occur independently of the requirements for increasing productive power, or the recognised constraints on doing so. However, the theoretical problem is more apparent than real. Historical materialism is a theory stressing the development of the productive forces subject to the constraints posed by humans' need for security and identity. And in the technological circumstances that have so far prevailed in the world, separate political entities and different group identities have been unavoidable. Consequently, historical materialism can legitimately recognise bootstrap processes because they are inscribed in the limited nature of productive power that has so far been developed.

On the third problem, Marx himself accepted that social systems could operate to block any natural tendency for the productive forces to develop. He believed that Western European history was *uniquely* dynamic. In the rest of the world (which he, along with everyone else in the West at the time, knew little about) he conjectured that the economic systems were sufficiently restraining in their incentive effects to bring about a situation very close to stagnation in the productive forces.[35] Characterising the non-Western world as one of extreme conservatism in this way is no longer accepted as accurate, but the belief that social relations can have inhibiting effects on the development of the productive forces has recently been given a persuasive new formulation. Robert Brenner has argued eloquently that European feudalism itself discouraged both lords and peasants from improving productivity. A lord's rational strategy favoured squeezing more resources from peasants coercively, while peasants saw it in their interests to resist and simply reproduce their material life without change.[36] In consequence, a situation resembling a 'low-level equilibrium trap' became evident.[37] Of course, capitalism did emerge and, indeed, first arose in Western Europe, but that does not compromise the point made by Brenner because he also argues that capitalism originated from class conflicts unconnected to the development thesis.

The most convincing way of countering this 'Brenner thesis' critical of the type of historical materialism presented here is to demonstrate that an all-encompassing barrier to increases in productive power in feudalism could not be a genuine self-sustaining 'low-level equilibrium trap'. Or, if it were, it would in all likelihood be both unstable and subject to disruption, succumbing then to a selection mechanism of change concordant with the development thesis. Therefore, we postpone dealing with this issue until Section 1.7, which takes up the matter of selection mechanisms.

1.5 The compatibility and fettering theses

The compatibility thesis rests as much on human nature and the character of the natural environment as does the development thesis. But it is best understood by providing examples of why specific types of economic systems can be said to be incompatible with particular types of productive forces. We look first at slavery and then at capitalism and feudalism.

One might easily imagine that a system of slavery could be made consonant with all levels of the productive forces, including the most advanced. Slaves could be trained in the appropriate skills and a sufficiently complex incentive system implemented to encourage conscientious performance. Markets might be present, even pronounced, as slaves were given some choice over their own consumption, and a market for different types of slave labour would be quite feasible, either on the basis of outright purchase and sale or for the renting of appropriately skilled slave workers. Nor is this wholly fanciful. There is evidence from the many studies of the *ante bellum* South in the United States that the system included examples of significant flexibility.[38] Why could this not have been generalised and refined as the developmental requirements of the productive forces changed?

The most convincing answer hinges on the existence of human needs for autonomy and dignified recognition by others. This requires that slavery be concentrated in activities involving unskilled physical labour, where the incentive system can rely heavily on coercion without adversely affecting labour productivity.[39] Thus neither the array of sophisticated skills associated with the development of the productive forces, nor the initiative called for in their exercise, could be widespread in a slave system. Or, to make the same point in a different way, even if the appropriate skills could be inculcated into slaves, and their behaviour modified appropriately, the costs of doing so on an extensive scale would exceed those required by systems of non-slave labour.[40]

Another thought experiment raising a challenge to the compatibility thesis centres on the late arrival of capitalist relations of production. Capitalism is associated with the very highest level of labour productivity in recorded history,[41] and there are sound reasons for believing that this productivity level is the result of capitalist productive relations.[42] But, precisely for this reason, it might be claimed that the failure of capitalism to emerge earlier shows that historical materialism cannot possibly be true. If the capitalist economic system could raise living standards by as much as ten times since the late nineteenth century, why could it not have accomplished a similar transformation many centuries before? Why has world history until very recently seemingly been dominated by inefficient economic systems?

The defence of the compatibility thesis in this case hinges on recognising that capitalism involves specialised producers who are dependent on markets for their consumption.[43] Such a pronounced division of labour and dense set of market relations, in turn, requires a transportation and communication infrastructure that is possible only when the productive forces have already significantly developed. And neither extensive specialisation nor market exchange will be encouraged unless there are considerable scale economies, which again indicates the need for relatively sophisticated technology. Moreover, capitalist relations of production are by definition based on contract between free persons, so that the possibility of using coercion to extract resources from others (as in slavery or serfdom) is circumscribed.[44] This is possible only when the productive forces have progressed to the point of allowing the emergence of modern states, which monopolise the means of legitimate violence, centralise political decision-making and administer well-defined territories bureaucratically. Relatively high labour productivity is also essential to overcome people's aversion to bearing the risks of specialisation and market dependence. Low standards of living encourage either self-sufficient production and/or relations of personal dependence, in which freedom is sacrificed for some assurance of survival. In short, capitalism came late in human history and there were good reasons for the delay.

A third example of the compatibility thesis and of the fettering thesis is provided by the classic materialist account of the transition from feudalism to capitalism. It begins by claiming that the feudal epoch in Western Europe saw significant improvements in the forces of production, as well as an expansion of markets.[45] Both phenomena certainly contributed to a growing incompatibility between feudal relations of production, based on a dependent peasantry in agriculture and the guilds in manufacture, and the further development of the productive forces. Large-scale productive establishments became both technically feasible and remunerative in each sector, requiring concentrations of specialised labourers that were inhibited by the bondage relations of serfdom, by the self-sufficiency possibilities allowed by petty production and by the restrictiveness of guild regulations. And all these feudal relations of production also restrained the mobility of labour which is essential to any production orientated to markets. Feudal relations of production had systematically fostered earlier productive improvements by allowing significant areas of discretion to the direct producers.[46] But, early into the second millennium, improvements already achieved, and further improvements rationally anticipated, engendered serious strains. Multiple crises ensued because overcoming the fettering of the forces of production required a radical change in relations of production along capitalist lines.[47]

1.6 The primacy, superstructure and uniqueness theses

One argument for the primacy of the productive forces over the production relations follows from the preceding two sections. If the productive forces have a transhistorical tendency to develop, and no system of production relations is compatible with all levels of such development, at some stage the economic system will have to change in order to facilitate the development of the productive forces.[48] Nonetheless, this is not by itself sufficient to justify the claim that the production relations are as they are by virtue of being those best for developing the productive forces, or, if they are not functional, that they will change to become so. The 'best' productive relations may be the most efficient for ensuring material development, but they are unlikely to be the only set of relations that could develop the productive forces. And, as we have already argued in Section 1.1, efficiency in the development of productivity might have to be compromised by attending to matters of security and identity. However, as we have also argued, these complications of security and identity constraining productive efficiency are not incompatible with historical materialism because the theory recognises that human needs for protection and meaning are always constraints on the development of the productive forces. The 'best' is defined as such only insofar as it is compatible with these constraints.

Something analogous can be said of the superstructure thesis. Because relations of production are not self-stabilising, they do require the institutions of the superstructure to consolidate them. Since powers and rights are so closely related conceptually and causally, a change in the powers defining the productive relations will act as a very powerful influence in ensuring a functional change in the superstructure. But, again, the 'best' superstructure may not be the only type of superstructure that is effective, while superstructural institutions, as much as productive relations, may be modified by the requirements of coping with matters of security and identity.

However, it should be recognised that the primacy and superstructural theses will be the more compelling the stronger are the mechanisms that engender a functional relationship between the productive forces and the productive relations, and between the productive relations and superstructure. In Section 1.7, we consider these selection mechanisms and suggest that they do strengthen with the development of the productive forces, and that this is supported by arguments in Section 2.3 of Chapter 2.

Nonetheless, the primacy thesis and the superstructural thesis are also threatened by the possibility of there being more than one type of productive relations, and more than one form of superstructure, that is 'best'. Any such occurrence of non-uniqueness would weaken historical materialism because it implies that the theory lacks determinacy.[49] However, even though a multiplicity of 'the best' cannot be ruled out in principle, in fact it does not appear to be a crippling problem. Empirically, there are recognisable types of social formation which indicate that the variations in the productive relations corresponding to particular forces of production, and variations in superstructures corresponding to particular productive relations, have actually been significantly bounded. 'Thus, hunter-gatherer societies are all fairly similar in their forms of distribution of power because their low level of resources implies that there is not much surplus power to distribute within them. The underlying thought is presumably that there is only one way of distributing nothing.'[50] There are also strong resemblances between the bulk of pre-industrial societies or agrarian civilisations,[51] and capitalist systems show pronounced uniformities.[52] It is simply not the case that, for the high level of abstraction at which the theses of historical materialism are formulated, there is a serious problem of non-uniqueness. At least, that is the evidence of history up to now.

So far, then, the discussion has provided credibility for the basic correctness of the development thesis, the primacy thesis and the superstructural thesis, but it falls far short of being definitive in each case.

To add more confidence requires examining the causal mechanisms through which economic systems and superstructures are maintained and changed.

1.7 Selection mechanisms

If the productive relations are to be functional for the development of the productive forces, and the superstructure is to be functional for consolidating the productive relations, there must be causal processes by which the 'best' structures are selected. Historical materialism recognises five such mechanisms: (1) the rational choice of individuals, (2) market competition, (3) exogenous shocks and the disruptive dynamics of existing systems, (4) group struggles, including the struggle of classes and (5) geopolitical rivalries. They are not mutually exclusive, and all may play a role in all types of change, but, even when effective, each and every one is likely to operate in a blunt fashion owing to the importance of false consciousness, the imperfections of information and the costs of bringing about change (as indicated in Sections 1.1 and 1.2).

If people are acquisitive and rational, any inefficiency in the productive relations or superstructures will tend to be recognised and there will be incentives to eliminate it. In this sense, rational choice theory supports historical materialism. But, nonetheless, the existence of inducements for change does not guarantee that they will be effective in bringing about the change. There will be opposition from those favouring the status quo, who may have substantial power. Consequently, change stemming from acquisitive motivation and rational action will occur only in special cases, where losers from the change can be easily overcome or can be guaranteed compensation for their losses so that their resistance is neutralised.

A similar verdict applies to market competition, which can be effective in eliminating inefficiency by compelling the less efficient to improve on the pain of bankruptcy. But special circumstances must prevail for it to work. Most obviously, markets must exist, and producers must be dependent on markets for their survival. If withdrawal from market relations is feasible, as it is with many peasants, who can easily become self-sufficient, the disciplining effect of competition will be muted. Additionally, markets must not be monopolised, or otherwise rigged, to such an extent that the compulsion of competition is seriously compromised.

Of more general significance than the preceding two mechanisms is the fact that all socioeconomic systems are susceptible to exogenous shocks stemming from climatic, demographic and biological events. In addition, they often exhibit endogenous processes of change that can disrupt the status quo. If either type of phenomenon occurs in circumstances where the productive forces are fettered by the existing relations of production, the prospects for functional change are increased. Alan Carling appeals to this mechanism in countering Robert Brenner's argument that the development thesis is not generally true because the incentives in the structure of European feudalism blocked change to more efficient productive relations (as outlined in Section 1.4 above). Even if the incentives were as Brenner claims, feudalism most certainly exhibited a Malthusian population cycle and was susceptible to outbreaks of plague. Indeed, this is heavily stressed by Brenner himself, who argues that the crises resulting from these disturbances in the fourteenth century brought about changes which varied with the relative strengths of the contending classes of lords and peasants. East of the Elbe the lords succeeded in intensifying serfdom, while in England they were able to retain direct control only of the land, not over peasant labour, and capitalist relations of production emerged as the unintended outcome of adjustments to this new situation. Carling's point is that, given variation among feudal systems across space and time, in the face of disruptive dynamics and exogenous shocks, the probability is that 'there'll always be an "England" '.[53] In other words, because feudal systems were never exactly the same, as time progressed there was an increasing probability of some exogenous shock or endogenous process bringing about a class struggle resulting in capitalist relations of production. And, it can be added, once the breakthrough to capitalism occurred, it created a powerful geopolitical selection mechanism that progressively extended capitalist relations of production.[54] So the essence of Brenner's argument could be accepted without damage to historical materialism.

Class struggles constitute an even more widespread mechanism of change than those involved in the transition from feudalism to capitalism. Marx regarded them as the principal selection mechanism, at least in Western European history during the modern era, and in doing so he exaggerated their significance. But conflicts, whether of classes, intra-class factions or non-class groups, are certainly general mechanisms of change. They may be treated as aggregate versions of the rational choice mechanism, although they can also be separated from any assumptions about individual rationality. However, in order for them to operate at all, group members must find some way of overcoming whatever free rider impediments to collective action exist.[55] And progressive groups always meet resistance from the more conservative ones. As with individual rational actions, how matters work out depends on the relative strengths of the contending parties, and whether or not some kind of acceptable and credible agreement is available to compensate losers. If it is, then the group representing the more efficient relationships and institutions will be definitely advantaged because they have larger resources to overcome the blocking of change. And even if agreements are not possible, association with economic relations and superstructural institutions promising higher productivity confers obvious advantages in attracting allies to the cause.

Geopolitical rivalries are group conflicts writ large and, through conquest or emulation, can work to align economic systems and superstructures to the developmental requirements of the productive forces.[56] The key requirements for this mechanism to operate efficiently are that economic productivity and military power be positively correlated, that different socioeconomic systems come into contact and that none is too securely protected by nature. When these conditions are met, the mechanism will work even if the Weberians are correct in arguing that in any particular society the logics of power and identity are separate from, and irreducible to, the 'economic' or the 'technological'. In all cases, those socioeconomic systems that fail to adopt relations of production and superstructural institutions which foster productive development comparable to that of rivals will tend to be eliminated.[57] Weber himself was acutely aware of the importance of geopolitical rivalry, but he was apparently not aware of the support it provides to historical materialism.

Nonetheless, it would be wrong to conclude that an appeal to these selection mechanisms can completely overcome doubts about the validity of historical materialism, since all these mechanisms might also effect change that is inefficient. The rational choices of acquisitive individuals and group actions can result in redistributions of productive assets that impede economic development.[58] Intense competition can bring about overinvestment and ruinous prices and thereby contribute to coordination failures, which adversely affect the utilisation of the productive forces.[59] So too can the consequences of exogenous shocks and military defeats. And geopolitical conflicts have sometimes brought about technological regressions as the primitive have defeated the more advanced.[60] It is also very clear that the selection mechanisms may take a very long time to operate. Thus, for example, prior to their conquest by European powers, many societies outside of Europe, including the Chinese empire, had relations of production that may not have systematically promoted the development of the productive forces at the maximal feasible rate. Of course, they did not survive in the face of capitalist imperialism, but prior to it they were long-enduring because their internal selection mechanisms were weak and their geopolitical conflicts did not involve systems where the productivity difference was large. So, even though the eventual outcome was as historical materialism specifies, where the productivity inefficient regimes were eliminated, the time scale involved was enormous.

Ultimately, the case for historical materialism as a theory applicable to all economic systems must rest upon two considerations. First, it depends on the importance to human beings of overcoming scarcity, and the importance of the development of labour productivity in achieving the satisfaction of other needs. We have made our position clear in believing these to be the dominant forces in the long run, but in the very nature of the case the argument cannot be made conclusive. Nonetheless, we take some satisfaction from the fact that those theorists furthest from historical materialism, the cultural determinists, who regard people's beliefs as the determinant of economic and political structures, tend to be concentrated among anthropologists and literary theorists (on the one hand, specialists in the study of peoples who are extinct, or becoming so, and, on the other hand, specialists in fictional texts).[61] Second, the case for historical materialism also depends on whether or not the selection mechanisms are biased towards progressive change. We argue in the next chapter that there is a tendency for this bias to strengthen with the development of the productive forces, which means that the case for historical materialism actually improves via the positive feedback effects that development itself creates.

Even at this stage, though, it is clear that the directionality of world history is broadly consistent with historical materialism. Although it has occurred at a variable rate of growth through time, and has always been unevenly distributed across space, over the course of human history there has been an immense expansion of productive power nearly everywhere. For example, Angus Maddison estimates that world output has increased over three hundred times in the previous two millennia alone.[62] Coupled with this, violence has been markedly reduced over large areas of the planet. The 'zone of peace', in which the prospects of interstate warfare, civil wars and other forms of violent disorder are very low, has never been larger.[63] At the same time peaceful human interaction has increased, both intensively and extensively, and cultural heterogeneity has contracted significantly. This is shown by many indices, including the spread of those phenomena of modernity that first arose in the West: capitalism, the modern state, science and nationalism. It is also made evident by such statistics as the halving of the number of languages spoken in the past 50 years, and in the global pre-eminence of English.[64] Thus the selection mechanisms *in toto* seem to have actually worked in the way specified by historical materialism. They have tended to adjust relations of production and superstructures to promote the development of the productive forces. Even if they have not done so perfectly, so that economic systems and superstructural institutions have not always been 'the best' because of the weakness of selection mechanisms operating to eliminate inefficiencies, a case can be made that these imperfections have been subsidiary and not powerful enough to override the main thrust of productive development. Moreover, as we will see in subsequent chapters, the strength of these selection mechanisms has increased in the modern era and strengthened even more in the late twentieth century.

1.8 Conclusion

This completes our argument for historical materialism as a general theory of economic systems. Insofar as we have been convincing, the case for explaining neoliberalism in terms of historical materialism gains strength, at least when neoliberalisation enhances the development of the productive forces. But the disparity between what is to be explained and the concepts in which the explanation is undertaken is enormous. Neoliberalism in advanced capitalism has been vividly evident only since the 1970s, and the population of advanced capitalism constitutes less than ten per cent of the world's total (although it commands over half of the world's output). Historical materialism, on the other hand, is a theory of world history since the emergence of *homo sapiens*. Thus it is desirable to close the gap by reducing the degree of abstraction in the account of historical materialism. We do this in the next chapter by confining attention to the topics considered by historical materialism as they have worked out in the modern era. This strengthens the case for explaining neoliberalisation in terms of historical materialism and provides the background for the more detailed arguments in succeeding chapters.

2
A Theory of Capitalist Economic Systems

2.1 Introduction

Social theorists have long regarded those production relations which we now call capitalist as especially well suited for generating economic dynamism. This is true of Adam Smith, Karl Marx and Max Weber, as well as virtually all lesser notables. Indeed, Marx went so far as to say that, compared to capitalism, all 'earlier modes of production were essentially conservative'.[1] So, if historical materialism is applicable to economic systems generally, as we tentatively claim it is in Chapter 1, it ought to be especially relevant for understanding capitalism. Our argument in this chapter is that the cogency of the theory does indeed improve significantly when applied solely to capitalism, but the high degree of persuasiveness still falls short of complete assurance. However, if the reference is narrowed further to advanced capitalism, confidence that historical materialism is essentially correct is again significantly raised. In this more restricted domain, the influences operating to constrain the development of the productive forces have weakened very significantly. This is true for both types of constraints: those recognised by historical materialism itself and those that qualify the validity of historical materialism as a theory of economic systems.

We begin the argument in Section 2.2 by considering the core properties of capitalism, which explain its productive dynamism relative to other types of economic system. Then, in Sections 2.3 and 2.4, we argue that the selection mechanisms that we discussed in Section 1.7 of Chapter 1 have operated in a manner more consistent with what is required for historical materialism to be true than they did in pre-capitalist times. The following two Sections, 2.5 and 2.6, outline the variations in capitalist systems across time and space, and claim that the differences evident between advanced capitalist economies are not evidence of different types of advanced capitalism, and that a convergence to a neoliberal form is presently occurring.

2.2 Core properties of capitalism

There are problems in defining any type of economic system, and problems especially in defining capitalism. What are conventionally referred to as capitalist economic systems have varied through time as well as across space. And historical materialism itself generates the expectation that productive relations will tend to undergo modification as productive power rises. Moreover, it suggests that this will be particularly true of capitalism because of its productive dynamism, and because one result of this dynamism is that the selection mechanisms operate to create an international division of labour consisting of many capitalist systems. Nonetheless, we argue here that it is sensible to treat all these variations in capitalist systems as particular examples of the general category of capitalism, so that whatever their differences they can still be regarded as members of the same species.

We argue below that the productive relations of all capitalist systems have common characteristics which can be designated as core properties because these properties underpin the unique productivity of capitalism. Thus they are not purely contingent similarities, but are characteristics essential for generating the rapid economic growth with which capitalist systems are associated, and which is documented in Table 2.1. These core properties also account for the marked similarities evident in the

Table 2.1 Gross domestic product per capita, 1820–2001 (1990 international Geary–Khamis dollars)

	1820	*1870*	*1920*	*1950*	*1970*	*2001*
	Advanced capitalist economies					
Austria	1218	1863	2412	3760	9747	20,225
Australia	518	3273	4766	7412	12,024	21,883
Belgium	1319	2692	3962	5462	10,611	20,924
Canada	904	1695	3861	7291	12,050	22,302
Denmark	1274	2003	3992	6943	12,686	23,161
Finland	781	1140	1846	4253	9577	20,344
France	1135	1876	3227	5271	11,664	21,092
Germany	1077	1839	2796	3881	10,839	18,677
Italy	1117	1499	2587	3502	9719	19,040
Japan	669	737	1696	1921	9714	20,683

Table 2.1 (Continued)

	1820	*1870*	*1920*	*1950*	*1970*	*2001*
Netherlands	1838	2757	4220	5996	11,967	21,721
New Zealand	400	3100	5641	8456	11,189	16,118
Norway	1104	1432	2780	5463	10,033	24,577
Sweden	1198	1662	2802	6739	12,716	20,562
Switzerland	1090	2102	4314	9064	16,904	22,263
UK	1706	3190	4548	6939	10,767	20,127
USA	1257	2445	5552	9561	15,030	27,948
		Other west European economies				
Greece	641	880	1918[a]	1915	6211	12,511
Ireland	877	1775	2533[a]	3453	6199	23,201
Portugal	923	975	1229	2086	5473	14,229
Spain	1008	1207	2177	2189	6319	15,659
		Former Eastern Europe and the USSR				
Average for seven Eastern European economies[b]	683	937	1695[c]	2111	4315	6027
USSR	688	943	1488[c]	2841	5575	4626
		Latin American countries				
Eight country average[d]	713	749	1635	2700	4309	6327
		East Asian countries				
Sixteen country average[e]	581	551	NA[f]	662	1420	3851
China	600	530	NA	439	783	3583
India	533	533	635	619	868	1957
		African countries				
Six country average[g]	441	657	1038[h]	1445	NA	3089
Fifty-seven country average[i]	NA	NA	NA	894	1357	1489

Source: Maddison (2003).

[a] Figures for 1921. From 1921 the figures refer to the Irish Republic.

[b] Albania, Bulgaria, Czechoslovakia, Hungary, Poland, Romania and Yugoslavia.

[c] Figures for 1913.

[d] Argentina, Brazil, Chile, Columbia, Mexico, Peru, Uruguay and Venezuela.

[e] Bangladesh, Burma, China, Hong Kong, India, Indonesia, Japan, Malaysia, Nepal, Pakistan, Philippines, Singapore, South Korea, Sri Lanka, Taiwan and Thailand.

[f] NA denotes not available.

[g] Algeria, Egypt, Ghana, Morocco, South Africa and Tunisia.

[h] Figure for 1913.

[i] See Maddison (2003), pp.189–224.

superstructures of particular capitalist systems, and for some common elements in the social consciousness of the people in these systems. Just as with the core productive relations, then, these features are not simply empirical regularities but are consistent with the claims of historical materialism in being functionally determined attributes of superstructures and cultures in capitalist systems.

In Section 2.5, we also contend that the changes in capitalist systems over time can be explained in terms of the propositions of historical materialism. Underpinning them all is the development of the productive forces. The spatial variations in capitalist systems, too, can be accounted for in materialist terms. The exact pre-capitalist circumstances from which particular capitalist systems first emerged, the specific selection mechanisms that were operating to bring this about and the technologies then most advanced are the crucial variables. But we also argue in Section 2.6 that there is a tendency for institutional convergence of capitalist systems to occur to the extent that catch-up to the same productivity levels takes place. In the context of the late twentieth century and the early twenty-first century, this means that neoliberalism is a powerful tendency operating in all advanced capitalist systems.

There are six core properties that define a set of productive relations as capitalist: a particular form of employment contract for wage labour prevails; property owners have specific types of powers over their property; market transactions are substantially free of restrictions imposed by family, kin and community; economic roles are market-dependent; productive organisations are rationalised; and money and finance take on an infrastructural role. These characteristics, in turn, require a superstructure centred on the modern state, and a social consciousness exhibiting an acceptance of cognitive freedom and a commitment to the politically constituted society usually thought of as 'the nation'. We now consider each of these characteristics before explaining how the selection mechanisms have operated in the capitalist era (Sections 2.3 and 2.4), what have been the main changes occurring through time (Section 2.5) and what variations across space are particularly evident (Section 2.6).

The capitalist employment contract is a core property and has a unique form. It does not involve the exchange of services for a remuneration, but the payment of a wage for obedience. Of course, both employer and employee may correctly anticipate what work will actually take place, but employers retain the power to redirect the activities of employees and will do so in the event of disturbances and innovations. Therefore, the employment contract involves a hierarchy, with unidirectional commands from employer to employees. This does not imply the absence of all constraints on the exercise of such power, and it is necessarily limited in duration because the employment contract is one between free persons. Nonetheless, the fact remains that the employment contract is a contract for obedience, and if it is not forthcoming the employer can terminate the employment of the employee.

Ernesto Screpani summarises the matter very well.

> The fundamental institution of capitalism is the *employment contract*. This is the nucleus of the labour utilisation subsystem. It can take different specific forms: it can be an individual or collective contract; a fixed-term or open-term contract; it can be defined implicitly in different measures; it can be combined with other kinds of labour utilisation transactions (contract for services, sharecropping contract etc.); it can give rise to different forms of payment (piecework and overtime pay, bonuses etc.); it can be stipulated by different categories of employers (private owners, public companies, state firms etc.) What cannot be changed is its fundamental characteristic, that is, its ability to generate the workers' obligation to obedience and the employers' prerogative to command.[2]

This is the essential point for many reasons, not least because it indicates that coordination through command is as integral to capitalism as is market coordination, and that the resulting superordinate and subordinate positions generate conflicting interests and give rise to a labour-management problem involving the use of incentives by the authorities to secure compliance and to strategies by employees to contest their power.

However, the powers inherent in capitalist private property must extend beyond those involved in the employment contract because the activities of employers and employees have to be coordinated outside the productive enterprise, and also connected with the actions of competitors, consumers and state bureaucrats. Markets of various sorts are the chief means of doing so. While they are not the only coordination mechanism in capitalism, markets are far more important than in any non-capitalist system, and a core property is that the powers of capitalist property owners accord with this prominence. People have control over what they own to an unprecedented degree and can exercise that control in a highly individualised manner. There are constraints on this freedom, but they stem overwhelmingly from political authorities that are distinct from civil society. There are virtually no institutional constraints arising from responsibilities to family, kin and local community, while the powers of property are formally separated from political and juridical power. All these features are in contrast to pre-capitalist systems. Furthermore, whatever restrictions there are on the powers over property and on market transactions, they are frequently promoted by the contracting parties themselves in order to ensure fair dealing. It is certainly wrong to see government rules as an invariably alien force, operating to undermine capitalist relations of production, or as impeding the dynamism that springs from them. Indeed, were it not for patent laws, the limited liability of corporations, the regulation of financial markets and many other forms of state intervention, modern capitalism would certainly perform less well than it actually does (as is fully understood by most business people despite their inclinations to use libertarian rhetoric and complaints of state interference).[3]

Irrespective of the extent of regulation, though, a core property of markets in capitalism is that they are impersonal. This does not imply that relationships between buyers and sellers are always at arms length or fleeting, only that they are not integrally connected with relations of kinship, or with communal ties, as was the case with most pre-capitalist markets. In capitalism, the main economic bond is the cash nexus, even though it may actually result in prolonged connections between particular purchasers and sellers. Whether or not this happens, a key feature of capitalism is that people can exit from established patterns of interaction and form new contractual relationships if and when they deem it to be in their interests to do so. That itself is an incentive for those who favour enduring associations to act cooperatively so as to preserve them, and since there are usually productive advantages in having long-term relationships they will tend to be pervasive, and contracts will be explicitly designed to preserve them.[4]

Another core feature of markets in capitalism is not only that they extend to the primary inputs of land and labour power along with produced commodities but that they do so in a manner that involves market dependence. People depend on markets for meeting the vast bulk of their needs, so that self-provisioning by individual households or by small groups shrinks significantly. This is in sharp contrast with bondage relationships, including slavery and serfdom, and with the petty production of free peasants and artisans, where many basic consumption requirements were met through home production or within local networks. And without the commercialisation of input supplies, and especially of labour power, there can be no market dependence. Instead, producers either face a real choice about entering exchange relationships and the extent to which they do so, because self-provisioning is a viable alternative or other coercively based systems of provisioning will be prominent. Only in capitalism are people obliged to depend on market exchange for their livelihood, and it is this that mandates them to adjust to market forces, which includes adaptation to more productive technologies.[5]

In this way, people's inclination to be rational is strengthened by 'the dull compulsion of economic relations'.[6] Since capitalism also involves people being released from the traditionalism inherent in kinship and local community bonds, individual acquisitiveness is promoted too. Of course, acquisitiveness has been evident in virtually all of history, as the development thesis of historical materialism suggests. But pre-capitalist property owners were usually oriented towards the accumulation of a narrow set of resources, such as precious metals, land, horses, retainers and servants. And they were normally circumscribed by traditional restrictions centred on family, kinship, bondage and patron–client relationships. The dominant motivation governing the objectives set for productive enterprises in capitalism, by contrast, is the disciplined acquisition of wealth in the abstract, measured in monetary terms, and there is little concern with the specific commodities that are bought and sold to maximise profits. Contractual relationships and market dependence provide the flexibilities that allow changes in both outputs and inputs so as to facilitate adjustment to new opportunities for gain. This makes productive enterprises highly rationalised organisations, which is the fifth core property of capitalist relations of production. The responsibilities of employees are specified as precisely as possible (although as we outlined above, they cannot be completely specified), and their effectiveness in carrying them out is promoted by their being selected for employment on criteria that emphasise competence in the assigned tasks, rather than some other characteristic like kinship or loyalty.

The sixth core property of capitalism is a specific type of finance (that is, of credits and debts), including money (which is a set of credits and debits with particular properties). Organisationally, financial instruments are themselves produced within capitalist relations of production: by rationalised financial companies exercising capitalist property rights, utilising labour through employment contracts and operating in impersonal markets on which they are dependent. A significant subset of these financial instruments constitutes money, defined as the measure of value, or wealth in the abstract, which acts as a means of payment in all transactions. It is true that in every advanced capitalist economy, money of the highest quality is issued by the state, but this forms a very small part of the total stock of money and in normal circumstances the money produced by financial institutions exchanges for state money without difficulty.

Functionally, money and finance are infrastructural in being necessary for all productive activity.[7] Money constitutes the measure of all value magnitudes, including profits, and the means of payment for all transactions, while financial companies allocate credits and manage debts, so facilitating both investment and consumption as well as the diversification of risk and intertemporal trading. Any crisis in the financial sector can induce serious malfunctioning throughout the economic system unless special measures are taken by political authorities to contain the adverse effects. And the specific type of regulation applied to the financial sector by the state has huge implications for capitalism generally (as we will see in Chapters 7 and 8).

We have already pointed out that the very nature of the employment relationship in capitalism generates conflicting interests and thus gives rise to a labour management problem. The five other core properties of capitalist relations of production – the powers of property owners, impersonal markets, market dependence, rationalised organisations and capitalist finance – make endemic two other problems: the coordination of future-oriented activities and the transfer of risks to those best able to deal with them. Although markets play a huge role in coordinating people's actions, markets cannot do so alone, no matter how sophisticated they are, because they can never be comprehensive. In particular, futures markets are relatively scarce (for very good reasons stemming ultimately from the existence of imperfect information), so that the integration of different investment activities needs supplementation by non-market mechanisms. Similarly, markets providing contracts for transferring risks are very thin (also as a consequence of imperfect information) and here too there has to be supplementation by non-market mechanisms.[8] And because kin and community regulation is attenuated in capitalism, these two problems, along with the problem of managing labour, become responsibilities of the state (although, as we will see in Sections 2.5 and 2.6 dealing with differences in capitalist systems, not solely the responsibilities of the state).

The state corresponding to the productive relations of capitalism is the so-called 'modern state', which monopolises the legitimate use of force in a well-defined territory, is constitutionally and bureaucratically organised, and claims to be the sovereign representative of the 'society' or the 'people', usually understood as 'the nation'. Only this type of political authority can guarantee a superstructure functional for securing capitalist relations of production. Such a state is a necessary complement to the exclusion of coercion from productive processes and market exchanges, and is also essential for the separation of a public realm of politics from a private realm of economic activities. Consequently, the fusion of property ownership in land with public authority that is evident in pre-capitalist systems like feudalism is wholly absent. Instead, the state in capitalism is the political counterpart of 'civil society' in which individuals are free of personal dependence on others, and whose economic relations with each other can be those of market contract based on law, where legal enactments are administered by state bureaucracies in a formally neutral and predictable manner. Laws specify the rights of various types of property owner, and, subject to some important qualifications, rights to exclusive control, benefit and disposal are established, so that those who do not possess what they require have to gain access through contracting with others.

Specifying and defending capitalist property rights necessarily includes dealing with the management of labour since the employment contract makes it a right of employers to exact obedience from employees. Thus the capitalist state has a structural bias in favour of employers, even though it is modified by the fact that employees have rights as free persons. Typically, there is also some degree of institutionalisation of conflict through the regulation of strikes, lockouts, working conditions, wages and the termination of employment contracts. And in advanced capitalism today, these are invariably supplemented with measures insuring citizens against the basic risks inherent in the operation of capitalist economic systems, including unemployment, the need for retraining and health coverage in the case of accidents. Thus the problem of managing labour has fused to some extent with the problem of risk transfer and has resulted in the creation of welfare states. Since these have come to be part of the means through which states manage effective demand, they also contribute to resolving the coordination problem inherent in capitalism.

Another way of stating all this is to say that capitalist states supply public goods. These are goods and services that cannot be provided profitably by private organisations, or would be inappropriately supplied (as has typically been true of policing and defence), even though the provision of such public goods is unambiguously productive. There need be nothing socialist about any of this; the principle of state financing as well as direct provision of public goods was accepted by Adam Smith, and few social theorists since, no matter how 'libertarian', have seriously questioned the principle (as distinct from its application).[9]

This characteristic raises the matter of state autonomy. Historical materialism is usually associated with two theories of the state: a superstructural organisation functional for sustaining the appropriate relations of production and the political instrument of the dominant class.[10] It should be clear from what has been said so far in this chapter and the preceding chapter that we are committed only to the first and not the second theory, which implies that the capitalist state will normally have the capacity to carry out its activities irrespective of how property owners conceive their interests. But, of course, this does not imply that such interests will be routinely ignored or countered. Indeed, there must be a class bias in the policy of capitalist states, both because the nature of the employment contact is hierarchic and gives authority to employers, and because the other property rights that capitalist states enforce invariably involve unequal holdings of property. This is true by the very nature of capitalism and irrespective of whether or not political authorities are believed to be legitimate.

Nonetheless, social consciousness in capitalist societies has to exhibit particular patterns. There must be widespread acceptance of cognitive freedom. This is because of the importance of science as a productive force, and of the scientific view of the world as an entity exhibiting complex regularities which are knowable through the use of reason and empirical testing open to the scrutiny of others. Thus, in capitalism, religious organisations are substantially drained of power and confined to propounding ideas and enacting rituals that place no important restrictions on either economic or political decisions. The churches become organisations of civil society, where membership cannot be ascribed but is a matter of individual allegiance. This privatisation of religion complements the weakened force of kin and community in promoting a highly individualistic conception of self. But, to date, this individualism is not completely cosmopolitan, and is instead joined to the idea of political communities being founded on 'nations'. And insofar as sacredness (in the sociological sense) remains vibrant in capitalist societies, it infuses conceptions of nationality.[11] Just as much as with capitalist relations of production and superstructures, then, the social consciousness of capitalist societies is very different from that of pre-capitalist societies, where religion is the dominant theme along with non-national group loyalties.[12]

However, there is a continuity between capitalism and non-capitalist systems in that many elements of social consciousness in capitalist societies conform to the general description of them in historical materialism. They are practically adequate, but simultaneously false by the standards of science and can be classed as ideological in being both theoretical and prescriptive.[13] For instance, the conception of people as individuals with a broad array of rights is confirmed as correct to people within capitalism by the actual exercise of their rights, and by the disapproval and punishments actually meted out to those who infringe the rights of others. But false consciousness is very evident, both in everyday conceptions and in 'high theory', when it is believed that social relations and political authority are founded on individuals' choices and rights. This cannot be true because the characteristics of individuals, including their beliefs and capacities, are formed as much by social relations and by political authorities as these relations and authorities reflect these characteristics of individuals.[14] And rights have themselves been historically variable, often taking non-liberal forms: as with nobles and commoners, who typically have different rights in pre-capitalist societies. Even in capitalism the rights of citizenship have changed significantly over time.[15]

Likewise the concept of 'the nation' may connote accurately what can be expected of any of its members, and thereby greatly facilitates cooperation and coordination in domestic social life. This is made most strikingly evident in wars and other emergencies. But, at the same time, the popular understanding of nationality is riddled with error. People think of themselves as naturally or normally having such a status, and nations are regarded as primordial entities, or divinely inspired, or both. The truth of the matter, however, is that nations are very recent creations, and from the perspective of modern social theory are the cultural complements to industrial capitalism and the modern state, both of which call for a suitably homogenised population.[16] Furthermore, beliefs about individuals and nations are ideological in being theoretical depictions inscribed with normative significance, justifying particular types of privilege and privation to the advantage of some groups and the disadvantage of others.

Michael Mann provides some dramatic illustrations of these characteristics.

> Only ... in the early 19th century in Britain and in the mid- to late 19th century elsewhere, did national identities spread out fully to the lowest classes. Eugene Weber's aptly titled book *Peasants into Frenchmen* .... has become a modern classic. In it he describes how most country-dwellers in France even in 1870 did not consider themselves members of the French nation. The regions around Paris, the home counties of France, did constitute a partial exception, since they

> were servicing the capital. But Weber concludes that most French men and women had much more local horizons. Peasants became Frenchmen only when state infrastructures actually penetrated their daily life, through military service, national education, and railways and motorised transport. I would also add national economic markets and production systems; national political infrastructures – routinised national parties, state institutions, and state services; and a national religion.... [Also there are]...revealing responses given by European migrants to U.S. immigration officers between 1880 and 1910. When asked where they came from, they overwhelmingly identified themselves in terms of 'locale, region, province and the like,' not in terms of a country. But the most convincing evidence derives from a battery of statistics on intimate family practices. Susan Cott Watkins....compared data for 1870 and 1960 across no less than 500 regions within 15 European countries. She collected data on rates of fertility, marriage, and illegitimacy. How often did people get married, how many children did they have, and were these legitimate? These are intimate practices indeed, resulting from millions of individual decisions taken by women and men in the privacy of their own relationships. But she found clear general trends. In 1870 differences were much greater within countries than between them. There was less of a French or a German family pattern than many varied local ones, some of which cut across national borders. But by 1960 the family had been substantially nationalised on all three issues. Now there was a French and a German and a British family norm regarding how many children one had, whether one married before children were born, and how frequently people got married. None of this had existed in 1870. The nation had been born very late – whether legitimately or illegitimately![17]

The different sectors of capitalist society are substantially insulated from each other, or, as the point is sometimes expressed, exhibit relative autonomy.[18] However, it is important not to misunderstand this last characteristic of capitalism. There is a separation of spheres of activity in the sense that economic, political and cultural functions are highly specialised and must be so in order to perform their respective roles, but this does not imply that they cease to affect each other in the manner already explained in Chapter 1. While acquisitiveness is the dominant economic force and is allowed relatively free rein, the fact that people feel the need to infuse what they do with transcendental significance means that cultural ideas, including those of religion, will tend to harmonise with material interests. And the maintenance of liberal property rights is likely to require their legitimisation through cultural sanctification and the minimisation of political influence by those groups who do relatively badly in capitalist conditions. Thus claiming that economic, political and cultural organisations are specialised and separated from each other does not imply the absence of cultural and political supports for capitalist economic activity, just as other types of economic systems are buttressed by non-economic structures.

However, the core properties of capitalist relations of production, and the associated forms of superstructure and social consciousness, are unique in having operated to generate rapid economic growth, as can be seen from Table 2.1. The historically unique form of acquisitiveness governing capitalist enterprises provides the drive to develop productive power, and it does so in general, rather than concentrating advance in just a few sectors. This is strongly reinforced by competition between enterprises, and by the relatively open access to their control by those who can marshal the assets and accept the risks of the market environment, which is continually subject to organisational and technological change. Inventiveness is itself promoted by conditions of cognitive freedom; in particular, no productively relevant knowledge can be inhibited by the charge of heresy, since religious organisations are politically weak. Moreover, any technical change which is widely adopted tends to be genuinely productive because economic activities are validated by market demands, and the costs of mistakes are concentrated upon those who undertake the wrong investments. Consequently, there is always a strong incentive for people to anticipate the consequences of their actions rationally, taking into account all the relevant information currently available. At the same time, contractual freedom and market dependence provide the adaptability required for the rational organisation of production in the light of the full array of available technologies. There are no legally enforceable distinctions of status in the form of caste, estate and guild prohibitions that systematically limit the efficient combination of inputs. Liberal property rights support this arrangement even when the results might weaken social cohesion, and any democratic participation that could seriously threaten these rights is usually constrained by repression, ideological conditioning and constitutional impediments. What Joseph Schumpeter called the 'creative destruction' of rapid innovation becomes very evident as existing investments and enduring relationships are destroyed economically by newer, more productive ones.[19]

2.3 Selection mechanisms in the capitalist era

In some very important respects, the selection mechanisms underpinning the theses of historical materialism (which we explained in Section 1.7 of Chapter 1) have strengthened markedly with the development of capitalism during the last few centuries. More of the mechanisms have operated, they have done so more comprehensively and powerfully, and the time taken for them to work out has shortened. Their increased effectiveness is outlined in this section of the chapter, while those features which continue to be problematic are deferred for consideration to the next section (2.4).

As already mentioned (in Section 2.2) rationality, joined to individual acquisitiveness, is intensified under capitalism. This is the result of the replacement of personal dependence by market dependence, the weakening of the traditional bonds of kinship and community, the 'separation' of politics and religion from the economy, as well as the erosion in the power of churches. Under capitalism, there is also so much more to be acquisitive of, and capacities for being rational, including calculating skills and access to information, are subject to significant improvement. Thus, as a selection mechanism through which economic relations become functional for the development of the productive forces, and superstructures become functional for the relations of production, individual rational choice is greatly strengthened. With capitalist relations of production and superstructures present, people who seek to use their resources to enhance productive power are less inhibited than in any other kind of system.

Competition complements this freedom by providing compulsions to exercise it. Market dependence implies that there are no economic alternatives to accepting technical progress, and the temporary superprofits which innovation brings encourage the search for new advances. This is inherent in capitalist relations of production in all circumstances, but it is significantly intensified with integration into the world market, a path taken by all capitalist economies from the very beginning (albeit, initially, in different ways). And, as we will argue later, neoliberalism in advanced capitalist economies represents a continuation of this trend. So, even though any individual capitalist economy may exhibit huge concentrations of market power, the process of globalisation ensures competitive pressure on most sectors of the economy.

Geopolitical rivalry has complemented market competition in two ways: by bringing about defensive modernisation among some laggards and by enforced adoption of capitalist relations and institutions through imperialism. In the nineteenth century, Germany, Japan and Russia all experienced 'revolutions from above' in order to eliminate military weaknesses.[20] This is true also for South Korea, Taiwan, Turkey and China during the twentieth century. Those countries which never attempted such a strategy, or which tried and failed, have often been colonised and had capitalist relations imposed upon them, albeit only partially, as in India under the Raj. These processes created the world market, and the space devoted in economics textbooks to the importance of the principle of comparative advantage in bringing about international trade is a relatively obvious example of false consciousness (which by no means implies that the principle of comparative advantage is itself illogical).

These potent effects of geopolitics are not accidental. Only under capitalist conditions have economic productivity and military power become highly correlated. Only under capitalist conditions have all socioeconomic systems come into regular contact with each other. Only under capitalist conditions has military technology advanced to the point of overcoming virtually all natural advantages in defence. Thus the limitations of the geopolitical selection mechanism discussed in Chapter 2 have been greatly weakened in the era of capitalism.

Class struggles and other group conflicts within capitalism are usually regarded as acting to degrade capitalist relations of production and superstructures.[21] But even with the success stories of working-class radicalism this is not wholly true. Both democratisation and welfare states have characteristics that run with the grain of capitalist social formations.[22] Democracy provides a means of mutual monitoring and control that acts to limit opportunism and corruption, and helps regulate domestic conflicts.[23] Welfare state measures, most of which are financed in a way that does not involve very much redistribution between classes, constitute the means of reproducing a healthy and skilled workforce, and also one homogenised into a single culture, which significantly improves its efficiency.[24] And, for much of the twentieth century, there were elements of market-eradicating technical change operating in capitalism. We will document in Chapters 3 and 4 how this misled many social theorists into doubting the continued viability of the capitalist system, but, more importantly, it provided space for the unionisation of working-class groups to contribute positively to orderly working relations by negotiating and enforcing collective agreements.[25]

Obviously this is not the whole story. But nowhere in actual history is any particular entity or event or sequence of events or structure purely one thing rather than another. Indeed, all the selection mechanisms evident within the capitalist era have features that qualify the primacy of the productive forces and the relations of production. In our view, they are all swamped in the long run by the effects supportive of historical materialism, and it remains broadly true to say that the selection mechanisms operating in the capitalist era have been especially favourable to productive development. But this is correct only in the aggregate, and there are particular counteracting effects, to which we now turn.

2.4 Real and imaginary imperfections in the selection mechanisms

Capitalist systems have endogenous processes of change and experience exogenous shocks which can be disruptive. One persistent characteristic of these economies has been fluctuations in economic activity levels due to business cycles. Normal upturns and downturns may not be of much significance for overall productive performance, but there have been extreme cases where slumps achieve proportions threatening the system itself. Most obviously, this was true of the Great Depression, beginning with the stock market crash on Wall Street in October 1929 and terminating only with the onset of war a decade later. It ushered in increased protectionism, the suppression of competition, more powerful state bureaucracies less accommodating to the needs of capital and an increasing non-market provision of basic subsistence. There were also beneficial economic initiatives, such as the abandonment of the Gold Standard, a more activist state administration of money and the beginnings of Keynesian demand management, all of which contributed positively to capitalist economic performance in the postwar years. But, at the time, all these were weak qualifications to what was a massive crisis for the world capitalist system, and one that was widely regarded as terminal (see Chapter 7). It did not turn out to be so, of course, and all threats to capitalism were defeated, but the process of doing so was very bloody and the after-effects were long-enduring. Expressed in the concepts of historical materialism it can all be summarised by saying that 'use fettering' of the productive forces as a result of effective demand failures may provoke a significant deviation in the path by which the productive forces continue to develop.[26] In other words, when the current use of the productive forces is significantly inhibited, but there is no fettering of their further development by capitalist relations, the economic system may undergo change in ways that, while not sustainable, prove to be more than fleeting.

Use fettering as a result of a deficiency of demand can be related to bootstrap factors that we referred to in Section 2.4 of Chapter 1, where we discussed militarism and identity politics. In financial markets particularly, it is easy to imagine self-fulfilling, optimistic expectations underpinning an asset price bubble, which, over time, faces an increasing probability of being popped by adverse news as to the state of the real economy. And, when this occurs, the resulting deflation of asset prices and bankruptcies can originate a set of pessimistic bootstrap expectations that are again self-sustaining but now operate to fetter the use of the productive forces. This means that bootstrap processes are inscribed in the core characteristics of capitalism, and any constraint they create for the development of productive power cannot be regarded as inconsistent with historical materialism. Likewise, the modification of capitalist relations of production that are implemented to contain these bootstrap processes is consistent with historical materialism.

The effects of geopolitical conflict can also be very destructive of the existing capitalist relations of production (as we explain in Chapter 7). But it is important to recognise that this is true for reasons that are consistent with historical materialism beyond the claim that bootstrap factors are inherent in superstructural relations. For example, neither the First World War nor the Second World War is clearly and obviously incompatible with historical materialism, irrespective of bootstrap matters. Capitalist relations of production were then, as now, nationally defined, and unchanging political jurisdictions can fetter the development of the productive forces. In a multi-polar world of several Great Powers lacking a hegemonic superpower, the negotiation and enforcement of agreements facilitating peaceful harmonisation and cooperation faces huge difficulties. And this was particular the case in circumstances of the first half of the twentieth century, where 'late starters', especially Germany and Japan, considered themselves disadvantaged by the extensive colonisation undertaken by European powers which had already taken place. But any change to the status quo which they could accept necessarily involved disadvantaging other Great Powers.[27] Furthermore, both Germany and Japan had plausible reasons for believing that aggression would secure their objectives.[28] They failed, but the outcome in 1945 in the West most certainly promoted the development of the productive forces subsequently, because it secured the preponderance of the United States, and American hegemony was exercised to promote capitalism in all the advanced countries (as we outline in Chapter 7). So the destruction and carnage of the three decades following 1914, then, are consistent with the central claims of historical materialism, both in terms of causal mechanisms and outcomes.[29]

Of course, while hostilities continued, the effect of these wars was sometimes to wholly eliminate capitalist relations of production or to severely compromise them, in all belligerent countries. But again, this is not incompatible with historical materialism, which stresses not the importance of preserving capitalist relations, but the primacy of developing the productive forces, including the importance of preserving past productivity achievements, and historical materialists recognise that this is always accomplished subject to important constraints, as we emphasised in Chapter 1. Capitalist relations of production and corresponding superstructures are but a means to achieve this end and are dependent on particular circumstances prevailing. Clearly, in times of industrialised warfare, circumstances favoured instead increases in the strength of states and in the scope of their activities, which involved command planning and the administrative allocation of resources outside of markets. We return to examine the economics of this transformation in Chapter 7.

However, some of the other consequences of these world wars, along with those of the Cold War thereafter, were less obviously favourable for the development of the productive forces. The requirements of mass mobilisation necessarily strengthened state bureaucracies and working-class organisations, whose cooperation was crucial to the war effort. Thereby, forces potentially hostile to capitalist relations of production were empowered, and the effects continued long after the cessation of fighting in 1945. As we have indicated (in Sections 2.2 and 2.3 above) they were not all contrary to the requirements of capitalism, but the strength attained by unions and socialist political parties in the early postwar years, and the expansion of welfare states that continued long after this, probably impeded the capacity of the relations of production in actual capitalism to develop the productive forces. In the very nature of the case, precise assessment is not possible, but given the historic working-class hostility to capitalism, and the delegitimisation of the system effected by the Great Depression, it would be purely coincidental if it all turned out to be fully functional to the requirements of capitalism. Most capitalist countries had welfare states that involved incentive structures significantly at variance with the requirements of market dependence.[30] Income support payments were divorced from productive contributions; schools, universities, hospitals and agencies of government were insulated from competition; secure employment in public bureaucracies was expanded; and the containment of employer power by unions was often effective even when it restrained technical progress.

Geopolitics also sets another problem for historical materialism. In the previous section, we explained how capitalist relations were extended via 'revolutions from above' initiating capitalist modernisations among late starters. We do not wish to withdraw anything that was said there, but it does gloss over a possible conceptual problem in historical materialism. The aim of modernising political elites in these cases was to elevate their countries' productive power, but it was not the level attained by the productive forces in their own jurisdictions alone that prompted them to do so. It was also the productive forces of others; so there is a discordance between the productive forces, the productive relations and the superstructure that may be held to be theoretically damaging to historical materialism in its present form. Even if this is not the case, there is a puzzle in explaining why some countries were able to defensively modernise while most failed to do so and succumbed to imperialism. This is not just a problem for historical materialism; it is a problem for all types of social theory, but it is nonetheless a problem.

As well as 'late starters', historical materialism has to face the issue of 'non-starters'.[31] In parts of the periphery, like sub-Saharan Africa, there remain hugely backward areas, typically riddled with violent conflicts and corrupt or powerless governments, which have failed to incorporate the more productive technologies that have long existed elsewhere. And in much larger areas of the periphery, economic development appears to have been less than was materially feasible. However, here, there is no serious theoretical problem for historical materialism, which is capable of persuasively diagnosing the constraints on modernisation in particular regions by pointing to how the selection mechanisms there operate. The theory emphasises explicitly that capitalist relations of production and superstructural institutions depend on the *domestic* productive forces having already achieved a moderately high degree of productivity.[32] But this condition is not satisfied in the most impoverished regions of the periphery. Historical materialism also points to the need for a consistency, or 'even development', between the technologies of production and of predacity for economic development to be possible, so that the 'rate of return' to the former activity dominates that of the latter for those who hold political and military power.[33] This clearly does not prevail in some areas of the backward South, where there is extensive importation of modern armaments, and a very limited importation of productive technologies, which are often used to fight for the control of natural resources that can be sold on the world market without any need to promote the development of productive power.[34]

In addition, historical materialism recognises that the inhabitants of any country must not be so diverse as to sustain autonomous political and military groupings which preclude the formation of effective states. But capitalist imperialism itself sometimes created the circumstances where this last presumption was undermined, and certainly failed to homogenise the populations involved to anywhere near the same degree as had been achieved in core societies, thereby allowing pre-capitalist forms of exploitation, corruption and violence to run rife.[35] Post-colonial interventions by advanced capitalist states, as well as the postwar regime of international economic relations crafted by the same states, have also sometimes helped to sustain the disorder and underdevelopment.[36] It is true that historical materialism provides no basis for claiming that economic growth in advanced capitalism *depends on* the poverty of the periphery, but the actual historical paths followed contributed to fostering affluence at one pole and deprivation at the other.[37]

According to historical materialism, the prospects for those who are most impoverished appear to be very bleak. Many of the conflicts and much of the corruption seem to have no productively progressive dimension. So the likely outcomes will be exceedingly unpleasant. Deaths through war, malnutrition and disease, along with the emigration of the more fortunate, are likely to be extensive and may eliminate some societies altogether.[38] Or those impoverished societies that do continue to exist will do so solely as a consequence of international aid extended for humanitarian purposes, and this is unlikely to encourage sustainable development. The only productively progressive prospects appear in the form of new imperial projects. These do carry the promise of more effective economic relations and superstructures being coercively imposed from above as a complement to imperialist exploitation or as a means of enhancing security in advanced capitalist societies by eliminating 'rogue states' and terrorist activities. To date, though, this is but a 'promise', and material gains have yet to emerge from the new imperial projects of the twenty-first century.[39]

Finally, running through much of the discussion of the 'imperfections' of actually existing capitalism, along with discussion of the selection mechanisms in Chapter 1, is a partial ignorance as to what is involved in the production relations being *functional* for the productive forces, and the superstructure being *functional* for the relations of production. This is a serious theoretical problem for historical materialism (but not only for historical materialism). Without clear and comprehensive criteria for separating constraints on the development of the productive forces that are compatible with historical materialism from those that are not, the theory remains in need of refinement. But, in any event, one substantive point is transparent. Whatever the exact role of material factors, depression and wars have distorted the relations of production and superstructures away from those core forms outlined in Section 2.2. One consequence has been that economists and other social theorists were misled as to the continued sustainability of capitalist economic systems, so that the onset of neoliberalism in the closing decades of the twentieth century came as a huge shock, as we document in Chapters 3 and 4.

2.5 Variations in capitalism over time

However serious may be the ambiguities in historical materialism, or the unfavourable evidence, it all has to be set against the fact that the selection mechanisms have operated upon the principal capitalist societies in a manner overwhelmingly favourable to the truth of historical materialism. On the whole the institutional and organisational changes within capitalism have been productive, and in this section we turn to considering these changes insofar as they are relevant to understanding neoliberalism. This is supplemented in Chapter 7, where we outline those changes in the international system through which the multi-polar world of Great Powers was replaced with a unipolar American hegemony. This geopolitical shift has been crucial to neoliberalism because it has pacified relations between advanced capitalist systems, and thus inhibited those security and identity imperatives that constrained and sometimes temporarily distorted the core properties of capitalism. In Section 2.6, we also consider some of the cross-sectional diversity of capitalist systems and indicate how these variations across space affect our argument about neoliberalism.

The primary source of historical change within capitalism has been rising productive power, operating through the channels specified in Section 1.3 of Chapter 1, and through the selection mechanisms discussed in Section 1.7 of Chapter 1 and the previous two sections of this chapter. We focus here on four developments which characterise the history of all advanced capitalist societies: the corporatisation of productive enterprises, the improvement in the conditions of wage labour, the democratisation of advanced capitalist states and the expanding range of public goods provided by them. Naturally, these are not the only changes to have occurred, but they are the changes central to understanding the neoliberal transformation of capitalism. This is frequently misunderstood as a return to the era of classical liberalism rather than what it actually is – the outcome of economic development in the twentieth century (as we explained in the Introduction).

The typical capitalist productive enterprise has undergone a change from being an owner-managed firm to a corporation. This is the result of technological change bringing complex production processes and economies of scale, which require huge amounts of capital and professional management. Consequently, there has been a separation of ownership and control, in which shareholders are dispersed and distinct from the managers who actually control the corporations. This creates a problem of corporate governance, so that incentive mechanisms have to be implemented to align the interests of managers with those of owners. We consider these mechanisms in the next section, but, however the problem is resolved, the bureaucratisation of productive establishments is certainly accentuated by corporate organisation. The firm itself becomes an abstract legal entity able to enter into contracts as a person, and employees are organised in multi-layered hierarchies. The governing rules include those on 'human resources', which are administered by specialised personnel, and aim to tame internal conflicts by resolving them in an institutionalised manner.

The employment contract retains its unique character in corporate capitalism, but the condition of most employees has been much improved. Taking a very long-term perspective, and on average, real wages rose at approximately the same rate as per capita incomes in all advanced capitalist countries during the twentieth century and the relative shares of labour and capital in national income did not change much in the period as a whole. This has created conditions of affluence, in which consumption itself has become a major cultural activity, and where many workers have accumulated a portfolio of assets. In the process, education has become very much more important for most occupations, which have multiplied into ever more specialisations requiring a diversified array of incentive systems to ensure conformity with corporate objectives.[40] At the same time, the rights allowed in capitalism, coupled to the conflictual nature of the employment contract, have facilitated the organisation of workers into unions, which have constrained the arbitrariness of management and sometimes contributed to the resolution of conflicts.

Organised labour movements have acted politically to promote democracy, and have been successful in doing so. Advanced capitalist states are no longer just constitutional and liberal; they are all mass democracies. This has brought some tension with capitalist property rights, but, in current circumstances, they operate at relatively low temperature. In large part, this is because democracy has institutionalised conflicts within the established political system as a macroeconomic complement to the microeconomic forms present in corporations. The long-run effect has probably been to attenuate the importance of class itself. While it remains a significant factor in explaining political and cultural divisions, it does seem to be dissipating. Party political loyalties have weakened since the end of the Second World War, and a differentiated mass culture is replacing distinct lifestyles centred on class.

Affluence has similar effects by expanding the size of discretionary purchasing power and therefore promoting behaviour less constrained by communal controls, including class controls. This has resulted in the atomisation and privatisation of consumption, and elevated the importance of this type of consumption in people's lives relative to their experiences in production activities. Thus the description of advanced capitalist societies as 'consumer societies' is apt. It points not only to the increase in consumption but also to its social and cultural organisation in individualist and family-centred forms.[41] Many of the changes we discuss in the next section and in Chapter 6 have had the same effect, so that, outside the return of a major crisis, the politics of class conflict appear to be in decline in all advanced capitalist societies. (However, such a crisis cannot be ruled out, as we will indicate in Chapter 8, and open class conflict could intensify again.)

The state itself has extended the provision of public goods, particularly education, health care and social security. This is evident from Table 2.2, which shows the growth of government expenditure in the twentieth century. On average, public expenditure as a percentage of gross domestic product trebled. The growth slows after 1980, but there has been no reversal of the upward trend in any country, except Ireland.

However, Table 2.2 both overstates and understates the importance of states in advanced capitalism. It exaggerates their importance because many of the expenditures are transfers, so the state itself does not absorb productive resources to anywhere near the level suggested by the figures.[42] At the same time it downplays the importance of states because the thicket of regulations that have come to surround most economic activities is not made evident. Regulation has been increasing through most of the twentieth century, and has certainly not been eliminated by the deregulation of the neoliberal phase since the 1970s, even under the avowedly economically libertarian governments of Margaret Thatcher and Ronald Reagan.[43] Furthermore, tax systems in all advanced capitalist

Table 2.2 General government expenditure (as share of GDP, per cent)[44]

Country	*1913*	*1937*	*1960*	*1980*	*1996*
Australia	16.5	14.8	21.2	34.1	35.9
Austria	17.0	20.6	35.7	48.1	51.6
Canada	NA	25.0	28.6	38.8	44.7
France	17.0	29.0	34.6	46.1	55.0
Germany	14.8	34.1	32.4	47.9	49.1
Italy	17.1	31.1	30.1	42.1	52.7
Ireland	NA	25.5	28.0	48.9	42.0
Japan	8.3	25.4	17.5	32.0	35.9
Norway	9.3	11.8	29.9	43.8	49.2
Sweden	10.4	16.5	31.0	60.1	64.2
Switzerland	14.0	24.1	17.2	32.8	39.4
UK	12.7	30.0	32.2	43.0	43.0
US	7.5	19.7	27.0	31.4	32.4
Simple average	13.1	23.8	28.0	41.9	45.0

societies provide incentives for particular types of private expenditures and inhibit others. So, while there are many reasons why particular groups have an interest in reversing neoliberalism, categorising it as an obvious reactionary trend is not one of them. As we have claimed in the Introduction and will argue throughout this book, neoliberalism is an outcome of economic developments in the twentieth century, not a reversion to the nineteenth.

2.6 Variations in capitalism across space

The changes outlined in Section 2.5 characterise the history of all present-day advanced capitalist societies. But in every period of time there have also been differences between them. These variations arise from a more complex set of factors than do the historical changes and, as we acknowledged in Section 2.4, are less well understood. What seem to have been particularly important were the differences in the pre-capitalist circumstances from which capitalist relations were formed and the exact array of selection mechanisms that operated most powerfully on them. Also, since the development of capitalism occurred at different times in different places, the level of technological sophistication of the productivity leaders had a huge impact on the organisational forms that were used to achieve catch-up.[44]

Describing the differences between capitalist systems is likewise more difficult than providing an account of common historical developments, because these differences have varied over time. In this section, we limit ourselves to considering what are generally regarded as the specific characteristics of American capitalism, German capitalism and Japanese capitalism in the 'golden age' years of the postwar period (1945–73). These are the variations emphasised by much of the literature in comparative political economy,[45] and those that are most relevant to our thesis on neoliberalism. But unlike this literature of comparative political economy, which stresses the autonomy of institutions and their difference between national capitalist systems, we will argue that most of the differences are more apparent than real or have been temporary devices to facilitate catch-up or stem from differences in the positions occupied within the world economy and system of states. In other words, we argue that the differences between American capitalism, German capitalism and Japanese capitalism have been exaggerated and that institutions are more endogenous and determined by material factors than is recognised in the literature of comparative political economy. Furthermore, we claim that there is a process under way bringing an institutional convergence towards neoliberal forms. Thus, as a general rule, when referring to American capitalism, German capitalism and Japanese capitalism, the noun capitalism is very much more significant than the adjectives.

Each form of capitalism provides an alternative solution to the problem of corporate governance where the disciplinary effect of competition in input and output markets is insufficiently powerful to align the interests of managers and owners. The notable feature of German capitalism is the importance of bank-centred finance, which provides a monitoring and control mechanism over managers as a result of the concentrated debt and equity holdings of banks. This is supplemented by the system of codetermination, in which the firm's employees along with the unions have legal rights to positions on the supervisory boards of corporations. So there is a monitoring of managers 'from below' as well as 'from above'. Furthermore, both bank-centred finance and codetermination inhibit the sway of market relations by impeding competitive access to credit for acquisitions and mergers, by privileging 'insiders' access to information, and in encouraging monopoly power.

Bank-centred finance is also important in Japanese capitalism, but here it is supplemented by networks of firms that hold equity in each other and have long-term economic relationships (the so-called *keiretsu*). Again, then, there are two forms of monitoring and control, one operating vertically and the other horizontally, which can initiate change in the event of inefficiency in particular firms. By contrast, the main mechanism of corporate control in the United States is simpler. It centres on profit-related incentive schemes for higher corporate executives and on the discipline exercised by financial markets. Especially important here are takeovers, or the threat of takeovers, which are made very much easier to implement compared to Germany and Japan by the greater transparency in corporate accounts, dispersed shareholding, the ease of raising finance and the absence of the other protections inherent in bank-centred finance, codetermination and *keiretsu* cross-shareholding.[46]

There are also differences in systems of labour control. German corporatism involves bargaining between encompassing federations of employers and employees, with participation by government ministers, resulting in sector-wide and economy-wide agreements that are legally enforceable. Part and parcel of this is that the union federations and federations of employers discipline their members so that agreements are actually implemented (subject to the details left open to enterprise bargaining by the agreements). This system has been able to manifest flexibility and bring about adjustments to changed circumstances in a relatively consensual manner because corporatism substitutes 'voice' and command through the federations of 'social partners' for market relations. At the other extreme is the Japanese system of enterprise unions and internal labour markets with lifetime employment for many employees in the flagship corporations. This engenders a pronounced common interest in the health of the firm and, because of this, flexibilities that allow adjustment to changed circumstances. By the same token there are strong incentives for employees to monitor each other's performance and report opportunism to the relevant authority in the hierarchy. The situation in the United States is again different from both Germany and Japan. Labour control relies more on hierarchic monitoring and disciplining, and flexibility is achieved through this, coupled with an easy hiring and firing environment, along with multiple credit and retraining facilities.[47]

Superstructural institutions and state economic policies differ, too. While Germany, Japan and the United States are all democratic, there are variations in the powers of national governments relative to sub-national governments, and in the power of the bureaucracy and judiciary compared to elected politicians, who are themselves organised into different structures of political parties. Alternative ways of providing public goods are evident as well. The hallmark divergence is typically considered to be in the industrial policies. German policy has been carried out via corporatist institutions, and much of the public aid to firms and industries has been provided through regional governments.

To describe it as unfocussed would be misleading, but it has been diffuse. By contrast, Japanese industrial policy in its postwar heyday involved very specific projects of industrial modernisation, carried out by an elite bureaucracy providing 'administrative guidance' via dense networks of relationships with *keiretsu* groups and backed by their control of bank credit and regulatory authority. In the United States, like Germany, regional governments enact many measures to foster business, as do Federal government agencies. Most significant of all, however, has been the Department of Defense's promotion of research and development and of technology transfer to American corporations within and outside of the defence sector.[48]

Each of these three sets of institutions and practices is associated with success, in that Germany, Japan and the United States are all advanced capitalist economies, now operating with similar overall productivity levels.[49] At the level of appearance they are clearly different, but exactly how different in reality and by what criteria and for what reasons are less obvious. Take industrial policies. The states of all present-day advanced capitalist systems have always used some form of industrial policy. But they have varied according to the sophistication of the productive forces then prevailing, along with state capacities for action and the problems that were identified at the time.[50] No particular set of policies has proved to be universally relevant. For example, in the 1970s and 1980s it was fashionable for American policy intellectuals to recommend the emulation of Japanese industrial policy. This was not well thought-out advice, quite irrespective of the substantial changes in the distribution of political power that would be required to implement any copying. Japanese industrial policy was a means of achieving catch-up to American productivity levels, and, indeed, has lost its distinguishing character as this has been achieved.[51] Much has also been made of the Japanese bureaucracy's policies of investment coordination, which markets alone cannot accomplish (as explained in Section 2.2).[52] But the Japanese employed only one mechanism of achieving this, and the problem is tackled in other capitalist economies too. German corporatist organisations obviously represent another means. But so too is there a resolution of the problem in the United States, operating through financial institutions, the interlocking directorships of corporations, industrial and trade associations, networks with government agencies, company reports, the business press and oligopolistic collusion.[53]

No doubt Japanese bureaucrats have provided a highly effective framework for the development of Japanese industry, and, equally without doubt, this has something to do with their intelligence and training. But the United States is not without its elite bureaucrats, who have provided the same species of service for American corporations. The character of the policy has been very different because the American economy was considerably more advanced than the Japanese for most of the postwar years, and has of course occupied a very different geopolitical position. The maintenance of American hegemony through the construction of worldwide military alliances and a globalised economy has not been a spontaneous process but has been crafted by leading public officials (as we outline in Chapter 7). They differ in character from their Japanese counterparts, rarely occupying career bureaucratic positions, but instead being recruited by successive administrations from the many prestigious universities, think tanks, the military, law firms and corporations in the United States, to which they generally return at the end of their government service. A bureaucratic structure similar to that of Japan would hardly suit American purposes, any more than the American system could have achieved Japanese objectives. But similar elite bureaucrats have been present in both cases, designing the 'public goods' relevant for their respective capitalist systems.[54]

The contrast between American corporations and Japanese networks has also been overdrawn. Even the vertically integrated, multi-divisional US behemoths that have long since begun restructuring closer to the Japanese model were themselves only differently organised networks. Each division had considerable autonomy, and the head office operated similar to a German and Japanese bank, concerned above all with financial issues, and with monitoring the performance of the divisions that actually did the production. Central personnel and services were provided in the event that restructuring was required, not unlike those provided in Japanese *keiretsu* and German corporatist organisations. Of course, all this took place within a single corporation, but the substantive similarity with the other systems is clear.[55] Neither could one seriously describe American capitalism in the twentieth century as being non-networked, given its origination of the modern system of franchising. Furthermore, US corporations generally have not operated in casual labour markets for executives or even for typical employees. *De facto*, there has been long-term, career employment associated with well-developed internal labour markets for those privileged to find themselves in 'core' or 'primary' employment, while those confined to the 'peripheral' or 'secondary' segment of the labour market enjoy very much less job security and lower rates of pay. A similar dual labour market has always existed in Japan, where only large companies offered lifetime employment, and relied heavily on small sub-contractors to achieve the necessary degree of wage and numerical flexibility.[56]

Nonetheless, the specific institutions of Germany and Japan that we have described are more at variance with market relations than those of the United States. And throughout Europe they have been supplemented by a relatively large number of state-owned enterprises, on which have been imposed public service obligations and patronage employment while budget constraints have been softened. Furthermore, all these institutions are 'dual use' in being both instruments to manage the affairs of the domestic economy and privileging citizens over foreigners in the absence of overt protectionism. Not surprisingly there have been rising tensions as Germany and Japan have integrated into the world market.

For this reason and others, some significant institutional convergence has taken place between the three forms of capitalist system. This is frequently depicted as 'Americanisation', which is a vulgar half-truth. It is not so much a result of American influence, which in the postwar years has always been immense, but of successful catch-up to American productivity levels. And the institutional convergence is not simply an emulation of American forms. In some cases, it is quite the reverse. For example, American corporations now resemble their Japanese counterparts in that they have become less vertically and horizontally integrated, and more networked through alliances.[57] At the same time, the neoliberal reform of the US financial sector has brought about less segmented markets and less specialised financial organisations. This has resulted in the accumulation of huge portfolios of assets under unified control, and increased the monitoring of corporate managers in a manner analogous to German and Japanese banks. And, increasingly, in all three economies similar systems of corporate governance are evident because there has been a contraction of bank-centred finance in both Germany and Japan as a result of economic development and globalisation, including deeper integration within the European Union, bringing about financial deregulation.[58]

German corporatism is also unravelling. Membership in unions and in employers associations is declining, the restrictiveness of peak-level agreements has weakened, so that there is more bargaining space at the level of the individual firm, and the dispersion of wage rates has increased as a result. This is hardly surprising given the failure of corporatism to overcome the problems of stagnation and unemployment that have bedevilled the German economy since the 1980s.[59] But corporatism elsewhere in Europe, notably in Sweden and the Netherlands, has also weakened in the same way as in Germany, so the phenomenon is not unique to Germany.[60] All economies have also privatised and deregulated in a neoliberal manner that has extended well beyond finance. The large public sectors of state-owned enterprises evident throughout Europe for most of the postwar years are a thing of the past.[61] All of these changes reflect the importance of those factors promoting neoliberalism more generally: non-Keynesian macroeconomic policies that have increased unemployment in Europe, more vibrant competition that has reduced the size of rents that are subject to bargaining, successful catch-up to American productivity levels, and new technologies which call for increasing flexibility at the enterprise level.

The type of Japanese industrial policy which prevailed in the years of high-speed growth has also been eroded. In manufacturing, there is very little, if any, modernisation left to do, and industrial policy has moved closer to the American pattern of concentrating on research and development and on technology transfer. Again this is not something peculiar to Japan. The same change has occurred in French industrial policy and for the same reason. Once catch-up has been substantially completed there are no more advanced industries overseas to emulate and surpass. Firms are themselves also stronger and less reliant on the state for subsidies, which, in any event, can no longer control the allocation of credit because of the larger retained profits of corporations and the global integration of financial markets.[62] Industrial policies of the Japanese and French type may still be relevant to more backward capitalist countries, but because of their effectiveness in overcoming backwardness, not for any more enduring reason.

Globalisation has been a corrosive force on all national political economies, but especially on those of Western Europe and Japan. It is also not an alien phenomenon imposed on the normal operation of distinctive national economies, but very much the consequence of the normal operation of capitalism.[63] Insofar as the capitalist mode of production operates on the logic of profit and brings about economic growth, it also tends to globalise because of the scale economies and other efficiencies brought by increased specialisation. And these were essential to the Europeans and Japanese in their endeavour to catch-up to American productivity levels. But globalisation, in turn, brings more interdependence and the need for a harmonisation of productive relations and state policies in order to reduce transaction costs and ensure a 'level playing field'.[64] It also tends to undermine trade union power and commitments to social democratic political projects. Rent-seeking activities not based on innovation have generally become more difficult to initiate and sustain (although farmers have proved particularly tenacious in the defence of their subsidies). And stronger incentives have been created to eliminate those aspects of welfare states most at variance with market dependence, and for promoting those elements that enhance the productivity of the workforce.[65]

Our argument throughout this book is that the principal causes behind these huge changes are materialistic.[66] The development of the productive forces has induced changes in all these institutions via the connections outlined in Section 1.3 of Chapter 1 and the selection mechanisms we have outlined in Section 2.3 of this chapter. Part and parcel of this has been the achievement of mass affluence as a result of rapid economic growth in the postwar years. Both the technologies underpinning the high productivity and the consequences of high incomes have atomised working-class populations, significantly privatising individuals into home-centred family lives and orientating them to consumerism. As producers, people have come to resemble the pieces of a Lego kit, homogenous in overall form, but differentiated by many specific features, and fully capable of being assembled together through market processes in different combinations very quickly and very cheaply.[67] As consumers, people have turned to markets not only to provision themselves on a more extensive scale but also to realise identities and to fashion distinctions from others.[68] Somewhat paradoxically, this has brought a significant cultural convergence within and between advanced capitalist societies, reducing the importance of both nationhood and class allegiances.[69] Working-class politics has also become much less threatening to capitalist relations of production, and the erosion of social democracy and the demise of Communism have brought a loss of confidence in there being any coherent alternative to neoliberal capitalism.

Nevertheless, differences are still evident between the capitalist systems of Germany, Japan and the United States. German corporatism is in a weakened condition, but important components still remain in place. The Japanese *keiretsu* and lifetime employment system may be unravelling but so far only slowly. Neoliberal measures have made much more headway in the United States, Britain, Australasia and elsewhere in Europe than in either Germany or Japan. However, if we are correct in the argument of this book, institutional convergence will continue and the differences will contract even further, even if they never completely disappear.[70] The most likely trajectories are a continuation of the recent past in which neoliberal reforms have been gradually introduced.[71] Certainly neither Germany nor Japan, in contrast to many peripheral economies in the past, can have a rapid neoliberal restructuring imposed upon them from outside as a result of unsustainable debt denominated in foreign currencies beyond domestic political control. Thus the most obvious prospect is a continuing slow expansion of neoliberalism, sometimes with later reversals, but on the whole relentlessly extending into more and more areas.

2.7 Conclusion

This completes our case for explaining neoliberalism in terms of historical materialism. We elaborate upon it extensively in the remainder of the book, in three broad strands of argument. First, in the next two chapters (Chapters 3 and 4), we consider why so many economists and social theorists believed that capitalism would exhibit a market-eradication tendency and failed to anticipate the neoliberalism that actually occurred. This includes Marxists, Keynesians, neoclassicals and institutionalists as well as those economic theorists most identified with neoliberalism, like Friedrich von Hayek. The prestige of these people is not thereby enhanced, but in exposing their erroneous ideas the analysis contributes to a much better understanding of the actual causes of neoliberalism. Second, in the subsequent two chapters (Chapters 5 and 6), we consider where the theorists of modern capitalism were correct in arguing that market elimination was taking place and why, ultimately, they were all wrong in believing that a reversal could not, or would not, occur. Third, in the final two chapters (Chapters 7 and 8), we look more closely at the historical trajectory of neoliberalism and why its onset was delayed until the 1970s and what might reverse it in the future. It follows from what we have said about the advanced capitalist economies today that the theses of historical materialism which were outlined in Section 1.2 of Chapter 1 hold in a less qualified form, and the corresponding selection mechanisms operate in a stronger manner, than at any earlier time. This implies that neoliberalism is far from being a transitory or fragile development. But, at the same time, it could be reversed by a resurgence of those types of factors which have brought a modification of capitalist relations of production and superstructures from their core forms in the past.

Part II

Theorists of Modern Capitalism on the Decline of the Market

3
Marx and the Marxists on the Decline of the Market

3.1 The puzzle

Marx is often and legitimately regarded as anticipating both the development of globalisation and the corrosive effects which market relations can have on other forms of economic and social organisation. But he also used the principles of historical materialism to predict the long-term decline of the market. Furthermore, Marx's arguments were accepted without significant criticism by later social democratic and Communist theorists, and similar ideas featured prominently in the work of many non-Marxian economists who were sometimes indirectly influenced by Marx's earlier analysis and supplemented it with other arguments. In some respects they were all correct, but ultimately they were fundamentally mistaken, as the development of neoliberalism during the final third of the twentieth century attests.

The main puzzle that we explore in the first part of this chapter can be stated very simply. Marx is often, and quite correctly, seen as the apostle of the market, most especially of the world market. The latest commentator to do so is Thomas Friedman,[1] but the argument has been made many times before by social theorists and economic historians, notably by Eric Hobsbawm.[2] In the century after his death, however, most of his followers were convinced that the market was in irreversible long-run decline. This prediction lies at the heart of Eduard Bernstein's revisionist challenge to the official theoretical position of the Second International, but it was also evident in Rudolf Hilferding's *Finance Capital*, published in 1910, in his post-1914 writings on 'organised capitalism', and in Nikolai Bukharin's thinking on 'state capitalism'.[3] Yet Hilferding and Bukharin, at least, claimed to be orthodox Marxists.

The puzzle can be resolved, also very simply. Marx's views changed significantly after 1848, first as a result of the failure of the revolutions of that year, and, second, due to the deepening of his knowledge of economics as a result of his studies in the 1850s and 1860s. The failure of the revolutions led to a shift in his theory of social and political change from a political voluntarist to a more economic determinist position. His intensive studies in political economy were reflected initially in the *Grundrisse* manuscripts of 1857, and culminated in the publication of volume I of *Capital* 10 years later. (After 1867, Marx did relatively little new thinking or writing on economic issues, but Engels continued to observe and to theorise right up to his death in 1895, and he maintained the emphasis on the economic determinism to which Marx had moved.) Marx's research brought many changes in his ideas: it led him away from philosophical speculation towards empirically informed economic theorisation, away from Adam Smith and towards David Ricardo, away from exchange and towards production as the dominant force in economic life, and away from proclaiming the political potential of the proletariat and towards the analysis of those political transformations initiated by the proletariat that could be sustained by material conditions. In this chapter we give detailed attention to Marx's analysis, not only because he adopts a materialist analysis most self-consciously, but also because he initiated the conception of market elimination, and provided compelling arguments justifying it.

Robert Brenner notes that in his pre-1848, 'Smithian' phase, the story that Marx told began with the growth of the market; this allowed the extension of the division of labour, which in turn gave rise to changes in the nature of social relations. 'By the end of the 1850s', however, 'Marx had significantly transformed his conception of historical materialism, precisely by transforming his understanding of the relationship between class and property relations and the development of the productive forces.'[4] The growth of the market, Marx now argued, was a revolutionary force only in appropriate circumstances, and these circumstances were determined by the nature of the mode of production.

Brenner's principal interest is in Marx's analysis of the transition from feudalism to capitalism, for which '[t]he results.... were far-reaching: essentially, they were to turn his first approach to transition upside down'.[5] But this theoretical inversion also had profound implications for Marx's and Engels's views on the transition from capitalism to socialism, which Brenner does not address. In their later economic writings, they claimed that socialism was maturing economically 'within the womb' of capitalism, just as capitalism had matured economically within the womb of the feudal mode of production. Market relations, especially, were being eradicated, so that economic processes were becoming less *commodified* in the specific Marxian sense: less atomistic, less impersonal and less anarchic. In the place of these characteristics, bureaucratic administration of resource allocation, the planning of activities in larger productive establishments, the rising significance of public goods relative to private goods, and greater state regulation of remaining market prices and conditions of contract were becoming more important. All this was seen to be a consequence of capitalist economic development, but also as transformative of capitalism itself.

More particularly, Marx and Engels argued, it was the result of five factors that could be seen to operate in contemporary capitalism. First, technical change brought enhanced economies of scale in modern industry, and this gave rise to increasing centralisation of capital, which transformed some market activities into undertakings within firms. Second, the growing importance of credit money and the related emergence of joint-stock companies were socialising some of the most important functions of capital. These two factors were engendering a third, the growth of cartels and trusts, which greatly reduced the intensity of competitive forces and tended to replace market processes with a form of private planning of prices and production. Fourth, the Factory Acts represented a fundamental reassertion of social control over the market for labour power. Fifth, and finally, the increased role of science in production meant that public goods, in the form of knowledge, were becoming more important relative to private goods, and was another force operating to socialise production.

3.2 Before 1848: the triumph of the market

The first full-scale account of the role of the market in Marxian writings comes in the opening chapter of *The German Ideology*, supposedly devoted to a critique of Ludwig Feuerbach but actually ranging over the whole of human history. Here Marx and Engels describe the development of the world market as an essential pre-condition for the achievement of communism, first because it is necessary for the development of the productive forces and second because it leads to the creation of 'the "propertyless" mass' on a global scale, that is, the formation of a world proletariat. 'Without this.... communism could only exist as a local phenomenon'.[6] This point is repeated in the next section, where they argue that the causal sequence runs from the development of the productive forces to the growth of the proletariat, and then to revolution.[7] There is no suggestion in either of these passages of any trend of market eradication, let alone of the emergence of socialist relations *within* the capitalist mode of production itself.

Later in the chapter Marx and Engels emphasise the importance for England of the growth of the world market in the early modern period: 'This demand, outgrowing the productive forces, was the motive power which, by producing large-scale industry – the application of elemental forces to industrial ends, machinery and the most extensive division of labour – called into existence the third period of private property since the Middle Ages' (This 'third period' was the Industrial Revolution). The result was 'universal competition', which 'forced all individuals to strain their energy to the utmost. It destroyed as far as possible ideology, religion, morality, etc., and, where it could not do this, made them into a palpable lie. It produced world history for the first time', and created a world proletariat, the first truly global class.[8] 'And finally, while the bourgeoisie of each nation still retained separate national interests, large-scale industry created a class which in all nations has the same interest and for which nationality is already dead.'[9]

The growth of the market is given an equally prominent place in the first section of the *Communist Manifesto*, where we learn that, after the discovery of America, 'The feudal system of industry ... now no longer sufficed for the growing wants of the new markets'.[10] 'Meantime the markets kept ever growing, the demand ever rising.... the need of a constantly expanding market for its products chases the bourgeoisie over the whole surface of the globe'.[11] Marx and Engels celebrate the achievements of this world market, which 'batters down all Chinese walls.... [and] compels all nations, on pain of extinction, to adopt the bourgeois mode of production.... In one word [*sic*], it creates a world after its own image'.[12]

But, they argue, this powerful process is also a contradictory one. Recurrent economic crises demonstrate that bourgeois production relations have become a fetter on the productive forces. 'And how does the bourgeoisie get over these crises? On the one hand by enforced destruction of a mass of productive forces; on the other, by the conquest of new markets, and by the more thorough exploitation of the old ones. That is to say, by paving the way for more extensive and more destructive crises.'[13] But the bourgeoisie has created its own grave-diggers in the form of the proletariat, which is becoming increasingly homogeneous, and its conditions increasingly desperate, in an increasingly polarised society. In consequence,

> the bourgeoisie is unfit any longer to be the ruling class in society, and to impose its conditions of existence upon society as an over-riding law. It is unfit to rule because it is incompetent to assure an existence to its slave within his slavery, because it cannot help letting him sink into such a state, that it has to feed him, instead of being fed by him.[14]

Three points should be stressed at this stage. The first is the brilliance of the *Manifesto*, both as literature and as social theory. Eric Hobsbawm rightly sees Marx and Engels as visionary prophets of the globalisation of our own epoch. The world they described

> is recognizably the world in which we live 150 years later.... what might in 1848 have struck an uncommitted reader as revolutionary rhetoric – or, at best, as plausible prediction – can now be read as a concise characterization of capitalism at the end of the twentieth century. Of what other document of the 1840s can this be said?[15]

The second point is the speculative, sketchy, underdeveloped nature of their arguments. Allen Oakley describes the economics of the *Manifesto* as '*impressionistic*', and comments that 'Marx made.... no attempt at this time to investigate the complex analysis that would be required rigorously to support his assertions'.[16] Hobsbawm refers to Marx as a 'communist Ricardian' at the time of the writing of the *Manifesto*, rather than a 'Marxian economist'.[17] The theory of revolution set out there, Hobsbawm argues, was derived from philosophical speculation: 'The aim of communism, adopted before Marx became "Marxist", was derived not from the analysis of the nature and development of capitalism but from a philosophical – indeed, an eschatological – argument about human nature and destiny.'[18] The third point is that political revolution, not economic processes, eradicates market relations, which may remain vibrant up till then.

Those few passages in the early writings of Marx and Engels that do refer to the concentration and centralisation of capital actually serve to reinforce these characteristics. In the *Economic and Philosophical Manuscripts* of 1844, for example, Marx follows Adam Smith in identifying a fall in the rate of profit as the consequence of increased competition; 'the first to suffer' from this 'is the small capitalist'.[19] He continues:

> If, however, the big capitalist wants to squeeze out the smaller capitalist, he has all the advantages over him which the capitalist has as a

> capitalist over the worker. The larger size of his capital compensates him for the smaller profits, and he can even bear temporary losses until the smaller capitalist is ruined and he finds himself freed from this competition. In this way, he accumulates the small capitalist's profits.
>
> Furthermore, the big capitalist always buys cheaper than the small one, because he buys bigger quantities. He can therefore well afford to sell cheaper.[20]

There is no suggestion here of economies of scale in production or of any role for technical progress in advantaging the big capitalist, or in reducing the importance of market relations in any other way. Marx again cites Smith on the effects of a fall in the rate of interest: 'When, therefore, this large capital is opposed by small capitalists with small profits, as it is under the presupposed condition of intense competition, it crushes them completely.'[21]

In his *Outlines of a Critique of Political Economy*, written at almost the same time as Marx's Paris manuscripts, Friedrich Engels does refer to monopoly as an innate tendency of the capitalist system:

> The opposite of *competition* is *monopoly*. Monopoly was the war cry of the mercantilists; competition the battle cry of the liberal economists. It is easy to see that this antithesis is again quite hollow. Every competitor *cannot but* desire to have the monopoly, be he worker, capitalist or landowner. Each smaller group of competitors cannot but desire to have the monopoly for itself against all others. Competition is based on self-interest, and self-interest in turn breeds monopoly. In short, competition passes over into monopoly. On the other hand, monopoly cannot stem the tide of competition – indeed, it itself breeds competition; just as high tariffs, for instance, or a prohibition of imports positively breed the competition of smuggling.[22]

There is no suggestion here of any long-run trend towards the growth of monopoly and reduction in the sway of market relations, still less one based on the nature of technical change in capitalist industry. On the contrary, Engels here sees the incentive to restrict competition as a universal feature, applicable to all points in time and to the owners of labour power and land no less than of capital.

Later he does seem to identify such a tendency:

> Moreover, the stronger worker drives the weaker out of the market, just as larger capital drives out smaller capital, and larger landed

> property drives out smaller landed property.... In crises of trade and agriculture, this centralization proceeds much more rapidly.... The middle class must increasingly disappear until the world is divided into millionaires and paupers, into large landowners and poor farm labourers.... Free competition, the key word of our present-day economists, is an impossibility.[23]

Even here, though, the drive to increased centralisation applies to merchant capital and landed property no less than to industrial capital, and even (somewhat bizarrely) to labour power. There is more rhetoric in this passage than there is analysis. As Oakley notes, with reference to the *Outlines* as a whole, 'the predominant influence of Adam Smith is noticeable here',[24] and the overall impression obtained from Marx's and Engels's early writings is that Robert Brenner is indeed correct in arguing that the role of the market is exaggerated, and the importance of the mode of production correspondingly underplayed, compared to later writings.

3.3 After 1848: the market in decline

After 1848 there were three subtle but cumulatively very important changes in Marx's thinking. The first involved his theory of revolution, and entailed a more considered articulation of the doctrine of historical materialism. It is most clearly expressed in the well-known 'Preface' to the *Critique of Political Economy*, published in 1859:

> No social order is ever destroyed before all the productive forces for which it is sufficient have been developed, and new superior relations of production never replace older ones before the material conditions for their existence have matured within the framework of the old society. Mankind thus inevitably sets itself only such tasks as it is able to solve, since closer examination will always show that the problem itself arises only when the material conditions for its solution are already present, or at least in the course of formation.[25]

This brings to mind the equally celebrated description of capitalism maturing 'within the womb' of the feudal order, but it is now asserted as a *general* principle, applicable to socialism no less than to capitalism.

Second, and very closely related to this first change, is Marx's new methodological insistence on the priority of production over exchange. As Maurice Dobb notes, Marx began (especially in the Paris manuscripts of 1844) with the concepts of supply and demand, competition and the market – in the *German Ideology* and the *Communist Manifesto*, the world market. His critique of these concepts, his reflections on the nature of a truly scientific political economy and the increasing influence of Ricardo at the expense of Smith, all led him to privilege relations of production over relations of exchange.[26] Again, this confirms Brenner's argument concerning the transformation of Marx's economic thought in the 1850s. It emerges very clearly from Marx's discussion of the world market in volume III of *Capital*, where he writes that it had 'contributed materially toward destroying the feudal fetters on production', but 'only where the conditions for [the modern mode of production] had taken shape within the Middle Ages. Compare, for instance, Holland with Portugal'. The effects of the development of the world market in the sixteenth and seventeenth centuries were 'accomplished conversely on the basis of the already existing capitalist mode of production .... it is not commerce in this case which revolutionises industry, but industry which constantly revolutionises commerce'.[27]

This, of course, is related to the third critical change: his analysis was now based on painstaking research into the origins of English capitalism, its contemporary characteristics, dynamic tendencies and the political economy literature that it had inspired. Between the early 1850s, when he began an intensive programme of research in economics, and 1867, when the first volume of *Capital* was published, Marx learned a very great deal about the capitalist mode of production. His research led him to uncover five reasons to expect the decline of the market as a result of capitalist development itself. And while this market eradication is never identified with the achievement of socialism, it is seen as its precondition. The five reasons are more or less clearly set out and more or less logically developed in his mature economic writings and they are, to a greater or lesser extent, inter-related. For convenience we shall deal with them separately in the remainder of this section.

3.3.1 Economies of scale and the centralisation of industrial capital

Marx distinguished what he termed 'modern industry' from 'manufacture'. His terminology here is rather unusual. By 'manufacture' he refers to the early stages of industrial production, in which craft skills are used, in conjunction with hand tools, in small workshops. 'Modern industry', by contrast, denotes large-scale production in factories, using machinery and steam power.[28] From his reading of Charles Babbage, he discovered the advantages that were enjoyed in modern industry by 'the collective labourer' over the individual workman.[29] Later in volume I of *Capital*, in the chapter on 'The general law of capitalist accumulation', Marx identifies a strong tendency for technical progress to increase the amount of constant capital used in production, relative to variable capital. (The 'general law' is the tendency thus created for unemployment to rise, as the supply of labour power outstrips the demand for it.) This reinforces the competitive advantage of large capitalist, and gives rise to 'concentration of capitals already formed, destruction of their individual independence, expropriation of capitalist by capitalist, transformation of many small into few large capitals'.[30]

Note that Marx's terminology is once more highly distinctive. By 'concentration' of capital he normally means an increase in the size of the individual unit of capital, while by 'centralisation' he denotes what is today referred to as industrial concentration. The trend to centralisation implied that a growing proportion of economic activity would be taken out of the market and internalised to the firm. As early as 1848 Marx and Engels were describing *nationalisation* as the ultimate limit of centralisation, predicting that the proletariat would soon use its political supremacy to 'centralise all instruments of production in the hands of the State', and making an immediate demand for the 'centralisation of credit in the hands of the State'.[31] Twenty-four years later, in a newspaper article on the nationalisation of the land, Marx repeated the point in a very clear statement that the development of capitalism is itself eradicating market relations and preparing the way for socialist relations of production, which Marx expects to be created in the not-too-distant future.[32]

Within capitalism, however, '[t]he battle of competition is fought by cheapening of commodities. The cheapness of commodities depends, *caeteris paribus*, on the productiveness of labour, and this again on the scale of production. Therefore, the larger capitals beat the smaller'.[33] And Marx has much more to say about economies of scale in volume III of *Capital*, especially in the opening chapters devoted to the theory of the falling rate of profit. In chapter V, where he discusses 'economy in the employment of constant capital', he gives a number of examples. The cost of motors does not rise in proportion to their horsepower. The cost of transmission equipment does not increase at the same rate as the number of labourers who work on it. The frame of a machine does not increase in cost as rapidly as the number of tools that it operates. There are savings in the cost of workshop and warehouse buildings as their size increases, and the same applies to expenditure on fuel and lighting. Finally, there are economies of scale in the recycling of waste products.[34]

As the ratio of constant capital to variable capital increases, Marx believes that the rate of profit tends to fall, and this reinforces the tendency towards the centralisation of capital. Accumulation increases the organic composition of capital, Marx writes. But '[o]n the other hand, a fall in the rate of profit again hastens the concentration of capital and its centralisation through expropriation of minor capitalists, the few direct producers who still have anything left to be expropriated'.[35] Indeed, this process 'would soon bring about the collapse of capitalist production if it were not for counter-acting tendencies, which have a continuous decentralising effect alongside the centripetal one'.[36]

3.3.2 Money, credit and joint-stock companies

In the chapter in volume I of *Capital* on 'the general law of capitalist accumulation', Marx introduces 'an altogether new force.... the credit system', which he describes as 'a new and terrible weapon.... an enormous social mechanism for the centralisation of capitals'. In consequence, 'the force of attraction, drawing together individual capitals, and the tendency to centralisation are stronger than ever before'. Unlike concentration, centralisation is not limited by the overall rate of capital accumulation. Indeed, '[i]n a given society the limit would be reached only when the entire social capital was united in the hands of either a single capitalist or a single capitalist company.'[37]

In volume II of *Capital,* writing about 'disturbances in the circuit of money-capital', Marx points to price fluctuations in the course of the business cycle as an additional factor increasing the centralisation of capital.[38] Later in volume II Marx suggests (in passing) that the credit system might also increase the concentration of capital,[39] and in volume III of *Capital* he returns to the question of its role in promoting centralisation. Credit gives 'absolute control within certain limits over the capital and property of others.... Success and failure both lead here to a centralisation of capital, and thus to expropriation on the most enormous scale'. In fact, 'the development of the credit system' amounts to 'the implicit latent abolition of capitalist property', albeit 'in a contradictory form'.[40]

Marx returns to this theme later in volume III: 'This social character of capital is first promoted and wholly realised through the full development of the credit and banking system.... [which] does away with the private character of capital and thus contains, in itself, but only in itself, the abolition of capital itself'. The relevance of this argument to his historical materialist theory of social transformation now becomes clear:

> Finally, there is no doubt that the credit system will serve as a powerful lever during the transition from the capitalist mode of production to the mode of production of associated labour; but only as one element in connection with other great organic revolution of the mode of production itself.[41]

The growth of credit, Marx maintains, is closely related to the rise of the joint-stock company. He cites Andrew Ure on the separation of ownership and control, which means that salaried managers, not capitalists, are now 'the soul of our industrial system'.[42] The work of supervision is now 'entirely divorced from the ownership of capital'. The success of cooperatively owned factories has demonstrated that 'the capitalist has become no less redundant as a functionary in production as he himself, looking down from his high perch, finds the big landowner redundant', while 'Stock companies in general – developed with the credit system – have an increasing tendency to separate this work of management as a function from the ownership of capital, be it self-owned or borrowed.... the capitalist disappears as superfluous from the production process.[43]

Marx regards these phenomena as fundamentally important, since 'the stock company is a transition towards the conversion of all functions in the reproduction process which still remain linked with capitalist property, into mere functions of associated producers, into social functions'.[44] Like cooperative factories, joint-stock companies 'should be considered as transitional forms from the capitalist mode of production to the associated one, with the only distinction that the antagonism is resolved negatively in the one and positively in the other'.[45] Oakley notes that Marx had already stated this striking principle in 1858, when he wrote to Engels setting out his plan for 'Book I, Capital': '*Share capital* as the most completed [*vollendetste*] form (passing over into communism) at the same time with all of its contradictions'.[46]

Engels returned to this theme in 1891 in his critique of the draft programme of the German Social Democratic Party (which was eventually known as the Erfurt Programme). Objecting to the phrase, 'The want of plan rooted in the nature of capitalist private production', he asked:

> What is capitalist *private* production? Production by *separate* entrepreneurs, which is increasingly becoming an exception. Capitalist

> production by *joint-stock companies* is no longer *private* production but production on behalf of many associated people. And when we pass on from joint-stock companies to trusts, which dominate and monopolise whole branches of industry, this puts an end not only to *private production* but also to *planlessness*. If the word '*private*' were deleted the sentence could pass.[47]

Along with market eradication, then, Engels clearly expected that the internal organisation of the firm and cooperative relations between firms to become more encompassing, and both phenomena were seen as preceding the transformation into socialism.

3.3.3 Cartels and trusts

Cartels were discussed only briefly by Marx. This was in volume III of *Capital*, to which Engels added extensive editorial notes. Marx refers to the cartels established by cotton manufacturers to stabilise or reduce the price of raw cotton, which survived only for a short period: 'And it must be admitted that such control [over the price of raw materials] is on the whole irreconcilable with the laws of capitalist production, and remains for ever a pious wish, or is limited to exceptional cooperation in times of great stress and confusion.'[48] This was written in 1865. Engels comments, 29 years later, that there has since been an increase in tariffs and in trusts. But he expects the latter to collapse in 'the first storm... and prove that, although production assuredly needs regulation, it is certainly not the capitalist class which is fitted for this task. Meanwhile, the trusts have no other mission but to see to it that the little fish are swallowed by the big fish still more rapidly than before'.[49] In a later editorial insertion, he observes that the instability of cartels has 'led, in some branches, where the scale of production permitted, to the concentration of the entire production of that branch of industry in one big joint-stock company under single management'. He cites as an example the United Alkali Trust. 'Thus, in this branch, which forms the basis of the whole chemical industry, competition has been replaced by monopoly in England, and the road has been paved, most gratifyingly, for future expropriation by the whole of society, the nation.'[50]

Engels had already written on these questions in 1880, in *Socialism Scientific and Utopian*, where he referred to a 'rebellion of the productive forces, as they grow more and more powerful, against their quality as capital', in which '*The mode of production rises in rebellion against the form of exchange*. The bourgeoisie are convicted of incapacity further to manage their own social productive forces.'[51] Economic crises encourage the development of trusts, in which 'The whole of the particular industry is turned into one gigantic joint-stock-company; internal competition gives place to the internal monopoly of this one company.' Again he cites the alkali industry as an example, in which the planlessness of competitive capitalism has been replaced by 'a definite plan of the invading socialistic society', and the exploitation of monopoly power has become so bare-faced that 'it must break down'. 'In any case', Engels continues, 'with trusts or without, the official representative of capitalist society – the state – will ultimately have to undertake the direction of production'.[52] Increasingly, the development of 'joint-stock companies, trusts and state property shows how unnecessary the bourgeoisie are' for the management of production. Having driven out the independent producers, in fact, capitalism is now driving out the capitalists and beginning the planning of production. But, Engels warns, 'the transformation, either into joint-stock companies or trusts, or into state ownership, does not do away with the capitalistic nature of the productive forces'. In the case of joint-stock companies and trusts this is obvious, but even the modern state is 'essentially a capitalist machine'.[53]

3.3.4 The Factory Acts

Capitalist machine or not, the British state had already intervened decisively in the market for that most important of commodities, human labour power. The introduction of the Factory Acts, Marx and Engels argued, represented a crucial curtailment of the power of capital. Marx deals with this question at some length in volume I of *Capital*, especially in section 5 of chapter X on 'the struggle for a normal working day'. Although he does not use the term, Marx here reveals an understanding that the establishment of a maximum working day is equivalent to the production of a public good, the physical well-being and ability to reproduce itself of the workforce. This public good is threatened by unrestricted competition because, 'in its blind unrestrainable passion, its were-wolf hunger for surplus-labour, capital oversteps not only the moral, but even the merely physical maximum bounds of the working-day'.[54] That there are no benefits to the individual capitalist from limiting the working day is recognised. 'Capital cares nothing for the length of life of labour-power. All that concerns it is simply and solely the maximum of labour-power that can be rendered fluent in a working-day. It attains this end by shortening the extent of the labourer's life, as a greedy farmer snatches increased produce from the soil by robbing it of its fertility.' Capitalism 'produces thus, with the extension of the working-day, not only the deterioration of human labour-power by robbing it of its normal, moral and physical, conditions of development and function. It produces also the premature exhaustion and death of this labour-power itself. It extends the labourer's time of production during a given period by shortening his actual life-time'.[55] '*Après-moi le deluge!* is the watchword of every capitalist and of every capitalist nation. Hence Capital is reckless of the health or length of life of the labourer, unless under compulsion from society.'[56] Though entirely rational for the individual capitalist, this is suicidal folly from the standpoint of the class as a whole. Marx draws a contrast here with slavery, where labourers, like horses, are private property, so that the slave-owner does have a material interest in humane treatment. 'It would seem therefore that the interest of capital itself points in the direction of a normal working-day.'[57]

Functional as it was for the system as a whole, the achievement of a normal working day was possible only after a prolonged struggle, and possessed a substantial symbolic and ideological significance. 'The creation of a normal working-day is, therefore, the product of a protracted civil war, more or less dissembled, between the capitalist class and the working-class.' It had begun in England, whose workers 'were the champions, not only of the English, but of the modern working-class generally, as their theorists were the first to throw down the gauntlet to the theory of capital'.[58] (He cites Robert Owen in a footnote.) As Marx said at the inaugural meeting of the International Working Men's Association in 1864, the Ten Hours' Bill was 'not only a great practical success; it was the victory of a principle; it was the first time that in broad daylight the political economy of the middle class succumbed to the political economy of the working class'.[59]

Once it had been achieved, the normal working day served to strengthen those forces that were already increasing the centralisation of capital and thus market eradication and bureaucratisation. As Engels put it in 1892, in a preface to a new edition of his *Condition of the Working Class in England*, manufacturing industry had been 'apparently moralised' in the 1840s. 'Thus the truck-system was suppressed, the Ten Hours' Bill was enacted, and a number of other secondary reforms introduced – much against the spirit of Free Trade and unbridled competition, but quite as much in favour of the giant capitalist in his competition with his less favoured brother.'[60] Capitalist acceptance of trade unions, and other concessions, are 'nothing else but means to accelerate the concentration of capital in the hands of the few.... and to crush all the quicker and all the safer the smaller competitors, who could not make both ends meet without such perquisites' as had previously been provided by a totally unregulated labour market.[61]

Marx, too, writes in volume I of *Capital* of '[t]he necessity for a generalisation of the Factory Acts' from cotton spinning and weaving to capitalist industry in its entirety, due to the way in which all branches of industry 'become, in a, comparatively speaking, wonderfully short time, dens of misery in which capitalistic exploitation obtains free play for the wildest excesses'. This generates a 'cry of the capitalists for equality in the conditions of competition, i.e., for equal restrain[t] on all exploitation of labour'.[62] The 'general extension' of the Factory Acts 'hastens on the general conversion of numerous isolated small industries into a few combined industries carried on upon a large scale; it therefore accelerates the concentration of capital and the exclusive predominance of the factory system'.[63]

3.3.5 The increasing role of science in production

The fifth and final factor tending to reduce the importance of market relations was the increasing role of science in capitalist production, which was seen to be expanding the public sphere at the expense of the private. In the *Grundrisse* manuscripts of 1857 there is a long discussion of 'the labour process and alienation in machinery and science', in the course of which Marx writes that

> The tendency of capitalism is thus to give a scientific character to production, reducing direct labour to a simple element in this process. As with the transformation of value into capital, we see when we examine the development of capital more closely that on the one hand it presupposes a definite historical development of the productive forces (science being included among these forces) and on the other hand accelerates and compels this development'.[64]

Or, as he put it 6 years later in *Wages, Price and Profit*, science has become the principal source of rising productivity and the most important means 'by which the social or cooperative character of labour is developed'.[65]

As a consequence, direct individual labour is becoming less and less important:

> It is reduced quantitatively to a smaller proportion, just as qualitatively it is reduced to an indispensable but subordinate role as compared with scientific labour in general, the technological application of the natural sciences, and the general productive forces arising from the social organisation of production. This force appears

> to be a natural gift of community labour, although it is a historical product. *In this way capital works for its own dissolution as the dominant form of production.*[66]

The significance of science in this context is brought out very clearly by Hal Draper, who emphasises Marx's comment that scientific knowledge 'costs it [capital] nothing'; in modern terminology, it is non-excludable and also non-rival, and is thus a public good. In volume III of *Capital*, Draper reminds us, as in the *Grundrisse*, Marx distinguishes 'general labour' from 'collective labour'. The latter is under the direct control of an individual unit of capital, and produces marketable commodities. The former refers to 'all scientific labour, all discovery and all invention', and is the common property of humanity as a whole.[67] This is described in the *Grundrisse* as 'the labour of the community – of its historical development, which does not proceed from the labour of individuals or the exchange of their labours'.[68] Since it costs nothing, capitalists tend to undervalue it.[69] As this general or universal labour becomes more and more important, commodity production and market exchange have become correspondingly less so.

3.4 The market in the revisionist controversy

We do not wish to overstate our case. Especially as far as Marx is concerned, this analysis of the decline of the market is based on fragmented reasoning and observations rather than fully developed arguments. This is hardly surprising, since with the exception of the Factory Acts they were hardly very developed in practice in 1867, when Marx's creative work in economics largely ceased. Engels, who lived until 1895 and was intellectually active and involved in political economy until the end, took things a little further. But it was only after his death that the claims of Marx and Engels were developed much more systematically by Bernstein and the revisionists, by Hilferding and by Bukharin.

The British Fabian socialists arrived at very similar conclusions about market elimination from different – not to say weaker – arguments, based very largely upon casual observation of the growth of state intervention throughout the nineteenth century.[70] The political inferences that the Fabians drew from this were, of course, totally different: since they were reformists, only a gradual, peaceful, 'evolutionary' movement towards socialism could be countenanced, not the proletarian revolution that lay at the heart of the Marxian political project. Similar arguments were at stake in the revisionist controversy that raged in the German socialist movement in the late 1890s and early years of the twentieth century.[71] The revisionist Eduard Bernstein (1850–1932) was exiled in London between 1888 and 1901, and debated the prospects for socialism with the leading Fabian theorists. He shared much of their vision, although he always denied having been influenced by them.[72] In his attack on orthodox Marxism, Bernstein has nothing to say about the increasing role of science in production, but he does refer to the other four arguments that Marx had advanced in predicting the decline of the market in effect endorsing three of them but expressing serious reservations about the increasing centralisation of capital. On this question Bernstein cites official data for Britain, France and Switzerland, concluding that

> If the relentless advance of technology and the centralisation of businesses in an increasing number of branches of industry is a fact the significance of which even obdurate reactionaries can hardly ignore nowadays, it is a no-less-well-established fact that in a whole range of branches of industry small and medium-sized businesses prove to be quite capable of surviving alongside large companies.[73]

Among the reasons for the survival of small business are the relative absence of economies of scale in many industries and the need in others for the producer to remain close to his consumers. Thus 'it looks today not as though large companies are constantly absorbing small and medium-sized companies but as though they are simply growing *alongside* them.'[74] According to Bernstein this is true in retailing and agriculture even more than in manufacturing. If the German state were to expropriate all enterprises employing more than 20 workers, a very large section of the economy would be unaffected.[75]

Despite these reservations about the centralisation process, however, Bernstein agrees with the orthodox Marxists that cartels are increasing in number and importance. Indeed, he welcomes them. Engels, he suggests, was uncertain as to whether cartels reduced the severity of cyclical fluctuations, or, as Rosa Luxemburg – a leading opponent of revisionism – now insisted, made them more severe. Bernstein is in no doubt that Luxemburg was wrong. Cartels can and do 'check the anarchy of production'[76] by replacing market instability with private planning of production, and especially planning of investment. Unlike tariffs, which represent an unnatural interference with economic life,

> The industrial cartel.... has grown out of the soil of the economy itself and is a characteristic means of adjusting production to the

> movements of the market. There is no question that at the same time it is, or can become, a means for monopolistic exploitation. But neither is there any question that, in its first capacity, it represents an enhancement of all previous remedies for overproduction. With much less risk than an individual enterprise, it can temporarily limit production in times of a glut on the market. What is better, it is also in a position to take steps against unfair competition from abroad. To deny this is to deny the superiority of organisation over anarchic competition. But that is what we do when we deny in principle that cartels can have a modifying effect on the nature and frequency of crises.[77]

Bernstein also acknowledges the rise of joint-stock companies. Against Marx, however, he argues that this has been accompanied by an increase rather than a reduction in the number of property owners.[78] These companies also contribute to economic stability by making possible an expansion in the use of credit. Again criticising Luxemburg, Bernstein suggests that 'credit abolishes the antagonism between the mode of production and the mode of exchange in that it periodically levels out the disparities between production and exchange.... by uniting many small capitalists, it transforms vast productive forces into collective property'.[79] Marx himself had recognised this, pointing to the way in which credit allows 'the gradual extension of cooperative enterprises on a more or less national scale'.[80] Bernstein also makes much of the growing capitalist acceptance of trade unions, in almost all advanced capitalist countries except in Germany, and of the need for state regulation of the labour market. This, he maintains, is connected to the growth of cartels, since their monopoly pricing often permits the workers to 'get a certain share of the booty'.[81] For both Bernstein and the Fabians, unions are 'indispensable organs of democracy and not merely transient coalitions'. They represent 'the democratic element in industry. Their tendency is to erode the absolute power of capital and to give the worker a direct influence in the management of industry',[82] thereby civilising the market for labour power.

Thus Bernstein, while a strong critic of Marxian orthodoxy on many important points, tended to agree with Marx on the decline of the market. In this, ironically, his position was close to that of the most influential defender of orthodox Marxism, Karl Kautsky (1854–1938), the principal theoretician of the German socialist party. Kautsky had already endorsed Marx's analysis in *The Class Struggle*, his gloss on the party's Erfurt Programme of 1891, arguing that the economies of scale that can be obtained from new technology lead inevitably to the concentration of the means of production in fewer and fewer hands.[83] At the same time, capitalists come to rely more and more on the state, destroying the validity of traditional liberal criticisms of state interference in economic life. Such is the growing need for 'regulation and management of the economic mechanism' that the 'economic omnipotence of the state, which appeared to the Manchester School as a socialist Utopia, has developed under the very eyes of that school into an inevitable result of the capitalist system of production itself'.[84]

However, Kautsky conceded very little to Bernstein and other revisionists. At the Stuttgart conference of the Social Democratic Party in 1898 he confined himself to criticising Bernstein for mistakenly generalising from the English experience, which was in fact quite exceptional, not least in the willingness of capitalists to tolerate trade union interference in the operation of the labour market. Things were quite different in Germany.[85] In his subsequent book-length reply to Bernstein, Kautsky asserts that the centralisation of capital is in fact increasing in all sectors of the economy. It is the direction of change that is crucial, not the survival of small business in some industries. Bernstein's is a theory of 'the barber's shop and the public house'.[86] These small enterprises are in any event completely dependent upon big business, Kautsky maintains; the economic centralisation of capital has thus gone much further than the purely technical centralisation.[87] Centralisation is proceeding also in agriculture, albeit more slowly and in a more complicated way than in industry. Thus Marx is right, and Bernstein is wrong. Indeed, according to Kautsky there is a curious contradiction in the latter's argument. Bernstein, like all other informed observers, agrees that the growth of cartels is 'the phenomenon which most characterises our economic life today'.[88] But this is possible only because of the increased centralisation of capital, which the revisionists perversely deny. (Bernstein had not, in fact, denied it; he had simply noted that it was a more gradual and more complex process than either Marx or Kautsky was prepared to admit.)

It was left to one of the youngest and most passionate participants in the controversy to take issue with both Bernstein and Kautsky on these important issues. Unwittingly – for she too claimed to be defending orthodox Marxism – Rosa Luxemburg (1877–1919) ended up attacking Marx as well. There has been no decline in competition, Luxemburg claims, and no weakening of competition in the market for labour power; neither joint-stock companies nor the increasing use of credit has made any significant difference to the operation of the capitalist mode of production or the market: 'we have not yet reached the state of full capitalist maturity presupposed in Marx's model of periodic crisis formation. The world market is still developing.'[89] Cartels are necessarily confined to individual industries, Luxemburg suggests, and are therefore incapable of restoring order to the system:

> According to Bernstein, they restrain anarchy and prevent crises by regulating production. This is, of course, true only to the extent that cartels, trusts, etc. become the general and dominant form of production. But that is rendered impossible by the very nature of the cartels themselves. The ultimate economic aim and consequence of employers' organisations is to exclude competition from a certain sector, thus influencing market profit in such a way as to increase the share gained by that branch of industry. Organisations of this kind can increase the rate of profit within one branch of industry, only at the expense of another, and they can therefore never become universal. If they were extended to all major branches of industry, they would cancel each other out.[90]

Neither is it the case that medium-sized business is tending to disappear:

> The conflict between medium-sized companies and big capital should not be envisaged as a regular battle in which the troops of the weaker party are steadily and continuously reduced, but rather as a periodic mowing-down of small capitals, which then shoot up again like weeds, only to be mown down once more by the scythe of big industry.[91]

And there are good reasons for this resilience, since

> .... there are two respects in which small capitals serve as factors in the technical revolution: they initiate new methods of production in traditional and well-established branches of industry, and they create new branches of production not yet exploited by the big capitalist. The idea that medium-scale capitalist enterprise is proceeding on a straight course of gradual decline is completely false.[92]

For Luxemburg, capitalism remains competitive to its core. This is true also of the labour market, for although in a few industries there may be 'a cartel of workers and employers against the consumer',[93] such a 'reactionary undertaking' can no more be extended across the entire economy than the product market cartels on which it relies. It is not clear that unions have a secure future, Luxemburg maintains, and in any case they do not abolish or even seriously alter the workings of the market for labour power. The trade union is

> ....the means whereby the workers actualise the capitalist law of wages, i.e. the sale of their labour power at current market prices. The unions serve the proletariat by exploiting, to its advantage, the market conditions which prevail at any given moment. However, these conditions themselves – i.e. the demand for labour power as determined by the state of production, the supply of labour power as provided by proletarianisation and natural reproduction, and, finally, the productivity of labour at any given time – all lie outside the sphere of trade union influence. The unions, therefore, cannot subvert the law of wages. They can, at best, keep capitalist exploitation within the current 'normal' bounds, but they cannot abolish exploitation itself, not even by stages.[94]

Thus unions can achieve 'nothing more than the regulation of capitalist exploitation according to market relationships'.[95]

Luxemburg was the only major participant in the revisionist debate who did not anticipate the decline of the market, and her major economic work, *The Accumulation of Capital*,[96] deals with a competitive capitalist system in which neither cartels, nor monopolies nor joint-stock companies play any essential role. In this, however, she was the exception. Luxemburg was never afraid to be her own woman. Of all the Marxian theorists of the Second International, she was the one who would have been least surprised by the onset of neoliberalism, more than half a century after her death. For all other leading Marxists, a tendency to market elimination was both clear and pronounced, including in the classic work of Rudolf Hilferding.

3.5 The market in Hilferding's *Finance Capital*

Rudolf Hilferding (1877–1941) studied economics under the eminent neoclassical economist Eugen von Böhm-Bawerk at the University of Vienna. His contemporaries included Joseph Schumpeter, on whom (as we shall see in Chapter 4) he had a significant influence. In *Finance Capital*, published in 1910, Hilferding reformulated Marx's analysis of the decline of the market in the context of a capitalist economy increasingly dominated by big business, and above all by big banks.

Hilferding never doubted that Marx had been correct in predicting the increased centralisation of capital and the resulting growth of cartels and trusts:

> ....there is a constant tendency for cartelization to be extended. As we have seen, the independent industries become increasingly dependent upon the cartelized industries until they are finally annexed by them. The ultimate outcome of this process would be the formation of a general cartel. The whole of capitalist production would then be consciously regulated by a single body which would determine the volume of production in all branches of industry. Price determination would become a purely nominal matter, involving only the distribution of the total product between the cartel magnates on one side and all the other member of society on the other. Price would then cease to be the outcome of factual relationships into which people have entered, and would become a mere accounting device by which things were allocated among people. Money would have no role.... This would be a consciously regulated society, but in an antagonistic form.[97]

Such a 'general cartel' is unlikely to endure, however, in the face of the conflicts of interest that would inevitably arise among its members.[98] And, while cartelisation makes possible the planning of production in individual industries and to this extent serves to 'diminish economic anarchy',[99] it worsens the problems faced by the system as a whole. Cartels can only shift the burden of any adjustment to change onto the remaining competitive industries, and will therefore make crises more severe, not less severe as revisionists like Bernstein claimed.[100]

The growth of monopoly is also associated with an increasing economic role for the state, since tariffs are required to protect cartels from import competition and permit them to dump their surplus output in foreign markets.[101] For this reason alone big capitalists are now much less hostile than they had once been to the state. More and more they depend on the state to defend their overseas interests, which are growing all the time with the massive export of capital. Thus finance capital needs a strong state. Liberal internationalism is no longer part of the bourgeoisie's world view: 'It has no faith in the harmony of capitalist interests, and knows well that competition is becoming increasingly a political power struggle.'[102]

These tendencies are reinforced by the growing use of credit and the rising power of the banks. Hilferding argues that credit is anti-capitalist and anti-market, since it involves a retreat from the impersonality of market relations, and thus foreshadows a post-capitalist society:

> In credit transactions the material, business relationship is always accompanied by a personal relationship, which appears as a direct relationship between members of society in contrast to the material social relations which categorize other economic categories such as money; namely, what is often called 'trust'. In this sense a fully developed credit system is the antithesis of capitalism, and represents organization and control as opposed to anarchy. It has its source in socialism, but has been adapted to capitalist society; it is a fraudulent kind of socialism, modified to suit the needs of capitalism.[103]

These trends of concentration and centralisation of capital are also evident in the financial sector, where

> there is a growing tendency to eliminate competition among the banks themselves, and on the other side, to concentrate all capital in the form of money capital, and to make it available to producers only through the banks. If this trend were to continue, it would finally result in a single bank or a group of banks establishing control over the entire money capital. Such a 'central bank' would then exercise control over social production as a whole.[104]

This growing control of industry and commerce by ever more concentrated and centralised banks, combined with increasing vertical integration in the industrial sector, 'involves a contraction of the social division of labour'[105] at the same time as there is an increasing 'technical division of labour within the combined enterprises'.[106] The jobs that workers do are more and more specialised, but the coordination of their work has been simplified; it is no longer carried out by impersonal market forces, and is no longer subject to the law of value which governs competitive capitalism.

These developments are to be welcomed by the socialist movement, since:

> The socializing function of finance capital facilitates enormously the task of overcoming capitalism. Once finance capital has brought the most important branches of production under its control, it is enough for society, through its conscious executive organ – the state conquered by the working class – to seize finance capital in order to

> gain immediate control of these branches of production.... taking possession of six large Berlin banks would mean taking possession of the most important spheres of large-scale industry, and would greatly facilitate the initial phases of socialist policy during the transition period, when capitalist accounting might still prove useful.[107]

Thus, for Hilferding, the development of capitalist society itself is very clearly pointing the way towards socialism, even as it is becoming more crisis-prone, more polarised and more antagonistic.

3.6 The impact of the First World War

Writing from exile in Switzerland, the Bolshevik economist and close associate of Lenin, Nikolai Bukharin (1888–1938) reaffirmed some of the central themes in Hilferding's *Finance Capital* and extended the argument to allow for the changes induced by the war. Bukharin points to the emergence before 1914 of a world economy with a strong tendency for prices of the same commodity, wage rates and rates of profit to be equalised on a global scale. The world economy remains 'an unorganised system of economies devoid of a conscious collective management where, on the contrary, the economic laws are the elemental laws of the market and of production subordinated to the market'.[108] The individual national economies, by contrast, have become highly organised. The elimination of competition within the nation, Bukharin argues, has only transferred the anarchy of capitalist production to the world stage, so that economic crises are now global rather than national, and war has emerged as 'one of the methods of capitalist competition'.[109] Thus it is not true that 'social progress has already reached a stage where "national" states can co-exist harmoniously. For the process of the internationalisation of economic life is by no means identical with the process of the internationalisation of capital interests'. In fact globalisation 'can and does sharpen, to a high degree, the conflict of interests among the various "national" groups of the bourgeoisie'.[110]

Within each nation, the continuing centralisation of capital has led to the growth of monopoly. Cartels and trusts 'must by no means be considered "abnormal" or "artificial" phenomena springing up in consequence of state aid like tariffs, freight rates, premiums, subsidies, or governmental orders, etc'. As a general rule, 'monopoly organisations are the strongest where productive forces are most developed',[111] with an important role being played by joint-stock companies and the expansion of credit. It is accelerated by means of vertical integration, which 'tends to turn the entire "national" economy into a single combined enterprise with an organisation [organic?] connection between all the branches of production'.[112] There is thus a 'very strong tendency towards transforming the entire national economy into one gigantic combined enterprise under the tutelage of the financial kings and the capitalist state, an enterprise which monopolises the national market and forms the prerequisite for organised production on a higher non-capitalist level'.[113]

Crucially, however, Bukharin denies that this process can be expected to extend to the international level. The uneven development of world capitalism in a system of territorial states precludes this, since 'the existing differences of economic structure and consequently of production-costs make agreements disadvantageous for the advanced "national" groups'.[114] Evidence of continuing national rivalry is provided by the increasing use of tariffs as a weapon of economic aggression. 'Thus, together with the internationalisation of [the] economy and the internationalisation of capital, there is going on a process of "national" intertwining of capital, a process of "nationalising" capital, fraught with the greatest consequences.'[115] These consequences include the growing export of capital, under the military and political protection of the state: 'the sharpening of competition between various states is most salient here. The internationalisation of economic life here, too, makes it necessary to settle controversial questions by fire and [the] sword.'[116] Thus imperialist rivalries must be seen as 'one of the forms of the competitive struggle' between national capitalist states.[117]

Bukharin sees the First World War as simply the culmination of this struggle. But it has also accelerated the underlying structural changes, promoting 'the appearance on the world arena of one of the largest state capitalist trusts, possessed of an unusually strong internal organisation. We mean the United States of America',[118] and further encouraging the 'national consolidation of capital in all the belligerent states:

> Thus if the war cannot halt the general development of world capital, if, on the contrary, it expresses the greatest expansion of the centralisation process, the war also influences the structure of individual 'national' economies in such a way as to intensify centralisation within the limits of every 'national' body and, while wasting productive forces on a colossal scale, it organises 'national economy' in that it places it more and more under the combined rule of finance capital and the state.[119]

The war has stimulated a further substantial increase in the economic activities of the state. This has not been seriously resisted by the capitalists, and will be maintained after hostilities cease:

> ....economic evolution, fortified at this point by the war, must and does lead to a situation where the bourgeoisie as a whole is more tolerant regarding monopolistic interference of the state power. The basic reason for this change is the ever growing closeness between state power and the leading spheres of finance capital. State and private monopoly enterprises merge into one entity within the framework of the state capitalist trust.[120]

Thus the war will prove to have profound material and ideological consequences. 'The exigencies of the war, and of imperialist preparations for war, force the bourgeoisie to adopt a new form of capitalism, to place production and distribution under state power, to destroy completely [the] old bourgeois individualism.'[121] But for Bukharin this does not represent the beginnings of a new socialist order, as some German theorists – the 'state socialists' – maintained. Commodity production remains, he concludes, at the level of the world economy, and with it the class division between workers and capitalists.

Rudolf Hilferding was not among the German 'state socialists' criticised by Bukharin at this point. Hilferding's interpretation of the German war economy lies somewhere between their optimism concerning the prospects for a peaceful evolution of socialism out of capitalism and Bukharin's revolutionary pessimism. He denies the optimists' naive assertion that the interests of workers, capitalists and the state are now identical. But he does agree that the growth of working-class power has lessened the intensity of class antagonisms, while the emergence of finance capital has reduced the anarchy of capitalist production. The war can only reinforce these tendencies:

> In place of the victory of socialism, there appears possible a society organised, indeed, but hierarchically and not democratically organised, at the apex of which stand the combined forces of the capitalist monopolies and the state, under whom the working masses are engaged in a hierarchy as agents of production. Instead of the triumph of socialism over capitalist society we would have an organised capitalism, better adapted than hitherto to meeting the immediate material needs of the masses.[122]

The impact that World War I had on Vladimir Ilyich Lenin (1870–1924) was heavily influenced by both Hilferding and Bukharin. Lenin, too, recognised that the system was becoming ever more 'organised' at the national level, resulting in a much reduced role for market relations. But his focus is concentrated on the international causes and consequences. He stresses even more than Bukharin, let alone Hilferding, that a new era has dawned, in which the destructiveness of war dominates the expansion of production. The leading capitalist powers have almost completed the colonisation of the world while the uneven development of national capitalist systems continues to change their power relative to each other, resulting in 'wars of redivision'. Thus any progressive features retained by capitalism have been eclipsed by its militarism, and revolutionary Marxists everywhere should no longer be inhibited by economic backwardness. The capitalist world economy is the relevant unit in terms of which the appropriateness of revolution is to be assessed, not any national unit of capitalism, whether it is advanced or backward. This doctrine became a key component of the theoretical foundations of the Bolshevik revolution in 1917.[123]

3.7 Between the wars

Hilferding returned to the notion of 'organised capitalism' in the mid-1920s, by which time he was a German citizen and a Socialist deputy in the Reichstag (he served as finance minister in the coalition governments of 1923 and 1928–9). The war has further increased the centralisation of capital and the power of the cartels and trusts, Hilferding now claims. Contrary to what he predicted in *Finance Capital*, this has improved the stability of the world economy and diminished the severity of the business cycle. (No more than any other Marxian – or mainstream – economist did Hilferding have any inkling of the impending Great Depression.) Private economic planning by big business, and the regulation of credit by the monetary authorities and the banks, has also contributed to greater economic stability. Internationally, conflict between the capitalist nations has become less menacing, with a new spirit of 'realistic pacifism' making a renewal of world war most unlikely. The growing political and trade union power of the working class has significantly improved its conditions of life. There remains an acute contradiction between the increasingly regulated character of production and the unorganised basis of capitalist property relations, but this can also be resolved peacefully, by progressive social reform. To some degree the market has already been tamed, Hilferding argues, and further moves in this direction are now politically and economically feasible.[124]

There are some ironies in all this. Hilferding had become, in effect, a Marxian revisionist, though he never lost sight of the importance of class conflict in the way that Bernstein had. As for Bukharin, he seized on the suppression of market relations in the period of War Communism in Russia (1918–21) as offering the prospect of a direct leap to post-capitalist society. However, his thinking soon changed dramatically. As a firm supporter of Lenin's New Economic Policy, initiated in 1921, he was associated – under Stalin's rule, fatally associated – with the liberal socialist position that market relations should be allowed a significant role in the gradual industrialisation of the Soviet economy.[125] But the official Communist line remained that taken by Bukharin in 1915 and affirmed by Lenin in the following year: the contradictions of the capitalist mode of production have been transferred from the national to the international plane, so that competition now takes place between nations, not between individual capitalists, and will inevitably flare up into renewed imperialist war.

Against the Leninist orthodoxy a minority of independent and anti-Stalinist Marxists in the West claimed, in effect, that it was business as usual, much as Rosa Luxemburg had argued. Capitalism remained basically competitive, anarchic, unorganised and driven by the same economic laws that Marx had identified. For the social democrat Henryk Grossmann, the most fundamental of these laws is the tendency for the rate of profit to fall as competition compels capitalists to introduce new techniques of production that increase the organic composition of capital more rapidly than the rate of exploitation. Neither finance capital, nor monopoly nor the large corporation play any essential part in this story; it is as if capitalism had not changed in any fundamental way since the middle of the nineteenth century.[126] However, none of these arguments proved very influential.

Moreover, the world *had* changed, if only because of the survival of the Bolshevik regime. What new mode of production was being created in the Soviet Union? And what were the implications, if indeed there were any, for the capitalist world? As early as 1919 Karl Kautsky was arguing that the October Revolution could not, in principle, result in the construction of socialism in Russia. History could not be short-circuited; socialism would come after capitalism had been fully developed, not before or instead of it. Hence the Bolsheviks were fated to restore capitalism in Russia, whatever their own intentions:

> It is only the old feudal large landed property which exists no longer. Conditions in Russia were ripe for its abolition but they were not ripe for the abolition of capitalism. Capitalism is now once again celebrating a resurrection, but in forms that are more oppressive and harrowing for the proletariat than of old. Instead of assuming higher industrialised forms, private capitalism has assumed the most wretched and shabby forms of black marketeering and money speculation. Industrial capitalism has developed to become state capitalism. Formerly state officials and officials from private capital were critical, often very hostile towards each other. Consequently the working man found that his advantage lay with one or the other in turn. Today the state bureaucracy and capitalist bureaucracy are merged into one – that is the upshot of the great socialist revolution brought about by the Bolsheviks, It constitutes the most oppressive of all despotisms that Russia has ever had to suffer.[127]

In effect, while Kautsky and the Bolsheviks agreed on the market-eradicating tendency of advanced capitalism, Kautsky's point here was that pre-revolutionary Russia had not been an advanced capitalist society, so that this tendency is irrelevant. If the country was not to succumb to a dreadful tyranny, the market had to be tolerated for quite some time.[128]

In the early 1920s criticism of the new 'state capitalism' in Russia came from dissident Bolsheviks inside the Soviet Union and from Menshevik exiles, Council Communists and others in Western Europe.[129] Once forced industrialisation began, with the first Five Year Plan in 1929, the state capitalist interpretation gained support from many other opponents of the Stalinist dictatorship. Although Leon Trotsky never abandoned his belief that the Soviet Union was a 'workers' state' (albeit one with severe bureaucratic deformations), his former secretary Raya Dunayevskaya came to disagree with him:

> The determining factor in analyzing the class nature of a society is not whether the means of production are the *private* property of the capitalist class or are state-owned, but whether the means of production are *capital*, that is, whether they are monopolized and alienated from the direct producers. The Soviet Government occupies in relation to the whole economic system the position which a capitalist occupies in relation to a single enterprise. Max Shachtman's designation of the class nature of the Soviet Union as 'bureaucratic state socialism' is

> an irrational expression behind which there exists the real economic relation of state-capitalist-exploiter to the propertyless exploited.[130]

She subsequently defended this position against Paul Baran, Oskar Lange and others in the pages of the *American Economic Review*.[131]

There were obvious parallels with contemporary developments in Western Europe and the United States. As Paul Mattick put it, there was 'an ever greater intrusion of the State into competitive society, a process resulting in "New Deals", "National-Socialism", and "Bolshevism", the various names for the different degrees and variations of the centralization and concentration processes of the capitalist system'.[132] The growth of state intervention was analysed in greater detail by Friedrich Pollock (1894–1970) in a series of articles in the theoretical journal of the Frankfurt School between 1932 and 1936. Economic liberalism is in decline, Pollock notes; even its former adherents now support a planned economy, often citing the success of Soviet planning in doing so. There are deep structural reasons for the decline of the free market, including the rise of giant corporations and administered pricing, together with the increasing tendency for the state to prop up failing private enterprises. This 'guaranteed capitalism' undermines the operation of market forces, since competition can only regulate a capitalist economy if it is allowed to be at least potentially ruinous. State interference, then, is both a symptom and a cause of the collapse of competitive capitalism. In its new monopolistic phase, planning will restore a reasonable level of economic performance. The concentration and centralisation of capital has made planning much easier, Pollock suggests. Planning is opposed by capitalists only because it would expose their lack of any economic function, and highlight their conversion into mere rentiers.[133]

A new 'state capitalist' stage is now emerging generally, Pollock argues.[134] Pointing to the growth of state enterprise in Britain and Germany, and the extension of state intervention in the early months of the New Deal in the United States, he claims that power is increasingly being concentrated in the hands of a smaller and smaller group of 'economic feudal lords',[135] while the middle class is losing what little remains of its economic independence and the proletariat is increasingly segmented and regulated. 'What is coming to an end', Pollock concludes, 'is not capitalism but only its liberal phase. Economically, politically and culturally, there will in future be ever less freedom for the majority of mankind'.[136]

This was written before the full implications of Hitler's rise to power could be discerned. Three years later, Pollock and his colleague

Kurt Mandelbaum (writing in exile under the joint pseudonym Erich Baumann) criticised John Maynard Keynes's *General Theory* for its sympathetic treatment of Mercantilist ideas and its unmistakable authoritarian tendencies: 'Keynes promises that private property, freedom, individual initiative and "efficiency" will be preserved, if we draw the necessary consequences from his revision of liberalism. The use which has been made of his proposals shows that these good things can be guaranteed only for a powerful minority and only if they are taken away from the great majority.'[137] (Keynes had opened himself to such criticism by writing, in the preface to the German translation of the *General Theory*, that his theory might be more appropriate to an authoritarian state than to a democratic one.)[138]

In 1940 Rudolf Hilferding, dismissing the concept of 'state capitalism' as self-contradictory, wrote instead of the emergence of a 'totalitarian state economy', which 'eliminates precisely the autonomy of economic laws'. In Nazi Germany and Stalin's Russia there is no longer a market economy: 'It is no longer price but rather a state planning commission that now determines what is produced and how. Formally, prices and wages still exist, but their function is no longer the same; they no longer determine the process of production, which is now controlled by a central power that fixes prices and wages.'[139] As the dissident Yugoslav Communist, Milovan Djilas, later put it, Lenin had been right to describe capitalist politics as 'concentrated economy'. But this had been reversed under Communism, when 'economy has become concentrated politics'.[140] In similar vein Herbert Marcuse characterised the National Socialist state as the enemy of the market. It represents 'a gigantic monopoly concern', which has introduced techniques of scientific management not only to the entire economy but also to education, culture and leisure activities.[141]

3.8 The view from 1941

In the 1930s James Burnham (1905–87) had been a prominent American Trotskyist. But, dissatisfied with the analysis of the Soviet Union offered by Trotsky and his followers, Burnham later developed an original and provocative interpretation of his own. His book *The Managerial Revolution* (1941), which became an immediate best-seller, was both heretical and evidently grounded in the principles of historical materialism. Burnham bases his thesis of a managerial revolution on a simple syllogism. Capitalism is evidently unsustainable; it shows no sign of changing into socialism; therefore it must be evolving into something else.[142]

While sympathetic to 'the similar theory of the bureaucratic revolution',[143] Burnham prefers the term 'managerial', since it is managers who have taken over the direction and coordination of production from capitalist financiers and stockholders (although he includes state bureaucrats in his 'managerial' class). Their rise to power is most obvious in Soviet Russia, and it is also evident in Nazi Germany; 'Leninism–Stalinism' and 'Fascism–Nazism' provide ideological support for the new rulers. The managers are also on the road to power in the United States, where 'Technocracy' and 'New Dealism' represent 'the most primitive and least organised' of the new managerial ideologies.[144] By 'New Dealism' Burnham was referring to the statist, anti-market tendencies of the Roosevelt administration; by 'Technocracy', he was describing a movement of North American professionals united in the belief that most important economic problems had engineering solutions, and that 'industrial waste' could be combated by the efforts of professional experts independently of (if not in outright opposition to) the market.

Burnham defines capitalism in terms that orthodox Marxism reserved for competitive capitalism, that is to say, as a two-class system of profit-driven commodity production in which money functions as capital and 'production as a whole is regulated, so far as it is regulated, primarily by "the market", both the internal and the international market. There is no person or group of persons who consciously and deliberately regulates production as a whole. The market decides, independently of the wills of human beings'.[145] Planning is thus 'incompatible with the nature of capitalism';[146] the role of the state is narrowly circumscribed, and the prevailing ideology emphasises individualism and a firm belief in progress. The increasingly crisis-prone nature of twentieth-century capitalism and the emergence of permanent mass unemployment have led to the collapse of the bourgeoisie's confidence in its own liberal ideology. But there is nothing to suggest that it will be replaced by socialism, as Marx predicted. The Soviet experience demonstrates that the abolition of capitalist property rights is not a sufficient condition for socialism, and indeed Russia is moving away from the classlessness, internationalism and freedom that are the principal characteristics of a socialist society. In both East and West it is the managers, not the proletariat, who are assuming control.

For Burnham, Nazi Germany is not a form of capitalism as the orthodox Marxists claimed, but rather 'a managerial state in an early stage'.[147] Whatever their formal legal rights might be, German capitalists have lost effective ownership of the means of production, since they are no longer able to make any important decisions according to normal capitalist criteria. Almost all economic enterprise is subject to rigid state control, so that

> The regulation of production in Germany is no longer left to the market. What is to be produced, and how much, is decided, deliberately, by groups of men, by the state boards and bureaus and commissions. It is they who decide whether a new plant shall be built or an old plant retired, how raw materials shall be alloted and orders distributed, what quotas must be fulfilled by various branches of industry, what goods shall be put aside for export, how prices shall be fixed and credit and exchange extended. There is no requirement that these decisions of the bureaus must be based on any profit aim in the capitalist sense.... It is literally true to say that the Nazi economy, already, is not a 'profit economy'.[148]

The proletariat, for its part, has lost what little freedom it once enjoyed, and now has absolutely no revolutionary potential.

The example of Nazi Germany demonstrates to Burnham the superiority of managerial economy over capitalist economy, and this means that all capitalist states will be forced to give way to it. He suggests that the managerial revolution, which began in 1914, will be complete by 1964.[149] It will culminate in state ownership; since the state is in effect the property of the managers, this will ensure their complete control over the means of production. Managerial society, in fact, entails the fusion of the state and the economy. The New Deal has already seen a huge increase in state intervention in the US economy:

> During the past seven or eight years, however, new capitalist investment in private enterprise has been almost eliminated, the annual amounts totalling only a few hundreds of million dollars, while vast idle funds have piled up in the banks. This does not mean that new investment has not taken place. It has done so through government, and in state enterprise, where it is in effect measured by the increase in the national debt. Federal government investment during these years has totalled more than five times private investment, a plain enough signal where the economic future lies.[150]

Meanwhile, the extension of state control over many aspects of economic life 'imposes restrictions upon capitalist property rights, [and] removes the objects and functions controlled to a greater or less degree from the unmixed reign of the market and capitalist property relations'.[151] The growth of capitalist opposition to Roosevelt is significant: 'the capitalists oppose the New Deal because they realize, without being wholly clear about the full problem, the truth: that the New Deal is in direction and tendency anti-capitalist'.[152]

In the decade after the publication of *The Managerial Revolution* Burnham moved sharply to the political right and became the very first of the neoconservatives. In 1941, though, his Marxian roots were still apparent. Thus he invokes changes in the forces of production to explain the rise of managerial society. It is 'the growth of large-scale public corporations along with the technical development of modern industry' that has all but wiped out the traditional owner-managed enterprise, and it is 'through changes in the technique of production' that 'the functions of management become more distinctive, more complex, more specialized, and more crucial to the whole process of production, thus serving to set off those who perform these functions as a separate group or class in society'.[153] This process has been accelerated by the Great Depression, which shows the urgency of the need for economic planning:

> In managerial economy, the regulation of production will not be left to the 'automatic' functioning of the market, but will be carried out deliberately and consciously by groups of men, by the appropriate institutions of the unlimited managerial state. As we saw, the necessarily decentralized economy of private enterprise makes impossible such deliberate regulation of production as a whole. Under the centralized economic structure of managerial society, regulation (planning) is a matter of course.[154]

Burnham objects to the term 'state capitalism' on the familiar grounds that it is contradictory as a description of the entire economic system; without private ownership, he argues, there can be no capitalists and thus no capitalism.[155] As we have seen, Friedrich Pollock had no such misgivings. The term is legitimate, Pollock maintains, because 'it indicates four items better than do all other suggested terms: that state capitalism is the successor of private capitalism, that the state assumes important functions of the private capitalist, that profit interests still play a significant role, and that it is not socialism'.[156] Nevertheless, terminology aside, the analysis of his 1941 article, 'State capitalism: its possibilities and limitations', is remarkably similar to that of Burnham. There are two critical characteristics of state capitalism, Pollock writes:

> (1) The market is deposed from its controlling function to coordinate production and distribution. This function has been taken over by a system of direct controls. Freedom of trade, enterprise and labor are subject to governmental interference of such a degree that they are practically abolished. With the autonomous market the so-called economic laws disappear.
> (2) These controls are vested in the state which uses a combination of old and new devices, including a 'pseudo-market', for regulating and expanding production and coordinating it with consumption. Full employment of all resources is claimed as the main achievement in the economic field. The state transgresses all the limits drawn for peacetime state activities.[157]

Pollock distinguishes democratic and totalitarian forms of state capitalism, with the state under the control either of the people or of 'a new ruling group, which has resulted from the merger of the most powerful vested interests, the top-ranking personnel in industrial and business management, the higher strata of the state bureaucracy (including the military) and the leading figures of the victorious party's bureaucracy'.[158] In either case, state capitalism is the result of long-term changes in the forces and the relations of production:

> Concentration of economic activity in giant enterprises, with its consequences of rigid prices, self-financing and ever growing concentration, government control of the credit system and foreign trade, quasi-monopoly positions of trade unions with the ensuing rigidity of the labor market, large-scale unemployment of labor and capital and enormous government expenses to care for the unemployed, are as many symptoms for the decline of the market system. They became characteristic in various degrees for all industrialized countries after the first world war.[159]

For Pollock the emergence of state capitalism 'signifies the transition from a predominantly economic to an essentially political era', in which 'the profit motive is superseded by the power motive'[160] and capitalists are reduced to mere rentiers. The limits to state capitalism are natural or political, not economic. 'Forewarned as we are', he concludes, 'we are unable to discover any inherent economic forces, "economic laws" of the old or a new type, which could prevent the functioning of state capitalism.... We may even say that under state capitalism economics as a social science has lost its object'.[161]

Neither Burnham nor Pollock is at all optimistic about the future. Authoritarianism is the order of the epoch for Burnham, although he suggests that some limited degree of democracy 'would be able to function, up to a point, without being a dangerous threat to the social rule, the power and privileges, of the managers or to the foundations of the new society',[162] and there is no reason why living standards might not slowly improve. Pollock's vision is bleaker, and foreshadows the dystopia of George Orwell's *Nineteen Eighty-Four.* Real wages will not increase under state capitalism, he argues, as this 'would imply more leisure time, more professional skill, more opportunity for critical thinking, out of which a revolutionary spirit might develop'. A permanent war economy is a more likely prospect, since neither mass unemployment nor a rising standard of living can be sustained.[163] We shall see in the next chapter how this deep pessimism was shared by contemporary conservative theorists of the decline of the market.

After 1941 the decline of the market no longer featured prominently in the Marxian literature, presumably because it was considered to be such an obvious phenomenon that it no longer needed to be emphasised. Most Marxists now believed themselves to be living in the final stage of capitalist development, which they variously described as 'imperialism', 'state monopoly capitalism' or simply 'monopoly capitalism'. One of the best-selling texts in the heyday of student radicalism in the late 1960s and early 1970s epitomised this consensus in its title: *Monopoly Capital.*[164] However, as late as 1979 Michel Aglietta, the founder of the 'regulation school' of French Marxism, explicitly ended his long survey of postwar global capitalism with the striking claim that the decline of the market was continuing. 'The coming massive socialization of the conditions of life will destroy free enterprise as the pillar of liberal ideology.'[165]

4

Neoclassicals, Keynesians and Heterodox Economists on the Decline of the Market

4.1 Introduction

Since they always adopted a perspective informed by historical materialism and concentrated on the capitalist mode of production, it is not surprising that writers with a Marxist background produced the most systematic and coherent analyses of the decline of the market. However, political economists from other schools of thought also covered much of the same ground and sometimes adopted a similar materialist perspective. In this chapter we discuss some prominent examples. We begin with Friedrich von Hayek and Joseph Schumpeter, classical liberal theorists, albeit with strong conservative inclinations, who in the 1940s accepted much of the validity of the Marxian prognosis, but bitterly regretted it. Then we assess the work of institutional economists in the United States who, from the 1930s to the 1970s, traced the far-reaching implications of the rise of the large corporation. In subsequent sections we deal with rather similar ideas in the work of John Maynard Keynes both before and after the publication of the *General Theory* in 1936, explore their influence during the so-called 'Keynesian revolution', and outline some of the ways in which mainstream, neoclassical economists were affected by these various currents of thought on the decline of the market and how they explained it.

4.2 The road to serfdom

Appointed to a chair at the London School of Economics in 1932, Friedrich von Hayek (1899–1992) was a powerful influence on British economics for the next 18 years, until his departure for the University of Chicago. Although he denied that he was a conservative, Hayek's unswerving opposition to any political interference with the existing distribution of income and wealth put him at odds with the great bulk of contemporary liberal opinion. In theoretical terms, though, he was indeed a classical liberal. Hayek was a convinced methodological individualist, an enemy of socialism in all forms, an opponent of expansionary government expenditure even in the most severe depression, and a resolute defender of *laissez-faire*. In 1944 he warned of the dangers threatening liberalism and the market in a pessimistic polemic that became a best-seller: *The Road to Serfdom*.

Hayek claims that England is much closer to Nazi-style totalitarianism than most of its citizens realised, and is moving further in that direction at an alarming pace. In fact he claims that the United Kingdom resembles Germany 20 or 30 years previously, when the intellectual seeds of Hitler's dictatorship were being sown by socialist theorists like Sombart and Spengler. This was a strange choice of adversaries. Werner Sombart (1863–1941), though close to Friedrich Engels in his youth, later broke with Marxism and by the 1920s had become a strong critic of German socialism, with anti-Semitic undertones.[1] The socialism advocated by Oswald Spengler (1880–1936) was of a distinctly Prussian variety, demanding 'obedience to the state, love of duty, and unflagging dedication to one's work'.[2] Neither man was remotely representative of mainstream German socialism, whether revolutionary or reformist.

However, unrestrained by the demands of scholarship, Hayek laments 'the increasing similarity between the economic views of the Right and Left and their common opposition to the Liberalism that used to be the common basis of most English politics'.[3] This growing hostility to economic freedom is promoted by 'the two great vested interests, organised capital and organised labour', but principally by the latter: 'the propaganda against competition by the Left', drawing on the support of organised labour, is at the core of 'the movement towards totalitarianism'.[4] In the past English people accepted the market, perhaps without knowing very much about how it worked. The new 'Economophobia', however, means that they now reject it, in the name of 'an incomplete and therefore erroneous rationalism' which demands that economic forces be subjected to social control. But it is 'men's submission to the impersonal forces of the market that in the past has made possible the growth of a civilisation which without this could not have developed'.[5] All these achievements are now at risk. Indeed, Hayek suggests, the battle is as good as lost: 'So long as Labour continues to assist in the destruction of the only order under which at least some degree of independence and freedom has been secured to every worker, there is indeed little hope for the future.'[6]

Why is this great disaster impending? Hayek is at pains to deny that there is any material basis for the decline of the market, thereby differentiating himself especially from the Marxists. The advocates of economic planning falsely claim that it is inevitable. 'The myth is deliberately cultivated that we are embarking on the new course not out of free will but because competition is spontaneously eliminated by technological changes which we neither can reverse nor should wish to prevent.' But, according to Hayek, this is simply untrue. 'The tendency towards monopoly and planning is not the result of any "objective facts" beyond our control, but the product of opinions fostered and propagated for half a century till they have come to dominate all our policy.'[7] Monopoly power is itself the result of political manipulation, not economies of scale; it is strongest in the most backward economies, and weakest in the most advanced. The myth has been created by analytical error. 'It is largely due to the influence of German socialist theoreticians, particularly Sombart... that the inevitable development of the competitive system into "monopoly capitalism" became widely accepted'.[8]

A second popular argument in favour of planning relies on the increasing complexity of modern civilisation, which, the enemies of the market claim, now requires conscious social regulation. 'This argument', however, 'is based on a complete misapprehension of the working of competition'. The price system, Hayek maintains, is in fact the only effective method of coordination for a complex economy. The support for planning of so many technical experts is easily explained: they have failed to understand the principle of opportunity cost, and cannot see that the pursuit of technical excellence will normally result in serious misallocation of resources. It is no accident that technocrats tend to be enemies of freedom. 'From the saintly and single-minded idealist to the fanatic is often but a step'.[9]

Hayek's account of the decline of the market is, therefore, rigorously idealist, not materialist: it has no foundation whatsoever in technology or economic relations, but is simply due to the prevalence of mistaken beliefs. 'It is because nearly everybody wants it that we are moving in this direction. There are no objective facts which make it inevitable'.[10] And again: 'The intellectual history of the last sixty or eighty years is indeed a perfect illustration of the truth that in social evolution nothing is inevitable but thinking makes it so.'[11]

4.3 Capitalism, socialism and democracy

His compatriot Joseph Schumpeter (1883–1950) arrived at a very similar conclusion by a very different route, one that was more materialist and heavily influenced by Marxists. In *Capitalism, Socialism and Democracy*, published in 1942, Schumpeter traces the material and cultural roots of the same ideological phenomena that Hayek identifies, and bemoans. 'Can capitalism survive?' he famously begins the prologue to the second part of his book. 'No. I do not think it can'. This is not because the system has failed, nor is it about to break down. On the contrary, 'its very success undermines the social institutions which protect it, and "inevitably" creates conditions in which it will not be able to live and which strongly point to socialism as the heir apparent'.[12]

Sixteen years older than Hayek, Schumpeter had a much deeper understanding of Marxism, derived from his own intensive reading and especially from personal contacts with Austro-Marxists like Max Adler, Otto Bauer and Rudolf Hilferding, whom he had encountered at Eugen von Böhm-Bawerk's graduate seminar at the University of Vienna in 1905–6.[13] Compared with Hayek, Schumpeter was a more consistent conservative, with distinctly aristocratic tastes and political views that made him sympathetic first to the Hapsburg empire and then to Catholic corporatism.[14] As another Austrian economist put it, long after his death: 'If we want to oversimplify we could say that while there exists any number of people who are non-Marxist socialists, there are very few specimens who can be regarded as non-socialist Marxists. Schumpeter is one of them. Or at least nearly so....'[15]

As early as 1928,[16] Schumpeter was pointing to a critical difference between entrepreneurial and 'trustified' capitalism.[17] In the latter stage, '[p]rogress becomes "automatised", increasingly impersonal and decreasingly a matter of leadership and individual initiative. This amounts to a fundamental change in many respects, some of which reach far out of the sphere of things economic'.[18] The entire social order, in fact, is likely to change:

> Capitalism, whilst economically stable, and even gaining in stability, creates, by rationalising the human mind, a mentality and a style of life incompatible with its own fundamental conditions, motives and social institutions, and will be changed, although not by economic necessity and probably even at some sacrifice of economic welfare, into an order of things which it will be merely [a] matter of taste and terminology to call Socialism or not.[19]

This was a rather Delphic utterance, coming at the end of a 20-page article on other themes and unsubstantiated by any detailed analysis. The missing arguments are supplied in chapter XII of *Capitalism, Socialism and Democracy*, which bears the dramatic title, 'Crumbling Walls'. Schumpeter begins by noting the 'obsolescence of the entrepreneurial function'. Entrepreneurship is all about innovation. But '[p]rogress itself may be mechanized as well as the management of a stationary economy, and this mechanization of progress may affect entrepreneurship and capitalist society nearly as much as the cessation of economic progress would'.[20] Innovation is becoming a matter of routine, 'the business of teams of trained specialists who turn out what is required and make it work in predictable ways'.[21] With the disappearance of any pressing need for 'the flash of genius', economic development has become 'depersonalized and autonomized. Bureau and committee work tends to replace individual action'.[22] Moreover, profit is no longer the reward for innovation but is reduced to mere wages for administrative labour. Thus

> Since capitalist enterprise, by its very achievements, tends to automatize progress, we conclude that it tends to make itself superfluous – to break to pieces under the pressure of its own success. The perfectly bureaucratized giant industrial unit not only ousts the small or medium-sized firm and 'expropriates' its owners, but in the end it also ousts the entrepreneur and 'expropriates' the bourgeoisie as a class which in the process stands to lose not only its income but also what is infinitely more important, its function. The true pacemakers of socialism were not the intellectuals or agitators who preached it but the Vanderbilts, Carnegies and Rockefellers.[23]

At this point Schumpeter acknowledges the influence of Marx. The contrast with Hayek's idealist views could not be more pronounced.

In a strikingly Marxian passage in section III, Schumpeter suggests that 'the capitalist process in much the same way as it destroyed the institutional framework of feudal society also undermines its own'.[24] It does so first by attacking small business and then, within the larger enterprise, by replacing the proprietor and the proprietary interest with salaried managers and small shareholders. Management 'tends to acquire the employee attitude and rarely if ever identifies itself with the stockholding interest', which does not count for very much. Freedom of contract has also been undermined, as it is now subject to the 'tropical growth of new legal structures' that is most evident with respect to labour contracts. In consequence 'the capitalist process pushes into the background all those institutions, the institutions of property and free contracting in particular, that expressed the needs and ways of the truly "private" economic activity'.[25] Before too long, no-one will care about property rights. 'Dematerialized, defunctionalized and absentee ownership does not impress and call forth moral allegiance as the vital form of property did.'[26]

Schumpeter does not neglect the cultural and ideological dimensions of the process. In chapter XI, 'The Civilization of Capitalism', he discusses the 'socio-psychological *superstructure*' and 'the mentality that is characteristic of capitalist society and in particular of the bourgeois class'.[27] The rise of capitalism brought with it the growth of rationality and 'adds a new edge to it in two interconnected ways'.[28] Money became the unit of account, allowing a cost–benefit calculus to be generally invoked in all manner of decisions; and science was applied to production as never before. 'Feminism, an essentially capitalist phenomenon, illustrates the point still more clearly.'[29] Only under capitalist relations of production has it been possible fully to exploit the productive power of one-half of the human race.

All this is now being transcended, as Schumpeter demonstrates in chapter XIII ('Growing Hostility'). Capitalism itself has produced an 'atmosphere of almost universal hostility to its own social order'. The peculiar sociology of the intellectual has engendered a deep hostility to capitalism that can no longer be controlled by patronage or repression. The intellectuals have 'invaded labour politics' and spread anti-capitalist values there.[30] Not only has 'the bourgeois fortress' become 'politically defenceless',[31] but the family itself is in irreversible decline. In chapter XIV ('Decomposition') Schumpeter writes eloquently about the erosion of '[t]he most glamorous of these bourgeois aims, the foundation of an industrial dynasty', and the impending 'disintegration of the bourgeois family'. This, he maintains, is 'wholly attributable to the rationalization of everything in life, which we have seen is one of the effects of capitalist evolution'.[32] The utilitarian calculation of the costs and benefits of family commitments has weakened the entire bourgeois social fabric, as can be seen from the growth of childlessness, the decline of the great bourgeois home and of the pride that was once taken in providing hospitality therein. Ideologically, Schumpeter detects the growth of 'an anti-saving frame of mind' and increased susceptibility of 'anti-saving *theories*'.[33] (This is presumably an oblique reference to Keynesian economics.) Thus anti-capitalist ideas are becoming more fashionable among the bourgeoisie itself, so that 'the typical bourgeois is rapidly losing faith in his own creed'. All these factors 'make not only for the destruction of the capitalist but for the emergence of a socialist civilization'. Marx's economic analysis might have been faulty, but his '*vision* was right'.[34]

4.4 The visible hand

Institutional economists were also concerned with the rise of the corporation.[35] Thorstein Veblen (1857–1929) wrote at great length on this subject, for example in his *Theory of Business Enterprise*,[36] but there is some disagreement on the precise arguments that he advanced.[37] The first unambiguous – and also extremely influential – text was that by Adolph A. Berle (1895–1976) and Gardiner C. Means (1896–1990), *The Modern Corporation and Private Property*, which begins by observing that

> The translation of perhaps two-thirds of the industrial wealth of the country from individual ownership to ownership by the large, publicly funded corporations vitally changes the lives of property owners, the lives of workers, and the methods of property tenure. The divorce of ownership from control consequent on that process almost necessarily involves a new form of economic organization of society.[38]

There is now a 'corporate system', as there was once a feudal system. It is characterised by the concentration of wealth and the separation of ownership and control, the latter raising the possibility that 'the interests of owner and of ultimate manager may, and often do, diverge', a state of affairs 'where many of the checks which formerly operated to limit the use of power disappear'.[39] The rise of the corporate system amounts to a veritable revolution, which 'destroys the very foundations on which the economic order of the past three centuries has rested'.[40] Repeating the metaphor, Berle and Means suggest that the new corporate system 'bids fair to be as all-embracing as was the feudal system in its time'.[41]

They identify several critical changes in the concentration of economic power. There is an increase in the size and market power of the business enterprise, and a corresponding shift in many industries from free competition to duopoly. Vertical integration has meant that '[a]n increasing proportion of production is carried on for use and not for sale'. And, finally, 'a society in which production is governed by blind economic forces is being replaced by one in which production is carried on under the ultimate control of a handful of individuals.'[42]

All this has led to a profound change in the nature of capitalism itself, since the organisations controlled by these powerful men 'have passed far beyond the realm of private enterprise – they have become more nearly social institutions'.[43] The policy implications, discussed in the final chapter of the book, are striking. 'Neither the claims of ownership nor those of control can stand against the paramount interests of the community.' Steps should be taken to make the modern corporation 'develop into a purely neutral technocracy, balancing a variety of claims by various groups in the community and assigning to each a portion of the income stream on the basis of public policy rather than private cupidity'.[44]

Adolphe Berle was a lawyer, whose interests focused on the implications of corporate property for legal theory and philosophy. Gardiner Means, though, was trained as an economist and was an important, if under-published, writer in the institutionalist tradition who had much more to say than Berle did on the economic significance of the corporation. He developed the concept of 'administered pricing', reflecting the fact that competition was weak in many industries and prices were no longer set impersonally by market forces, but administratively through the decisions of a few individuals in the dominant corporations.[45] Administered prices tended to be much less flexible than competitive prices. This had important macroeconomic consequences, Means maintained, because the elimination of downward price flexibility had removed the principal method by which the capitalist economy had formerly been able to adjust to reductions in aggregate demand.[46] To the end of his life Means regarded his macroeconomic analysis as an alternative to that proposed by Keynes in the *General Theory*, and this it certainly is, since Keynes denied that falling prices and wages were either desirable or likely to be effective in restoring full employment in a recession (see Section 4.6 below). Means's approach actually foreshadows the 'New Keynesian' models of the 1980s and 1990s, which also placed all their analytical eggs in the fragile basket of wage and price flexibility.[47]

When Berle and Means came to reconsider their earlier views, in the second (1968) edition of *The Modern Corporation and Private Property*, they found little reason to make fundamental revisions. Berle simply claims that 'the trend toward dominance of that collective capitalism we call the "corporate system" has continued unabated',[48] with 90% of non-farm output now controlled by corporations. 'There is increasing recognition of the fact that collective operations, and those predominantly conducted by large corporations, are like operations carried out by the state itself. Corporations are essentially political constructs.... they are an adjunct of the state itself'.[49] For his part, Means suggests that administered prices have been a major factor in the postwar inflation. Excess demand pushes prices up, but excess supply does not result in price decreases. The overall price level tends to increase whenever there is excess demand in a few important sectors of the economy, and thus in the absence of *general* excess demand. This model of 'administrative inflation'[50] is similar in some respects to the 'structuralist' models that were popular in the late 1950s and early 1960s. In policy terms, it seems to require the imposition of permanent wage and price controls, like those introduced in the 1960s by the Johnson and (more reluctantly) the Nixon administrations.[51] Means himself concludes that 'competition among the few' is no longer sufficient to protect the public interest, and that a strong case can be made for some form of economic planning in the United States.[52]

The institutionalists played an important role in the formulation and implementation of economic policy during the New Deal, where they found common ground with the Technocrats (see Chapter 3, Section 3.8). The latter, led by Stuart Chase and Howard Scott, emphasised the contribution of engineers and other technical experts in promoting efficiency against the pernicious influence of the 'vested interests', and in reducing the waste that was produced by competition. They had very little faith in the ability of the market to serve the public interest, and Scott even claimed to have discovered a replacement for market price as a measure of social value.[53] Both the institutionalists and the Technocrats were supporters of economic planning.[54]

The implications for the price system of the growth in corporate power were further explored by Arthur R. Burns (1895–1981) in his massive book *The Decline of Competition* (1936). Burns was more conservative than most institutionalists of his generation, serving as Chairman of the Council of Economic Advisers in the Eisenhower administration between 1953 and 1956. Elements of monopoly, Burns argues, have increased so greatly that '[t]hey can no longer be regarded as occasional and relatively unimportant aberrations from competition. They are such an organic part of the industrial system that it is useless to hope that they can be removed by law and the industrial system thus brought into conformity with the ideal of perfect competition.'[55] Like Gardiner Means, Burns is worried by the macroeconomic effects of monopoly. Price rigidity can only increase the instability of output and employment: 'If the demand for a product is at all elastic the maintenance of an unchanged price throughout cycles of increasing and decreasing demand must increase the amplitude of fluctuations in the volume of production beyond what it would be if the price were increased in times of increasing demand and reduced in times of falling demand.'[56] Moreover, price stabilisation in periods of rising productivity results in rising profit margins. This reduces the demand for consumer goods, since '[i]ncreases in wages tend to divert incomes from those who save much to those who save less'.[57] The 'collapse of business from 1929 to 1933', Burns concludes, can be 'attributed to the stabilization of prices while costs were falling'.[58]

A more sociological perspective was taken by R.A. Gordon (1908–78) in his *Business Leadership in the Large Corporation* (1945), which seeks to provide a very detailed empirical confirmation of the principal theses of Berle and Means. The corporate board of directors has 'for the most part.... surrendered its function of active decision-making in the large corporation' to professional managers.[59] These managers seem not to be strongly motivated by financial gain, and there is little evidence of a link between managerial salaries and profits. Non-monetary incentives are much more powerful, Gordon argues, including the urge for power, the desire for prestige, emulation, creativity, group loyalty, security, the urge for adventure and the desire to serve others.[60] He discusses the role of various 'interest groups' – the modern term would be stakeholders – including stock owners, financiers, suppliers, customers, other firms in the industry, labour and government. While the influence of government and labour is growing, that of financiers has been undermined by the increasing independence of management and its ability to generate internal finance.[61] In his (1960) preface to the second edition of the book, Gordon reaffirms his earlier conclusions: the corporation remains dominant, the separation of ownership and control has continued, stockholder influence remains slight, and there has been no reversal of the decline in the power of banks and bankers. Despite the recent growth of stock options, profits are still not very important in managerial motivation, and if anything price inflexibility has increased further since 1945.[62]

4.5 A new industrial state

By far the best-known of all the institutionalist writers on the giant corporation is John Kenneth Galbraith (1908–2006), who obtained direct practical experience of corporate power during his tenure as deputy administrator of the Office of Price Administration in the United States between 1941 and 1943. In his first of many popular books, *American Capitalism: The Concept of Countervailing Power*, Galbraith takes a relatively optimistic view of the changes wrought by the growth of the corporation. Like Schumpeter, he maintains that monopoly is associated with a faster rate of technical progress than that prevailing under free competition, and these dynamic benefits more than offset the static disadvantages of higher prices and lower levels of output. Moreover, competition has given way not to unrestrained monopoly but rather to a system of 'countervailing power', in which producers are compelled to pay close attention to the interests of suppliers (especially organised labour) and customers (large retailers and powerful trade buyers). This is generally supported by the state: 'the provision of state assistance to the development of countervailing power has become a major function of government – perhaps *the* major domestic function of government';[63] it is most evident in the farm and labour legislation of the New Deal. The principal difficulty with this new stage of American capitalism, Galbraith concludes, is its chronic inflationary bias, which will require increasing state interference in private decision-making. 'It is inflation, not deflation or depression, that will cause capitalism to be modified by extensive centralized decision.... Boom and inflation, in our time, are the proper focus of conservative fears.'[64]

He presents a different and much more elaborate analysis in *The New Industrial State*,[65] which provoked a lively reaction from some important neoclassical economists. Galbraith now identifies a clear technological imperative leading to the decline of the market. The increased capital-intensity of production and the lengthening of the production process impose a requirement for long-range planning. The 'increasing unreliability of markets'[66] poses problems for the corporate planners, which can be overcome in three ways: by superseding the market altogether, by means of vertical integration; by controlling it, through administered prices; and through eliminating uncertainty by entering into long-term contracts with customers and suppliers. Galbraith suggests that

> ....the enemy of the market is not ideology but the engineer.... rarely in social matters has there been such a case of mistaken identity. It is not socialists. It is advanced technology and the specialization of men and process that this requires and the resulting commitment of time and capital. These make the market work badly when the need is for greatly enhanced reliability – when planning is essential.[67]

There is a clear parallel with the management of Soviet-type economies: 'The modern large corporation and the modern apparatus of socialist planning are variant accommodations to the same need.'[68]

The result of this technological imperative, Galbraith continues, is a significant shift in power from the owners of capital to what he terms the 'technostructure'. This is 'a new factor of production', an 'association of men of diverse technical knowledge, experience or other talent which modern industrial technology and planning require'.[69] Like Schumpeter, Galbraith points to the decline of the traditional entrepreneur, who 'must, in fact, be compared in life with the male *Apis mellifera*. He accomplishes his act of conception at the price of his own extinction'.[70] The needs of modern technology for greater planning and control mean that

> ....what the entrepreneur created passed inexorably beyond the scope of his authority. He could build. And he could exert influence for a time. But his creation, were it to serve the purposes for which it was brought into being, required his replacement. What the entrepreneur created, only a group of men sharing specialized information could ultimately operate.[71]

The technostructure relies on retained earnings to finance investment projects, and is thereby protected from interference by financial markets. These profits are themselves protected by planning, giving the large corporation a substantial degree of long-term stability. The increasing autonomy of the technostructure is apparent even in Eastern Europe, making the very concept of socialism 'an overture to nostalgia'.[72]

Like Robert Gordon, Galbraith argues that the textbook neoclassical model of the firm and its goals is no longer relevant: 'Subordination to the market, and to the instruction that it conveys, has disappeared. So there is no longer, a priori, reason to believe that profit maximization will be the goal of the technostructure.'[73] Instead, 'identification – the voluntary exchange of one's goals for the preferable ones of organization – and adaptation – the association with organization in the hope of influencing its goals to accord more closely with one's own – are strong motivating forces in the technostructure and become increasingly so in the inner circles'.[74] In practice this means that preserving the technostructure's autonomy is the most important corporate goal, leading it to pursue growth, subject only to a profit constraint.[75] Contrary to 'the theology of the market',[76] prices are administered by the technostructure in order to cover its investment requirements. Anti-trust laws 'do not preserve the market. They preserve rather the illusion of the market'.[77]

The political repercussions are substantial, according to Galbraith. The technostructure generates profits on such a huge scale that saving tends to rise even more rapidly than investment. Regulation of aggregate demand by the state is thus much more urgent than it was in an economy dominated by small, owner-managed firms. Galbraith repeats his earlier claim that corporate capitalism is especially prone to inflation. The disappearance of profit maximisation generates a wage-price spiral, in which pay rises are freely conceded because they can be easily passed on to customers: 'The entrepreneur had reason to resist'.[78] Thus 'a system of wage and price controls is inevitable in the industrial system'.[79] The technostructure has shown itself to be much less concerned by the growth of state intervention than the traditional entrepreneurs. Indeed, when 'planning replaces the market',[80] the boundaries between the firm and the state become fuzzy: 'Each organization ... is an extension of the other',[81] as can be seen most clearly in the relationship between the military and their large contractors. Galbraith points to the existing tendency for the convergence of capitalism and communism, which 'occurs at all fundamental points',[82] and expects there to be a further blurring of the boundaries between the corporations and the state. These developments 'are leading, if the harshest term may be employed, to the socialization of the mature corporation'.[83]

Galbraith's vision was attacked by conventional economic liberals[84] and by liberal socialists.[85] His views did not change appreciably as a result of their objections, but in *Economics and the Public Purpose* (1973) he amended his terminology and also slightly revised the argument, now attributing more significance to the competitive, small-business sector. Drawing on the work of Robert Averitt,[86] Galbraith suggests that the United States has a dual economy, and distinguishes the 'market system' from the 'planning system'. The latter is what he termed 'the industrial system' in *The New Industrial State*. Only in the former are the traditional forces of free competition still to be observed.[87] Galbraith is never in doubt as to which system will predominate. As he wrote in the first issue of the *Journal of Post Keynesian Economics*, which he had helped to finance:

> The relevant historical change to which there must now be accommodation is in the nature of the industrial market. The market, with the maturing of industrial society and associated political institutions, loses and loses radically its authority as a regulatory force. Partly this is inherent in industrial development – in the institutions that modern large-scale production, technology and planning require.[88]

In all essentials, the institutionalist analysis of the corporation is endorsed by the eminent business historian Alfred Chandler (1918–2007), who owed no allegiance to any particular school of economic theory. In a series of books between 1962 and 1990, Chandler described how the 'modern business enterprise took the place of market mechanisms in coordinating the activities of the economy and allocating its resources. In many sectors of the economy the visible hand of management replaced what Adam Smith referred to as the invisible hand of market forces.'[89] The modern business enterprise is a complex, multi-divisional organisation controlled by a hierarchy of salaried managers. It largely replaced the traditional firm in the first half of the twentieth century because 'administrative coordination permitted greater productivity, lower costs, and higher profits than coordination by market mechanisms',[90] favouring the internalisation of activities previously carried out by several firms. Vertical integration is thus a crucial part of Chandler's historical narrative. The modern enterprise has not replaced the market altogether, but it does 'take over from the market the coordination and integration of the flow of goods and services from the production of the raw materials through the several processes of production [and then on] to the sale to the ultimate consumer'.[91] The result is a 'managerial revolution in American business' (the title of Chandler's concluding chapter), so that by the 1950s 'managerial capitalism had gained ascendancy over family and financial capitalism'.[92] Similar processes took place in Europe and in Japan, albeit rather more slowly. Chandler emphasises the 'economies of scale and scope' that were made possible by the multi-divisional enterprise, taking as an example the experience of the computer industry after 1950, which 'parallels that of the American machinery industry a half-century earlier'.[93]

In sum, the institutionalists asserted the death of both the market and the owner-managed business. The latter has been supplanted by giant corporations that enjoy considerable product market power and substantial protection from outside pressures, especially those emanating from financial markets and shareholders. Prices are administered rather than set by competition, and private planning has replaced the market as the principal determinant of output, investment and prices. Alfred Eichner (1937–88), who had a foot in both the institutionalist and Post Keynesian camps, generalised from the experience of the Soviet Union to draw an intriguing parallel between corporate pricing behaviour and the Soviet turnover tax. The former is really a 'corporate levy', Eichner argues, used by management to raise internally the funds needed for its investment projects, in much the same way as the Stalinist state tax the enterprises that it controls to meet its budgetary requirements. In neither case, Eichner concludes, do prices have anything to do with marginal utilities or marginal costs; in both cases, resources are allocated by administrative decisions, not by any invisible hand.[94]

4.6 The end of laissez-faire

By 1945 the Austrian and institutionalist economists whose views were outlined in the previous sections of this Chapter were clearly outside the mainstream of economic theory, and their heterodoxy became even more evident in subsequent decades. On the future of the market, however, many of their ideas were shared by leaders of the profession, including some of the most respected neoclassical theorists. Among the early neoclassical economists Alfred Marshall (1842–1924) took the rise of corporate capitalism very seriously, writing about it at length not in his *Principles of Economics* but in *Industry and Trade*,[95] which deals 'essentially with the economics of oligopolies, cartels, combinations, and "conditional monopolies" forced to practice limit entry pricing'.[96] Marshall's treatment is more nuanced than that of the Marxists. Large firms enjoy significant technical advantages over small ones, but also suffer from organisational inertia and tend to be slower to adopt new technologies. For Marshall the outcome of competition between them is uncertain, and it is by no means inevitable that small firms will be crushed by the power of their larger rivals.[97]

Marshall's most eminent disciple, John Maynard Keynes (1883–1946), possibly the greatest of all twentieth-century economists, was more definite. He is not someone who is normally considered as an apostle of the decline of the market, but, in fact, he was precisely that. In a well-known essay, the 1926 'End of Laissez-Faire', Keynes distinguishes the 'Agenda of government' from the 'Non-Agenda': 'I believe that in many cases the ideal size for the unit of control and organization lies somewhere between the individual and the modern State. I suggest, therefore, that progress lies in the growth and the recognition of semi-autonomous bodies within the State', such as the Universities, the Bank of England, the Port of London Authority, 'even perhaps the railway companies'.[98] In 1926 the Bank of England and the railway companies were, of course, still privately owned, though the latter had been forced to submit to compulsory amalgamation under the 'grouping' legislation of 1921. 'But more interesting than these', Keynes continues:

> is the trend of joint-stock institutions, when they have reached a certain age and size, to approximate to the status of public corporations rather than that of individualistic private enterprise. One of the most interesting and unnoticed developments of recent decades has been the tendency of big enterprise to socialise itself.[99]

To justify this striking assertion Keynes points to the separation of ownership and control, which means that 'the making of great profit becomes quite secondary' to other goals. Subject only to the need to maintain a minimum dividend payment, 'the direct interest of the management often consists in avoiding criticism from the public and from the customers of the concern'.[100]

Keynes is no supporter of what he invariably denotes, with deliberate use of capital letters, as State Socialism. 'Nevertheless', he argues, 'we see here, I think, a natural line of evolution. The battle of Socialism against unlimited private profit is being won in detail hour by hour'.[101] To the extent that State Socialism hinges on the nationalisation of institutions like the Bank of England and the railway companies, it is simply out of date, since it 'misses the significance of what is actually happening', which is that large private corporations are increasingly being run in the public interest rather than for the exclusive benefit of their shareholders.[102] As he had written in the previous year, in 'Am I a Liberal?' (1925): 'The transition from economic anarchy to a régime which deliberately aims at controlling and directing economic forces in the interests of social justice and social stability, will present enormous difficulties both technical and political. I suggest, nevertheless, that the true destiny of New Liberalism is to seek their solution.'[103] One reason for this is that there are important activities that can only be undertaken by the State. They include controlling the currency, influencing the level and rate of growth of population, and – crucially – coordinating saving and investment.

Many of these ideas were carried over into the *General Theory of Employment, Interest and Money* (1936). The principal policy message of Keynes's greatest book is not the merit of counter-cyclical fiscal policy, nor even the virtues of cheap money, but rather the inescapable necessity of 'a somewhat comprehensive socialisation of investment' as 'the only means of securing an approximation to full employment'.[104] While he has no objection to what is wrongly described as '"wasteful" loan expenditure',[105] and favours the eventual 'euthanasia of the rentier',[106] Keynes's policy priorities lie elsewhere.[107] This is the conclusion of chapter 12, on 'The State of Long-Term Expectation':

> For my own part I am now somewhat sceptical of the success of a merely monetary policy directed towards influencing the rate of interest. I expect to see the State, which is in a position to calculate the marginal efficiency of capital-goods on long views and on the basis of the general social advantage, taking an ever greater responsibility for directly organising investment; since it seems likely that the fluctuations in the market estimation of the marginal efficiency of different types of capital, calculated on the principles I have described above, will be too great to be offset by any practicable changes in the rate of interest.[108]

And in chapter 22, 'Notes on the Trade Cycle', he again argues that businessmen's expectations of future profitability fluctuate so wildly that 'the duty of ordering the current volume of investment cannot safely be left in private hands'.[109]

Keynes's analysis is not without its problems. One might wonder what further institutional changes were necessary, given the existing tendency for private capital to socialise itself. (Why had private investment collapsed in the early stages of the Great Depression, if profitability was no longer the crucial factor in managerial decisions?). Keynes himself tends to minimise the radical nature of his conclusions, famously describing the *General Theory* as 'moderately conservative in its implications',[110] and denying any intention of attacking the orthodox microeconomic theory of resource allocation. To this a liberal critic like Hayek might well object that, if private profit no longer determines investment decisions, we have already moved a long way from a market economy towards a state-controlled one. Keynes's sympathy for permanent wage and (perhaps) price controls would have added to liberal misgivings.[111]

Neither would such critics have been comforted by the knowledge that

> Keynes's 'state' was defined, not by legal prerogative but by what we might call 'degree of publicness'. By the 'state', he meant not the government and its servants, but that group of institutions, whether privately or publicly owned, which pursue public interest aims rather than short-term profits.... He believed that the state, in this sense, was a growing force in economic life.[112]

Keynes was nevertheless much more favourably disposed towards Hayek's *Road to Serfdom* than many of his followers, describing it in correspondence with Hayek as a 'grand book.... Morally and philosophically I find myself in agreement with virtually the whole of it; and not only in agreement, but in a deeply moved agreement'. But he drew very different conclusions:

> I should say that what we want is not no planning, or even less planning, I should say that we almost certainly want more. But the planning should take place in a community in which, as many people as possible, both leaders and followers, share your own moral position. Moderate planning will be safe if those carrying it out are rightly orientated in their own minds and hearts to your own moral position...
>
> ....Dangerous acts can be done safely in a community which thinks and feels rightly which would be the way to hell if they were executed by those who think and feel wrongly.[113]

Keynes's elitist statism alarmed the left no less than the right, with Robert Brady attacking Keynes's 'British version of National Socialism',[114] a characterisation of Keynes's ideas that he shared with the (then) Marxist Eric Roll and with the Frankfurt School theorists Kurt Mandelbaum and Friedrich Pollock.[115] But many of Keynes's younger colleagues were democratic socialists with strong egalitarian convictions, and were enthusiastic supporters of a greatly expanded public sector and of planning not merely for postwar reconstruction but as a permanent feature of a just and efficient society.[116] Some of them, though, shared some of Hayek's misgivings. Barbara Wootton, a long-standing advocate of planning, wrote a surprisingly sympathetic critique of his book,[117] while Joan Robinson was especially concerned by the emergence of a powerful movement emanating from big business for what she termed 'monopoly planning'. The word 'planning', she complained, was increasingly used as a smokescreen to disguise the gulf between socialist and anti-socialist proposals.[118] Some of the capitalist support for planning had clear Fascist connotations, Robinson argued, while even the less objectionable ideas of the British industrialist Samuel Courtauld amounted to 'a mildly benevolent version of the Corporative State'.[119]

Most economists sympathetic to the *General Theory*, however, would have agreed with the social democratic Australian economist Douglas Copland that

> Capitalism under the control of the entrepreneur guided mainly by considerations of maximum profit is now completely discredited. It

> does not give economic security to the masses of the people; it does not provide the administrative machinery whereby increased technical efficiency is transformed easily into a generally higher standard of living; it does not furnish society with the social institutions required to meet the strains imposed by economic fluctuations and rapid technical progress; it does not provide the increasing range of free or collective goods that enter more and more into the standard of living. Countries have been able to absorb the shocks of depression and improved technique in inverse proportion to their dominance by the capitalistic entrepreneur.[120]

The British Tory politician – and later Prime Minister – Harold Macmillan (1894–1986) went even further. Macmillan sees the growing interest in economic planning as 'merely an extension of that principle of interference and regulation which has been common to the political thought of England since the first Factory Act was passed'.[121] Heavily influenced by Keynes, Macmillan believes that

> the doctrine of *laissez-faire* has been abandoned in practice; that the boundaries of 'public enterprise' have been very greatly extended; and that intervention by the Government in the economic life of the nation is increasing rapidly.... in private industry the theory of free competition is also being very largely abandoned in practice. Great efforts have been made with or without the assistance of legislation to enforce schemes of regulation and control which are contrary to the whole conception of free competition. These movements have arisen, it must be remembered, not in obedience to new theories, but as the reaction of practical business men to the changed circumstances in which industry and commerce have to be conducted.[122]

Even in the private sector, '[t]he whole trend of development is in the direction of greater integration, and the supersession of unrestrained competition by methods of cooperation.'[123]

Macmillan calls for the establishment of a National Investment Board, with functions that would 'include the regulation of the capital market by estimation of the savings available, determination of the volume of foreign lending, coordination and supervision of the issue of loans for the Government, local authorities, and other public bodies, and discouragement of "semi-fraudulent" issues';[124] the Board would take over many of the functions of the Stock Exchange. He further proposes the setting up of a Ministry of Economics as 'the keystone of the structure of a planned economy'.[125] The author of this self-proclaimed 'middle way', to repeat, was also a prominent Conservative politician, and later served for 7 years as Prime Minister (1956–63).

The period from 1945 to the mid-1970s is often described as 'the age of Keynes',[126] in the sense that a middle way had indeed been found between laissez-faire and State Socialism. In the process, it appeared to many others that the role of the market had been very greatly diminished. As early as 1956 the social democrat Anthony Crosland claimed that the contemporary economic order was no longer a capitalist one. Power has been transferred from the private owners of capital to the state, through nationalisation and direct intervention in the private sector; to organised labour; and to the newly influential class of technicians and professional managers. The latter are much less aggressive in the pursuit of profit than traditionalist capitalists once were, and much more inclined to accept their social responsibilities. Full employment has brought with it a shift from a buyers' market to a sellers' market for labour power. Almost everyone now agrees, Crosland claims, on the need for some measure of economic planning by the state to supplement, if not entirely to replace decentralised decision-making by private owners driven by profit maximisation.[127]

Twenty years later, Keynes's future biographer Robert Skidelsky edited a series of articles for the London *Spectator* on 'the end of the Keynesian era', which now seemed non-viable due to the severity of stagflation. It was an era, Skidelsky suggests, of 'decline in the power of private capital', which

> has steadily receded in face of the growth of working-class organisation and the state. It was this change in the balance of social power that enabled Keynesian ideas to triumph in the first place. No doubt big business needed Keynes too, and appropriated Keynesian spending policies for its own advantage. But need for state economic support is a sign of weakness, not strength; and full employment was a labour, not business, demand, commitment to which has, in turn, strengthened labour's bargaining power. Of course, concentrated private capital is still immensely strong. But it no longer dominates the stage as it did fifty or sixty years ago; and in Britain and Italy it has been substantially, perhaps fatally, weakened.[128]

Most of Skidelsky's contributors anticipate a further increase in the economic role of the state, and a corresponding decline in the role of the market. Thus the sociologist J.T. Winkler points to the continuing growth of 'corporatist "state control"' as

> the outcome of continuous, often covert, bargaining between the state and private economic groups possessing real power. There will always be compromise, but over time, as the state adds new instruments of control and increases the effectiveness of their application, the prospect is for an incremental expansion of the state's control over the economy and a corresponding diminution in the realm of private discretion.[129]

This was not a prospect that Keynes would have completely welcomed, but for many it seemed, in the 1970s, to be the logical culmination of 'the end of laissez-faire'.

4.7 Neoclassical economics and the decline of the market

In one of his more conservative moments Keynes wrote, at the end of the *General Theory*, that

> if our central controls succeed in establishing an aggregate volume of output corresponding to full employment as nearly as is practicable, the classical theory comes into its own again from this point onwards.... there is no objection to be raised against the classical analysis of the manner in which private self-interest will determine what in particular is produced, in what proportions the factors of production will be combined to produce it, and how the value of the final product will be distributed between them.[130]

This is a surprising judgement, both in the light of what he himself had stated elsewhere and because several of his own colleagues had already produced a series of cogent arguments that denied it. By 1936 the concept of 'market failure' was very clearly identified with Cambridge microeconomics, and it had been developed in almost complete independence from any form of macroeconomic analysis, and was thoroughly neoclassical.

There were at least four reasons, derived from neoclassical economics itself, for supposing that the capitalist market might fail to supply the social benefits that Keynes claimed for it. The first was the already familiar problem of externalities: benefits and (especially) costs that are not taken into account by the individual decision-maker although they have a significant impact on social well-being. The classic example, of course, is pollution. The implications were set out very clearly by A.C. Pigou (1877–1959), in his *Wealth and Welfare* (1912), later expanded into the massive *Economics of Welfare* (1920). As Pigou demonstrates, the more extensive and substantial these externalities are believed to be, the greater the degree of state interference in the market that is required. For some theorists in this tradition, externalities give rise to such a systematic and widespread divergence between market outcomes and social optima that the necessary combination of taxes and subsidies seriously weakens the case for the market. Thus, for Andreas Papandreou,

> ....damaging externalities are ubiquitous. Nothing less will do than an economy-wide structure of indirect taxes designed to transform private marginal costs into social marginal costs. But this task, informationally, imposes as much strain on the governmental authority as a detailed quantitative plan would impose on it in a planned economy. The informational economies guaranteed by decentralization in the market economy would suddenly disappear... it is hard to avoid the conclusion that effective confrontation of the problem leads either to large-scale regulation or to the *internalization* of externalities through reliance on some form of social planning.[131]

Second, there is the question of market power. Perfect competition is viable only under unreasonable assumptions about technology: the size of the individual enterprise must be restricted by rising average costs to a level of output that is modest relative to the demand for the product of the industry, or only a few large firms can survive. The 'costs controversy' that raged in the *Economic Journal* in the early 1920s seemed to indicate that this was not generally the case, famously leading one participant to conclude that 'It is necessary, therefore, to abandon the path of free competition and turn in the opposite direction, namely, towards monopoly'.[132] Such a turn might have led the neoclassicals to the quasi-institutionalist conclusion that the determination of prices in the market had already been replaced by 'conscious authoritarian manipulation of prices and quantities'.[133]

The theory of imperfect or monopolistic competition, articulated in the early 1930s by Joan Robinson and Edward H. Chamberlin, appeared to offer a slightly less alarming alternative. Under imperfect competition the market continues to operate, and with an expanded domain, since competition now extends to product quality and the encouragement of consumer demand through advertising rather than being confined solely to prices. Ultimately, however, the new theories offered cold comfort to believers in the benefits of the market. Even if the economies of large-scale production are limited, allowing many firms to survive in any particular industry, the efficiency properties of perfect competition are invariably violated: workers, to take the most important case, are inevitably paid less than the value of their marginal products.[134] If economies of scale are greater, 'large-group' monopolistic competition gives way to oligopoly. With 'competition among the few', however, the spectre of administered prices cannot be avoided, since the illusion of competition now conceals the reality, which is tacit collusion to set the monopoly price.[135] Excess capacity, which is also predicted by models of imperfect competition, makes the temptation to collude even stronger. Finally, in one celebrated model, oligopolists are supposed to assume that their rivals will match price cuts but not price increases. The resulting 'kinked demand curve' entails a vertical discontinuity in the firm's marginal revenue function and, by extension, in its marginal revenue product function. Since the latter is, on the innocuous assumption of perfect competition in the labour market, also its labour demand curve, it follows that the elasticity of demand for labour is zero over what might be a substantial range of wage rates. It follows that wage cuts will not increase employment.[136] This alarming result is derived on purely microeconomic grounds and without any reference to macroeconomic theory, Keynesian or otherwise.

Robinson later set out three reasons for her belief in 'The impossibility of competition':

> These three tendencies – the tendency for competition to make markets imperfect by product differentiation, the tendency towards oligopoly where advantages of scale exist, and the tendency for excess capacity to lead to collusion – between them leave only narrow areas in the economy where conditions are such that competition can normally prevail. All three tendencies are deeply rooted in the very nature of the competitive system. It therefore seems very dubious whether it is proper to treat competition as a normal equilibrium state of affairs.[137]

This conclusion is closely related to the third and fourth sources of market failure, which centre on questions of income distribution and on the instability of equilibrium. The earliest critics of the marginal productivity theory of distribution had objected, back in the late nineteenth century, that all non-wage incomes contain very large components of economic rent, or 'surplus', so that the owners of capital and land receive much more than their productive contributions could hope to justify. In the case of George Bernard Shaw, a devoted follower of Jevonian economics, this inspired a marginalist theory of surplus value that is difficult to distinguish, in its implications for economic justice, from the Marxian theory of exploitation.[138]

The same complaint resurfaced, via a quite different route, in Robinson's *Economics of Imperfect Competition.* Although she later repudiated her early support for neoclassical microeconomics, writing a new preface to the 1969 edition in a mood of severe self-criticism, she reaffirms her treatment of exploitation, which she now believes to be almost the only part of the book that had any lasting merit.[139] The problem for more orthodox neoclassical economists is that an unjust distribution of income renders the entire market-determined allocation of resources unjustifiable too. As Pigou acknowledged:

> The maldistribution of productive resources as between essential and superfluous *things* is not, of course, as is sometimes loosely supposed, a *further* evil, superimposed upon and additional to the evil of unequal distribution of incomes among persons. It is the same evil viewed from a different angle. But it is, none the less, real and exceedingly important. The reason why widely unequal distribution of income is an evil is that it entails resources being wasted, in the sense that they are used to satisfy less urgent needs while more urgent needs are neglected. Obviously the evil is a very grave one.[140]

Once again, very significant state interference with market outcomes is called for and, on impeccable neoclassical reasoning.

Moreover, on the logic of traditional neoclassical economics there need be no costs to state interference with market outcomes through the redistribution of wealth (which, obviously, could have significant effects on the distribution of income). An efficient allocation of resources is possible with *any* distribution of ownership rights in the productive forces.[141] Nor is any significance attached to capitalist relations of production. It does not matter whether 'workers rent capital' or 'capital hires workers'.[142] Oskar Lange was to use this flexibility to argue for socialism on the basis of neoclassical theory itself (as we explain below).

Fourth, and finally, there is the problem of the stability of market equilibria. This is especially important in the context of investment decisions. The expected profitability of an investment project depends on the expected price at which future flows of output can be sold;

this depends on the capacity of the industry, that is, on the number of firms and the quantity of capital at their disposal; this depends on past expectations about the profitability of investment, which in turn depends on expectations in earlier periods. There is no reason to expect that entrepreneurs' independent decisions, based on individual expectations, will be consistent with each other in any one period, let alone over many periods. The difficulty is obvious and, under conditions of free competition, insoluble.[143] It is compounded, but not created, by Keynesian uncertainty with respect to future macroeconomic conditions. The simplest way of theorising about this problem is in terms of the cobweb cycle, or hog cycle, to which Robinson referred in her contribution to a conference on monopoly and competition:[144] 'what was needed to break the cycle in the shipbuilding industry – where keels were laid when freight rates were high, and building ceased altogether when freight rates came down in response to the appearance of the newly built shipping space – was not more information, but investment planning'.[145] Two decades earlier Pigou had conceded that errors of foresight would be considerably reduced if investment plans were centrally coordinated, under capitalism or socialism.[146]

There are, in fact, three possible neoclassical responses to the market failures that have been identified. Two are supportive of capitalism, and the other of socialism. The first capitalist reaction is to assert that the costs of 'state failure' are always greater than the costs of market failure, so that regulation and control represent a cure much worse than the disease. Better to allow the market free rein: sooner or later, competition will prevail – unless monopoly power is reinforced by unnecessary state interference. The Chicago School (Milton Friedman, George Stigler and their associates) have always argued in this manner. The Virginia School, led by James Buchanan, takes the story a little further by explaining the growth of the state in terms of rational, selfish behaviour by the minority private interests that profit from it. The Chicago theorists offer no clear historical analysis of the decline of the market, which they tend to see (rather like Hayek) as an inexplicable and essentially timeless mistake that only sound economic education can put right. Even Buchanan, in his account of the collapse of Soviet communism, sees the great popularity of socialism earlier in the twentieth century as nothing more than a 'monumental folly', strengthened by the innate human proclivity for rent-seeking but having nothing to do with the real historical development of capitalism.[147] As mourners for the market in decline, both Chicago and Virginia compare very poorly with the materialist lament of Joseph Schumpeter.

The second neoclassical response to market failure places much less emphasis on the dangers of state failure, arguing instead for the retention of capitalist property relations, and also the market, but with its failures corrected by comprehensive state intervention, up to and including central planning of investment. This conclusion, to repeat, could be derived from exclusively microeconomic arguments, independently of any commitment to Keynesian macroeconomics. In this spirit Paul Samuelson (b. 1915) echoes Pigou in noting that the existence of a perfectly competitive general equilibrium is only a necessary, but clearly not a sufficient, condition for the maximisation of social welfare. There are an infinite number of such equilibria, all but one of which are the products of (actual or potential) redistributions of income and wealth by the government.[148] Put slightly differently, the supposed optimality properties of market equilibria can be shown to rest on truly 'heroic assumptions':

> 1. Each person's tastes (and values) depend only upon his separable consumptions of goods. That is, there must be no 'consumption externalities'.
> 2. Strict constant-returns-to-scale prevails.
> 3. Perfect competition, in senses too numerous to list here, prevails.
> 4. The interpersonal distribution of property (inclusive of personal attributes) is ethically correct initially or is to be made so by ideal lump sum transfers of a perfectly non-distorting type.
>
> Then, and only then, has it been rigorously proved that perfect competitive equilibrium is indeed optimal. So strict are these conditions that one would have thought that the elementary consideration that a line is infinitely thinner than a plane would make it a miracle for these conditions to be met.[149]

The macroeconomic problems emphasised by Keynes compound these difficulties. There is no 'invisible hand' to solve them: 'deliberate, purposive, intelligent social action' is required to achieve full employment.[150]

In his discussion of 'the economic role of private activity' Samuelson points to the dominance of non-market allocation mechanisms in 'many circles' that Americans belong to: 'the Elks, the Samuelson family, the office pool, etc. In almost none of these relationships is the organizing principle that of decentralized competitive pricing'.[151] Another eminent neoclassical economist, Kenneth Arrow (b. 1921) reminds his readers that 'in no society does as much as half the population receive income from the market'.[152] As one of the founding fathers of modern general equilibrium theory, Arrow knew the limitations of Walrasian theory better than most. 'Market failure', he repeatedly argues, goes far beyond the classic examples of pollution and other environmental externalities to encompass the unavoidable *absence* of markets for many important future contingencies, and the consequent and quite inescapable need for non-market mechanisms, including such institutions as hierarchy and authority relationships. 'Trust', for example, 'is an important lubricant of a social system.... Unfortunately this is not a commodity which can be bought very easily. If you have to buy it, you already have some doubts about what you've bought'.[153] Similarly, the well-known problems of adverse selection and moral hazard make it impossible to insure against bankruptcy. Although uncertainty about the future is pervasive, it is not adequately dealt with by the market, and this constitutes

> ....an even more severe shortcoming of the actual capitalist system compared with an ideally efficient economic system. The uncertainties themselves are relevant commodities and should be priced in such an economy... In the absence of suitable markets, other coordinating and communicating mechanisms are needed for efficiency. These come close to defining the socialist economy, although admittedly wide variations in the meaning of that expression are possible.[154]

Even assuming that this difficulty can be overcome, the social benefits of the market rely heavily on the existence of perfect competition. In an early paper Arrow demonstrates that perfect competition exists only when equilibrium has been achieved. Outside equilibrium, individual firms have some market power, even if output is homogeneous and the number of firms is large: 'In disequilibrium, the market consists of a number of monopolists facing a number of monopsonists. The most general picture is that of a shifting set of bilateral monopolies. The range of indeterminacy in each bargaining situation is limited but not completely eliminated by the possibilities of other bargains.'[155] With smaller numbers of firms, the existence of oligopoly poses very severe problems for neoclassical theory, since rational behaviour in conditions of strategic interdependence demands very high levels of knowledge on the part of all actors:

> Each agent must not only know that the other agents (at least those with significant power) are rational but know that each other agent knows that every other agent is rational, and so forth....

> ....It should be obvious how vastly these knowledge requirements exceed those required for the price system. The classic economists were quite right in emphasizing the importance of limited knowledge. If every agent has a complete model of the economy, the hand running the economy is very visible indeed.
> Indeed, under these knowledge conditions, the superiority of the market over centralized planning disappears. Each individual agent is in effect using as much information as would be required for a central planner.[156]

One implication of this, Arrow continues, is to undermine the Coase Theorem, according to which any externality can be internalised through a suitable allocation of property rights and contracting between their owners, so that the Pigovian complex of taxes and subsidies becomes unnecessary.[157] Samuelson, too, denies the validity of the Coase Theorem, on very similar grounds, since '[u]nconstrained self-interest will in such cases lead to the insoluble bilateral monopoly problem with all its indeterminacies and non-optimalities'.[158]

Samuelson's ironic conclusion invoked 'A final law...There are no rules concerning the proper role of government that can be established by *a priori* reasoning'.[159] His colleague Wassily Leontief, however, was an active campaigner for the introduction of economic planning in the United States. Leontief concedes that the price mechanism, which operates through a process of trial and error, still has its supporters:

> In some markets and under certain conditions this actually works. But considering the lack of any reliable information on which to base their expectations, many business leaders have come to recognize that this trial and error game instead of bringing about a desired state of stable equilibrium results in misallocation of resources, underutilization of productive capacity and periodic unemployment.[160]

This makes a strong case for 'steering' the economy, rather than relying on the invisible hand of the market.[161]

But it was still a capitalist economy that would be steered in this manner. The alternative was to acknowledge that the age of capitalism was over, and that the potential advantages of free competition could only be achieved under socialism. As we have seen, Kenneth Arrow concluded that socialism was the way in which the ideal market outcome could be achieved in practice. However, this was a restatement of a principle of some antiquity. So far as we know, the first to formulate it explicitly was the English neoclassical socialist H.D. Dickinson (1899–1969) in his criticism of the liberal Austrian economist Ludwig von Mises, who had argued that rational economic decision-making was impossible under socialism. On the contrary, Dickinson replied:

> .... only in a socialist community, where production can be carried on in the full light of statistical measurement and publicity, is it possible to realise the true principles of economic valuation.... The beautiful systems of economic equilibrium described by Böhm-Bawerk, Wieser, Marshall and Cassel are not descriptions of society as it is but prophetic visions of a socialist economy of the future.[162]

Something very similar to this was implicit in Fred Taylor's presidential address to the American Economic Association in December 1928,[163] and Taylor's argument was repeated in a more sophisticated form a few years later by Oskar Lange (1904–65) in his celebrated defence of market socialism: 'The difference between the traditional Marxist and the modern position on the problem [of resource allocation under socialism] is thus but a difference as to the technique applied.' The traditional Marxists had nothing but the – wholly inadequate – labour theory of value at their disposal. 'Only the technique provided by the modern method of marginal analysis enables us to solve the problem satisfactorily.'[164] As Lange's Marxist critics were quick to point out, this argument was something of a two-edged sword: was it the market *process* that was to be simulated, or simply the market *outcome*? If the former, as Lange suggested in the 1930s, then his version of socialism was the polar opposite of that envisaged by Marx, Engels and their followers. Towards the end of his life Lange came down emphatically in favour of the latter interpretation. He had shown that the anti-socialists were wrong, since the simultaneous equations of general equilibrium theory could be solved by trial and error through a socialist market mechanism. But this has been overtaken by technical progress:

> Were I to rewrite my essay today my task would be much simpler. My answer to Hayek and Robbins would be: so what's the trouble? Let us put the simultaneous equations on an electronic computer and we shall obtain the solution in less than a second. The market process with its cumbersome *tatônnements* appears old-fashioned. Indeed, it may be considered as a computing device of the pre-electronic age.[165]

Lange's conclusion could have been strengthened by reference to the literature on linear programming, a set of optimising techniques developed simultaneously but independently by Western and Soviet economists in the late 1940s and early 1950s, often with military applications in mind. The 1975 Nobel prize in economics was shared by L.L. Kantorovich (1912–) and by the Dutch-American economist Tjalling Koopmans (born 1910) for their work on the theory of programming.[166] As Paul Samuelson had earlier observed, 'no one who understands both economic theory and programming theory is likely to deny that the latter's fundamental duality theorems have added to his understanding of the pricing mechanism *and its limitations*'.[167]

4.8 The corporate economy revisited

Somewhat surprisingly, these arguments took place in almost total isolation from the contemporary debate on the implications of the corporatisation of the capitalist economy. That is to say, the neoclassical microeconomists continued to assume that 'the firm' was an owner-managed enterprise with the single goal of profit maximisation, with no separation of ownership and control, goal conflict or principal-agency problems. The first serious neoclassical consideration of these questions came as late as 1959, when William Baumol (born 1922) proposed sales revenue maximisation (subject to a profit constraint) as an alternative to the conventional goal of profit maximisation.[168] This was an ingenious and elaborate, but methodologically completely orthodox, extension of the standard constrained optimisation framework to the corporate economy, where ownership of the firm was separated from effective control. A somewhat more elaborate analysis, in similar mould, came from Oliver Williamson (born 1932), who proposed a managerial utility function in which 'expense preference' featured prominently. Items which the owner-managed enterprise treated as costs – such as the size of the head office staff or the managerial salary bill – now become the principal goals of the firm. That is to say, managers try to maximise staff and salary levels, subject again to a profit constraint. Only when the external competitive environment is unusually unfavourable does the managerial firm come close to maximising profit.[169]

These early managerial theories of the firm are open to criticism from two different perspectives. Organisational theorists complain that they are sociologically naïve, and also assume incredible powers of information gathering and processing on the part of the managers. Under conditions of 'bounded rationality' and pervasive conflicts of interest between different fractions of the managerial elite, only "satisfactory" rather than optimal solutions are likely to be sought, and the relevance of the traditional theory of the firm becomes doubtful.[170] The precise implications of this are, however, rather unclear: 'many of the attacks on the theory of the firm are not so much proper critiques of existing theory as they are suggestions for the development of a new theory appropriate to this different set of questions. Ultimately, a new theory of firm decision-making behaviour might be used as a basis for a theory of markets',[171] but no such theory has yet emerged from the work of the organisational theorists.

The neoclassical economist Robin Marris, by contrast, objected not to the maximising assumption but rather to the static nature of the analysis. A growing firm offers important advantages to managers – above all, the opportunity for more rapid promotion – that a stagnant firm cannot. Thus, Marris suggests, it is reasonable to suppose that the corporation maximises the rate of growth of sales revenue, not the level of sales, subject to the usual profit constraint. There is very little difference between 'managerial capitalism' and 'managerial socialism' in this regard.[172] More sociologically aware than Baumol or Williamson, Marris applies the Weberian theory of bureaucracy to the problems of managerial motivation and compensation. While he rejects both satisficing and Galbraithian institutionalism as anti-theoretical, Marris therefore proposes what he describes as a 'bureconic' theory of the managerial firm.[173]

Initially denying that managerial capitalism had produced 'a whole new system of social relationships',[174] Marris subsequently widened the scope of his analysis to 'the corporate society', endorsing the sociologist Tom Burns's description of 'a new model of society which eventually superimposed bureaucratic organisation on the old market society'.[175] Marris's 'final conclusion' is that market processes are no longer able to cope with the problems of increased social interdependence and increased externalities that characterise corporate societies. These problems can only be solved by 'social benefit corporations', which would operate like Yugoslav self-managed enterprises (but with more attention paid to social benefits and less to the workers' private incomes) or 'the better class of government agency'. There is still some role for 'old-style small profit seeking enterprises', Marris suggests, but 'Increasingly, I think, the days of the stockholder corporation must be numbered'.[176] This is a judgement with which Keynes, Galbraith and Schumpeter might all have concurred.

Like the Marxists, the institutionalists and the Austrians, then, eminent neoclassical economists failed to anticipate the rise of neoliberalism. When they thought about the future of the market at all, they, too, saw it in as being in long-term decline. True, there were some notable exceptions to this general rule. James Meade, for example, asserted the *increased* salience of market solutions in his critique of *The New Industrial State*,[177] and Oliver Williamson soon had second thoughts about the market-suppressing tendencies of the multi-divisional corporation.[178] We shall return to these authors in Chapter 6. First, however, we must move from theory to practice, and investigate developments within the capitalist mode of production itself.

Part III

Neoliberalism and Modern Capitalism

5
Market Elimination in Modern Capitalism: Where the Theorists were Right

5.1 Introduction

In previous chapters, we have shown how Marx, his followers, and subsequently economists and social theorists of other schools all predicted the decline of the market, and most did so from a broadly historical materialist perspective. They identified fundamental changes in the forces of production that would tend to eradicate market relations, including new technologies generating huge economies of scale and scope and the growing use of science – considered to be a public good that could not be easily or efficiently privately appropriated – as the basis of modern industry. At the level of the productive relations, they expected the market-dependent petite bourgeoisie to be replaced by a new professionalised middle class indifferent or actively hostile to the market, while the economic role of the state would grow for a variety of reasons and contribute to the increasing socialisation of production and consumption within the capitalist mode of production itself. This would be accompanied by changes to the superstructure, with legal doctrines, political institutions and ideology all adjusting to the basic transformation of society that was under way. In this chapter, we show how these expectations could be justified for much of the twentieth century, but were then obviously and comprehensively falsified by profound changes in the opposite direction. These changes were in accord with, and are best understood in terms of, the concepts and propositions of historical materialism, which we outlined in Chapters 1 and 2.

5.2 The productive forces

The evidence on the concentration of capital[1] in the United Kingdom between 1909 and 1970 was summarised by S.J. Prais, who found a strong increasing tendency over the period as a whole, interrupted in the interwar years but accelerating after 1949. The share of the 100 largest enterprises in manufacturing output rose from 16% in 1909 to 41% in 1970; one half of total output was produced by the 2000 largest enterprises at the beginning of the century, and by only 800 in 1970.[2] A similar (if rather slower) trend was identified in the United States, where the share of the 100 largest enterprises in total manufacturing output rose from 21% in 1910 to 33% in 1970.[3] By 1968 the 200 largest companies owned 60.9% of US corporate assets, compared with 47.2% in 1947.[4] In France, the share in total employment of firms with ten or fewer workers fell from 32.2% in 1906 to 16.2% in 1954, while the share of firms with 500 or more rose from 18.5 to 27.1%.[5] These are just three examples; similar developments can be observed in almost all advanced capitalist economies over a broadly similar period.

This was associated with an increase in concentration at the industry level. In UK manufacturing, for example, the share of the three largest enterprises in the total employment of the typical industry grew from 26% in 1935 to 41% in 1968, after which any further increase was minimal.[6] It was a continuation of a tendency that had begun in the latter decades of the nineteenth century and manifested itself in almost all advanced capitalist countries.[7] There is every reason to suppose that it was also connected with increased vertical integration, thereby creating a strong tendency for administrative hierarchies to replace markets in the coordination of economic activity. As we saw in Chapter 4, the business historian Alfred Chandler, who documented this process in the United States, emphasised that social and organisational innovation has been no less important than technical innovation (narrowly defined in the engineering sense) in promoting the concentration of capital.

Empirical studies of concentration are often restricted to manufacturing, which is the sector of the economy with the greatest average firm size. This is a less significant limitation than it might appear to be, since it was precisely manufacturing that was increasing its share of employment and output in the late nineteenth and early twentieth centuries, largely at the expense of agriculture. In the United Kingdom, the industrial sector (manufacturing, mining and construction) already accounted for 35% of national product in 1850–4; its share continued to rise until 1955–9, when it contributed 48% of total output.[8] In Germany, the industry share was 21% in 1850–4, 40% in 1900–4, 50% in 1935–9 and (for West Germany only) 51% in 1950–4.[9] Industry accounted for 44.5% of total UK employment in 1891, peaking at 49.4% in 1971; in

Germany, the corresponding figures are 32.9% in 1882, 42.1% in 1939 and 48.9% in 1970.[10]

There is a huge literature on the growth of monopolies, cartels and trusts, and the associated weakening or outright disappearance of price competition. Classic accounts include those of Berle and Means,[11] Bain[12] and Baran and Sweezy[13] for the United States, and Aaronovitch and Sawyer[14] for the United Kingdom. It was not a simple process, since it provoked deep public hostility, and there were recurrent and partially successful attempts to regulate or even reverse the growth of market power. Early monopolies were challenged by new competitors and by courts and politicians, and the steady state, at least in the United States, was oligopoly, or 'competition among the few'.[15] Oligopolistic prices were set administratively,[16] often being stabilised through tacit collusion at a level close to that which would have been established by a single, profit-maximising monopolist. Competition was confined to such non-price dimensions as product specification, innovation and marketing. The administered pricing procedures of the giant corporation were so different from the impersonal 'higgling of the market' that Alfred Eichner, the historian of the Sugar Trust, wrote of the fixing of a 'corporate levy' comparable to the Soviet turnover tax.[17] This 'oligopolistic margin' provided profits well in excess of those that truly competitive firms would have obtained, and was used in part to finance research and development operations that allowed for continual reduction in production costs.

Marx was also prescient in his prediction that science would become increasingly important as a source of improvements in the productive forces:

> ....until about 1875, or even later, the technology used in the economies of the West was mostly traceable to individuals who were not scientists, and who often had little scientific training. The occupational separation between science and industry was substantially complete except for chemists who were engaged in analyzing, testing, and measuring some industrial processes.
>
> This situation changed in the last part of the nineteenth century.... The derivation of new or improved products and processes from the esoteric explanations of science became the work of industrial scientists, whose efforts were driven and shaped by estimates of their potential economic value.[18]

Joel Mokyr confirms the increasing importance of science to technological change in the twentieth century, driven by the profit motive, and also notes a growing optimism in the ability of technology to solve all social problems. The nature of technological advance had now changed, and was linked in a way that it had never been before to economies of scale and declining average costs.[19] By the end of the century, research and development accounted for some 4% of United States GNP, or $227 billion in 1998, and on some estimates more than 60% of the labour force was engaged in the 'information sector', compared with only 20% in agriculture and manufacturing.[20] 'It can be argued that virtually all of the economic growth that has occurred since the eighteenth century is ultimately attributable to innovation.'[21]

The scientific method was also applied to the management of production and the control of the labour process.[22] As we shall suggest in the next section, this had important implications for the nature of work and also – or so many thinkers believed – for the social and political characteristics of the working class itself. The broader repercussions of the growth of science as a productive force seemed to be twofold. On the one hand, by generating economies of scale it buttressed the monopoly position of big business. On the other hand, it testified to the increasing socialisation of production within capitalism: scientific knowledge was created by society, and could not be securely or efficiently privately appropriated. Thus the patent system, which allows the (temporary) conversion of scientific discoveries into private property, has always been contentious. In mid-nineteenth century Britain, the anti-patent movement enjoyed considerable support.[23] As J.D. Bernal noted in 1939, intellectual property was a subject that made scientists distinctly uneasy:

> The taking out of patents by scientists is a practice on which opinion is much divided. The general ethics of the profession is definitely against it. It is felt that in the first place no individual scientist can honestly claim such an exclusive right to a discovery as entitles him to sole profit from it, and in the second, that a scientist has no right to block in any way the progress of application. On the other hand, it is felt only just that science should receive some return from the new values it gives to the community. The first difficulty could be, and has been, overcome, by the taking out of patents by institutions rather than individuals, but this only enhances the second difficulty.[24]

The result was continuing tension between science and the market, and resistance to the notion that ideas might be tradable commodities.

5.3 The productive relations

Just as Marx had predicted, the century after his death saw a rapid decline in the petite bourgeoisie: peasant farmers, petty traders, artisans and small manufacturers were giving way to big business. This can be documented in terms of their numbers, their share in total output and their political and social influence. In the case of the peasantry, there was also an increase in their dependence on the market due to a reduction in self-provisioning.[25] In Western Europe, this decline was probably fastest in France, where 'independent' workers represented 40.1% of the labour force in 1881 but only 13.9% in 1975 (a further 3.4% were 'family workers'). In Germany, independent and family workers fell from 35.9% of the labour force in 1882 to 16% in 1970, while in Great Britain the decline was from an already low 12.8% in 1891 to 7.7% in 1971.[26] The decline of the *petite* bourgeoisie accelerated after 1945. In the OECD countries, 31% of those working were classified as self-employed in 1954, but only 17% in 1973.[27] There was a continuing fall in their contribution to total output. Long-term data on the share of 'entrepreneurial income' in national income are available only for Britain. As expected, they reveal a protracted and continuing decline, from 21.8% in 1889 to a nadir of 7.1% in 1968.[28] A similar process was unfolding in other advanced capitalist countries and in all likelihood even more rapidly.

As the old middle class declined, a 'new middle class' was rising in its place, characterised by the possession of educational qualifications, specialised knowledge and technical expertise rather than the ownership of property. The historian Harold Perkin identifies the emergence of 'professional society' as the most important social development of the twentieth century. Professionals derive their status and self-esteem from the possession and exercise of expertise, not capital. Perkin also claims that they were motivated more by an ethic of professional service than by the quest for profit, and their attitude to the market was one of neutrality, if not suspicion or outright hostility.[29] In arguing that professionals were at least potentially anti-capitalist, Perkin was part of a long intellectual tradition. As early as 1910, Rudolf Hilferding was pointing to 'a deterioration in the position of salaried employees', so that 'the opposition of these strata to capital (for which they perform the most important as well as the most useless functions in production) will increase'.[30] The belief that the new middle class could be won over to the cause of socialism was central to the political strategy of European social democracy and the British Fabians alike.[31]

For the institutionalist Thorstein Veblen, too, 'the engineers' were profoundly hostile to 'the price system'. Their professional instinct was to use their skills to increase production, and this brought them into conflict with the output-restricting policies of the corporate elite, whose 'sabotage' they bitterly resented.[32] Credence was given to Veblen's argument by the emergence in the interwar years of the 'Technocracy' movement.[33] In effect, the technocrats had written the manifesto for James Burnham's 'managerial revolution' (which we discussed in Chapter 3). They provided evidence of a profound change in both the social position and the ideological outlook of the middle class, creating an anti-market orientation that would have been totally alien to the classic petite bourgeoisie of an earlier epoch.

Most nineteenth-century proletarians experienced no pleasure from active participation in the market for their labour power, and the same was true of their involvement in markets for consumer goods. Working hours were long and time was scarce. In 1850, 'average normal hours' in Britain ranged from 57.6 per week in the cigar and tobacco industry to 60.8 in tailoring. The only significant reductions in the second half of the century came in the strong boom of 1872–4, when craft unions for once enjoyed real power. By 1880 the range of normal hours was from 52.6 (cigar and tobacco workers again being the most favoured) to 58.1 (in the iron and steel industry. There were no further reductions of any consequence until 1919–20.[34] It should be noted that overtime working was common, and that unskilled and semi-skilled workers probably enjoyed even less leisure than the better-documented craftsmen.

Incomes were also simply too low to permit any significant discretionary expenditure. A semi-skilled urban worker in Britain in the middle of the century would earn between 15s and £1 a week, if fortunate enough to be in steady employment. A typical family with three children, earning 15s, would spend 72% of its income on food, almost half of that on bread and potatoes. 'There are a few "luxuries" here', in the form of cheap meat and beer, John Burnett concludes from an examination of the budget of one such household, 'though nothing for fresh vegetables or milk, sickness or insurance'. Even for skilled workers food accounted for 60% of their income, admittedly with a slightly more pleasant diet. This fortunate minority enjoyed 'a reasonable margin of about 6s a week for clothing, education and occasional indulgence in tobacco.... and beer'.[35] These English workers, it must be remembered, were the best paid in Europe and among the most affluent in the world; only in North America and Australia did the working class live better.

Fifty years later working-class life had improved, so that 'the standards of the skilled of 1850 had become those of the average in 1900', with protein now representing a significant part of the diet. But food still took up three-quarters of the typical household budget, and a large minority of the working class (including the sick, unemployed and intermittently employed) fell short of the most minimal level of nutrition.[36] Seebohm Rowntree described the living conditions of one York family, 'poorer-paid, though by no means the poorest'. The husband was a lorry-driver and his wife did casual cleaning and sewing jobs; there were two young children:

> Their house, rented at 3s. a week, had 3 rooms, 1 on each storey: from the living-room stairs led to a bedroom and from that, a ladder to the attic above. There was a tap, but no sink, in the living-room, from which drippings fell on to an uneven brick floor partly covered with linoleum and rag mats. Furniture consisted of a table, 2 wooden easy chairs, a sofa covered with American cloth and an occasional table under the front window displaying family treasures such as a glass vase and a few photographs. This was existence in 1900 at 'round about £1 a week'.[37]

A similar pattern of poverty while in employment and destitution when out of work was movingly described in Robert Tressall's magnificent novel of working-class life in early twentieth-century 'Mugsborough' (Hastings). Unlike Rowntree's lorry-driver, Tressall's 'ragged trousered philanthropists' were housepainters, that is, skilled men who had served an apprenticeship. Nonetheless, they and their families were appallingly badly dressed and could seldom afford to eat meat. For people like these, 'shopping' was evidently not a source of 'identity', or of profound sociopsychological satisfaction, as it was to become as general affluence spread to the working class after 1945 (see Chapter 6).

If incomes were low, wealth was non-existent for the workers. At the risk of stating the exceedingly obvious, it is a simple matter to document the fact that the working class owned no assets of any consequence, and hence had no direct material interest whatsoever in the operation of financial markets. Long-term evidence on the distribution of wealth exists only for the United Kingdom, the United States and Sweden. In 1875, the richest 5% of individuals in Britain owned 84% of the nation's wealth. By 1911–13 this had risen to 87%, but the bottom 90% of the population still owned only 8% of the wealth. As late as 1954, when the share of the top 1% had been reduced to 43%, the poorest 90% had a mere 21%.[38] A similar story can be told for the United States. While in 1860 the top 1% of Americans had to be content with a trifling 24% of the country's wealth, the top 40% owned 97 or 98% of it and the bottom 50% had approximately zero.[39] In Sweden, where the earliest data are for 1920, the poorest 80% had no wealth at all; 25 years later, after a long period of socialist government, this was no longer the case, and their share had risen – to precisely 4%.[40]

The only assets of any consequence that might be owned by working people, as late as the middle of the twentieth century, was some proportion of the value of their (heavily mortgaged) house. Once again we can take the British case as broadly representative. Over the previous hundred years building clubs had grown up to offer 'a dream, which very few realized, of escape from the landlord'.[41] By 1900, owner-occupation was still confined to a very small minority of all dwellings: 1.3% in central Birmingham, for example. Detailed research in the city of York found 6% of the working class to be owner-occupiers, but on closer examination this figure included clerks and shopkeepers in addition to skilled artisans. Nationally, too, most 'working-class' home-owners were actually lower middle-class.[42] Not until the 1930s were rising real wages combined with cheap houses and low interest rates, so that 'the possibility of a mortgage spread from white-collar occupations to at least some higher-paid manual workers'. In 1945, however, barely one quarter of all houses in England and Wales were owner-occupied, and the great majority of working people were still tenants.[43]

If real wages were rising slowly, and the growth of disposable income did allow the working class some modest involvement in the market for consumer goods, it could be argued that their engagement in the market for labour power was declining. This process had two dimensions. The first was linked to political developments, including the growth of trade unions, which will be discussed in the next section. The second took the form of a slow but inexorable tendency towards homogenisation, with traditional skills being threatened by mechanisation, craft privileges attacked by employers and customary wage differentials also under threat. In addition, the concentration of capital and the increasing professionalisation of management were reducing the opportunities for modest upward occupational mobility that had once existed for a minority of skilled workers. This was a gradual and very uneven process, but perceptive observers like Sidney and Beatrice Webb had identified it by the end of the nineteenth century.[44] It gathered strength in the early years of the twentieth century, spurred on by Frederic Winslow Taylor's propagation of the principles of 'scientific management', with its dogmatic separation of job execution and job design and the associated crusade to eliminate all discretion from the performance of the worker's designated task.[45]

Where significant differentiation between workers did persist, it took on a quite different and distinctively modern form. Once craft privileges had been destroyed, as for example in the United States steel industry, job hierarchies were deliberately re-created with the double intention of tying the worker to the company by rewarding 'loyalty' and long service, thereby reducing costly labour turnover, and of eliminating the threat of collective resistance by creating a culture of individualism – divide-and-rule at the workplace, in other words.[46] The effect was to offer 'insiders' a degree of protection from outside competition, making the so-called 'internal labour market' a shelter of sorts from the external market for labour power. In fact the metaphor is an unfortunate one, since the discipline of the market was largely replaced by bureaucratic control and administrative procedures. By the middle of the twentieth century, liberal academics were beginning to invoke quite different images: the 'balkanisation' of labour markets[47] or even 'a new industrial feudalism'.[48] Later theorists of 'dual' or 'segmented' labour markets drew attention to the way in which those workers who were excluded from the 'internal labour market' found themselves at a very serious disadvantage by comparison with those who were included.[49]

These developments were reinforced in a number of ways by the rise of the state.[50] The quantitative evidence on the growth of the capitalist state is overwhelming. Tanzi and Schuknecht report that the share of GDP accounted for by 'general government expenditure' in 14 advanced capitalist countries[51] rose from 10.8% at the beginning of the 1870s to 19.6% in 1920, 28.0% in 1960, 41.9% in 1980 and 45.0% in 1996. Outside Ireland, New Zealand and (very marginally) the United Kingdom, where the government share was lower in 1996 than it had been in 1980, the rise of the state continued without interruption into the neoliberal era. The smallest of the 14 governments was the United States, with 32.4% of GDP in 1996, compared with 7.3% in 1870; the biggest was Sweden, where the government share had increased from 5.7% to no less than 64.2%, more than double the 31.0% reported for 1960.[52] This prompted Assar Lindbeck to describe Sweden as a 'mini-transition' economy by 1990, with neoliberals reacting against what they saw as an almost Soviet level of government intervention. In the previous two decades, the Swedish state had come to function as an employer of last resort, providing a shelter from the labour market for a very substantial minority of the working population. In addition, tight controls over capital markets and very high taxes on profits had been introduced, with the aim of creating 'capitalism without capitalists'.[53] This, of course, was an extreme case. In the 14 countries as a whole, the state employed 2.4% of the total labour force in 1870, 17.5% in 1980 and 18.4% in 1994, in which year government employment was lowest in Japan (6.9%) and greatest in Sweden (32.0%).[54]

What Winston Churchill described as the 'second Thirty Years War' (1914–45) was a crucial watershed in the growth of the British state, as we explain in Chapter 7. After being roughly static between 1880 and 1914 the government's share in total output rose sharply during the First World War, and this was only partially reversed with the coming of peace. There were further modest increases in the interwar years in state expenditure on pensions and housing.[55] To a very large extent the rise of the state in the twentieth century reflected precisely those factors that the Marxists and other economists proclaiming the elimination of the market had identified, sometimes as early as the nineteenth century. They included the provision of public goods, or goods with a pronounced 'public' dimension, that the market failed to deliver (education, health and social insurance); regulation of the market for labour power; the costs of administering, defending and expanding colonial empires; and the increasingly large costs of wars. There was also a small but significant element of income redistribution, defended by many liberal economists. As A.C. Pigou told a Manchester audience on the eve of the Great War: 'I believe it to be right that the well-to-do should be summoned by the State to help their poorer neighbours whenever that summons can be enforced without evoking gravely injurious reactions upon the production of wealth and, therewith, ultimately upon the fortunes of the poor themselves.... This proposition seems to me to hold good of State subsidies upon education, insurance, housing, food and clothing equally.'[56]

5.4 The superstructure

These profound changes in the forces and the relations of production were reflected in the superstructure. The law moved in a collectivist direction, with new statutes being enacted to protect labour, and many fractions of capital, from full exposure to the market. The evolution of law in the United States in response to the 'state capitalist' phase that began in the 1930s is described by Chase.[57] Elsewhere, decisions by judges, as well as legislators, imposed new and onerous restrictions on the rights of property-owners, provoking bitter complaints from liberal legal theorists like A.V. Dicey.[58] We can illustrate this by reference to industrial law in the United Kingdom, where the formerly severe sanctions on trade union activities gave way, from the 1870s onwards, to a legal environment in which union interference with free competition between workers was increasingly tolerated, if not actively encouraged. For the most part this required Acts of Parliament to reverse hostile judicial decisions. Even after the repeal of the repressive Combination Acts in 1824–5, the English common law had continued to regard trade unions as criminal conspiracies 'in restraint of trade'. The Acts of 1871, 1875 and 1876 effectively took the criminal law out of industrial relations. 'By legalizing trade unions, the state implicitly recognized the anti-competitive objectives which they pursued.' This was despite the strong opposition of employer representatives; it enjoyed the support of both Conservative and Liberal politicians.[59]

The judges, however, continued to defend the operation of a competitive market for labour power, at the end of the century using the doctrine of civil (rather than criminal) conspiracy to spectacular effect in the celebrated Taff Vale case. Once again Parliament intervened to protect the right of unions to interfere with freedom of contract. Section 3 of the Trade Disputes Act of 1906 provided that

> An act done by a person, in contemplation or furtherance of a trade dispute, shall not be actionable on the ground only that it induces some other person to break a contract of employment or that it is an interference with the trade business or employment of some other person or with the right of some other person to dispose of his capital or his labour as he wills.[60]

This made it virtually impossible for any capitalist to sue any union or individual union member for any non-violent action undertaken in the course of a strike. The language could not have been clearer. Even the judges finally relented in their hostility to 'labour monopolies', as can be seen by the remarkable judgement of the House of Lords in the 1942 Crofters' Case, when a union embargo on the supply of yarn to non-union weavers was declared to be a legitimate tactic in the promotion of the membership's interests:

> The weavers alleged that the whole arrangement was a conspiracy to injure; but the House of Lords said that it was not. All the parties were pursuing their legitimate interests, the mill owners to increase

> their control of the market and their profits, the union to improve wages and extend membership – all, said Viscount Simon, 'to create a better basis for collective bargaining.... A combination with such an object is not unlawful, because the object is the legitimate promotion of the interests of the combiners'. The union could use the dockers to help the mill workers; and any combination between employers and union could not be invalid merely because each has, in Viscount Maugham's phrase, 'his own axe to grind'.[61]

The market for labour power had certainly not been abolished but, as the law now recognised, it had been very substantially socialised and tamed. Judges now treated workers' collective interests as being no less valid than those of employers; they themselves abstained from the battle, so long as each side pursued its own self-interest by acts lawful in themselves. Lord Wright even added: 'The right of workmen to strike is an essential element in the principle of collective bargaining.'[62]

At least in Britain the judiciary were content to allow wage determination to be decided by collective bargaining. In the newly federated Commonwealth of Australia, it was the Conciliation and Arbitration Court that decided the minimum, or 'basic', wage. Its long-time President, Justice H.B. Higgins, saw industrial arbitration as a 'new province for law and order', and one which left little room for market forces.[63] Higgins conducted an early household expenditure survey as a preliminary to the determination of a 'living wage', defined in terms of the 'fair and reasonable' needs of the workman and his family, independently of the industry's capacity to pay and with the explicit implication that bankruptcy was preferable to under-payment: 'If a man cannot maintain his enterprise without cutting down the wages which are *proper* to be paid to his employees.... it would be better that he should abandon the enterprise.'[64] Both 'Higgins's decisions and the language he used were Aristotelian and mediaevalist in doctrine and sentiment', reflecting a 'mediaeval vision of economic "justice" '.[65] Not surprisingly, his hostility to the operation of an unfettered labour market made him very popular with the trade unions.

During the First World War compulsory arbitration was used to fix wages by all the major combatant nations, and it was extended to peacetime in the case of Weimar Germany. Elsewhere, the labour market was increasingly subject to regulation by the state, in the form of legislation restricting hours of work, protecting occupational health and safety and (eventually) prohibiting discrimination against women and minority workers and offering protection against unfair dismissal. This was due in large part to the increased power of trade unions, which proved able to use their political and industrial influence to secure favourable changes in the law.[66] The growth of mass trade unionism led to the spread of collective bargaining, with the state either offering active encouragement and support, as in the United States after 1935, or maintaining a position of benevolent neutrality, as in Britain.[67]

As unions 'matured', and their professional salaried officers began to operate less as agitators and more as 'managers of discontent', employers came to see the benefits that might accrue from the institutionalisation of industrial conflict. Industrial relations became both pluralistic and bureaucratic. Formalised procedures for regulating employment relationships and resolving disputes contributed substantially to the smooth operation of big business in the Golden Age of growth during the three decades after the Second World War, in both Europe and North America. If this meant a considerable reduction in the importance of the market for labour power, it was seen by many capitalists as a small price to pay for economic and social stability.[68]

The rise of the welfare state drove a further wedge between working-class incomes and returns from the labour market. This took the form both of cash payments (unemployment, sickness and disability benefits; income support; aged pensions; child and maternity allowances) and of benefits in kind (especially in the provision of education, health and housing). Many conservative and some liberal critics worried about the disincentive effects of the welfare state, and with good reason.[69] Between 1960–4 and 1975–9 unemployment benefits rose from 28.0% of average pay to 43.2% in the OECD countries, and an index of employment protection legislation increased steadily, from 0.79 to 1.09.[70] By the 1970s, these changes in the superstructure of advanced capitalist societies meant that the working class was substantially sheltered from the vagaries of the labour market, which was no longer the sole determinant of their standard of material comfort.

5.5 Social consciousness

All this had profound repercussions for social consciousness. Rather than attempting the daunting task of writing a comprehensive history of ideas over more than a century, we will simply illustrate with one important example and highlight the way in which neoclassical economics accommodated itself to the new productive forces and productive relations after 1870. Since this question was discussed extensively in Chapter 4, we can be brief here. Although marginalism was both widely interpreted and frequently intended as an assault on Marxian political economy, it also proved attractive to many socialists, who claimed that 'marginalist economics should simply be seen as *the* form of economic analysis which socialists should use to argue their case'.[71] Advocates of this position included Mikhail Tugan-Baranovsky in Russia, Eduard Bernstein and Conrad Schmidt in Germany, and Achille Loria and Arturo Labriola in Italy, together with lesser-known theorists in countries like Denmark and the Netherlands. Even Knut Wicksell and Léon Walras, who were radical egalitarians rather than orthodox socialists, had socialist friends and socialist sympathies. Since it could be argued persuasively that the marginal utility of a dollar was much greater for poor people than for the wealthy, marginalism could easily be invoked to justify tax-and-spend policies to redistribute income and wealth.[72] The difficulty, in fact, was to find a convincing argument against complete equality; not until John Rawls's formulation of a new theory of social justice was this satisfactorily achieved, and it, too, implied support for a very substantial degree of redistribution.[73] Once the Pigovian distinction was drawn between private and social benefits and costs, vast possibilities were also opened up for welfare-improving intervention by the state to deal with externalities and rectify market failures.[74]

Even the Walrasian model of competitive general equilibrium was reclaimed by the left: the market-clearing auctioneer was a phantom of the theorist's imagination, but it could be given flesh and blood in the form of a central planning bureau.[75] Thus general equilibrium analysis was reinterpreted as the economics of socialism, not capitalism.[76] Theorists much more sympathetic to the market, like the self-proclaimed 'liberal-socialist' (and future Nobel laureate) James Meade, could also see advantages in some forms of planning. In the 1940s, Meade focussed on macroeconomic planning, largely restricted to broad aggregates like total consumption, investment, exports and imports.[77] By 1970, however, he was advocating 'indicative planning' at the industry level. In principle, he argued, indicative planning would produce results identical to those of the comprehensive contingent futures markets that were assumed by general equilibrium modellers. In practice, since such markets did not (and realistically, could not) exist, planning offered firms a more reliable means of dealing with uncertainty than the unfettered market mechanism could provide.[78]

Microeconomic planning was intended to supplement macroeconomic management, not to replace it. It is significant that Meade was an early disciple of John Maynard Keynes, whose great plan to save capitalism from itself required 'a somewhat comprehensive socialization of investment'[79] and thereby pointed to the suppression of market forces in the determination of the rate of capital accumulation. Small wonder that Communist theoreticians like Keynes's Cambridge colleague Maurice Dobb drew heavily on orthodox economic theory in their writings on socialism.[80]

6
The Return of the Market: Where They All Went Wrong

6.1 Introduction

As we saw in the previous chapter, there was considerable evidence to support the contention that the market was in long-run decline. For much of the twentieth century, the development of the productive forces could plausibly be interpreted as predominantly market-eradicating. The corresponding changes in the productive relations, in the superstructure, and in social consciousness appeared to be reinforcing this tendency. Indeed, down to the late 1970s, economists of many analytical and political persuasions believed that it was irreversible. But there was already evidence to the contrary. Throughout the twentieth century, and especially during the postwar years, there were many changes in the productive forces and productive relations that promoted markets, and to which all schools of economists paid insufficient attention.

6.2 The productive forces

As far as the productive forces were concerned, the seemingly inexorable increase in the concentration of capital had ceased by the late 1960s, and had then gone into reverse. The share in UK manufacturing output of the 100 largest firms peaked at 41% in 1968, and by 1991 it had fallen to 36%, while the average five-firm concentration ratio had declined from 45.3% in 1980 to 29.8% in 1994. Surveying the literature, Malcolm Sawyer concluded that 'the predominant factor in the decline of concentration was estimated to be a decline in the extent of economies of scale'.[1] In their comprehensive study of 'downsizing' in the United States, Baumol, Blinder and Wolff[2] came to broadly similar conclusions. In France the employment share of firms with 500 or more workers peaked in 1954 and thereafter declined, as did the share of very small enterprises (with 10 or fewer employees); employment in the remaining, medium-sized enterprises rose significantly.[3]

In fact there had long been doubt about the extent of technical economies of scale. Austin Robinson ended his textbook on *The Structure of Competitive Industry* 'published in 1958' with a complaint:

> But we know far less than we ought to know about the extent of the economies of scale. How much does a firm's cost of production increase if it is, say, 25 per cent below the optimum size? Is it a matter of 2–3 per cent? Is it a matter of 10 per cent? Are we, as consumers, wasting sixpence in the pound [2.5%] or five shillings in the pound [25%] by demanding variety.... it would be greatly for the benefit both of policy-making and of clarity of economic thinking if more quantitative information were widely available.[4]

Similarly, 20 years later, Sig Prais inferred from the growth of multi-plant companies that 'plant-economies of scale are not of critical significance' in explaining the growth of concentration, and that 'there is scope today for a wider absolute range of [plant] sizes than previously'.[5] This conclusion has been confirmed by more recent studies. After a detailed survey of the literature on economies of scale and their effects on competition in car production, banking, electric power generation, health care, railways, telecommunications and many other industries, Stephen Martin concluded that:

> Despite the attention given in the theoretical literature to the consequences of economies of scale in the traditional sense, there is no evidence of their general importance. There is little reason to think that diseconomies of scale will set a limit to the expansion of firms in global markets, and there is little reason to think that the attainment of minimum average cost mandates high levels of seller concentration in global markets.
>
> Network externalities are likely to be present in a few sectors (telecommunications; distribution of electric power and natural gas). Such externalities have many of the effects traditionally ascribed to economies of scale.
>
> Outside of such sectors, there is no compelling evidence for the presence of natural monopoly.[6]

Prais argued that the falling cost of communications was a force for increasing concentration, since it reduced the administrative expenses of multi-plant companies.[7] He was probably mistaken in this. In the final decades of the twentieth century, in fact, 'smaller companies did as much to drive globalization.... as bigger ones. The lowering of trade barriers, the spread of deregulation, the plummeting cost of transport and communication: all made it possible for Davids to challenge Goliaths'.[8] At the global level, the reversal of the previous trend towards the concentration of capital was striking. 'Far from gaining economic clout, the biggest multinationals were losing it. In the period from 1980 to 2000, the world's biggest fifty firms grew more slowly than the world economy as a whole.'[9] And there were strong grounds for supposing that the future lay with smaller rather than with bigger business: 'the more futuristic the industry, the less the evidence of concentration. In computer hardware, computer software, and long-distance telephony, the market share of the top five firms in America has been declining.'[10]

These developments were associated with another, rather more subtle, growth in the relative importance of markets. Chicago economists like Ronald Coase and George Stigler had always been sceptical of the supposed inexorable growth of vertical integration, pointing to the very powerful forces of increased specialisation that favoured vertical disintegration. Thus Stigler criticised '[t]hose too numerous people who believe that transactions between firms are expensive and those within firms are free', citing as a counter-example the metal trades in nineteenth-century Birmingham, where 'specialism was carried out to an almost unbelievable extent'.[11] Vertical integration, Stigler maintained, was more often the effect of monopoly – itself frequently the result of misguided government intervention – than the cause. This 'minimalist school', which contended that 'companies make sense when the "transactions costs" associated with buying things on the market exceed the hierarchical costs of maintaining a bureaucracy', claims to have been vindicated by modern technology, which 'is generally shifting the balance of advantage away from companies and towards markets and individuals'.[12] The 'global outsourcing model' was used to immensely profitable effect by retailers like Walmart to drive down the cost of almost everything sold in its stores, not to mention the wages of its US labour force.[13] The movement towards radical vertical disintegration soon extended well beyond trade in manufactured products:

> It is now becoming clear that the global outsourcing business model can also be applied to the service sector. Owing to improvements in electronic communications and the Internet, many services that were previously nontradable have become tradable. These include basic computer systems maintenance and software programming, tax preparation and accounting, architectural planning, and telephone call centres. Even retail sales is potentially tradable, as indicated by the success of the Amazon.com business model. This means that services will be the next area where the global sourcing model will be applied, with corresponding effects on compensation and employment security [in the United States].[14]

Even professional legal and medical services have begun to be outsourced to India.

This helps to explain why 'recent scholarship has produced a revised view that identifies entrepreneurial small firms as making a crucial contribution to innovative activity and technological change'.[15] A few years before Stigler's analysis of vertical disintegration, in fact, Josef Steindl had noted a number of other reasons why small firms had managed to survive even in the face of the supposed technical and financial advantages enjoyed by their big competitors. First, they benefited from product market imperfections which, Steindl suspected, were a reflection of consumer irrationality. A second factor was imperfect competition in the labour market, which allowed small firms to pay lower wages. Third, there were political and public relations considerations that inhibited big business from attempting to eliminate smaller rivals. Finally, Steindl pointed to 'the gambling attitude' of small entrepreneurs, who were prepared to 'accept high risks at very low remunerations'. All in all, 'the survival of small firms is .... dependent on a series of factors not very creditable to our economic system', since they involved the exploitation of consumers and workers and a substantial degree of self-exploitation of the small business owners themselves.[16]

A more or less contemporary study of the British rayon industry, carried out at the suggestion of Samuel Courtauld, owner of the dominant firm in the industry, painted a very similar picture. The survival of small firms was 'very much against the weight of technical factors', Philip Andrews reported, but was 'very largely the result of Courtaulds' marketing and price-policy'. Courtauld's profit margins were so large that small producers could still operate successfully, especially since they were 'free to devote themselves to the more profitable parts of the general market for rayon, and [had] no obligation to sell to the market as a whole'.[17] And Courtaulds' 'live-and-let-live attitude' must itself have been motivated in part by a desire to avoid regulatory intervention.

However true these claims may have been they are not matters connected to the productive forces, and the overwhelmingly important fact is that many technological developments were already beginning to favour small-scale production, as Bertrand Russell noted with approval as early as 1949: 'Electricity and motor-transport have made small units of industry not only economically permissible but even desirable, for they obviate immense expenditure on transportation and organisation. Where a rural industry still flourishes, it should be gradually mechanized, but be left *in situ* and in small units.'[18] Here Russell identifies two of the technologies of the early twentieth century that reduced the cost of organisational specialisation and dispersion. Other technologies having similar and huge effects include refrigeration, containerisation and jet aircraft. The result was to reduce the relative benefits of vertical integration, and thus to make market relations more dense.[19] Similar consequences flowed from technical changes that reduced the cost of impersonal communication: telephones and cables at the end of the nineteenth century, faxes, emails and video links 100 years later:

> For most of the 20th century, the cost of telecommunications services declined at a real rate of 4–5 % per year. For long-distance services, the decline was even more rapid – around 10 % per year. Over a period of 100 years, the compound effect of these declines yields a reduction in costs by a factor of one million or more.[20]

By the late 1980s it was evident that information technology was greatly reducing the costs of decentralised coordination, thereby encouraging the use of markets at the expense of hierarchies. 'Low cost computation favors electronic markets by simplifying complex product descriptions and reducing asset specificity.'[21] There were clear implications for corporate strategy: 'All firms should consider whether more of the activities they currently perform internally could be performed less expensively or more flexibly by outside suppliers whose selection and work could be coordinated by computer-based systems.'[22] Increasingly this was precisely what happened: 'enhanced information control methods through computers and lowered transportation costs made it possible for firms to subcontract whole stages of the production process to producers across the world. Not only, then, was the production process itself fragmented and transformed, but the social communities tied to formerly integrated production sites were fragmented and disrupted in an economic–social process widely understood as "deindustrialisation"'.[23] This has already been mentioned in this section regarding vertical disintegration. As we have already seen, corporations increasingly focussed on what they believed to be their 'core competencies', subcontracting everything from cleaning and catering to professional activities like accounting, and legal services. And the internet spawned a massive e-commerce sector, involving business-to-business transactions in 'market spaces', both horizontal (steel tubing for many applications) and vertical (aerospace industry parts); consumer-to-consumer transactions (such as EBay); and business-to-consumer transactions, sometimes involving online sellers with no presence in any physical marketplace (an example is again provided by Amazon.com).[24]

More than coordination and communication costs were affected by the new technologies. Opportunities for surveillance and monitoring were used by credit rating agencies to expand financial markets by making impersonal transactions less dangerous and principal–agent relations less risky. Technologies of exclusion permitted the privatisation of commodities with public good characteristics, such as electronic tolls on roads, signal scrambling and unscrambling devices and gated consumption of club goods.[25] As early as the 1960s James Meade was using the example of road pricing to illustrate the new technological possibilities for the extension of market relations.[26] Forty years later, digital broadcasting holds out a similar prospect, threatening 'free to air' transmissions and enhancing the growth of pay-per-view and video on demand services that are sometimes described as 'narrowcasting'.[27]

Market-promoting technical change has long permeated household production no less than consumption, with new forms of birth control and the introduction of new domestic appliances (themselves the product of electrification) permitting the commodification of domestic labour and a huge expansion in waged labour by women who, in previous generations, would have been confined to the home.[28] Finally, technologies provided by economics itself have contributed to the growth of market relations. Meade saw 'advances in mathematical economics' as fundamental in extending the realm of the price mechanism. Improvements in the design of incentive systems, auctions and financial engineering have allowed a more focussed enforcement of profitability as the sole criterion determining the allocation of resources.[29]

While business-to-business transactions initially dominated e-commerce, they began to be overtaken by business-to-consumer transactions, operating through 'the market choice box.... the consumer's interface between the many electronic devices in the home, such as television, cable, telephone and computer, and the information superhighway. In turn, this market choice box makes access possible to the vast variety of market choices'.[30] Within a decade this ambitious prediction already looked rather dated: there is no reference to the use of mobile phones to connect buyers and sellers. However, a substantial decline in vertical integration was already apparent:

> firms in some industries have come to rely on external sources for a larger number of components and for administrative and support services, which often results in the disaggregation or "spinning off" of portions of these activities to other organisations. Some of the production functions and many of the staff functions performed by professionals in large organisations are now being contracted out to smaller, more specialized firms,

or carried out by temporary workers on a contract basis.[31] And there are important implications for the nature and extent of product market competition. While the 'industrial economy' was dominated by oligopolists, whose market shares rose and fell only slowly, the 'information economy' is distinguished by temporary monopolies, which are highly profitable for a while but are rapidly destroyed by new competitors with superior technology. Economies of scale give way to network economies – or, to put it another way, demand-side economies of scale replace supply-side economies, where cost savings result from the number of buyers rather than the size of the production unit.[32]

As Manuel Castells documents, there was a corresponding change in the internal structure of the enterprise,

> from vertical bureaucracies to the horizontal corporation.... To manoeuver in the new global economy, characterized by an endless flurry of new competitors using new technologies and cost-cutting capabilities, the large corporations had to become primarily more effective rather than more thrifty.... To be able to internalize the benefits of network flexibility the corporation had to become a network itself.[33]

In other words, to make the most of markets, corporations have to organise themselves as markets. These changes, Castells emphasises, 'were not the mechanical consequence of technological change'; if anything, organisational change preceded and even 'induced to some extent the technical trajectory'. Once underway, however, organisational change 'was extraordinarily enhanced by new information technologies', which made it possible to eliminate entire layers of management.[34] We shall return to this question in the following section, when we consider the associated changes in the relations of production.[35] Networking also affected relations between enterprises, where 'strategic alliances' have largely replaced the traditional cartels.

> Such alliances concern specific times, markets, products, and processes, and they do not exclude competition in all the areas (the majority) not covered by the agreements.... Rather, strategic alliances are decisive instruments in this competition, with today's partners becoming tomorrow's foes, while collaboration in a given market is in sharp contrast to the ferocious struggle for market share in another region of the world.[36]

By the 1980s it was very evident that fundamental changes were indeed occurring in the forces of production. In particular, the advantages of 'flexible specialisation', involving small-batch production for rapidly changing 'niche' consumer markets, were increasingly apparent.[37] It was frequently claimed that this constituted a new stage in the development of capitalism: 'post-Fordism' had replaced the earlier stage of 'Fordism', with its mass production technology, mass markets and stable, giant, vertically integrated oligopolies. As two sociologists put it, in a book dramatically proclaiming 'the death of class', the final decades of the twentieth century saw 'the extinction of the lumbering Fordist dinosaurs' through 'their dissolution into networks of relatively small but skilled-up production companies that engage in product innovation on a competitive basis'.[38] Management theorists distinguished business strategies of 'innovation' and 'quality enhancement' from the relentless pursuit of 'cost reduction' that had characterised the classic Fordist enterprise.[39]

Some of the more ambitious claims of the early enthusiasts for flexible specialisation have proved to be unjustified. Few now believe that the new technologies entail a brave new world of work, dissolving the social relations of wage labour and capital or overcoming alienation, subordination and work intensification.[40] Flexible specialisation itself proves to be an ancient phenomenon, found in 'the artisanal and putting-out manufacturing systems of proto-industrialisation'.[41] Even Fordist mass production has been found to be more flexible than it originally appeared.[42]

But it is important not to go too far in the opposite direction. There is, for example, something distinctive about the new techniques of motor manufacturing described by the *Economist* in 2002. As vehicle producers become more responsive to consumer demand for variety, there will be a shift in emphasis 'from huge plants seeking maximum economies of scale to smaller, more widely distributed plants that are closer to their markets'. These developments also affect business customers, with fleet buyers beginning to design their own trucks, specifying the engines, gearboxes and braking systems that they require. In future, cars too will be made in 'modules that are simply snapped together in small assembly lines close to the consumer, where details can be adapted to local tastes'. This has been facilitated by the emergence of 'space-frame technology', which 'uses extruded metal parts, which are riveted or even glued together to make up the skeleton of a car body, to which plastic or other lightweight panels can be attached. This dispenses with the expensive machines needed to stamp out load-bearing panels, and so favours the use of smaller, cheaper factories'. Huge plants like Volkswagen's Wolfsburg factory, with a maximum output of 750,000 vehicles per year, are now obsolete. New car factories are built to operate at one-quarter of this capacity. 'According to some visionaries, there could be many more built at a tenth of that size, as suppliers take over more of the construction of cars, and car companies themselves move towards a snap-together final assembly much less complex than today's.'[43]

None of this would have been possible with the Fordist technology and management systems of the 1920s. Yet it was precisely that technology and those management systems that were copied, with great success, in Stalin's Russia. Fordism lent itself to hierarchies rather than markets. The initial economic triumph of the Soviet Union, and later of its satellites, began to dissolve in the late 1960s as the new post-Fordist technologies adopted in the capitalist West favoured horizontal links between productive units (and hence market relationships, often via networks), rather than vertical links and the corresponding administrative controls. In the East, as in the West, the belief of Marx and many other economists of all schools that technological change inevitably promoted vertical integration and market eradication proved to be false.[44]

There was an additional problem with the Marxian argument, also widely supported by non-Marxists, which was at its strongest when dealing with industrial production. In the more advanced capitalist economies of North America and Western Europe the relative importance of manufacturing peaked in the third quarter of the twentieth century. Thereafter the share of industry in both total output and total employment began to fall rapidly as tertiary output and employment grew. There are some difficult conceptual issues here, since 'the service sector' is a portmanteau term that includes the supply of inputs for manufacturing business in addition to the provision of personal services for individuals.[45] Nevertheless, the general picture is very clear. In the UK, for example, where de-industrialisation proceeded most rapidly and was recognised earliest,[46] the share of manufacturing, mining, construction and utilities in national product fell from 48% in 1955–9 to only 29% in 1989–93. In (West) Germany, which by the 1990s was still unusually heavily dependent on manufacturing, the decline was from 51% in 1955–9 to 38% in 1989–93, while for the US the corresponding figures (this time excluding utilities) were 39% in 1950–4 and 30% in 1989–93.[47] The employment share declined even more rapidly, since labour productivity grew more slowly on average in the tertiary sector. Industry accounted for 49.1% of all UK jobs in 1951 but for only 27.9% 40 years later. In the US the decline was from 34.6% in 1950 to 25.9% in 1990 (again excluding utilities).[48] Futurologists had been proclaiming the emergence of a 'post-industrial society' for several decades.[49] There is no need to imitate their hyperbole, but it is important to recognise that, by the end of the twentieth century, the typical wage- and salary-earner was no longer a factory worker.[50]

Finally, in the development of the productive forces, there proved to be serious defects in treating science applied to capitalist production as a public good. There is absolutely no doubt that scientific knowledge has come to play an ever greater role in the production of both goods (agricultural and industrial) and services. This is evident both from the increased employment of scientists and technicians and from the accelerating growth of research and development expenditure in all advanced capitalist economies.[51] The difficulty arises with the assumption that scientific knowledge is inevitably, or normally, a public good that cannot be appropriated. On the contrary: 'Almost all technical progress.... starts by being the result of efforts made by a single enterprise, and is initially *private*.' Indeed, it makes sense to define the firm itself in terms of 'its accumulated private technology. Just as patterns of behaviour and memory ultimately define the differences between people, so the stock of accumulated private technology largely defines the differences between enterprises. This is the irreducible "core", without which an enterprise ceases to be itself'.[52]

If knowledge is private then it can be appropriated, and the more easily, and cheaply, the more sophisticated are the monitoring and surveillance technologies. If this were not so, it would be difficult to explain why rational capitalists would ever incur any expenditure on research and development, and the very notion of intellectual property would be oxymoronic. By the end of the twentieth century, however, the capitalised value of technical knowledge, broadly defined, probably exceeded the value of all the physical capital owned by US corporations,[53] and the United States government was energetically promoting bilateral so-called 'free trade' agreements where the principal benefit to US companies was the recognition and protection of their intellectual property rights rather than the 'opening of markets' more conventionally associated with free trade.[54] 'Recently', Michael Perelman notes,

> claims to informational property rights have been expanding by leaps and bounds....The impulse to make such claims is not necessarily new. Karl Marx claimed that the invention of the windmill caused the emperor, the nobility, and the priests to squabble over who owned the wind...What is new is the degree to which the legal system has sanctioned such demands.[55]

We have to assume that Marx's tongue was in his cheek when he wrote these words. Perelman's is not. 'The courts are moving to protect more and more claims of intellectual property', he complains, 'even though the broader circulation of information is better for society as a whole'.[56]

The objection that intellectual property represents a fetter on the productive forces is an old one, and would be endorsed by many economists of all schools, including neoclassicals.[57] It is, though, open to serious question. If something can be appropriated then it can be traded, even if it is intangible, and this is true also of knowledge. The critical issue affecting the speed of diffusion of new ideas is the degree to which competition drives down their price. Thus William Baumol accepts the Schumpeterian view that innovation has become routinised in corporate capitalism (see Chapter 4, Section 4.3), but he sees this as a positive phenomenon, since it greatly reduces the level of uncertainty associated with research and development and therefore encourages more investment in new technology. Moreover the ability to assert intellectual property rights enables the corporation to internalise what would otherwise be some of the externalities resulting from innovation, if only for a limited period. The threat of losing its new and private technology by imitation or theft provides a strong incentive for the firm to sell access to it while it still commands a price. Baumol thus identifies the sale of intellectual property through technology licensing as an important source of the accelerated diffusion of new productive ideas, which can be documented in practice and modelled in theory, in profit-maximising terms.[58] Similarly, the 'commercialisation' of university research is now well-known, if often lamented.[59] It would not be seen as either a threat or an opportunity for academe if science, applied to production, was in fact the public good that Marx – tongue *out* of cheek – believed it to be.

Writing in the 1850s, Marx cannot reasonably be expected to have anticipated the emergence of intellectual property rights, which by the late twentieth century had become the most rapidly growing form of capitalist property in the most advanced capitalist countries (above all in the United States). He simply followed the great majority of writers in his day and assumed that knowledge was for the most part inherently non-appropriable, so that property rights in it could not, in principle, be defined. Hence, he concluded, science and technology were not and would not become the subjects of market transactions. It followed that this increasingly important part of the productive forces lay outside the market, and on this basis he buttressed the case for believing there to be a market eradication tendency in capitalist development.[60]

6.3 The productive relations

Neither did changes in the productive relations proceed precisely as the classical Marxists, and other social and economic theorists, had expected. For one thing, the petty bourgeoisie survived much longer than anyone had anticipated, partly because the economies of large-scale activity in agriculture and retailing were slow to become apparent, but more especially because of the protection that small business obtained by the astute exercise of its political influence.[61] In Western Europe, the European Union's Common Agricultural Policy represented a massive and continuing transfer of resources from urban taxpayers to farmers. Although large landowners and corporate agribusiness benefited most in absolute terms, the CAP was also a lifeline for millions of small farmers, whose attachment to the market – however protected and distorted that market might be – was beyond question.[62] In retailing, the remorseless advance of first the supermarket and then the hypermarket was slowed, in Europe and Japan, by legal restrictions on competition, including the fiercely defended prohibition of evening and weekend trading that survived in Germany, for example, until the early years of the twenty-first century.

As neoliberalism began to attack the institutions of labour market regulation, some growth in self-employment occurred, this time because it enhanced flexibility for big business. In the UK, to take the one example for which long data series are available, the share in total employment of 'independent and family workers' reached its lowest point as early as 1951 and then began to rise, while the share of entrepreneurial income in GNP continued to fall until 1968, after which it increased rapidly.[63] This should not be exaggerated. In the OECD

> self-employment [had] only grown from 9.8% of non-agricultural employment in 1979 to 11.9% by the end of the 1990s, and fell in agriculture. Moreover, it is striking that in the USA, thought of as a model for entrepreneurial opportunity, the share of self-employment in non-agricultural employment fell in the later 1980s and 1990s and is probably no higher than in 1973.[64]

The 'flexible firm' that began to attract the attention of academic researchers in the 1980s has a core of permanent full-time employees surrounded by a periphery of workers on casual and fixed-term arrangements, agency 'temps' and self-employed contractors.[65] The refinements of contract-writing and incentive provision coupled to enhanced monitoring capabilities that were outlined earlier in this chapter (Section 6.2 above) also encouraged the spread of franchising arrangements at the expense of the traditional, hierarchical multi-site corporation in activities as diverse as fast food restaurants and home maintenance. The franchisees constituted a new petite bourgeoisie, totally dependent upon and wholly committed to the market for their services.[66]

By 1994 the sociologist Alberto Martinelli was able to cite a substantial literature on the growth of small business. Writing on 'entrepreneurship and management', he distinguished three distinct classes: the leaders of large corporations; small entrepreneurs; and middle- and lower-level managers.[67] Of these three categories, the small entrepreneurs had always been dependent upon the market. But the corporate elite were no longer the modest and largely propertyless bureaucrats that Berle and Means had described. The Chief Executive Officers of the largest US companies – to take the most flagrant example, but one which was rapidly extending throughout the world – had seen their incomes rise from 42 times that of the average employee in 1980 to a multiple of more than 500 in 2003.[68] They had also become significant shareholders, and stock options tied their large fortunes very closely to the equity value of their corporations, which in the long run depends on profitability (see also Chapter 8).

What of Martinelli's third class, the middle- and lower-level managers? They, too, were much less insulated from the market than their professional status might once have implied. There was a subtle but profound change in the ethos of professional society, resulting from a struggle between two professional groups: the managers of big business and their supporters in the right-wing media and think tanks who preached the free market but did not practise it, and the 'one-nation' professionals.... who believed in social justice and social cohesion as the best means of invoking the willing cooperation on which economic growth depended.[69]

The outcome was 'the victory of the private sector professionals over the rest of society. It represents a dangerous aspect of professional society, indeed of all societies: the tendency of all dominant elites who control the flows of income to steer more and more and more of it to themselves'.[70]

This struggle was linked to a fundamental change in the nature of the corporation itself, from the traditional unitary structure (the 'U-form') to a multi-divisional structure (the 'M-form'). The inventor of these terms, Oliver Williamson, had begun by arguing for the irrelevance of the conventional neoclassical, profit-maximising model of the firm, which needed to be replaced by a theory of managerial discretion based on the relative insulation of the corporation from the market (see Chapter 4). After a conversion experience in the late 1960s – his personal 'vision on the road to Damascus'[71] – he came to believe that the principal–agent problems that had so impressed Berle and Means had been overcome by new forces of 'internal control', stronger than the 'external control' supposedly exercised by financial markets over managerial performance. The M-form corporation restricted the degree of managerial discretion by mimicking the operation of financial markets inside the firm, substituting internal resource allocation rules for the threat of takeover as the most effective constraint on the behaviour of managers. Each division was required to compete for funds, to employ them profitably, to report on its performance and to subject itself to rigorous auditing, just as if it were an independent legal entity.[72] The transformation of the large corporation, which had begun as early as the 1920s in the United States, had gone largely unnoticed. This, Williamson suggested, was because 'the benefits of organizational innovation are more difficult to appropriate than for most technical innovations: patents are unavailable and imitation is relatively easy'.[73]

If the capitalist class was becoming not less but more dependent on the market, the relationship of the working class to the market also confounded the expectations of economic and social theorists. Instead of occupational homogenisation there emerged a complicated pattern of labour market segmentation that went far beyond the traditional labour aristocracy. This tendency had been noted as early as the 1890s by the revisionist Marxist Eduard Bernstein, but it was ignored in the torrent of condemnation that his reformist political agenda brought down upon him. Far from becoming increasingly similar in (lack of) skill, pay and status, the working class was more and more differentiated in the nature of the work that it performed and the rewards that this work provided. To a certain extent this was the result of a conscious 'divide-and-rule' strategy by employers.[74] In very large part, however, it simply reflected the growing complexity of the capitalist economy, which could no longer be viewed as a sort of giant enlargement of the Engels family's cotton mills. The consequence was that working people became more individualistic and less solidaristic. Instead of exposure to markets having a radicalising effect, as in the past,[75] the opposite occurred.

As this growing passivity has been joined to an increasingly acquisitive and privatised life, the rapid decline in trade union membership in most advanced capitalist countries should hardly seem surprising.[76] Only in the Nordic countries has union membership held up. The decline has been greatest in the so-called 'liberal countries': the United States, UK, Australia and New Zealand. In the United States, union density – membership as a proportion of the labour force – peaked at 35.5% as early as 1945 and has been in steady decline since 1954.[77] In Australia, where as late as 1982, 49% of all employees were union members, 20 years later only 23% belonged; and the decline is continuing.[78] The fall in union membership in New Zealand owed much to repressive legislation in the 1990s. In the decade during which the 1991 Employment Contracts Act was effective, union density fell from 45% to 17% and it shows no sign of recovery, despite the passage of pro-union laws by the incoming Labour government in 2001.[79] Elsewhere

> ....the last two decades of the twentieth century were a period of relentless, sustained corrosion of British unionization. Membership fell by 5.5 million and density from one-half to under one-third of employees. The fraction of workers whose pay was set by collective bargaining halved from around 70 per cent to 35 per cent.[80]

A similar story can be told for Germany, although here the decline was from a lower base and proceeded more slowly; union density fell from 38.4% in 1977 to 25.4% in 2000.[81]

This had real consequences. As one study of the decline of British unionism noted:

> Many trade unions, whose power to capture economic rent was once reflected in high pay, jointly controlled working practices and considerable job security, have seen their influence decline in every respect. The scope and impact of bargaining and, by implication, the depth of trade union recognition, have diminished substantially.[82]

There is scope for argument concerning the extent to which workers have become more individualistic, and hence less collectively minded, than they once were.[83] But it is indisputable that they have become more willing to take a free ride during the postwar years, accepting whatever benefits that might accrue from labour market regulation without accepting any corresponding obligation to bear their share of the costs. And this increased individualism reflected a change in the underlying economic and social reality.

Workers increasingly perceived, quite correctly, that there was something to gain from active individual involvement in the labour market: job search and 'human investment' were risky activities, to be sure, but they often paid off in the form of higher wages, improved promotion prospects and better working conditions. While success in the market for labour power brought increased rewards, failure was punished more and more severely, at least in relative terms. Around 1970 there was 'a great U turn' in the distribution of income from employment in the United States, with decades of increasing equality giving way to a sharply widening dispersion.[84] Thus the average real hourly wage for non-supervisory workers was no higher in the Clinton years (1993–2000) than it had been in the Kennedy-Johnson era (1961–8), despite the big increase in labour productivity that had occurred. At the tenth percentile, real wages were 9% lower in the 1990s than they had been in 1973, while the ratio of wages at 90th percentile to those at the 10th percentile rose from 3.7 to 4.4.[85] The growth in inequality was not confined to the United States. A similar story can be told for other Anglo-Saxon countries. In Australia earnings at the 90th percentile were 142.2% of the median in 1975 and 164.3% in 2002, while earnings at the 10th percentile had fallen from 76.0% to 65.9% of the median. For women, where inequality was slightly less pronounced, there was a corresponding increase at the top end of the distribution (from 136.5% to 152.0%) and decrease at the bottom (from 80.2% to 70.6%).[86] And in New Zealand, where the effects of labour market deregulation were compounded by severely regressive changes in taxation and welfare policies, the bottom tenth of the population experienced a 5.8% fall in real income between 1984 and 1998, while the top decile saw their incomes rise by 32%.[87]

An important qualification must be registered at this point. The growth of inequality, along with the tendency towards individualism and the decline in collectivism, was most pronounced in the Anglo-Saxon or 'market liberal' economies. Union density and collective bargaining held up better, and inequality rose less, from a lower base, in the 'social market economies' of continental Western Europe, especially in the Nordic countries.[88] As we saw in Chapter 2, Section 2.6, there are differences between national capitalisms, with divergent socio-political institutions and (as we shall see later in this chapter) contrasting records of income redistribution, poverty reduction and maintenance of a generous welfare state. The changes discussed in this chapter have resulted in a significant degree of convergence. In terms of industrial relations, though, the persistence of diversity also needs to be recognised. 'It is even possible that, despite common changes overall, variation in the nature and extent of change has actually increased the amount of diversity across advanced nations.'[89] Most particularly the corporatist forms in much of Europe may continue to function at the microeconomic level even if they completely cease to operate at the macro level.[90]

The changing relationship between the working class and the market was not confined to the sale of labour power. Rising real incomes and increased leisure time – both undeniable features of capitalist development in the very long run, if less clearly and universally evident in the last 20 years or so – transformed the position of the proletarian as consumer. One aspect of this was predicted (and welcomed) by socialists: the commodification of domestic labour, which replaced much of the unpaid work of the housewife with goods and services purchased from the market.[91] But they had not anticipated the cultural and ideological implications of the emergence of a 'consumer society' in which many working-class people, no less than the middle and upper classes, derive both their principal satisfactions and their sense of identity less from what they do at work than from what and how they consume.[92] There occurred both a MacDonaldisation of society, in which standardised, mass-produced consumer opportunities were extended to the great mass of the population,[93] and a subsequent, more subtle process of Disneyisation in which differentiated and customised consumption, associated with emotional or performative labour, appeared to offer much greater scope for consumer sovereignty and individual choice.[94] These processes corresponded, very approximately, to the Fordist and post-Fordist eras in the development of the productive forces.

The social geographer Saskia Sassen has identified a close and dialectical relationship between productive technologies, the nature of consumption and the organisation of work:

> Customized production, small runs, specialty items, and fine food dishes are generally produced through labor-intensive methods and sold through small, full-service outlets. Subcontracting part of this production to low-cost operations, including sweatshops and households, is common. The types of firms and labor that serve this market are distinct from the large department stores and supermarkets that serve the middle-income market. Department stores and supermarkets typically sell standardized products, which they acquire from large, standardized factories located outside the city or region. Proximity to retailers is of far greater importance to customized producers. These producers rely heavily on specific customer input in designing their product line, and their small scales of production raise the relative costs of transportation and national distribution.....The expansion of the low-income consumer population in large cities has also contributed to the proliferation of small operations and the move away from large-scale standardized factories and large chain stores for the low-priced goods. The consumption needs of the low-income population are met in large part by small manufacturing and retail establishments that rely on family labor and often fall below minimum safety and health standards.[95]

Thus 'flexible specialisation' in production, growing inequality in earnings and increasing diversity in consumption needs and experiences all complement and reinforce each other, and all intensify the pervasiveness of market relations.

There has also been a pronounced increase in working-class involvement in asset markets. To some extent this has been the inevitable consequence of debt-financed purchases of durable consumer goods. Workers now behave 'like little capitalists', as Geoff Harcourt puts it, varying their expenditures more rapidly than their incomes and acquiring both assets and liabilities. By severing the link between income and expenditure this has probably contributed to the increasing instability of the system;[96] it has certainly helped to transform the relationship between the worker and the market. While the distribution of wealth continued – and indeed continues – to be very much more unequal than the distribution of income, in the second half of the twentieth century the working class began to accumulate financial assets, first in housing and then in the form of pension rights. We again take the UK to illustrate the growth of the first of these. In the first two postwar decades the proportion of houses that were owner-occupied almost doubled, rising from 26% in 1945 to 47% in 1966. By 1983 there had been a further increase, to 63%. Now almost half of all skilled manual workers owned their own home, and a quarter of the unskilled. White-collar workers were even more likely to be owner occupiers, and among 'employers and managers' only 13% did not own their own home.[97] These figures already reflected to some extent the decision of the Thatcher government in the 1980s to give local authority tenants the right to buy, at a very substantial discount, which encouraged a further rise in working-class home ownership. 'In the two decades between 1981 and 2001 the number of owner-occupied dwellings in the UK increased by more than 40%, while the number of rented dwellings fell by around 15%.' In 2001 almost two-thirds of dwellings in the UK were owner-occupied; this was slightly above the European Union average.[98]

The dramatic growth of owner-occupation did not make Britain the 'property-owning democracy' that Conservative election propaganda had claimed it to be as early as 1964. But it did give a majority of the working class a significant stake in the market – the ability to gain (and in some cases to lose) large sums from buying and selling, an ability that had previously been restricted to the landed gentry and to the bourgeoisie and some elements of the petite bourgeoisie. Towards the end of the twentieth century, the privatisation of pensions began to create a substantial working-class interest in the operation of financial markets more generally. Initially pensions were provided almost exclusively by the state, and the prevention of poverty in old age was the result of social policies entirely disconnected from the market. Beginning in the 1940s this, too, began to change with the growth of private pension schemes largely financed by employers, in the UK, the US and some parts of Western Europe.[99] The proportion of the British labour force covered by such 'occupational pension schemes' rose from 13% in 1936 to 33% in 1956 and 49% in 1967, declining somewhat thereafter. Coverage was much greater in the public sector (90%) than in the private sector (50% of men and only 25% of women).[100] By 1999–2000, 61% of male and 52% of female employees in the UK had rights either to an occupational pension or a personal pension, or both.[101]

Down to the 1980s pension rights were much less important in increasing working-class attachment to the market than the growth of owner-occupied housing, since decisions were made, and risks borne, predominantly by employers and their professional fund managers. Benefits were almost invariably 'defined', that is to say, fixed as a proportion of salary on retirement, so that retirees had nothing to gain (or lose) from fluctuations in the value of the funds' portfolios. Only quite recently, with the contraction of defined-benefit schemes and the introduction of 'consumer choice' in pension provision, have working people been enabled – or in many cases required – to play the financial markets with their prospective retirement incomes. The practical and ideological consequences of these important changes have yet to fully work themselves out.[102]

The trend towards the growing dependence of all social classes upon the market was considerably strengthened by the great changes in the nature of the capitalist state that began in the late 1970s and are still continuing. Their most obvious manifestation has been the privatisation of state-owned enterprises. In the 1990s alone, revenues of $600 billion were generated by privatisation in the OECD countries. As a proportion of GDP, privatisation receipts ranged from 0.5% in Spain (1986–91) to a remarkable 14.1% in New Zealand (1987–91).[103] Perhaps surprisingly, there was no overall reduction in the state's share of national income. Taking a slightly longer perspective, the state's share in total output was significantly greater in 1999 than it had been in 1983 in both Western Europe and Japan, and only slightly lower in the United States.[104] Despite the privatisations, the government also continued to increase its share of total employment, for which 17 rich countries stood at 17.5% in 1980 and 18.4% in 1994, the extreme cases in the latter year being Japan, at 6.9%, and Sweden, at 32.0%. Not until the early 1990s was there any clear indication that state employment might at last be in decline.[105]

These quantitative indices are, however, more than a little misleading. They mask much more important qualitative changes, which involved the marketisation of state activities and the introduction of market-mimicking arrangements similar to – and often borrowed from – those developed in the 'M-form' private corporations described in the previous section. Beginning around 1980 there was a fundamental alteration in the organisation and management of state activities, taking a variety of forms (compulsory competitive tendering, subcontracting, build-own-operate-transfer projects, private finance initiatives) but always including an attack on the concept of public employment as a shelter from the market.[106] The relative advantages of markets and hierarchies were now being debated by political scientists as well as economists, and their conclusions were influencing politicians. Principal–agent models were used to decide which government services might appropriately be purchased from private suppliers. 'The contractual paradigm suggests, among other things, that government is more likely to prefer the private contracting method when contractor "types" (reputations, expertise, honesty) are well known, service outputs are easily measured, and negotiations are not plagued by the small-numbers problem.'[107] Garbage collection was a case in point. 'When these conditions are not met, however, the government may find it more efficient to internalize contracting relationships by setting up its own bureaucracy. Consider the provision of policing services',[108] where adverse selection problems are acute and behavioural outputs are difficult to measure. Since this passage was written, however, there has in fact been a pronounced shift towards the market for the provision of 'security services',[109] leading one Italian author to draw uncomfortable historical parallels with the emergence of the Mafia as a private contractor offering protection, for a fee, to Sicilian capitalists.[110]

The neoliberal transformation of the state was taken furthest in New Zealand, whose State Services Commission reported proudly on 'a decade of change'. State enterprises had been subjected to corporatisation (or commercialisation), deregulation and privatisation. Simultaneously the public service was transformed by the introduction of

> many of the positive features and incentives of the private sector. The key principle was that managers, if they were permitted to make all *input* decisions – pay, appointments, organisational structures, production systems, etc. – would respond by accepting personal accountability for producing substantially higher quality *outputs* – the goods and services provided for Government and other users....
>
> This has led to considerably more structural changes in departments – and turnover of personnel, especially at senior levels – than was the case before 1984. Incoming chief executives tend to want to reshape their organisations to meet their own preferences and priorities, and some make further refinements and re-tunings as

> time goes by. A number of departments have been through several restructurings.... each of which has generated transactions costs. These sorts of restructurings do appear to be an integral part of the new environment.[111]

New Zealand public finances were also transformed by the introduction of the purchaser–provider principle to govern the relationship between Ministers and their departments and agencies. 'The positive incentives in these arrangements are powerful – they resemble, in effect, the arrangements and incentives of the commercial marketplace.'[112] There were corresponding changes in employment relations:

> The shift that has taken place in a short time away from a centralised, tightly regulated, highly bureaucratic human resource management tradition could hardly have been more profound. Public Service managers now have very much the same latitude – and accountability – in personnel business as their private sector counterparts. They can decide what sort of staff they need, and in what numbers, they can select them and engage them, and they can negotiate terms and conditions of employment. They can do whatever is necessary to train and develop their staff, they can reward them, and if need be they can sanction them.[113]

Clearly public sector employment no longer offered a shelter from the market. If New Zealand had gone further in the marketisation of its public sector than any other nation, the direction of change was the same everywhere. By the mid-1990s it was engulfing even the Scandinavian countries.[114]

The processes that transformed the economic role of the state were not without their apparently paradoxical aspects. In an era of supposedly wide-ranging deregulation there was also an inescapable increase in the scope of regulation and the number of regulators, since many of the newly privatised enterprises enjoyed substantial market power that would otherwise have been used against the interests of influential customers and suppliers.[115] And within the velvet glove of increased liberalisation an iron fist could be found, since the repression of the dangerous 'underclass'[116] proved to be an urgent task for the new, supposedly slimmed-down state. Neoliberal think tanks like the Institute of Economic Affairs in London helped to promote a new authoritarian attitude towards the poor.[117] While the bulk of the welfare state remains in place, so far as treatment of the very disadvantaged is concerned, there were very clear parallels with the triumph of the Whigs in the England of the 1830s, when liberal economists and politicians insisted that the rewards offered by market freedoms must be complemented by the workhouse as the penalty for failure.[118]

6.4 The superstructure

As the productive relations changed, so too did the superstructure. The law adapted itself rather effortlessly to the new constellation of productive forces and relations, offering much greater protection for intellectual property rights, relaxing antitrust laws and the constraints that they imposed on corporate activities, and undermining collectivism in the market for labour power. This was evident in judicial decisions concerning industrial disputes, where (for example) the unusually pro-union doctrines enunciated by the courts in Britain and Australia earlier in the twentieth century (see Chapter 5) gave way to a renewed defence of private property and an insistence on the priority of individual rights. In the celebrated British case of *Rookes vs. Barnard* in 1964 the courts created an entirely new tort of 'civil intimidation' to circumvent the protection afforded to trade unions by the statute law and offer employers civil remedies for union actions that interfered with their right to enter into contracts.[119] In an echo of the Taff Vale case 60 years earlier, the judges' decision had to be overturned by legislation, which survived only until Margaret Thatcher's neoliberal assault on the unions in the early 1980s removed all discretion from the judiciary. In Australia the evidence of changing judicial attitudes came two decades later than in the UK, with a series of judgements extending the scope of the federal Trade Practices Act to union activities in several high-profile cases, with the enthusiastic support of neoliberal politicians.[120] Once again legislation was needed to overrule the judges, but in this instance the respite lasted for just 3 years.[121]

In the US, too, the window of opportunity for collective bargaining that had opened under the New Deal in the 1930s was rapidly closed as the language of individualism, market forces and 'the right to work' – free of any union influence, it was understood – reflected the new spirit and practice of labour law.[122] This was a significant part of a more general improvement in the legal climate for American corporations, as Carl Kaysen suggested in 1996:

> ....business law is in important part derivative of a society's view of the corporation. If a society views its corporations as powerful

> creatures whose strength rivals that of government, that society will tend to constrain the corporation's actions and focus on antitrust and other rules that tranquilize the most powerful firms. If a society views its corporations as weak from internal decay and under siege from international competitors and takeover entrepreneurs, that society will tend to help those firms experiment with alternative organizational forms, relax its antitrust laws, and protect firms and their managers from takeovers. In very broad outline this is what happened in the thirty-five years between 1959 and today.[123]

The law had previously taken a much more sceptical view of corporate activities, as demonstrated by contributors to *The Corporation in Modern Society*,[124] the volume to which Kaysen was alluding. He himself was no radical critic of US capitalism. Indeed, he was best known for his earlier writings on the 'soulful corporation', which had supposedly come to place social responsibility ahead of the single-minded pursuit of profits and was subject to excessive regulation by an over-sensitive legal system.[125] Now he worried that the pendulum had swung too far in the opposite direction.[126]

In politics, the most important changes associated with neoliberalism included the transformation of Social Democratic and Labour parties into neoliberal clones;[127] serious challenges to the parts of the welfare state; the greater authority and alleged 'independence' of central banks; and the rise of international economic institutions dedicated to the promotion of the neoliberal project, from the IMF and the World Bank to the OECD and the WTO.

The most obvious of these changes was the adoption of pre-Keynesian macroeconomic policies by governments of both 'Right' and 'Left'. This involved the abandonment of full employment as the over-riding policy goal, often accompanied by open or tacit acceptance of the monetarist notion that there exists a 'natural' rate of unemployment 'ground out', in Milton Friedman's notorious words, 'by the Walrasian system of general equilibrium equations'[128] and thus determined by purely microeconomic considerations and immune to influence by macroeconomic policy. Full employment was replaced by low inflation as the fundamental – indeed, almost the only – policy goal, and monetary policy effectively became the only policy instrument. Again the monetarist influence was apparent, with accelerating inflation seen as the inevitable consequence of misguided efforts to force unemployment down below the natural rate. Related to this was a repudiation of any role for discretionary fiscal policy and the replacement of 'functional finance' by a return to 'sound finance', with balanced budgets and/or structural surpluses as the proclaimed policy rule – even if, in practice, sustained deficits have proved difficult to avoid.[129]

Discretionary monetary policy gave way to rules, most recently the 'Taylor rule' linking interest rates to expected inflation, and to a dogmatic insistence on 'central bank independence', which removed monetary policy from government control and instead subjected it to the insidious influence of the financial markets.[130] These same markets were comprehensively deregulated, both domestically and with respect to international transactions (as we explain in Chapter 7). The removal of quantitative and qualitative controls over the volume of lending meant that interest rates became the only instrument of monetary policy, with the consequence that asset price bubbles could not be burst without the danger of severe damage to output and employment (a point to which we return in Chapter 8). There was thus an inherent deflationary bias in macroeconomic policy, which reinforced the abandonment of the full employment goal. All these tendencies were promoted and reinforced by the international economic institutions, whose own sharp neoliberal turn will be discussed shortly.

To a limited extent some of the corporatist 'social partnership' economies resisted these tendencies,[131] but their ability (and willingness) to do so should not be exaggerated. Nor should too much be made of the differences between avowedly bourgeois and supposedly social democratic or Labour governments. The Scandinavian countries did defend full employment for a decade or more after the onset of the great stagflation in the early 1970s,[132] but they too were eventually overwhelmed by the neoliberal flood-tide. The Labour governments in New Zealand (1984–91, 2000–), Australia (1983–96) and the United Kingdom (1975–9, 1997–) were as 'sound' in their macroeconomic policies as any of the more conservative regimes. Not to mention Italy, where the 'centre-Left' coalitions in power during 1996–2001 and since April 2006 proved to be considerably more 'fiscally responsible' than the right-wing Berlusconi governments that they defeated.[133]

A similar but less dramatic story of change and reversal can be told about the 'reform' of the welfare state, which involved both retrenchment (expenditure cuts) and restructuring ('workfare' in place of welfare). There were reductions in benefit levels, tightening of eligibility conditions and a general harshening of both the welfare regime and the intellectual climate in which it operated, including an increased emphasis on duties as against rights and greater stigmatisation of welfare recipients. The major changes were focussed on the least advantaged. Again there was substantial diversity in the experience of different countries, with Sweden at one extreme and the United States at the other,[134] but the direction of change was unambiguous. As a broad generalisation, welfare cuts were introduced by bourgeois governments but accepted and often reinforced by their social democratic and Labour successors; in some cases (notably Germany after 2002) it was the latter which made most of the running.

This has led to claims that there are strong pressures from 'globalisation' for a 'fiscal race to the bottom'.[135] But the restructuring of welfare was more important than retrenchment, given the continued need for all advanced capitalist economies to retain a substantial welfare system in order to shift the burden of labour market flexibility from employers to the state, and also to maintain the health and educational levels of the working-class, along with its purchasing power. Work, training and job-seeking tests for welfare recipients were more rigorously enforced and penalties for non-compliance substantially increased.[136] And, generally, the welfare state has been reorganised along market lines. There is no doubt that the much higher levels of unemployment (open and disguised) since 1973 added to the neoliberal pressure on the welfare state. Thus the apparently quite separate spheres of macroeconomics and social policy changes were in fact very closely related. They amounted to a real 'bourgeois revolution' in economic and social policy.[137]

The international economic institutions also shifted fundamentally in a neoliberal direction. Down to about 1970 the World Bank, to take the best-documented example, was profoundly influenced by theorists like Gunnar Myrdal (1898–1987) and Hollis Chenery (b. 1918), who mistrusted the market and favoured a substantial element of development planning. The Bank took a relatively open, eclectic and pluralist position on many questions of development policy, tolerating if not encouraging government intervention, capital controls and even a limited measure of protection against manufacturing imports.[138] By 1980 the emergence of a 'Washington Consensus' had swept all this away, with the Bank, the IMF, the WTO (formerly GATT) and the US Treasury now agreeing that poor countries should be required to obey the so-called 'ten commandments' of neoliberal development policy: deregulation and increased competition; privatisation of public enterprises; a guarantee of secure property rights; fiscal discipline; the reform of government expenditure; tax reform to favour private enterprise; financial liberalisation; a unified (and devalued) exchange rate; trade liberalisation and the encouragement of foreign direct investment.[139] The Washington Consensus became a matter of faith[140] that spilled over also to rich countries, which were themselves required to play the game. At the ideological level this transformed the OECD, once a bastion of

Keynesian thinking, into an increasingly influential advocate of neoliberal ideas. At the political level the various organs of the European Union promoted neoliberal policies in both macroeconomics (the so-called Growth and Stability Pact; the European Central Bank) and microeconomics (mandating competition in all sectors, including formerly sacrosanct areas of public services).[141] After 2003 the accession of Eastern European countries with a strong governmental commitment to neoliberalism strengthened these tendencies. The few remaining international agencies which held out either lost what little influence they had once enjoyed (the International Labour Organisation) or began to accommodate themselves to the new intellectual climate (a revealing example is provided by UNCTAD, initially established as a counterweight to the neoliberal institutions but increasingly adopting the same outlook as the IMF and the Bank).[142]

6.5 Social consciousness

The rise of neoliberalism was also accompanied by far-reaching changes in social consciousness. We again restrict ourselves to the important case of neoclassical economics, and since the most important developments have been lucidly surveyed by Roger Backhouse[143] we can be quite brief. In essence, neoliberal ideas have been in the ascendant in academic economics since the late 1960s. In the United States, at least, this process of ideological mutation goes back to the 1940s and 1950s, when institutionalism was expunged from Ivy League institutions and faith in the market mechanism began to revive.[144] But it was in the 1960s that the 'neoclassical synthesis' of Keynesian macroeconomics and Walrasian microeconomics gave way first to monetarism and then to New Classical macroeconomics and 'real business cycle' theory, all insistent on the underlying stability of the private sector and hostile to the discretionary use of fiscal or monetary policy to increase output and employment.[145] The development of the new area of 'public choice theory' emphasised 'state failure' as a much more dangerous prospect than the market failures that had been stressed by earlier generations. Government intervention was now viewed as the primary cause of inflation and as a major source of inefficiency, rent-seeking opportunism and bureaucratic waste.[146] The Coase Theorem purported to show that all externalities can, under appropriate assumptions, be internalised, so that redefinition of property rights made it possible for efficient market contracts to replace the battery of regulations, subsidies and taxes that was required by Pigovian welfare economics.[147] Even the previous general acceptance of the need for antitrust laws and close regulation of monopoly power succumbed to a Panglossian belief in the efficacy of potential competition in what were believed to be normally 'contestable markets'.[148] These were the ideas that influenced Margaret Thatcher and the circle of advisers around Ronald Reagan in the period leading up to their election triumphs in 1979–80, and since then they have gone from strength to strength.[149]

6.6 Conclusion

Looking back on the rise of neoliberalism at the very end of the twentieth century, the radical development economist Susan George invoked the Gramscian notion of 'cultural hegemony' to explain what had occurred: 'this vast neo-liberal experiment we are all being forced to live under has been created by people with a purpose', she maintained. 'Neo-liberalism is not a force like gravity but a totally artificial construct.' It had been created by pro-market intellectuals and propagated by their wealthy supporters:

> .... neo-liberals have bought and paid for their own vicious and regressive 'Great Transformation'. They have understood, as progressives have not, that ideas have consequences. Starting from a tiny embryo at the University of Chicago with the philosopher-economist Friedrich von Hayek and his students like Milton Friedman [*sic*] at its nucleus, the neo-liberals and their funders have created a huge international network of foundations, institutes, research centers, publications, scholars, writers and public relations hacks to develop, package and push their ideas and doctrine relentlessly.[150]

A similar argument has been made by Pierre Bourdieu and Goran Therborn.[151] Of course, ideas *do* matter. But Susan George and those who take the same line exaggerate their case. As we have extensively documented in Chapters 3 and 4, the ideas of most economists for most of the twentieth century were not neoliberal. Rather they believed that market elimination was the dominant trend. Moreover, as we have argued throughout, neoliberalism was clearly not a 'totally artificial construction'. On the contrary, it had very deep roots in twentieth-century technological and social change. Why it took so long for these roots to generate any visible foliage is the theme of the next chapter.

Part IV

Neoliberalism: Past, Present and Future

7
Why Was Neoliberalism Delayed?

7.1 The problem

Our argument, to repeat, is that neoliberalism in advanced capitalist economies was the product of a long period in the development of the productive forces and associated changes in the production relations, which modified the superstructure and had significant effects on social consciousness. However, this points to a potentially serious problem for us in accounting for the timing of neoliberalism. Why was it delayed until the 1970s? In previous chapters, we have documented the technological and economic forces that operated to reduce or eliminate market relations, but these chapters also showed that they coexisted for a long time with changes working in the opposite direction to promote market relations. Certainly, the latter strengthened from the 1970s, with the emergence of information technologies centred on the computer,[1] but it seems reasonable nonetheless to expect that neoliberalism would have begun earlier than it actually did.

7.2 An outline of our argument

Our argument has four components. We deal with them here in summary form and elaborate upon them in subsequent sections of this chapter and also in Chapter 8.

First, as we explained in the Introduction, neoliberalism in advanced capitalist economies is not a return to classical liberalism, but is compatible with, and indeed requires, the maintenance of welfare states as well as extensive regulation of most economic activity. There have been reductions in unemployment benefits and welfare payments to the poor in order to promote market dependence, but, on the whole, welfare states have been restructured rather than reduced in provision. Most of their programmes contribute to the high productivity of advanced capitalist societies, and remain very popular with their electorates. The same holds true for deregulation. This has been pronounced in finance and other important sectors, but it usually involves re-regulation rather than the rescinding of regulation. And both imply that neoliberalism in advanced capitalism is a different phenomenon from that characterising peripheral countries, including former communist 'transitional' economies. Neoliberalism in advanced capitalism is a matter of extending markets and market dependency, but it occurs in contexts involving sophisticated technologies and political democracy, which make it very different from what goes by the same name in less-developed areas. It is misleading to treat neoliberalism as a singular entity having similar causes and consequences the world over, irrespective of the levels of economic development and type of political system.[2]

Second, neoliberal changes were delayed by the consequences of the 'age of catastrophe', defined by the two World Wars and the Great Depression.[3] All three events accelerated the protectionist tendencies countering market dependence that were emerging in advanced capitalist economies before 1914.[4] But these two wars and severe depression also added new and powerful market-eradicating forces that continued to have significant effects in the postwar years, where they were reinforced by those of the Cold War. What proved to be especially important for their enduring influence was the economic and military predominance of the United States and its adoption of a 'grand strategy' accepting Keynesian constraints, both (to a rather limited extent) within America and (to a rather greater extent) in other capitalist economies. This included the maintenance of significant 'financial repression', in which financial institutions and financial markets were severely restrained in what influence they could exercise on other economic sectors and on state policies. (We examine this in more detail in Section 7.3 below.)

It is true that there was a market-eliminating trend operating independently of the Great Depression, World Wars and the Cold War, which stemmed from those technological and economic changes documented in Chapter 5. However, this market-eliminating trend was reinforced by the 'age of catastrophe' and its aftermath, and the contrary forces actually promoting markets were considerably constrained and weakened. Consequently, the significance of much of the market elimination that actually took place was misspecified by economists of all the schools discussed in Chapters 3 and 4.

Third, it was the financial changes initiated by the United States in the early 1970s which inaugurated neoliberalism. These changes arose from the limitations placed upon its own policy autonomy by the international monetary system that America had itself fashioned after the Second World War. Beginning in the second Nixon administration, financial repression was first lessened and then substantially removed in subsequent years. This brought economically defensive reactions in a neoliberal direction on the part of other advanced capitalist countries which were, in fact, already poised to institute change as a result of their convergence to American productivity levels.[5] The ending of financial repression in the United States was not the only cause of neoliberalism, as should be very clear from what we have said in previous chapters, but more than any other single set of events, it was responsible for *initiating* the neoliberal turn.

Since the end of the Second World War in 1945, the United States has been much more than simply the largest capitalist economy. It has also been hegemonic, designing and enforcing the rules of the Western international order for both economics and security. However, relative size has underpinned this dominant role. In 1950, the GDP of the United States constituted 27% of world GDP, compared to 26% for the whole of Western Europe and 3% for Japan. The predominance of America in industrial production, with 50% of world output, was even more pronounced. By 1973, the United States contributed 22% of world GDP, Western Europe 26% and Japan nearly 8%. Even in 2001 America's share had decreased only marginally to 21%, but this was now more than that of Western Europe's 20% and still three times the size of Japan, which had fallen slightly to 7%.[6] Moreover, the United States had a single national government throughout this period and one that controlled overwhelming military force.[7]

Analogous to America not being 'just a capitalist economy', finance is not 'just another sector of capitalist economies'. Within the framework of capitalist relations of production, finance exercises an influence far exceeding its relative size. It is not only infrastructural in being essential to the operation of virtually all other sectors of the economy,[8] it is peculiarly infrastructural. The financial requirements of firms typically cannot be met independently of financial institutions or financial markets. Complete self-financing is usually impossible and would normally be imprudent even if feasible. Moreover, the supply of finance from outside the firm is joined to rights over revenues that entail control over matters connected to bankruptcy, and these often connote power over much more mundane matters. If firms cannot pay the interest on their loans from banks or bondholders, these creditors can force a bankruptcy if they choose to do so. This can provide them with general influence over company policies. And holders of equity have rights to select directors and top managers, which allows them to exercise power more directly. Only the 'repression' of these rights through state regulation, or their modification through state ownership or state direction of financial institutions, or their *de facto* restriction as a result of inhibiting the concentration of equity, can free industrial capital from the 'hegemony of finance'. And, unconstrained, the rights of finance work strongly to promote profitability. Supplying finance is a circuit of 'money in–money out', exempt from many of the goal-displacement possibilities inherent in actually producing commodities induced by professional and productivist cultures that qualify the priority of profit.[9] Consequently, the lifting of financial repression is a powerful source of neoliberalism generally when the productive forces and production relations favour the extension of markets.

So it proved in the 1970s. Lifting financial repression within the international monetary system, and then domestically, introduced forces corrosive of the prevailing Keynesian regime. Over the next quarter-century there were many other changes in a neoliberal direction, and a new set of rules, usually described simply as 'neoliberal' or as 'globalisation', emerged. Insofar as the new system has been designed, it has been fashioned principally to secure American power and prosperity in a new form, with significant adjustments made by other advanced capitalist economies to retain their own affluence and influence.[10] In the early 1970s, it is doubtful that US strategic planners, or anyone else, were able to anticipate all the parameters of the new system. But the debt crises in Latin America during the 1980s and the end of the Cold War with the collapse of the Soviet Union in the early 1990s, both of which allowed neoliberal measures to be imposed on less-developed countries, provided much illumination of what was possible. Certainly, by the end of the twentieth century, the main properties of the new order had clearly emerged, although they are typically obscured by employing ideological terms stressing the promotion of democracy and freedom and securing the will of the 'international community'.

Fourth, from the perspective of historical materialism, there were multiple contradictions present in the initial postwar order. This does not imply that it was a failure. In fact it performed exceptionally well, as we acknowledge in Section 7.4. But no structure of productive relations has ever proved enduring, for the reasons we outlined in Chapters 1 and 2. The development of the productive forces requires new forms of productive relations from time to time. And the institutional embodiment of the productive relations sometimes necessitates change to preserve and expand productive power. These contradictions also typically generate crises rather than smooth, gradual adaption. The many reasons explaining why 'change through crises' is normal can best be understood negatively, by outlining the perspective of traditional neoclassical economics in which there are no crises. In this theory, economic agents are optimisers, always acting in contexts where all valued attributes of goods are divisible, neither exhibiting benevolence or malevolence, nor subject to major information deficiencies, and never having discontinuous behavioural responses, nor organising collectively to preserve or change political power. If the world were actually like this, then crises would not occur. The fact that it is not explains why there are multiple sources of crises, and why they occur so frequently.[11]

However, crises do appear to be less than fully deterministic as to timing, since they depend on all manner of contingent factors to trigger them, and any account of the beginnings of neoliberalism should recognise this. It could have begun earlier or, indeed, have been delayed longer. Neoliberalism began in the 1970s because this is when crises promoting neoliberal changes first appeared, as we explain in Section 7.4 below. Before we do so, however, we consider the events responsible for the regime prevailing before neoliberalism and from whose contradictions neoliberalism emerged.

7.3 The age of catastrophe

For all the importance of the crises of the 1970s they were dwarfed by those of the 'age of catastrophe', which began with the First World War in 1914, continued through the Great Depression in the 1930s and ended with the defeat of the Axis powers in 1945. From virtually any perspective, all of these events are of world-historic significance. They are certainly central for us, even though we are concerned with understanding the onset of neoliberalism in advanced capitalist economies a quarter of a century later. This is because the 'age of catastrophe' had enduring effects in altering international relations between the great powers and in changing the role of markets in all capitalist economies.

The Great Depression was a 'market failure' of such severity that it made many of the core characteristics of capitalism appear to be dysfunctional: irrespective of their earlier role in expanding productive power, it seemed they now fettered its full utilisation. Between 1929 and 1933 the real GDP of the United States declined by nearly a third, and even in 1939 it remained below the level of a decade earlier.[12] Unemployment reached almost 25% in 1933 and remained high throughout the 1930s.[13] In most of Western Europe and in Japan, the collapse was less pronounced but nonetheless substantial.[14] In these circumstances, capitalist property rights, competition, the discipline provided by market dependence and bankruptcies, all became parts of the problem, not a solution to it. By contrast, the core properties of modern states – their capacity for resource mobilisation through command and their universal administrative reach within their own jurisdiction – proved to be massive advantages,[15] and governments everywhere intervened to an extent unprecedented in peacetime. All abandoned commitments to the Gold Standard and reorientated their monetary policies towards the needs of their domestic economies, imposed restrictions on international trade, repressed domestic finance and capital mobility, promoted cartelisation and placed other limits on competition, and compromised market dependence through the provision of emergency relief, public works schemes and social welfare programmes.[16]

The two World Wars had an even greater immediate impact. Despite orthodox economists' celebration of the market, very few have believed that fighting major wars in the industrial age would be more effective if conducted on commercial principles, and with good reason. Market contracts often have to be very detailed, specifying obligations and remunerations over a wide variety of future circumstances. And the more detailed they are, the higher the transaction costs in time and resources.[17] Not surprisingly, markets have usually been considered unsuitable for organising activities in times of war, when the range and depth of possible contingencies increase massively. The greater uncertainty dramatically raises both the length of the period required freely to negotiate contracts and the resources used in doing so, while raising doubts as to whether agreements will be honoured, so destroying possibilities for voluntary contracting altogether. As a result, centralised coercive authority, bureaucratic administration and resource allocation through command were extensively employed in the two World Wars, which also restricted and fragmented trade and capital flows and thereby promoted autarky in national economic life. Total war encouraged the expansion of precisely those industries – steel, chemicals, heavy engineering – where the economies of large-scale production were greatest, making centralised planning easier and competition least viable. It also promoted national, inter-class coalitions in which welfare state provisions were offered in exchange for patriotic commitment by the working class. The conscription of individuals into the military, the requisitioning of assets, large increases in taxation and restraints on the use of bargaining power by labour in conditions of full employment were accompanied by a vast growth in governmental responsibilities for citizens' well-being: comprehensive price and rent controls, the rationing of necessities, support for families of combatants and extensions of social programmes. So much so, in fact, that many elements of the welfare state have their origin in war.[18] For the same reasons, war tended to bring the incorporation of trade union officials into decision-making structures, encouraged more equality in income distribution and expanded the franchise.[19] Nationalism and other collectivist ideologies were deepened and radicalised in ways that devalued the atomistic individualism of liberalism, and, to a lesser extent, the class politics of socialists.[20]

These were the general effects of depression and war, many of them evident in virtually all capitalist economies. Most probably some of the changes would have occurred as a result of economic development under peaceful conditions. Institutionalising union rights, further democratisation, the extension of some social welfare programmes, restrictions on international migration and the strengthening of national cultures would have likely happened in several capitalist societies without wars and depression,[21] but the 'age of catastrophe' accelerated and deepened these changes. Moreover, it had a pronounced effect on two other matters crucial to the later development of neoliberalism: the structure of geopolitical power and the repression of finance.

Wars have dramatic effects on hierarchical relations between states. Some are victorious; others are defeated. The victors can often occupy the territory of the losers and write the rules of interaction for the postwar era. The defeated have little choice but to make the best of a subordinate position. But even states on the winning side may find themselves in reduced circumstances, their resources depleted by the destruction and carnage. So it was after the Second World War. In Western Europe and Japan, the United States was supreme. Its own territory (apart from Hawaii in 1941) had experienced no war damage, hostilities in Europe had ended the Great Depression and the Soviet Union had borne most of the human costs of defeating the Nazi armies. At the end of the 'age of catastrophe', then, the United States was by far the richest and most powerful nation in the world, occupying both major Axis powers – all of Japan and a substantial area of Germany – and having troops throughout Western Europe and East Asia. Some of its allies, especially Britain and France, were markedly changed in a different way. France had been conquered, and Britain suffered extensive war damage, had liquidated its foreign investments and borrowed heavily to prosecute the war.[22]

As a consequence, the interests of the United States could easily prevail in the whole Western bloc. While the 'age of catastrophe' had huge effects on other capitalist powers, which were relevant to what happened in the immediate postwar years, they were secondary to the shaping of the international economic and security regimes which emerged. Both were essentially American impositions, with the economic and military power of the United States marshalled to make them more or less acceptable to its allies, old and new.[23] Because it was so rich, it could afford to be less coercive. Hence the effects that wars and depression had on the United States were more significant than elsewhere.[24]

These effects not only substantially increased the geopolitical power of America relative to other states, they also ensured that this power would not be employed to attempt a return to the classical liberal era preceding the First World War. In this regard, the Great Depression, rather than the two wars, had the more enduring impact. Partly because the Great Depression was more severe in the United States than elsewhere, it had more radical consequences, ushering in extensive financial repression within a Keynesian political economy. After 1945, in the interests of economic stability and security, the United States also promoted this 'mixed economy' capitalism amongst its allies, while designing an international economic regime of selective openness helping to preserve it for several decades.[25]

However, the 'age of catastrophe' as a whole is important for understanding the Great Depression itself and its influence into the postwar years. Although far less than that of the Second World War, the First World War clearly had an impact on the United States. Many markets were suspended or restructured to facilitate the war effort, and the activities of the federal government expanded substantially. But hostilities did not last very long for America (less than 2 years, since the United States remained neutral until 1917), and most wartime measures were quickly dismantled after 1918. The economic standing of the United States rose relative to European economies because the war damage in Europe was extensive, and the United States had been transformed from a net debtor to a net creditor, with Wall Street replacing the City of London as the foremost financial centre. Nevertheless, even in 1918 the GDP of Western Europe was nearly 50% larger than that of America,[26] and the war did not fundamentally transform the geopolitical position of the United States despite the important role it played in the Versailles peace agreements.

Charles Kindleberger has traced the interwar economic disasters to this circumstance.[27] He argues that a capitalist world economy requires a hegemonic power to provide the 'public goods' promoting stability: an open market, access to finance, orderly exchange rates, some coordination of macroeconomic policies and lender of last resort facilities in an international financial crisis. This 'hegemonic stability thesis' makes eminent sense, and Kindleberger argues that interwar problems can be traced to the fact that Britain was a declining hegemon and the United States was a rising hegemon, with neither the decline nor the rise large enough to settle the issue. This is true, but American 'isolationism' after the First World War also reflected the fact that there were no major threats to American national security until the late 1930s, and that the world order was largely one of European empires which the United States had little interest in stabilising or securing, since this conflicted with the 'open door' policy consistent with American productive efficiency.[28] Thus the United States lacked both the power and the interest to become hegemonic in the interwar period.

The effects of the Second World War were more pronounced in every respect and thoroughly transformed the geopolitical situation. It was a much longer conflict for the United States, fought across the Pacific as well as the Atlantic, and required a far more extensive mobilisation.[29] Roosevelt himself described America as 'the arsenal of democracy', and in the circumstances it is difficult to accuse him of exaggeration. 'At the news of the US entry into the war, Winston Churchill openly rejoiced – and with good reason. As he later explained it, "Hitler's fate was sealed. Mussolini's fate was sealed. As for the Japanese, they would be ground to powder. All the rest was merely the application of overwhelming force".'[30] Victory also brought to the United States a sufficient increase in all forms of power to sustain a postwar hegemony over the entire capitalist world and one that could be used to favour its economic interests, including the ending of the European empires. And the economic interest in forging a new order was buttressed by the security threat posed to Western capitalism by the Soviet Union and its allies.

It was in this geopolitical context that the American experience of the Great Depression proved to be crucial. The collapse in output was larger than that suffered by all other capitalist economies apart from Germany, and like governments everywhere, the American government did not know how to reverse it. But, among the democracies, the Roosevelt administrations were much more active and radical. Of particular importance for the later fashioning of the postwar hegemonic order was the empowering of trade unions and the containment of the financial sector, so reversing the pre-depression structure of production relations in two very significant respects.

The Wagner Act of 1935 was highly supportive of union rights, and by 1939 membership had tripled to over 15% of the labour force, rising to 35% during the next 10 years. This was one of the many measures helping to contain political unrest, but it also had an economic rationale in establishing a countervailing power to the corporations, which were encouraged to collude in the hope that this would reverse the deflationary spiral.[31] The system never advanced to the level of a corporatism of social partners, European style, but it increased the power of labour relative to capital, as did the extension that took place in the American welfare state, which, along with the effects of war, also reduced income inequality.[32] And it is true that the empowering of unions was a partial substitute in corporate governance for the weakened role of finance due to the new restraints placed upon it. Unions were much more able to monitor managers than could unorganised labour and had an interest in doing so in order to ensure the viability of firms and the employment of their members. As we have seen in Chapter 4, John Kenneth Galbraith later provided a theory of 'countervailing power' which explained this as one example of new forms of corporate control appropriate to an era in which the market was in decline.

The measures implemented to suppress the autonomy of finance were extensive. 'Firewalls' were erected to separate commercial and investment banking and to sever all banking from other financial institutions (trusts, insurance companies and securities firms). The activities considered legitimate for each type of organisation were specified, along with the rules to which they had to conform. Federal deposit insurance was established and competition between banks inhibited. Bond and equity markets had stricter regulations imposed and a new regulatory body, the Securities and Exchange Commission, was established. Financial practices deemed to be manipulative or speculative were outlawed.[33] The bubble in asset prices that accompanied the boom of the 1920s, along with the stock market crash of October 1929, had led to the belief that financial laxity and malpractice were heavily implicated in causing the depression.[34] This was reinforced by the disastrous deflationary policy pursued by the bankers of the Federal Reserve.[35] Populists, who had long regarded financial capital as uniquely parasitic, argued persuasively that the depression provided compelling new evidence that this was so. This was later buttressed by the combination of large federal deficits and rapid recovery from the depression during the early years of the Second World War, which lent great credence to Keynesian economics.

The 'age of catastrophe' was thus hugely transformative, including of economics itself, with Keynesian theory coming to supplement neoclassical analysis. (It never did *supplant* pre-Keynesian ideas, despite the best efforts of radical Keynesians.) At the time of the Great Depression, neoclassical orthodoxy proved wholly inadequate to the task of providing remedial measures, and the advice of economic purists, when implemented, actually worsened the effective demand failure. Both at the time, and subsequently, neoclassical economists have regarded all of the turbulence as the consequence of exogenous shocks. From their perspective, this is understandable. But, from the broader perspective of historical materialism, wars and depressions clearly have endogenous features. We have already explained this in Chapters 1 and 2, but it is a sufficiently important point to justify stating it again.

Jack Levy provides a succinct summary of the history of warfare which reflects its systemic nature:

> War has been a frequent and persistent pattern of behaviour among and within states for millennia and has been enormously destructive of human life and property... Certain empirical regularities have emerged... [in] ... patterns of warfare in the modern state system, the origins of which most historians trace to about 1500 A.D.... There have been approximately 120 wars involving a great power against another state since 1500, or about one every four years. Of these, about half have been wars between great powers... [These] ... have been declining in frequency but increasing in seriousness... [involving] ... a larger number of great powers, more nation-months of war, and much higher casualties... Wars involving the great powers against non-powers have become less frequent and shorter but only somewhat more severe in terms of casualties... The frequency of colonial or imperial wars increased gradually, exploded in the nineteenth century, and then declined with the liquidation of the European colonial empires in the twentieth century... [The] pattern of warfare in the nuclear age appears to be different from the patterns of earlier ages. There are fewer great power wars but an increased number of wars between medium and smaller states, some of which are essentially proxy wars between the superpowers. There are also more civil wars.[36]

The disruption inflicted on the world economy by the First World War also helps explain the endogeneity of the Great Depression. It brought a new pattern of international indebtedness in the 1920s without the hegemonic interventions necessary to set bounds to instability. Also, while the Great Depression was clearly exceptional in terms of its severity, there has been a very long history of financial crises and effective demand failures.[37] Hence the recurrent nature of the phenomenon makes it difficult to regard it as simply stemming from exogenous shocks. Most historians today accept that the causes of the Second World War had a great deal to do with the outcome of the First World War, and that the likelihood of a serious depression was increased by the nature of the first postwar settlement which, in turn, promoted fascism in Germany. The whole period between 1914 and 1945 was aptly described by Winston Churchill as 'the second thirty years war'.

At all events, it is certainly true that the United States was a very different country at the end of this period than at the outset. Of course, in this it was not alone. However, it was unique among capitalist powers in being powerful enough to fashion a new international order. And what it did create was heavily affected by the way it defined its interests as a result of the experiences in the preceding three decades.

7.4 The postwar order and 'The Golden Age'

The post-1945 international regime that America fashioned was not totally new. There remained two important characteristics of the world before 1914: a system of separate states and of capitalist relations of production. However, both states and capitalism were modified. The United States had no interest in establishing a colonial empire for itself, but instead favoured the decolonisation of existing empires, so expanding the states system and weakening many other great powers.[38] All economies of 'the West' were to be integrated into a relatively open world market, and all Western states were to be organised into new security alliances, with the United States at the hub of both.[39]

The new states system and capitalism were also changed as a result of American experiences in the 'age of catastrophe'. Within the core Western bloc, capitalist relations of production were remodelled in a 'New Deal' form, providing rights for organised labour and social welfare provisions, and with significant constraints placed on finance, all within a context of mass democratisation. Economic liberalism was promoted, but gradually and selectively. Some wartime measures were retained in many countries for some years after the end of hostilities, strict controls on international capital movements were accepted as legitimate, and exchange rates were fixed (although adjustable in conditions of 'fundamental disequilibrium'). Full convertibility of currencies did not occur until 1958, and then only for current account transactions, while freer international trade was fashioned in a manner that allowed many differences between national capitalist systems to flower. These included the indicative planning and administrative guidance models of France and Japan; corporatist social partnership arrangements in Germany, Scandinavia, Austria and the Netherlands; and less-coherent versions of the 'mixed economy' in Britain and Italy, all of which were utilised by national governments to promote economic modernisation and catch-up to American productivity levels.[40] There can be little doubt that the Cold War contributed to this restraint on liberalisation and to capitalist diversity. By requiring the United States to cultivate allies, it provided Europeans and Japanese with more domestic autonomy than America would otherwise have found acceptable and made the postwar world less economically liberal than it would have been in the absence of conflict.[41] It was also responsible for maintaining the state capacities for mass mobilisation that had been developed in the 'age of catastrophe', which tended to be market-eliminating.[42] In addition, the Cold War brought about the resocialisation of science in the United States (and, we suspect, in many other NATO countries). The period 1940–80 saw a massive increase in federal funding for scientific research, especially in universities, which operated as a sort of surrogate industry policy. After 1980, this went into reverse, despite the huge increase in military expenditure by the Reagan administration. The 'Cold War model' now gave way to a 'competitiveness model' in which science was regarded as a private, not a public, good.[43]

The threats from Communism were threefold. First, the hugely expanded military power of the Soviet Union consequent upon its victory in the Second World War posed a danger of invasion for Western Europe. Second, Communist parties within Western European countries and Japan, many of which had also been empowered by the leading role they had played in resisting fascism, were viewed as subversive forces inside capitalist societies. Third, anti-colonial movements in the periphery often coupled social revolution to national liberation, and were typically classified as 'communist' as a result. All threats were regarded with the upmost seriousness by the United States. The principal security alliances were those with Europe and Japan, and they kept American military power extended across the globe. The relations established between the US forces and peripheral governments to counter radical insurgencies had the same effect. Within advanced capitalist societies the United States encouraged moderate governments, including those involving social democrats, to adopt policies incorporating the working classes of their respective countries into mainstream politics and the national culture. Generous aid was provided for all purposes, in the form of dollars, and in assistance with the establishment of suitable military forces, political parties and 'civil societies', including trade unions.[44]

In effect, a two-tiered 'grand bargain' or 'implicit contract' characterised advanced capitalist countries. The Europeans and Japanese accepted subordination to American geopolitical leadership, while the United States accepted that these countries could exercise considerable autonomy in their domestic affairs. And within each capitalist society there was broad agreement on the need for state activism and class cooperation to promote economic development, welfare programmes and centrist politics.[45]

This postwar order proved very successful. There was no return of depression conditions. Indeed, economic growth was so rapid that the first three decades of the postwar period have has been characterised as a 'golden age'.[46] International trade expanded even faster, but this increasing openness was joined to extensive social programmes reducing market dependence, including within the United States.[47] Democracy and peace were preserved throughout the heartlands of the capitalist world, and communism was successfully contained in most areas of the globe.[48] A dense network of international organisations was established to institutionalise cooperation between the United States and its allies.[49] Nevertheless, the economic components of the system began to unravel in the early 1970s, first in the international monetary system, and then more generally, resulting in the lifting of financial repression. So began the neoliberal era with finance at the forefront, first being liberalised itself and then acting as a market-promoting force elsewhere. We now turn to consider the multiple crises which brought this about. Then, in Section 7.6, we analyse the deeper contradictions from which these crises arose, concluding with an outline of some key aspects of non-financial liberalisation in Section 7.7.

7.5 The unravelling of the postwar economic order and the beginning of neoliberalism

Beginning at Bretton Woods, New Hampshire, in 1944, the international monetary institutions were designed by the United States for multiple purposes. One of these purposes was to promote the US dollar as the main international currency, from which major seigniorage benefits could be derived. Another was to concentrate the burden of adjustment of payment imbalances on deficit countries, not the surplus countries of which the United States expected to be the chief representative for some time.[50] Not surprisingly, then, when America itself began to experience serious deficits in the 1960s, other leading capitalist states sought to ensure that adjustment was concentrated on the United States. But, in fact, this was difficult for America to accomplish in an acceptable way. Since all currency values were specified in terms of the dollar, it could not itself devalue within the rules of the system without the cooperation of other states. In the absence of this cooperation, and it was not actually forthcoming to the extent thought to be appropriate by the United States government, it would be forced to adjust by deflating the American economy, and this would have compromised domestic policies connected to the civil rights movement and the war in Vietnam. The United States chose instead to break with the international monetary system so as to preserve its policy autonomy, and gamble on its ability to preserve hegemony in new form. As we explain below, the Bretton Woods system would have collapsed at some point during the 1970s even if the United States had been inclined to preserve it in the early 1970s. But America was not so inclined for the many reasons we will consider in this section and the next, and it was this unilateralist stance which triggered neoliberal changes more generally.

Between August 1971 and March 1973, the Bretton Woods system fell apart: the United States was no longer obliged to provide gold in exchange for dollars held by other central banks, and all currencies began to float. This took away a major rationale for maintaining international capital controls. Significant autonomy in domestic policy could still be preserved even if exchange controls were lifted completely because the constraint of maintaining fixed exchange rates had been extinguished. The United States effectively ended capital controls in 1974, Britain did so in 1979, and most other advanced capitalist countries followed in the 1980s. Underpinning this liberalisation was the material fact that the productivity gap between the United States and the other advanced capitalist economies, which had resulted in large part from the effects of the 'age of catastrophe', had been substantially closed. This catch-up to American productivity levels had significantly lessened the effectiveness of state-managed economic development for Europeans and Japanese. As convergence occurred and the technical frontier was approached, it became less clear to planners what allocation of capital would prove most productive. The ending of domestic financial repression took place during the same time period, in response to the same influences. And it was all made more imperative by the onset of many other crises during the 1970s.

Ultimately the most fundamental change of all during this decade lay with the productive forces. It is now clear that in the late 1960s or early 1970s a significant reduction in productivity growth and in profitability began throughout advanced capitalism. Many features still remain puzzling, including the speed with which the decline occurred. But part of what was happening was the exhaustion of improvement possibilities within Fordist technologies. The deleterious effects on productivity growth and profitability were reinforced by a marked increase in the militancy of the working class, and a corresponding increase in its wage demands, throughout advanced capitalism from the late 1960s, and this continued into the 1970s.[51] At the same time there was the emergence of a new general-purpose technology centred on the computer, which proved to be far more market-promoting than did Fordist technologies.[52] And simultaneously, the requirements of limiting markets in the interest of preserving the mass mobilisation capacities appropriate for industrialised warfare (which we explained in Section 7.3) started to wane. A new 'revolution in military affairs' began, also stemming from computers. This promised a qualitative leap in surveillance capacities and information processing, joined to precision-guided munitions of enhanced firepower and stealth delivery. The need for large conscript armies suited to industrialised warfare was reduced, along with the value of the collectivist measures required to sustain them.[53] Thus both productive and destructive technologies moved towards favouring more coordination through markets. This was reinforced by the breakdown of discipline exercised by organised labour, which encouraged employers to see an intensified market discipline as the better option. All this meant that resolving other crises would tend to proceed in a neoliberal direction, even if this direction was far from obvious initially.[54]

Indeed, the implications of the technological changes were very unclear at the time. Attention was focussed elsewhere, on the widespread acceleration in inflation and the rise in unemployment, along with the oil price increases in 1973 and 1979. All of this has led to the 1970s being described as the decade of 'stagflation'. It also meant that the system of fixed exchange rates would have broken down even if the United States had conformed to the disciplinary rules of the Bretton Woods system, and even if the other advanced capitalist countries had fully accepted a uniquely privileged role for America not to do so. By the same token, many systems of domestic financial repression would also have been compromised, because they were premised on maintaining low, stable, inflation rates (about which more is said below).

Simultaneously, the recycling of petro-dollars through Western banks consequent upon the large increases in the price of oil provided further incentives for governments to liberalise financial systems in order to attract the new business for 'their' banks. The selfsame petro-dollars also added to the funds available for speculation on foreign-exchange markets and thus initially reinforced the need for flexible exchange rates. However, these speculative balances had already grown substantially in the era of the Bretton Woods system, especially after 1958 when there was full convertibility for current-account transactions, and most notably with the development of the euro–dollar market (about which, again, we say more below). Speculation in favour of dollar devaluation had contributed to the demise of the international monetary system between 1971 and 1973 and would have finished it off later even if governments had acted to preserve it after 1973.

While international crises and the ending of the Bretton Woods system introduced corrosive influences into systems of domestic financial repression, there were also developments within national economies that worked in a complementary manner. In the United States, the regulatory structure introduced by the New Deal brought significant changes in the relative weight of different types of financial institutions. In particular, commercial banks declined,[55] and in order to offset their competitive disadvantages, the American government concurred in the formation of the euro–dollar market in the late 1950s, where dollar-denominated deposits could be held outside the jurisdiction of the monetary authorities of the United States.[56] As we have already pointed out, these deposits facilitated the speculation which helped bring the collapse of the Bretton Woods system.

Rising inflation in the United States also contributed to the relaxation of restrictions on the activities of American banks.[57] Since the Great Depression, they had faced a ceiling on the interest rates which could be paid on deposits (in order to inhibit competition, which, it was believed, contributed to financial instability). The rise in nominal rates occasioned by the inflation forced a deregulation of the interest rates which banks could pay.[58] This, in turn, advantaged banks relative to other institutions and disturbed the overall regulatory structure of finance,[59] promoting further liberalising reform. A similar dynamic of financial deregulation is evident in other countries as well.[60]

The pressure that financial institutions could exert on governments in favour of deregulation also came with the promise of an enhanced productive contribution. All the crises of the 1970s increased risks to profitability in virtually every sector of all capitalist economies. Not only were there reductions in the share of profits and in the rate of profit, but floating exchange rates, unstable inflation and volatile interest rates made for increased risk at the microeconomic level. New financial instruments (which today are referred to as derivatives) offered expanded opportunities for hedging, and their cost was reduced significantly by the rapid advances in computational technology used to calculate risks. But these innovative forms of insurance were not easily accommodated by the prevailing regulatory structures and, not surprisingly, it was the regulation, and not the innovations, that were removed.[61]

Thus for several reasons it became progressively more difficult to justify the full range of financial regulations, and particularly so in the light of the great boom of the postwar years, in which growth had been rapid and recessions mild, so making the return of depression conditions a remote prospect. Preventing a slump no longer seemed so difficult, and a fundamental re-evaluation of the objectives to be served by such regulation was undertaken from the 1970s. The United States led the way but was followed closely by other advanced capitalist economies, especially as continuing globalisation required the harmonisation of such rules. Clearly, there was no longer an overwhelming need to accept the microeconomic inefficiencies inherent in a system that had been designed to neutralise the specific problems of the 1930s, while there were greater incentives to provide an environment encouraging financial innovation.[62] A new consensus developed in which the key objectives to be served by regulation were seen to be the protection of systemic financial integrity and the control of fraud. Consequently, state deposit insurance has been preserved, together with lender of last resort facilities, along with regulations enforcing proper practices in financial institutions and financial markets, while the barriers segmenting different types of financial institutions and markets and protecting them from competition have been significantly lowered. The trend has been towards allowing all financial companies to be able to compete by offering a full array of services, and being similarly regulated to ensure fair dealing and prudent risk management.[63] This second objective has relied heavily on information technology and would have been difficult, if not impossible, to implement with any sophistication before the 1970s. However, the changes have clearly made finance much more powerful vis-à-vis other economic sectors, and this has promoted liberalisation generally.

7.6 The underlying contradictions

The crises discussed in the preceding section were no accident, unfortunate or otherwise. They reflected deeper incompatibilities. The most fundamental contradiction was the one between the productive forces and the productive relations. Economic development during the 'golden age' occurred with strengthened market-enhancing forces which we have documented in Chapter 6. Moreover, a radical new general-purpose technology emerged. Similar technical revolutions have happened several times before, and have done so with increasing frequency under capitalist relations of production because they are so promoting of innovation.[64] Exactly when prevailing technologies will begin exhibiting diminished productivity growth is hard to anticipate, as is the speed with which new technologies will attain their full potential, along with people's understanding of how productive relations have to be modified or changed to realise it.[65] However, it was clear by the 1980s, if not before, that information technologies centred on the computer tended to be market-promoting, in both financial and non-financial activities, and this realisation has brought a neoliberal reorientation of economic policies implemented by political authorities in advanced capitalist societies.

This was reinforced by working-class militancy fostered during the high employment years of the 'golden age'. Michal Kalecki had anticipated the contradiction as early as 1943:

> .... under a regime of permanent full employment, the 'sack' would cease to play its role as a disciplinary measure. The social position of the boss would be undermined, and the self-assurance and class consciousness of the working class would grow. Strikes for wage increases and improvements in conditions of work would create political tensions ... 'discipline in the factories' and 'political stability' are more appreciated than profits by business leaders. Their class instinct tells them that lasting full employment is unsound from their point of view, and that unemployment is an integral part of a 'normal' capitalist system.[66]

However, the severity of this problem varied between countries. Those with corporatist social partnership systems were affected least; those without them but with strong unions, as in Britain, were affected most. This accounts for much of the prominence achieved by neoliberalism in the UK. Successive governments, especially under Prime

Minister Thatcher, introduced liberalising economic measures (joined to increasing political authoritarianism) in order to tame organised labour as well as to facilitate the incorporation of new technologies. But this has been a current in neoliberalism everywhere to some extent, although it is usually described in less conflictual terms as 'enhancing flexibility', and has been pursued more moderately in Europe and Japan.[67]

The other primary contradiction within the productive relations was that the postwar regime was one of selective openness designed to promote economic growth, but the growth actually achieved put the selectivity under mounting pressure:

> The framers of Bretton Woods envisaged a combination of trade liberalization and capital controls. But I doubt if it is possible to have free trade without relatively free capital movements. For once large payments across the exchanges are permitted for one purpose, it is difficult to stop them for other purposes ... [enabling] ... owners of capital to speculate against currencies which were overvalued.[68]

Thus the state's capacity to control finance weakened as the speculative resources destructive of restrictions strengthened, making the maintenance of any set of fixed exchange rates difficult and costly, especially after the move to full convertibility on current account in the late 1950s. The specific crisis of the early 1970s ended them, but another scenario of crises could easily have been similarly destructive. Indeed, in the same context, anything that affected different economies asymmetrically on a significant scale could have done it. And once fixed exchange rates disappeared there was less benefit, if any, to be derived from many other financial restrictions.

The status of the US dollar as the principal source of international liquidity provided America with seigniorage benefits, but it also created another contradiction:

> In an influential book that appeared in 1960, economist Robert Triffin of Yale University called attention to a fundamental long-run problem of the Bretton Woods system, the **confidence problem**. Triffin realized that as central banks' international reserve needs grew over time, their holdings of dollars would necessarily grow until they exceeded the U.S. gold stock. Since the United States had promised to redeem these dollars at $35 an ounce, it would no longer have the ability to meet its obligations should all dollar holders simultaneously try to convert their dollars into gold. This would lead to a

> confidence problem: Central banks, knowing that their dollars were no longer "as good as gold," might become unwilling to accumulate more dollars and might even bring down the system by attempting to cash in the dollars they already held.
>
> One possible solution at the time was an increase in the official price of gold in terms of the dollar and all other currencies. But such an increase would have been inflationary and would have had the politically unattractive consequence of enriching the main gold-producing countries. Further, an increase in gold's price would have caused central banks to expect further decreases in the gold value of their dollar reserve holdings in the future, thereby possibly worsening the confidence problem rather than solving it![69]

Thus, there was a structural basis for the kind of speculation that helped end the Bretton Woods system between 1971 and 1973. It would have been possible to introduce new sources of international liquidity, which many European governments favoured. But this would have undermined the advantages the United States derived from the dollar being the main international currency, and hegemonic states do not accept reductions in their own privileges and power unless forced to do so.[70] The United States was far from being in such desperate straits in the 1970s and chose instead to end the Bretton Woods system.

Nonetheless, there was a marked extension in the anxiety exhibited by American strategic planners during the 1970s, and it continued into the 1990s. This was important in encouraging the United States to restructure its economic hegemony on a more liberal basis, although exactly how important is difficult to know. The problem was the rapid growth of other advanced capitalist economies in the postwar era, and especially the truly spectacular performance of Japan, which suggested that a complete convergence to American productivity levels was very close, and then some degree of 'overtaking' might occur thereafter, all thought to be the result in the case of Japan of its uniquely productive system of 'administrative guidance'.[71] At first the concern was principally economic, but it quickly turned to include the threat of hegemonic rivalry at the geopolitical level.[72] Both made the United States more inclined to view its relationship to other advanced capitalist systems in less-cooperative and more conflictual terms, bringing a unilateralist turn to American policy, which included (but was not confined to) an initiation of neoliberal measures.[73] Not until the recovery of productivity growth in the United States in the early 1990s[74] and the onset of stagnation in Japan during the same decade did the fears subside. (In fact, they were soon replaced by different ones focussing on the long-term threat posed by China.)[75] Again there is a structural basis to such anxieties, as no hegemon can take kindly to 'peer competitors', while the sources of uneven development are very powerful in generating them.[76]

Geopolitics were also present in the particular crises of the 1970s that triggered the liberalisation of finance, and played a role, too, in the reaction of the EU to the way the United States responded to these crises, which had the effect of spreading neoliberalism throughout advanced capitalist economies. The deterioration of the US balance of payments and the increase in inflation in the second half of the 1960s had their origin in a combination of federal government expenditures on the Vietnam War and the extension of the American welfare state in the 'Great Society' programme which, in large part, was a response to the civil rights movement. Neither the war nor the domestic conflict was destined to happen exactly when they did. But the imperatives of the containment strategy meant that the United States had to fight wars in the periphery whose resource demands would be domestically unpopular. And the civil rights movement aiming to incorporate African-Americans into 'the nation' was inevitable, given their geographical dispersal during the 'age of catastrophe' and the consequent loss of coercive control by Southern reactionaries.[77]

Even the oil price 'shocks' of 1973 and 1979 had a systematic geopolitical dimension. As economic and military hegemon of the West, the United States deemed control of Middle Eastern oil supplies to be a vital interest of the United States (as it still is). This required privileging Israel and the Shah of Iran over the Arab states. Regional conflicts and the Iranian revolution of 1979 thereby came to encompass the United States and its allies (as they still do). In the 1970s, oil prices were used as a weapon. It failed to shift US policy very much, but trying was not irrational and it made its own contribution to economic disruption.

Geopolitics and economics merged more powerfully in the reaction of the EU to the general turbulence of the 1970s and to the unilateralist moves of the United States in ending the Bretton Woods system. The abandonment of fixed exchange rates threatened the degree of European integration already achieved, since cross-border trade became riskier and member states faced the temptation of protectionism via currency manipulation. Moreover, the events ending the Bretton Woods system were interpreted by the Europeans as the United States being less willing, and perhaps less able, to provide the public goods associated with economic hegemony. Thus, from the second half of the

1970s the EU made moves to deepen integration by fixing exchange rates in the European Monetary System (which culminated in the European Monetary Union at the turn of the twenty-first century). And, in the mid-1980s, the new attempt to fix exchange rates was joined to the Single Market programme, which implied significant financial liberalisation at some point and, indeed, neoliberal measures much more generally. Controls on international capital movements were no longer consistent with the deeper integration envisaged within the EU, and financial services were denationalised and harmonised as part of the endeavour to extend cross-border trade to services.

European integration had been promoted by the United States after the Second World War as part and parcel of its own hegemonic project. Integration was regarded as encouraging economic recovery, helping to secure peace on the continent and as a complement to the NATO alliance, once described as intended 'to keep the Americans in, the Russians out, and the Germans down'. However, success on all counts meant that the creation began to escape the control of the creator. Such an event has happened many times before (including two centuries earlier when the United States itself emerged), and it was probably not unexpected by American strategic planners. But, more certainly, it was what the US interpreted as threats to its own economic hegemony from other advanced capitalist economies that led it to undermine the Bretton Woods system in the early 1970s, and to embrace a market promoting strategy in order to reconstitute hegemony as a new basis.[78] The EU reacted by deepening, and liberalising, its own integration.

More generally, even if they are allies, states compete with each other, and not just because economic variables are relevant to issues of power.[79] Political jurisdictions embody the property rights which secure the productive relations. They can be more or less efficiency-promoting, which, of course, affects the profits and wages received by citizens. Obvious inefficiencies will engender demands for change, and they will likely be stronger the more open is the world market. Rivalry with competitors operating within alternative jurisdictions will be more intense, and those in areas of greater institutional efficiency will be advantaged. Consequently, there will be a tendency to liberalise laws and regulations whenever they promise productivity improvements, as they have done since at least the 1970s. This has resulted in the different variants of capitalism converging institutionally.

Thus institutions compete with each other, not just companies and individuals, and no more so than in finance when it is opened to the world market. During the 'age of catastrophe' and in the early years of the 'golden age', national financial systems could be very different because they were all principally made to serve national economies and insulated from international competition.[80] The increasing integration of all capitalist economies into the world market after 1945, and especially the crises of the 1970s and the reactions to these crises, changed this situation radically. Financial institutions in different countries and geographically separated financial markets increasingly became competitors, bringing more similarity in organisation, behaviour and regulation. This can be regarded as a triumph of Anglo-American 'exit'-based models over European and Japanese 'voice'-based models, because the former can be extended internationally much more easily and cheaply than the latter, since they are more market-based and impersonal.[81] This is true, but neglects to recognise that the deregulation of American and British financial institutions has made them more like the universal banks of continental Europe. In other words, there has been a process of mutual convergence, rather than any simple copying of an Anglo-Saxon model.[82]

However, whatever the relative weight of the particular influences discussed in this chapter, our argument throughout has been an application of what we said concerning selection mechanisms in Chapter 2 and Chapter 3. That these mechanisms have operated in the postwar years, and in the neoliberal era, should occasion no surprise as they are universally present and are strengthened by the economic development which they promote. We have concentrated on finance for the reasons already explained in Section 7.2, and now turn to consider neoliberalism in other infrastructural areas. Although this has been treated systematically in Chapter 6, our focus here is different in that we concentrate attention on the selection mechanisms at work, and thus the role of crises and contradictions, as well as the leading role played by the United States.

7.7 The role of crises and contradictions in the neoliberalism of other parts of the infrastructure: telecommunications, transportation and energy

While the same forces were present in bringing neoliberalism to non-financial sectors of capitalist economies, the role played by crises was much less prominent. But the United States has, again, frequently been in the lead, especially in the deregulation, of telecommunications, transportation and energy.[83] The American regulatory structure appeared to be more out-of-date than those in other advanced capitalist economies because the industries regulated were not joined to any industrial policy orchestrating them in catch-up modernisation plans. Indeed, it was the success of European countries, and especially of Japan, in implementing such policies that provoked US strategic planners during the 1970s to seek an American rejuvenation through market liberalisation. In the case of telecommunications, there was also the effect of the latest 'revolution in military affairs'. Many of the computerised information technologies were 'dual use', with spillover possibilities in both directions, so that economic and military needs went hand in hand, not an unusual circumstance in modern history.

Nonetheless, beginning in the 1980s the neoliberal measures adopted by other advanced capitalist countries became more dramatic. Public sectors of state-owned enterprises subjected to privatisation and re-regulation were larger, unions hostile to both neoliberal policies were more powerful, and there was a more pronounced 'anti-market' social consciousness fashioned during the days of catch-up growth.[84] Especially in Europe, neoliberalism has met with more resistance than in the United States but, somewhat ironically, neoliberalism itself has been hugely boosted by the process of European integration.[85] To minimise possibilities of protection being extended to domestic companies by national governments, the deepening of European integration has encouraged the reduction of state subsidisation to 'national champions' and thus promoted hard budget constraints through privatisation and the harmonisation of neoliberal re-regulation.

Behind the whole process of neoliberalism, however, has been the same change in the position of other capitalist economies relative to the United States that has brought financial liberalisation. The catch-up to American productivity levels made large public sectors (apart from some programmes of social welfare, defence and education) redundant.[86] They could no longer be used successfully for activist industrial policies geared to modernisation, because this had been achieved, and the enhanced market discipline associated with financial liberalisation was envisaged to be applicable even to former publicly owned monopolies and quasi-monopolies. The profitability demands from liberalised finance could promote productive efficiency, while re-regulation could concentrate on correcting for imperfect competition in product markets (or so it was claimed).

The influence of new technologies has also been obvious. These technologies were involved in the liberalisation of finance, since they made available the much cheaper and faster computation required for sophisticated asset pricing and risk-based re-regulation. But the lifting of financial repression could have occurred without this, and it was actually triggered by the crises of the 1970s, which played a much less direct role in neoliberalism outside the financial sector, where new technologies were crucial, especially in telecommunications. 'Three technological challenges transformed the sector: the development of advanced terminal equipment, the advent of microwave and satellite transmission, and the creation of sophisticated "value added" services combining data processing with communications.'[87] These undermined the natural monopoly character of the industry, along with the preference for uniform service provision at uniform prices and made established regulatory categories outdated.[88] The influence of new technologies on telecommunications was evident as early as the 1950s but reached avalanche proportions in the 1970s and 1980s, in all advanced capitalist economies. And once telecommunications were liberalised, they facilitated huge market-promoting changes in virtually every other sector of these economies, both in production and in consumption activities.

Similar technological changes favoured enhancing commercialisation elsewhere in the publicly owned or heavily regulated, infrastructural industries. The development of a much wider range of jet aircraft, both small and large, coupled to increasing integration of national and international markets requiring more transportation of people and goods, lay behind the airline privatisation and re-regulation that began in the 1970s. As with finance, the changes in one area have also driven liberalising moves in competitive sectors, such as road and rail transportation and ports. And, parallel to the effects of neoliberalism in telecommunications, market-promoting changes in other industries have occurred in consequence, most obviously in tourism, courier services, 'fast foods' and security provision. The effects on mass consumption and on popular and political culture have been equally huge. For example, the reality of a European identity complementing economic integration has probably been brought much closer by budget airlines than anything actively promoted in Brussels.[89]

Energy production and distribution were affected by the crises of the 1970s as well as by new technologies. The oil 'shocks' of 1973 and 1979 initiated the decontrol of energy prices in the endeavour to reduce demand and expand supplies. Information technologies have since provided more effective and cheaper means of metering usage, more economic use of supply networks and the expansion of the number of suppliers into such networks. The overall effect has been to expand markets and make them more competitive. As a result, there have been important secondary effects on other sectors of the economy, many of them market-promoting, just as with finance, telecommunications and transportation.

7.8 State and market

The emergence of a new general-purpose technology centred on the computer in the 1970s clearly promoted neoliberalism in both finance and elsewhere. But as we have argued in previous chapters, and documented in Chapter 6, there were many earlier changes in the productive forces and productive relations which favoured a neoliberal turn in advanced capitalism. The delay resulted from the enduring effects of the 'age of catastrophe' and, conceivably, could have been even longer because crises played such an important role in initiating the change, and the timing of crises is never fully deterministic. Nonetheless, the contradictions of the postwar regime ensured that they would appear at some point, and that they would usher in a neoliberal turn given that the underlying material conditions were favourable to expanding markets. In the absence of the new information technologies, neoliberalism would have been less pronounced, but market-promoting changes in the productive forces and productive relations were already sufficiently well developed to ensure that the recovery from crises would proceed in a neoliberal direction.

This argument should also help dispel some widespread misconceptions. Neoliberal measures in advanced capitalist economies have not simply been the result of globalisation, nor are they the consequence of an enhanced power of markets relative to states. Neoliberal measures have facilitated globalisation and market expansion as much as they have been a response to them. Rather than reflecting any reduction in the power of states, they were initiated by the most powerful of all states as part of a grand strategy to retain hegemony. While this strategy often reduced the power of political authorities elsewhere, it also sometimes prompted them to reorganise in a way that recovered the power, as in the case of the EU, and this, too, given the technological circumstances, has involved the promotion of markets. It is usually naive to lump all states together into a single category or to regard markets as much the same the world over. There are huge differences in both cases, and an increase in the power of one does not imply a reduction in the power of the other. Well-functioning markets can promote state power, and states encourage the development of markets for this reason. Both are part and parcel of the selection mechanisms recognised by historical materialism, and they help to account for the continuing rise in overall productivity. If, instead, markets constrained the productive forces, states would endeavour to reduce their role, as they did in the 'age of catastrophe'. It is to a renewal of this possibility that we now turn in the next chapter, where we investigate what might reverse neoliberalism in advanced capitalism.

8
What Might Reverse Neoliberalism?

8.1 Some difficulties with answering the question

Intellectual history is littered with predictions of an assured future for trends that turned out to be temporary and reversible. We have seen many examples of such mistakes in earlier chapters, where it was shown how leading economists in diverse schools of thought all failed to anticipate the onset of neoliberalism and, instead, predicted a long-run decline in market relations.[1] Since none of these people could be sensibly described as stupid, their erroneous expectations serve as a warning to anyone who would offer forecasts about the future of neoliberal capitalism.

Nevertheless, we cannot legitimately shirk the issue because we have claimed there to be a definite causal structure explaining the development of neoliberalism, and this has implications for its continuance or reversal. However, we do need to proceed with caution, and the predictions we make can only be conditional and coarse-grained. Our materialist stance allows little else, because some of the most important determinants of the economic phenomena with which we are concerned are themselves subject to historical change in ways that are difficult to anticipate. While it is true that those characteristics of human nature which anchor historical materialism[2] can be treated as transhistorical constants for the time scale with which we are concerned, the other components of the causal structure – the selection mechanisms – which actually determine much of the specific course of history inside the bounds set by human nature cannot be treated as unchanging.[3] Nor, more obviously, can the technological, economic and political conditions in which they operate. At any particular time the productive forces, the productive relations, superstructures and social consciousness are all modified by one or more selection mechanism. But this process brings about new contexts of possibility and constraint in which the (possibly changing) selection mechanisms do their work once again.

Thus in forecasting the future of neoliberal capitalism we have two sets of difficulties to contend with: both the selection mechanisms and the phenomena on which they act may evolve in ways that can be difficult to foresee. In this section we focus on how the selection mechanisms of human rationality, market competition, collective action by groups and geopolitical rivalry can change. In Sections 8.2–8.7 we turn to consider how these (possibly changing) mechanisms could interact with changes in the productive forces, the productive relations and superstructures, either to preserve or to reverse neoliberalism.

Consider first the changing nature of rationality. Acquisitiveness may be an invariant quality of the human character and thereby contribute to the tendency for the productive forces to develop through time, but the degree of rationality with which it is combined is clearly variable. Economic development itself involves improvements in the techniques by which knowledge of the world expands, including knowledge of how to be rational. This is evidenced by the advances in mathematical programming, statistics and the other tools of rational choice theory. But, as with other forms of knowledge, future improvements cannot be predicted (otherwise they would not then lie in the future).[4] Hence the manner in which rational people will behave is subject to variation through time and this, ironically, impedes the capacity to rationally forecast all the future consequences of rational behaviour, because previously established empirical regularities may be dissolved as behaviour changes. Given the pervasiveness of rational behaviour in modern capitalism, this complication is generally relevant, but it is most clearly so in our discussion of financial crises (in Section 8.5 below) and geopolitical conflict (in Section 8.7).

Change also occurs in market competition, and economists of all schools recognise the importance which the type and degree of competition have for the functioning of capitalist economies. Competition acts as a compulsive force on human choice by reducing the degrees of freedom that would prevail if its impact were lessened. This means that there are huge incentives for those subjected to competition to seek some insulation that protects them.[5] But success is difficult to foresee, because private information and the relative powers of the parties involved play a large part in determining the outcome. Thus forecasting the events and trends affected by the extent of competition is also very difficult. This is especially important for our discussion of political opposition to neoliberalism (in Section 8.6) and environmental deterioration (in Section 8.4), as is the formation of collective action groups.

The formation of groups, including classes, has invariant features. Collective action by a group is made more likely, the more similar are the circumstances of its potential members, the smaller the number of these members, the greater is their interaction with each other, and the fewer options there are for individual strategies to ameliorate discontent.[6] But there is also a dimension of indeterminacy, so that the intensity with which common interests are prosecuted is changeable, even in identical structural conditions. The formation of a group tends to produce conflict with other groups, and the conflict can feed back to promote solidarity and radicalism. However, while the formal properties of these positive feedback processes are clear, the empirical events that can act as tipping points initiating cumulative causation are much less well understood.[7]

Geopolitics also exhibits discontinuities. We have seen an important example of this in Chapter 7, where we explained how the armed conflict between advanced capitalist states in the first half of the twentieth century was replaced by *Pax Americana*. Rivalry between advanced capitalist systems did not then disappear, but it has become overwhelmingly economic since the mid-twentieth century because any serious military challenge to the United States became self-evidently futile. This pacification will continue if American hegemony remains in place. It could well do so, at least for many decades. All the sources of American power – military, political, economic and ideological – remain fundamentally strong,[8] but there are also persuasive scenarios of long-term hegemonic decline.[9] And, if and when the erosion is pronounced, previous patterns of conflict could emerge once again. We discuss this issue in Section 8.7 below.

Finally, 'exogenous shocks' always remain to complicate all predictions. Perhaps they do not literally exist, and all events really are fully determined,[10] but in the present state of knowledge there is no alternative but to accept randomness, and also to accept that it may be more or less prevalent. At the very least, this makes the timing of events very difficult to forecast exactly. Even if there can be great confidence that some particular phenomenon will occur because the mechanisms working to bring it about are very strong, there may still be a huge degree of indeterminacy as to when it will actually make an appearance.

For all these reasons, then, there is uncertainty as to how the selection mechanisms will operate in the future, making the forecasting of what will happen to neoliberal capitalism precarious. Sections 8.3–8.7 buttress this conclusion by examining the uncertainties surrounding the technological, economic and political contexts in which the selection mechanisms will operate. As a consequence, the only sensible type of prediction is conditional, incorporating an 'if ... then' structure. And the 'ifs' will typically involve assumptions of *ceteris paribus*, while the 'thens' may not include exact dating, owing to the importance of 'accidents' which constitute randomness.[11]

Subject to these qualifications, our theory of neoliberalism provides forecasts of its future in three forms. First, we believe that there are clear limits to neoliberalism in advanced capitalist economies: markets will always remain incomplete; welfare states will be substantially preserved and no 'race to the bottom' in taxation and regulation will occur. Second, neoliberal capitalism will malfunction in ways that bring reforms, but these reforms will often not be system-changing. This will be the case with recurrent problems of corporate governance and managerial opportunism, as well as with inappropriate policies of privatisation, outsourcing and deregulation. Third, neoliberalism will be subject to some degree of reversal if technical change becomes market-eliminating; if the productive forces are seriously degraded by global warming; if large financial crises occur; if popular opposition to neoliberalism is provoked by increasing inequality and if future wars become heavily resource-absorbing. We consider each of these three types of forecast in the following sections of this chapter.

8.2 The limits and excesses of neoliberalism

Neoliberalism is necessarily limited, because it is impossible for markets to encompass all human activity. The provision of justice and defence, of emergency services and public administration, as well as the electoral process and legislative deliberation must be substantially shielded from commercial influence if they are to be effective. Many types of contract have to be prohibited because they conflict with the understanding of personhood and individual freedom which constitutes the legal foundation of agreements within capitalism. Futures markets will always be thin owing to the uncertainties people face as to their preferences and production technologies beyond the current period, and because the problems of fraud and opportunism multiply in intertemporal trading. Contingent commodity contracts are inevitably constrained for the same reasons of fraud and opportunism, including in the forms of adverse selection and moral hazard. And, as we have explained in Chapter 2, Section 2.2, command is intrinsic to the employment contract. So, all in all, much of advanced capitalism cannot be subordinated to the market without serious malfunctioning occurring.

Furthermore, some economic activity which could be organised on more pronounced market lines may continue to successfully resist neoliberalism as a result of superior efficiency, and therefore superior profitability. Most importantly, as we have already suggested in Chapter 2 and Chapter 6, some pockets of microeconomic corporatism may survive the unravelling of economy-wide corporatist organisations. But the key to achieving this is higher efficiency. Without this no corporatist elements can endure in a world of market-promoting technologies, weakened unions, globalising capital and neoliberalised political parties.

By the same token, the major programmes of the welfare state will be preserved because they are productive and cannot be more efficiently provided through genuine markets. These programmes are also very popular with electorates and are protected by a myriad of interest groups.[12] Only those transfers involving income entitlements to the able-bodied poor are likely to face much retrenchment. State-financed health care and education at all levels, along with income support organised on insurance principles, are most unlikely to face serious cut-backs in the bulk of advanced capitalist countries.[13] As a consequence there will be no 'race to the bottom' in taxation to improve competitiveness, because it would prove to be counter-productive. However, what is likely to continue changing is the organisation of the welfare state. It will become more market-friendly through the greater provision of publicly financed services utilising private suppliers, more internal resource allocation governed by pricing formulae, as well as a wider set of user charges for particular services.

Other important impediments to the domain of markets will also remain in place, at least for some considerable time. Judged solely from the perspective of orthodox microeconomics, neoliberal capitalism would work most efficiently if national laws and regulations were harmonised with each other, and there was a single monetary system. This would minimise transaction costs and maximally expand markets.[14] But, apart from impinging on the interests of a myriad of professional groups privileged by national credentials, it would detract from the power of most states to fulfil their functions regarding security and the maintenance of national identity. While this might not matter unduly for smaller jurisdictions, it conflicts with the interests of the hegemonic power unless its own national standards become generalised, and the judicial, administrative and monetary authorities of the hegemon hold sway internationally. This would certainly prove unacceptable to other states with hegemonic ambitions, and to those states with interests that favour the containment of hegemonic power.

All these limits to neoliberalism, however, will constitute sources of political tension. Sometimes government policies will go awry, with overzealous retrenchment and the promotion of neoliberal measures that are economically inappropriate. This will generate protests and calls for reversal, although actually bringing about repeal may prove difficult. Ideologically, neoliberal capitalism involves both the celebration of the market and the cult of the businessman. Thus, compared to other lobbying groups, business organisations encounter less resistance from governments. And this is likely to be enduring, since the countervailing power of labour unions, social democratic parties, the professions, universities and churches, along with state bureaucracies modelled on Weberian principles, have all been weakened.[15] Not surprisingly, then, there will be a tendency for neoliberal excess.

Already there are many examples of inappropriate privatisations, unsuitable deregulations, excessive governmental outsourcing and silly rules requiring private–public partnerships in new investments. Sometimes the public sector has been looted through the privatisation of natural monopolies at artificially low sale prices, and the deregulation process has often been captured by business groups to yield powers with which to fleece consumers. At the same time neoliberal measures have been promoted simply to reduce the current expenditures and current debt levels of governments, contrary to any sensible concept of economic efficiency.[16] Furthermore, institutions requiring a degree of autonomy so as to properly execute their responsibilities have been overly subordinated to markets. Especially destructive have been the pressures and incentives for university research to be funded by commercial organisations. The undesirable consequences have been most obvious in the case of medical research.[17] No doubt these mistakes have been more easily implemented because the onset of neoliberalism coincided with the emergence of a new general-purpose technology (which we discussed in Chapter 6). As a consequence, there has been greater uncertainty as to the manner in which public policy should proceed. But, despite all the fog, the malevolent influence of business interests is also clearly detectable.

An important element of positive feedback is evident in these developments. Neoliberal policies increase inequality in both income and wealth;[18] the power of the very rich grows at least as rapidly as their bank balances; public policy is biased even more in the interests of the wealthy; and so inequality increases further. In this way plutocracy and neoliberalism become mutually reinforcing phenomena. The tendency can be seen most clearly in the United States, where all types of election (state and federal, and for the executive and the legislative branches of government) have become ever more costly, and thus place a premium on attracting rich supporters, so that lobbyists for corporate interests can exercise influence over policy to a degree that would have been inconceivable to those political scientists who studied the emergence of 'pressure group politics' in the early decades of the twentieth century.[19] But it is apparent, to a greater or lesser extent, across the whole globe. And it is not just a question of grossly inequitable distribution. The efficiency of markets is also threatened, and in the same cumulative manner: market failures (which engender vast inequalities in wealth) give rise to state failures (defective regulation and privileged monopolies), which reinforce market failures, and so on. One especially important example of this occurs in finance, where increasing inequality reduces the risk aversion of the very rich, leading them to invest more in private equity funds and hedge funds which have high rates of return on average, so reinforcing the trend to inequality. There is also a danger here because these funds are the least regulated and can more easily go bankrupt, so posing threats to the integrity of the financial system as a whole.[20]

Even among orthodox economists, suspicion of 'business' has long been evident. Over 200 years ago, Adam Smith wrote of the opportunistic proclivities of merchants and manufacturers in terms not very different from those of modern economists.[21] And, since Smith, much evidence has accumulated indicating that business constitutes a set of very special interests, not the embodiment of the universal. Even limiting attention to the twenty-first century yields many examples of corporate fraud, as in the case of Enron, Worldcom, Tyco and other large companies. Shareholders have been defrauded by executives creating misinformation, or acting on insider information for their own benefit. Implicit contracts with employees have been terminated for the short-term financial advantage of those at the top of the hierarchy. At the same time the members of corporate 'compensation committees' have often been chosen by those whose remuneration they determine. And all this has been facilitated by business lobbying for weakened corporate law, the degrading of accounting standards and the emasculation of state bureaucracies.[22]

The separation of ownership and control is especially problematic for corporate governance. Professional managers who control the assets of others need to be provided with incentives, or otherwise disciplined, to act in the interest of asset owners. This has proved difficult to 'get right'. For example, one of the most widely-used set of schemes involves linking managerial incomes to the share price of what they manage. But this has failed to align managerial interests with shareholder interests (let alone with the interest of other stakeholders). Managers can themselves influence share prices independently of actually raising future earnings per share because they control much of the information on which market assessments are made. Nor are markets always efficient in the use of information that is available. The profits of financial capital depend not only on estimating the 'fundamentals' of corporate value but also on the expectations of others' assessment of market sentiments, so that the anticipation of capital gains can create self-reinforcing asset price bubbles. As we will argue in Section 8.5, these can be dangerous because they can engender financial crises, but bubbles also undermine attempts to align managerial remuneration with long-term profitability.

However, in normal circumstances these excesses of neoliberal capitalism – both the policy errors and the opportunism – are unlikely to bring about system-transforming change.[23] In advanced capitalism the productive forces and the productive relations each favour neoliberalism, and no form of capitalism could function devoid of corporations run by professional managers, or without information provided to governments from business lobbyists. This implies that system-preserving reform will prevail in response to the problems discussed in this section. Only if policy errors and managerial malpractice contribute to a serious financial crisis might there be more radical re-engineering of the system. We now turn to consider this and other possible developments that could induce a significant reversal of neoliberalism in advanced capitalism. We begin by considering possible changes in the productive forces, then turn to consider the productive relations and, finally, the superstructure.

8.3 Market-eliminating technical change

There are multiple mechanisms of coordination, including various kinds of markets, hierarchic command, voting, 'voice' and violence. One way of appreciating why advanced capitalism has proved to be so successful is to recognise that its core characteristics[24] advantage the system over alternatives by allowing the various forms of coordination to be blended together and to be altered in relative importance as comparative efficiencies change. The possibility of forming contractual relations obviously facilitates the development of markets, while the nature of the employment contract allows the strengths of hierarchy to be realised. 'Voice' can easily play a role in many circumstances, and is especially important in contexts where there are long-term relationships within firms or between firms.[25] Shareholder voting power allows the control of managers, and while it operates very imperfectly it does eliminate some of the most obvious inefficiencies that would otherwise occur.[26] Violence is excluded from playing an economic role within capitalist systems, which helps explain why they attain such high productivity, but this high productivity ensures the political and military domination of capitalist states in the world as a whole.

Many influences change the relative efficiency of different forms of coordination. We consider these in terms of changes in the productive forces, the productive relations and superstructures, analogous to our previous discussions of market elimination and the expansion of markets with the onset of neoliberalism. We begin in this section by focussing on technical change. Currently it takes a form which promotes markets, but this could change with the development of a new general-purpose technology.[27] We have no particular reason to believe that the bias of technical change will shift against markets and become more favourable for the use of alternative coordination mechanisms, but we have no reason to rule it out either.

Other things being equal, neoliberalism could be expected to go into reverse if economies of scale and scope expand, so promoting the concentration of capital; if agglomeration economies increase, bringing a reduction in the geographical dispersion of economic activity; if there are improvements in the surveillance and monitoring of personnel within organisations, so enhancing the benefits of hierarchical command; and if the 'publicness' of scientific knowledge becomes more pronounced while the capacity to exclude others from its benefits deteriorates. Markets would also contract if new technologies reduce the degree of substitutability between inputs; if firm-specific or product-specific capital, including human capital, increases in relative importance; and if 'design' characteristics in cooperative endeavours intensify.[28]

All these changes would have a directly contracting effect upon the extensiveness of market relations. But other technological forces could have similar consequences indirectly. If automation, particularly robotics, substantially reduced the demand for human labour then more of the remuneration of the non-propertied classes would have to take the form of welfare state transfers. And if rising productivity and further increases in affluence induce those remaining in employment to demand that their work contribute more to achieving substantive values, formal rationalisation and, therefore, markets will encounter a less hospitable space in which to operate.

In these ways some types of improvement in the productive forces could act to eliminate markets, and many of those economists we discussed in Chapters 3 and 4 would appear, once again, full of insights stretching beyond their own times. But, paradoxically, it is also true that particular types of deterioration in the productive forces could also eliminate markets. The prospect of a general reversal in productivity growth in advanced capitalism is remote, but a significant and sudden deterioration in environmental quality as a result of global warming could mean that markets would fare much less well, and other coordination mechanisms would expand to deal with new problems. This may not be the most important effect of rapid global warming, but an effect it almost certainly will be.

8.4 Environmental deterioration

Threats to humanity from a hostile natural environment, and from changes in the environment, have been present since the dawn of history.[29] Economic development, and especially the rapid economic growth generated by capitalism, has reduced many of these dangers, but it has exacerbated others. Some of the hazards have been subjected to strict legal controls in which market forces play no role, or a highly constrained role. This is the case with toxic wastes, carcinogens, the protection of biodiversity, transportation of dangerous materials, travel speeds and noise levels. But market mechanisms have been used too, as in the case of road pricing, tradable pollution permits and subsidies to encourage recycling.[30] No doubt both types of response will continue to be employed. However, there are also compelling grounds for expecting new environmental crises which will undermine markets in a much more dramatic fashion than has so far been experienced.

This claim is founded on predictions of global warming as a result of greenhouse gases being generated in the process of economic growth, especially through the use of fossil fuels. These gases alter the earth's atmosphere in a way that traps heat from the sun and thus warms the planet. True, there are likely to be some benefits from this because the Arctic, Northern Canada and Siberia would yield their natural resources at lower cost and become more habitable. But areas which presently have dense populations will suffer massive disruptions as a consequence of rising sea levels, changing ocean currents, more hurricanes and less productive agriculture. Creating markets to price carbon emissions and subsidising the development of more environmentally friendly technologies might play a role in restraining global warming, but it is possible that it is already too late for such measures to have much impact. Powerful processes of positive feedback may have already been set in motion, in which warming promotes further warming, and possibly at an accelerating rate.[31] There is no certainty that this is actually the case, but more and more scientists believe it to be prudent to assume that worst-case scenarios will materialise.[32] And, in all these cases, neoliberalism will suffer serious reverses.

Moreover, even if global warming could be put into reverse through the use of green taxes and other market-friendly pricing measures, these measures may not actually be implemented. The negative effects of environmental change lie in the future and adversely affect very many countries, so there are two types of free-rider problem inhibiting the appropriate types of collective action.[33] The present generation, and perhaps several generations that follow, may calculate that since *their* benefits from ameliorative measures will be less than *their* costs it is not worthwhile for them to contribute much to reversing the process. A similar logic applies to the world's population as a whole at any particular time, because it is divided between different jurisdictions and there are no institutions that can assign burden-sharing. Each nation may seek to minimise its own costs in providing a solution so that there is, overall, an inadequate global response.

Either way, the market-eradicating effects of global warming will stem from two sources. First, the consequences of the process will be calamitous. Second, there will be uncertainties as to the timing and location of the catastrophes. Consequently, planning will have to rest heavily upon a military model of hierarchic command:

> Climate change is complicated and uncertain, but…the underlying calculation is fairly straightforward. The global average temperature is expected to increase by between 1.4°C and 5.8°C this century…Anything much higher [than the bottom end of the range] could lead to catastrophic rises in sea levels, increases in extreme weather events such as hurricanes, flooding and drought, falling agricultural production and, perhaps, famine and mass population movements.[34]
>
> The rise in sea levels … could become the most serious consequence of climate change…. If all of Greenland's ice were to melt, sea levels would rise around 7 metres; if West Antarctica's were to go, that

> would add another 6 metres; and if East Antarctica's ice melted – which nobody thinks likely for the foreseeable future – sea levels would go up by a devastating further 70 metres. Even a 1 metre rise would flood 17% of Bangladesh's land mass and cause serious problems for coastal cities such as London and New York.[35]

It is not just warming that will occur. So far as Northern European countries and Britain are concerned, there is the possibility that changes in the Gulf Stream could produce a significant cooling effect upon them 'With its huge volumes and sharp temperature difference to surrounding waters, it carries so much tropical heat from the mid-Atlantic to Western Europe that Norway's coastline is, in winter, 20°C warmer than similar latitudes in Canada... [and without the Gulf Stream there could be]... icebergs around Britain'. In America, hurricanes are the main climatological hazard to the east coast, but 'establishing trends in hurricane frequency and intensity is much more difficult than in temperature'.[36]

Conceivably, global warming (and localised coolings) could usher in a new Fordist-type era, in which the 'end of affluence' engenders a widespread contraction of markets.[37] But even if productive power continues its upward trajectory in advanced capitalism, there will be major reversals imposed on neoliberalism. The frequency distributions of catastrophic events which underpin the probabilistic calculations in insurance and capital markets will become unreliable, so these markets will contract. Since people's risk aversion and the need for investment will not change in tandem, new demands will be placed upon public authorities to fill the void. More dramatically, the sheer scale of property damage and asset destruction could cause huge increases in the number of bankruptcies and in unemployment. This, in turn, would require states to extend their 'lender of last resort' function, along with accompanying regulation, beyond the financial sector. And, of course, there would have to be increases in taxation to relieve destitution and fund public works.

The catastrophes of global warming will also bring an expansion of state capacities for mass mobilisation not dissimilar to those of World War Two.[38] Millions of people may have to be rapidly evacuated from coastal cities, and they will require transportation, shelter, sustenance and relocation. In addition there will have to be extensive policing to counter threats to 'law and order'. The magnitude, complexity and uncertainty of these undertakings suggest that outsourcing the responsibilities to the private sector would not be feasible. Likewise with providing the new public goods of flood control and irrigation.

Furthermore, there will be indirect effects of environmental crises, bringing a roll-back in neoliberalism. It is not unusual for one type of crisis to induce others. Financial crises could easily be triggered by the destruction inflicted by global warming and, if not contained, would result in serious failures of effective demand, as in the 1930s. The inequitable distribution of the costs of global warming might provoke new regional conflicts, or other group hostilities, within capitalist polities. And conflict could easily extend into geopolitics, with new colonisations and 'wars of redivision'. But it is also true that all these phenomena which have the effect of contracting markets might occur independently of global warming, and it is to these possibilities that we turn in the next three sections.

8.5 Financial crises and depression

A financial sector wholly free of state regulation and intervention would be a uniquely important source of instability, stagnation and depression in capitalist economies. Especially damaging bankruptcies can more easily occur as a result of the activities of financial companies than those of other types of capitalist enterprise. And both the prospect and the actual occurrence of bankruptcies within the financial sector itself can have a huge impact on the economy as a whole. Finance is infrastructural in providing necessary services to virtually every form of production, as well as many types of consumption, so that any malfunction within finance has harmful effects virtually everywhere.

'Free' finance would be prone to cause damaging bankruptcies for several reasons. First, fraud is easier to perpetrate and mistakes are more likely, because financial transactions involve promises to pay at various dates in the future. The unwillingness or inability to meet contractual obligations is thus more prevalent in financial activities than in other types of capitalist business.[39] Second, the size of price changes in securities can be very large, since they are the capitalised equivalents of changes in expected income flows. As a result, changes in the value of portfolios can easily compromise the ability to meet obligations to others in a world where budget constraints are finite. Third, both the tendency towards fraud and mistakes, as well as large price changes, mean that speculation plays an especially large role in financial markets. This sometimes brings about price bubbles that divorce asset values from the fundamental determinants of value inherent in technology and consumption. While they continue, these bubbles draw resources away from productive activity, and when they burst they bring capital losses that can induce widespread and cascading bankruptcies everywhere.[40] Fourth, and finally, the products of the financial sector exhibit two peculiarities. The sector produces money at close to zero marginal cost, yet it cannot produce the highest quality money (state money) at any cost.[41] As a result the confidence of depositors in financial institutions is fragile; they know that there is a tendency to produce too much money, and they also know that in a crisis there will be insufficient 'high quality money' available to satisfy all claimants simultaneously.

Of course, the failure of business enterprises is a normal part of capitalist dynamics, often classified as part of the 'creative destruction' in which resources are reallocated to more productive endeavours. But bankruptcies are also seriously problematic. In themselves, they involve only the certainty of unemployed resources, not the assurance of re-employment elsewhere, and one bankruptcy can induce many more because the unpaid debts are the assets of others. This chain reaction will be pronounced in the case of insolvency of financial companies themselves since they are the custodians of 'other peoples' money', and contagion will be the more pronounced the greater is the integration of the financial institutions. Indeed, the mere prospect of bankruptcies of financial institutions, rather than their actual occurrence, can bring about a 'credit crunch' as existing loans are recalled and new loans curtailed, so contracting investment and consumption throughout the economy. Even worse, the expectation of a bankruptcy in a financial institution can be self-realising as depositors demand high-quality money which the institution alone cannot provide in sufficient quantity.

State regulation and intervention can reduce all these risks and mitigate the destructive consequences if problems do arise. But regulation and intervention may not always be appropriately structured, or applied with sufficient zeal. The most serious examples of failure occurred in the early 1930s. Fraud, expectations unhinged from fundamentals, bubbles and their bursting, and bankruptcies all played a part in the onset of the Great Depression. But the intervention of the monetary authorities throughout the capitalist world failed dismally. 'Lender of last resort' facilities were overly restrained and deflationary policies were often favoured in circumstances which called for their exact opposite.[42] State failures thus reinforced market failures, and together they were front and centre in causing depression. As we have explained in Chapter 7 this, as much as the two world wars, brought about a reversal of liberalism in advanced capitalism for much of the twentieth century.

The obvious question is, 'Can it happen again?'.[43] It is a query especially apt in the neoliberal era. Whereas the experience of the Great Depression brought the end of the Gold Standard and much stricter state control of finance in all capitalist countries in order to limit fraud, price volatility and bubbles, while maintaining the solvency of financial institutions in virtually all circumstances, neoliberal measures have dismantled many of these safeguards.[44] The 1930s also gave birth to Keynesian macroeconomics, which provided the knowledge by which financial systems could be more appropriately managed to ensure that severe failures in effective demand do not occur again. But neoliberal theory has repudiated much of this and returned to advertising the quality of pre-Keynesian thought.[45]

Nevertheless, despite these grounds for concern, the fiscal and monetary authorities in advanced capitalism are today much more competent and powerful than were their predecessors during the 1930s. Basic Keynesian ideas remain orthodoxy for the macroeconomic management of capitalist economies, despite the pre-Keynesian rhetoric of politicians, bankers and many economists, and the range of policy instruments potentially available in an emergency is much larger.[46] Any financial crises that threaten the overall economy could be contained and reversed. And any adverse effects on economic activity generally would be limited by the size and extensiveness of government expenditures, the ease of running large budget deficits if required to do so, the many automatic stabilisers inherent in fiscal policies and the pervasiveness of welfare state programmes.[47] Thus any recurrence of either very serious financial crises, or of a deep and prolonged depression, in advanced capitalism is unlikely.

But it is impossible to be completely sure. Certainly there have been changes in the nature of finance itself, and many of these reinforce the potential for financial crises. The existence of a large stock of government debt and new financial instruments do allow better risk management, and that is a source of greater stability. But the underlying frequency distributions, on which basis probabilities are calculated, may be unstable because financial innovations themselves can change them in unknown ways.[48] As a result of neoliberal deregulation, levels of private debt as a percentage of income are now very much higher in many advanced capitalist systems, which implies an increased vulnerability to bankruptcies.[49] And financial interdependencies are once again much more global, while regulation and control remains overwhelmingly national, so that cooperation is required between independent authorities.[50] This occurs extensively, but such cooperation is always inherently problematic because no agreements can cover all contingencies. There is also a greater variety of financial institutions, not all of which are protected with state deposit insurance, and there are uncertainties as to how wide the protection of 'lender of last resort' facility extends,[51] and how many insolvencies monetary authorities could cope with simultaneously.

The deflationary impact that any financial crisis might have upon the economy generally is also potentially very serious. The recent experience of Japan has been instructive. Stagnation and deflation were allowed to continue for over a decade after the bursting of the bubbles in the financial and property markets in the early 1990s. Large budget deficits were allowed to occur, but the monetary policies required to renew growth were never enacted because they were unorthodox and required moving beyond the manipulation of short-term interest rates to deliberately increasing the rate of inflation.[52] The institutional structure and the policy constraints operative in the European Union are also causes for concern. Both the path to monetary union and the 'Stability and Growth Pact' governing that union have been deflationary. The EU is not an optimum currency area, so the various regions will fare very differently under a single monetary policy. In the event of a failure of effective demand, the EU lacks a large and powerful political centre to enact expansionary fiscal policies, or to dictate appropriate monetary policy to the European Central Bank.

A serious depression in advanced capitalism would be a huge body blow to neoliberalism. When markets fail in so dramatic a fashion, alternative coordination mechanisms come into their own. Although the exact sequence of actions that would be taken is unpredictable, there cannot be much doubt that neoliberalism would be reversed on a wide front. Moreover, even a major financial crisis that is successfully contained so as not to have a harsh impact on the overall economy is likely to bring the reversal of financial liberalisation. Such crises are frightening and costly, and would call for stricter regulation, higher reserve ratios, varied and variable margin requirements for borrowers in different sectors, limits placed upon the activities which financial institutions could undertake, the imposition of taxes on financial transactions and heavier capital gains taxation.

The impact of such measures would not be limited to the financial sector, precisely because finance is infrastructural. In particular, if the role of finance in disciplining the managers of corporations is diminished, alternative governance structures would be sought. More and stricter laws constraining executive behaviour, tightening up company accounting, strengthening the independence of auditors and providing incentives for employees to provide evidence of managerial malpractice, might not greatly damage neoliberalism. But reform might move towards more radical measures, seeking to strengthen the supervisory capacities of shareholders and workers. Even new forms of corporatism, including the encouragement of unions, might be promoted. And, precisely here, there would be supporting forces arising from the effects of globalisation on labour markets in neoliberal capitalism. It is to this prospect that we turn in the next section.

8.6 Political opposition

There is clearly a basis for political opposition to neoliberalism. Privatisation, deregulation, outsourcing, corporate and government restructuring, along with macroeconomic policies fixated on inflation, have produced many casualties the world over. But, so far, no political force has emerged to channel the discontents into a coherent programme. The leaders of the 'anti-globalisation movement', of course, seek to constitute such a vanguard. However, the dramatic spectacles orchestrated since the Seattle riots in 1999[53] are not matched by the quality of their analyses or the persuasiveness of their programme. True, some of the specific pathologies described by intellectuals of the anti-globalisation movement are valid enough: sweat shops in the South involve appalling conditions for labour; corporate marketing is an attempt at mind control which sometimes results in stupefaction; and governments have frequently abandoned their duties in the face of business pressure.[54] But the 'theory' offered to reveal the 'deep structure' and guidance for effective political agency is genuinely absurd.[55] Neoliberalism is seen simply as the predation of elites on 'the multitude', which in turn is diagnosed as a manifestation of 'Empire', which itself is left undefined and opaque. Radical democratisation is proposed as a counter strategy, but there is no serious analysis of the limits to any form of democracy, especially in circumstances of diverse interests extending across different states, which continue to act as containers separating privilege and deprivation.[56]

Within the advanced capitalist countries opposition to globalisation is virtually non-existent. (Or, perhaps more accurately stated, it exists but is subdued and only voices opposition 'when asked', as with the rejection of the EU constitution in 2005.)[57] There are many characteristics of advanced capitalism which make this passivity understandable. The working population is ever more segmented by occupational diversity. Some degree of labour market regulation remains, offering protection from the full rigours of competition, while social welfare programmes for the vast bulk of people continue. Liberal democracy allows policy adjustments to occur in the face of the most serious discomforts, and most of people live exceedingly privatised lives in conditions of affluence. The organisations of the historic labour movement are in tatters, formerly radical parties have been neoliberalised, and previously autonomous institutions of civil society – universities, churches, professional associations and the media – have been subordinated to the discipline of the market.[58]

This provides the backdrop for two literatures of 'endism', the 'end of history' and the 'death of class', both of which represent neoliberalism as a terminal point in modern history.[59] They are most certainly premature. On present trends, mass opposition to neoliberalism from within advanced capitalist societies will surely be provoked from a source additional to those already discussed in previous sections of this chapter.

Since the mid-1970s, income inequality has increased in virtually all advanced capitalist societies. It has been most dramatic in the United States, but only France appears to be wholly exempt from the trend.[60] The underlying changes are all intimately related to neoliberalism: lessened constraints upon corporate executive remuneration,[61] the decline of unions and the deregulation of the labour market,[62] an increase in the share of profits in national income and a corresponding fall in the wage share,[63] a skill bias in technical progress[64] and the effects of increased international trade and capital flows. Since it is these forces of globalisation which are most amenable to political intervention, we turn to examine them in more detail.

According to traditional international economics, some increase in inequality within the advanced capitalist economies is to be expected from international trade.[65] Countries will specialise where they have comparative advantage, which is determined by the factors of production of which they have a relative abundance. Advanced capitalist countries are well-endowed with capital, including human capital (skilled labour), whereas countries of the South have abundant unskilled labour. Thus, with globalisation, traditional trade theory predicts that the rich countries will specialise in capital-intensive and skill-intensive products, while the poor countries will specialise in labour-intensive products. One distributional effect of this will be that the lower-skilled workers in advanced capitalist countries will face reduced wages compared to the levels that would have prevailed in the absence of globalisation. The orthodox theory of international trade does not venture far into politics,[66] but since the unskilled workers in capitalism are relatively less powerful politically, the interests in favour of protectionism will be weak compared to the contrary interests of the skilled workers and owners of capital who gain from increased trade.

However, as is now well known, traditional trade theory is incomplete, misleading and empirically false, with the result that the adverse distributional impacts of globalisation within advanced capitalist societies will not be confined to the least skilled, and can in consequence be more politically significant. Factor flows occur as well as trade flows, and many countries of the South are now large net recipients of foreign direct investment from advanced capitalist countries, increasing the capital endowment in poor countries and reducing it in the rich countries. In addition, many production activities have military implications, so the capital-intensity and skill-intensity levels of these sectors will be raised within poor states that face security threats, through state-induced forced savings and investments in education.[67] This means that some of their exports to advanced capitalist economies will be directly rivalrous with those in the comparative advantage of the rich countries and will have a depressing effect on wage levels well beyond those of the low-skilled. There are also purely economic reasons associated with indivisibilities and network effects which imply that the techniques of production adopted by poor countries will be closer to those of the rich countries in some activities than traditional trade theory recognises, again posing a more general threat to living standards of the working population in advanced capitalism.[68]

It is not possible to determine precisely how large in aggregate these effects will be in the future. But the integration of China and India into the world economy has brought a 40% increase in the global labour force, and their rapid rates of economic growth suggest that the effects will be far from marginal. This conclusion is buttressed by the implications of information technology, which has significantly expanded the range of tradable commodities. Any information that can be digitised can have associated tasks outsourced internationally. This includes software programming, engineering design, legal opinions, medical diagnostics and accounting, all of which presently involve relatively well-paid occupations in advanced capitalism.[69] Thus, before too long, large sections of the middle class and labour aristocracy are going to experience neoliberalism in a much less pleasant form than they have done hitherto.

There is a public policy response to this issue which runs somewhat with the grain of neoliberalism: namely, expanding welfare state programmes in a way that provides further support for the needs of the market while simultaneously neutralising the threat of opposition to globalisation. The most obvious manner in which this could be achieved would be to emulate the 'active labour market' policies of the Scandinavian countries by extending more generous support for displaced workers through expanded unemployment benefits coupled to heavily subsidised retraining programmes and relocation schemes. But even this would involve an increase in taxation and a transfer of income from the 'winners' to the 'losers' in a counter-trend towards increasing inequality. And it may very well be insufficient. After all, the problem of globalisation is not only lost jobs for workers in advanced capitalist economies, but also lower wage rates, and active labour market policies do not address this dimension of the problem. Since all advanced capitalist systems are democracies, there is thus the real possibility that welfare state expansion may turn towards more radical redistribution, and to measures that clearly run against the grain of neoliberalism by expanding the universalistic rights of citizenship.

This response might very well be joined to an increase in national or regional protectionism, through the restriction of imports from poor countries, raising impediments to international outsourcing and the curtailment of capital exports. This is even more at variance with neoliberalism, and especially so because it would likely spread into measures that counter neoliberalism *within* advanced capitalist economies, and not be confined to international economic relations. Limiting capital exports would necessarily mean increased monitoring and regulation of finance. The reduction in competition would encourage a more activist stance against the market power of corporations. There would also be improved incentives for union organisation to expand, as the threat of moving production offshore would be weakened and there would be more profits that could be captured through wage bargaining. Indeed, organised labour might even be supported by state authorities which, in the face of declining market discipline, sought to promote alternative corporatist arrangements in order to deal with the problem of corporate governance and macroeconomic management.

There are, however, several huge dangers in the resort to protectionism. Obviously, there would be retaliation and the increased chance of trade wars. Moreover, any trade war might be the precursor of real war, analogous to the way in which limitations on international economic relations in the 1930s fostered inter-state conflicts. This is by no means a remote possibility. Today, as then, there are several other factors at work undermining state cooperation beyond those we have discussed in this section and in Sections 8.4 and 8.5, and these can have their own deliberalising effects.

8.7 War

In the twentieth century wars had a huge impact, eliminating market relations and delaying neoliberalism in advanced capitalism. But they were very specific types of war, involving industrialised great powers, which made enormous resource demands, and required extensive command planning and large conscripted military forces. The world market was fragmented and the productivity levels of national capitalist economies had diverged significantly by the time of peace in 1945, resulting in the construction of 'catch-up' models that entailed a great deal of market suppression until convergence was achieved.[70] Some of the deliberalising social and political effects of these wars and their aftermath are also still with us in the form of citizenship entitlements, and therefore will not be re-enacted with the onset of new wars.

Wars like World Wars I and II will not recur. Military technology has been revolutionised with the invention of nuclear weapons, information technologies, precision-guided munitions and the professionalisation of military forces. Of course, wars are very unlikely to cease, because they are integral to attaining security and political domination in a context of multiple states, especially where the productive forces require ever larger spheres of unimpeded operation for their efficient utilisation. But future wars will be very different, and any deliberalising effects are unlikely to match those of the great conflicts during the twentieth century. They could be more or less radical, depending on the types of war that do occur.

At one extreme would be wars involving the large-scale use of nuclear weapons. One version could stem from hegemonic challenges to the United States, most obviously from China, but also possibly involving a reinvigorated Russia, or even a transformed and centralised EU.[71] Another version could occur as a consequence of waning American power resulting in nuclear proliferation and thus a heightened chance of nuclear wars throughout the globe. But even with no more proliferation, or a very limited proliferation, there would be openings for nuclear war not directly involving the United States. Least surprising would be a war between India and Pakistan, or between China and Taiwan. But a nuclear war between China and Russia, or China and Japan, would not be much more of a surprise. In all cases the effects would be devastating. Nothing would remain unaffected, if only because of the disastrous environmental effects of many nuclear explosions.[72] Reversals of neoliberalism would likely occur on a broad front and, equally likely, would be a very long way down the list of concerns of most people, irrespective of whether they were enthusiasts or opponents of neoliberalism.

How probable such conflicts are is unknowable. Wars have been a regular occurrence in the past, but the sheer destructiveness of nuclear weaponry is a change of such significance that it may wholly disrupt historical patterns. From one perspective the existence of several heavily armed nuclear powers destroys the rationale for war because any sensible notion of victory seems impossible to achieve. Thus nuclear weapons make war non-Clausewitzian and eliminate it as a rational political option.[73] But, from another perspective, 'there are no ultimate weapons'[74] and the basis for warfare remains essentially unchanged.[75] Moreover, the 'thinking' of neoconservatives associated with the Bush Administration in the early twenty-first century is a reminder that rationality, and even a minimal attachment to reality, can fail.[76]

At the other extreme are wars in which the military forces of advanced capitalist states are limited to 'surgical strikes' at enemy bases in 'failed states' or 'rogue states' through the use of air power and special forces, with most of the 'boots on the ground' tasks undertaken through the use of military power drawn from outside the advanced capitalist states. This was the type of warfare employed in Afghanistan immediately after the 9/11 attacks on the United States. It was also used against Islamic forces in Somalia early in 2007, where Ethiopian troops did most of the ground fighting. American military power was limited to air strikes, a naval blockade and the use of special forces. But those are just two examples of this 'limited' type of warfare, which has a long history.[77] It is likely to continue in the future, and, equally likely, will have no discernable effect upon neoliberalism in advanced capitalism.

Between these two extremes there are types of warfare which could have a limited but significant deliberalising effect. Most obviously this would be true of wars involving advanced capitalist states undertaking large-scale and enduring occupations of other countries' territory in order to re-engineer their societies in a way that eliminates the basis for anti-Western terrorism.[78] The extensive use of military forces other than those of advanced capitalist countries would not be feasible, because detailed control of the reconstruction would be required. And, if coupled with an 'enemy within' phenomenon where terrorist attacks occur inside advanced capitalist societies, this type of warfare could erode neoliberalism quite markedly.[79] Not only would conscription and heavy taxation be required for fighting abroad, with a resultant boost to entitlements stemming from the rights of nationality trumping those of private property and consumer choice, but the increased transactions costs of using markets within advanced capitalism would tend to erode these markets.

This scenario is the most probable way in which future wars might reverse neoliberalism in advanced capitalism, at least during the next few decades during which US hegemony cannot be seriously challenged. But the scenario itself is not very likely to materialise. The second Iraq war beginning in 2003 has been a sobering experience for all who entertained notions of dealing with terroristic enemies of 'the West' by rapidly Westernising the world from which they emerge. When wars occur they are much more likely to be of the 'surgical strike-subcontracting ground forces' variety. And the effect of these wars on neoliberalism, even if there are very many of them happening simultaneously, will in all probability be minimal.

8.8 The most likely sequence of reversals: immediate, intermediate and long-term

The greatest immediate threat to neoliberalism in advanced capitalism is a serious financial crisis. But it is also a continuing danger as long as neoliberal deregulation remains in place. Unless heavily repressed, capitalist finance is especially prone to generating crises. And if they occur, there will be a renewed wave of deliberalising regulation of finance. This could well be followed by complementary changes in the rest of the economy because of the infrastructural nature of finance. However, whether or not a new institutional equilibrium emerges is another matter. If financial stability returns and memories of the crises fade, or memories are reframed to portray the damage done by crises as less than it actually has been, there will be fresh set of neoliberal changes. There is a cyclical element in all this: as we have stressed in Section 8.2, in normal circumstances there is a disposition towards excess in neoliberal capitalism, and the excesses are often centred in finance.

The strongest threat to neoliberal capitalism in the intermediate term is protectionism designed to limit global competition from less-developed capitalist countries. However, it too is a continuing threat. If it fails to materialise during the next couple of decades, the causes promoting it are likely to remain in place, and whenever it does emerge the deliberalising effects will not be limited to the international sector (as we have explained in Section 8.6). The alternative policy of expanding the welfare state in advanced capitalism to engineer a significant redistribution through subsidising those whose incomes are under pressure would provoke more opposition than would protectionism. The costs of protectionism are more easily hidden, the 'national' character of democracy facilitates its implementation, and mythologies of personal identities centred on individual independence are more easily preserved with protectionism than they are with government transfers.

In the long run, stretching throughout the bulk of the twenty-first century, the really serious threat to neoliberalism appears to come from global warming. No doubt, there will be agreements made between political authorities to limit their greenhouse gas emissions and, equally without doubt, collective action problems will ensure that they are inadequate. So it can be expected that alternative modes of coordination to that provided by markets have an auspicious future. The catastrophes which underpin this deliberalisation may also bring about more dramatic attempts to reverse global warming, but then it will be too late for them to have a significant impact in much less than a century or two. And, in this case, the effects of past warming and strengthened attempts to curtail it may combine to intensify market elimination beyond what would have occurred if appropriate corrective policies had been in place from the beginning.

The most disastrous form of neoliberal reversal – a return of large-scale warfare carried out with the latest vintage of weaponry – is very difficult to assess in terms of likelihood. Wars have been endemic in the past, but the new military technologies may well have transformed the generating causal structure. There is also huge uncertainty surrounding the most benign form of reversal – a new wave of market-eliminating technical progress. Historically, general-purpose technologies have changed frequently, but future alterations in their market-promoting or market-eliminating biases are impossible to forecast. Such properties rest upon new knowledge which, by definition, cannot be known in advance. Overall, then, the extremes are least predictable, but the three forces of the middle – financial crises, protectionism and global warming – could prove to be very significant in curtailing markets, especially if they interact and reinforce each other.

Notes

Introduction

1. Anderson (2000), p.17.
2. The advanced capitalist economies include those of North America above the Mexican border, Western Europe, Scandinavia, Japan and Australasia. See Klein (2007) for an account of neoliberalism elsewhere.
3. Marx (1867), pp.8–9.
4. Arblaster (1984); Conway (1995); Marshall (1950).
5. Mann (1993); Tilly (1990); Searle (1999).
6. See Table 2.2 in Section 2.5 of Chapter 2.
7. See Chapter 2, Section 2.3.
8. Perkin (1989); Readings (1997); Suleiman (2003).
9. Vogel (1996).
10. This is frequently referred to as 'deregulation'. Despite the obvious inaccuracy of the terminology, it would be pedantic to avoid using it.
11. Hobsbawm (1994).
12. See Chapter 7.
13. Glyn (2001); Przeworski (1985); Przeworski and Sprague (1987); Sassoon (1997).
14. Gilmour (1992); Holmes (1993); Muller (1997).
15. See Chapter 2, Section 2.6.
16. Anderson (2000).
17. See also Rosenberg (2000).
18. See Chapter 7. Another term for 'positive feedback' is 'cumulative causation' (see Kaldor (1996) and Myrdal (1957)), and the basic idea is the opposite of diminishing returns: the expansion of an activity creates feedback that promotes itself rather than inducing dampening effects on further expansion.
19. Glyn (2001) and (2006); Sassoon (1996) and (1997).
20. See Bardhan and Roemer (1993); Douglas (1993); and Giddens (1994) and (2000). See also Lukes (2003) cited in Ball and Bellamy (2003).
21. Carling (2006); Esping-Anderson (1990); Howard and King (1985), pp.16–25. See also Chapter 8, Section 8.6. However, Marxists have been unique in recognising that the elimination of markets, if it is to be sustained, requires a material foundation. See Chapter 3, and Howard and King (1994).
22. Scruton (1990) and (1991). See also Bell (1968), MacIntyre (1985) and Muller (1997) and (2002).
23. Arrow and Hahn (1971); Stiglitz (1994).
24. Clower (1965), cited in Hahn and Brechling (1965); Leijonhuvud (1968).
25. King (2002).
26. See Chapter 2, Section 2.2; Chapter 7 and Chapter 8, Section 8.5.

27. See Chapter 8, Section 8.5.
28. Our position is similar to that of Foucault in relation to Nietzsche. 'I prefer to utilise the writers I like. The only valid tribute to thought such as Nietzche's is precisely to use it, to deform it, to make it groan and protest. And if commentators then say that I am being faithful or unfaithful to Nietzsche, that is of absolutely no importance' Foucault (1980), pp.53–4.
29. Armstrong *et al.* (1991); Brenner (1998); Duménil and Lévy (2004a); Glyn (2006); Kotz (2003); Overbeek (1993).
30. Gamble (1988); Eichengreen (2007), chapter 9.
31. The orthodox version of the same theory in Olson (1982) suffers from similar problems and, moreover, provides no mechanism through which neoliberal measures could actually be implemented. Olson deals with the sclerosis induced by interest groups successfully exercising influence on governments to redistribute income in their favour, but he neglects to explain what could reverse the process and rejuvenate economic growth. The same deficiency is evident in the work of the Chicago school of economics and the Virginia school of political economy, who are often credited with anticipating neoliberalism. In actual fact they fashioned theories of regulatory capture and rent-seeking behaviour, which induce economic stagnation in the same way as Olson claims, but they too provide no account of the mechanism that can reverse this by restructuring incentives for people to produce wealth rather than using their resources to induce governments to redistribute it. See also Chapter 4, Section 4.7.
32. The best account is that of Gowan (1999). See also Helleiner (1994).
33. See, for example, Bourdieu (1998); George (1999) and Therborn (2001).
34. See Chapter 1, Section 1.1 and Chapter 2, Section 2.2. The materialism we adopt to explain neoliberalism is often classified as structuralist and determinist, and thereby as devaluing human agency in the historical process. Those who make these charges typically do not provide convincing reasons to justify their belief that history really is 'open', which is a very different matter from accepting that people themselves make choices. There are good grounds for believing that human agency can have important historical effects, but only in special circumstances where decision-makers wield enormous power, or where crises open up various trajectories of change analogous to switch points on a railway line. See the classic texts of Mills (1959) and Weber (1946), p.280.
35. Of course, there were economists who stood apart from the main schools of thought. So far as influencing the onset of neoliberalism is concerned, Milton Friedman and Friedrich von Hayek are usually regarded as most important. However, as we show in Chapter 4, Hayek believed that advanced capitalism exhibited tendencies of market elimination. Moreover, until the late 1960s, both Friedman and Hayek, along with many other libertarians of the Right, such as Ludwig von Mises, were widely regarded as cranks within the economics profession. They were most certainly closer to classical liberalism than to neoliberalism, and many of their ideas still seem 'cranky' in the neoliberal age. Also see note 31 above.
36. Hobsbawm (1994).

1 A general theory of economic systems

1. Broadie (1997); Macfarlane (2000); Meek (1973), (1976).
2. Howard and King (1989), Chapters 5, 12 and 13.
3. Blackledge and Kirkpatrick (2002); Bertram (1990); Carling (2004), (2006); Gellner (1980a); Semenov (1980), cited in Gellner (1980b).
4. Löwry (1996); Sayer (1991).
5. The pathbreaking work here is Cohen (1978). See also Cohen (1988).
6. As is done, for example, by Winch (1958) and Sahlins (1995).
7. As is attempted to some extent in Braudel (1981), (1982), (1984); in Weber (1978), (1981); in Mann (1986), (1993); in Gellner (1988) and in Hicks (1969).
8. Marx makes this point in Marx (1867), p.82.
9. See, for example, Cohen (1995), (2000) and also Carling (2006).
10. Cohen (1988), chapter XI; Eagleton (1996).
11. This phrase is the title of Tilly (1984).
12. Historical materialists do not maintain that all historical events have been inevitable, as we have explained. What they do claim is that the increase in productive power, the enlargement of pacified areas of the world, the expansion of human interactions and the decline in heterogeneity are not contingent features of the historical process, but 'had to occur', given the way that human beings and their environment are constituted. They also claim that factors limiting the development of productive power, insofar as they are amenable to alteration through human actions, will tend to succumb to mechanisms of change that will eliminate the inhibiting factors.
13. There are good reasons for scepticism, since human nature is not directly observable and has to be inferred from human actions or from experiments or from introspection. At the same time, what is deemed to be human nature carries huge implications for social and ethical theory. Not surprisingly, then, there have been very different descriptions of what constitutes its central characteristics. See, for example, Lopson (2001); Pinker (2002); Stevenson and Haberman (1998); Stevenson (2000) and Trigg (1999). However, our argument for historical materialism in terms of human nature does not involve the more contentious issues; for example, see Section 1.2 below.
14. See, for example, Mills (1962).
15. Marx (1859), pp.20–1.
16. Cohen (1978), pp.32, 45, 55.
17. Cohen (1978), pp.63–6.
18. Cohen (1978), pp.216–17.
19. Cohen (1978), pp.45–7; Mills (1989); Taylor (1966); Torrance (1995). See also Chapter 2, Section 2.2.
20. For a succinct account of what is required for action to be fully rational, see Elster (1985) See also Hargreaves Heap and Varoufakis (1995) and Rubinstein (1998).
21. Cohen (1978), chapter IV.
22. In other formulations of the principles of historical materialism some characteristics attributed to human nature would not be generally accepted. For example, Marx seems to have believed that human acquisitiveness would be pronounced only in conditions of abject scarcity, and would begin to wither

away once a moderately sophisticated level of technological development had been accomplished.

23. Károly Takács (2002), p.3, tells the following story, 'I passed by a graffiti in the center of Budapest during the Serb-Croatian war, which claimed that "Milosevic is a pig". Under this text, there was a sagacious response also in English stating that "Human beings are the problem"...Human beings are the problem in the sense that despite the painful consequences they choose to make sacrifices for their group and participate in an action that results in intergroup conflict'.
24. There are various ways of stating the main theses of historical materialism. We choose the form most suitable for our purpose, which is to explain the development of neoliberalism in advanced capitalism.
25. Howard and King (2001a).
26. Of course, this is distressingly imprecise, but the problem is endemic to all social and economic theory that is not either purely structuralist or fully economistic. See, for example, Hargreaves Heap *et al.* (1992); Rubinstein (1998) and Williamson (1996). Perhaps the clearest example of non-optimality is the huge range of variability in the size of modern territorial states. Nonetheless, historical materialism predicts that there will be powerful forces at work promoting efficiency, and this is also evident. For example, the economies of different jurisdictions are today significantly integrated, and the efficiency losses attributable to there being separate polities resulting from historical causes that are no longer economically relevant are probably quite small. However, small or large, they create incentives for even deeper integration in order to eliminate them, just as historical materialism claims will occur with any obvious inefficiency.
27. See Chapter 2, Section 2.5.
28. See Maddison (2001), for other examples of 'setbacks' to economic development.
29. See Chapter 2, Section 2.3.
30. Cohen (1978), pp.152–3.
31. Searle (1995).
32. McNeill (1982). To recognise that the productive forces have developed as a consequence of military activities is no refutation of historical materialism, which claims that the productive forces tend to develop, not that they do so only for economic reasons.
33. Tilly (1985), cited in Evans *et al.* (1985); Olson (2000). References to 'rates of return' are of course metaphorical and are used here only for brevity.
34. See Schelling (1978). The term 'bootstrap' comes from the expression 'to pull oneself up by one's own bootstraps', and it points to situations where decision-makers' expectations are self-fulfilling, and so cause the phenomena that were expected in the first place. The most eminent economist who tended to view the economy as exhibiting marked bootstrap characteristics was John Maynard Keynes, and the most prominent bootstrap theory within the social sciences is Realist international relations theory.
35. Howard and King (1985), chapter 14.
36. Aston and Philpin (1985); Brenner (1986).
37. A 'low-level equilibrium trap' occurs when the incentives people face lead them to act in ways that preserve the existing situation, even though

alternative arrangements that would develop the productive forces at a faster rate are feasible.

38. Davis (2003).
39. Fukuyama (1992), part III.
40. Of course, all this might change as a result of technical progress itself. Mind-altering drugs and genetic engineering seem to carry the threat of being able to modify human nature to such an extent that slavery is no longer anachronistic because it fetters the development of the productive forces. See Fukuyama (2002).
41. See Chapter 2, Section 2.2.
42. See Chapter 2, Section 2.2.
43. See Chapter 2, Section 2.2.
44. See Chapter 2, Section 2.2.
45. See Maddison (2001), pp.44–52.
46. Marx (1894), p.794.
47. Dobb (1964); Hilton (1976); Aston and Philpin (1985).
48. Cohen (1978), pp.158–9.
49. The uniqueness thesis applies only to 'types' of production relations, superstructures and social consciousness. It does not claim that there are no variations within types, which would be absurd. The uniqueness thesis is thus compatible with the existence of 'path dependency' because it can occur without changing the 'type' of economic system that prevails.
50. Carling (2004), p.77.
51. Crone (2003); Gellner (1988); Diamond (1997).
52. See Chapter 2, Sections 2.2, 2.5 and 2.6. See also Hirschman (1991).
53. Carling (1991), Part 1.
54. See Chapter 2, Section 2.3.
55. Olson (1965); Howard and King (2001a).
56. Blackburn (1990); Diamond (1997); Carling and Nolan (2000); Greenfeld (2001).
57. Bertram (1990); Carling (1993); Carling and Nolan (2000).
58. Bhagwati (1991), part II.
59. Kindleberger (1987).
60. Casal (1994) cited in Bertram and Chitty (1994); Dyer (2005), Chapter 5; McNeill (1982).
61. This is not to say that all anthropologists and literary theorists, or even a majority of them, are cultural determinists.
62. Maddison (2001), p.28. See also Fogel (2004) and Warsh (2006), chapter 24.
63. Fukuyama (2002).
64. Mann (2004), p.523.

2 A theory of capitalist economic systems

1. Marx (1867), p.486. This description of pre-capitalist systems as 'essentially conservative' does not imply that development of the productive forces was absent, nor that any improvement would be rolled back. What Marx's statement does highlight is that pre-capitalist relations of production were not well suited to generating vigorous growth, but were more effective in

preserving the fruits of what growth had already occurred, whether as a result of a systematic tendency to develop the productive forces or for other reasons. Given the precariousness of human survival prior to modern times, this was the central imperative and an immense achievement in the face of the hugely destructive forces present in the natural world.

2. Screpani (2001), p.258. Chapter 1 of this book provides extensive elucidation of the points made in the quotation. See also Earl (2001); Simon (1951) and Williamson (1985).
3. Vogel (1996).
4. Williamson (1985).
5. Neoclassical economic theory, despite its concentration upon market processes, is especially open to criticism for not stressing the importance of market dependence. See Howard and King (2001a), pp.794–6. Markets are not specific to capitalism, but have existed in most pre-capitalist societies. However, capitalist markets are unique in exhibiting general market dependence, and this is crucial for the dynamism of capitalism, as we demonstrate more fully below.
6. Marx (1867), p.737.
7. Schumpeter (1934), p.126, expressed this point by saying that the 'money market is always, as it were, the headquarters of the capitalist system, from which orders go out to its individual divisions....'.
8. As we have seen, this applies to the employment relationship as well, and worker obedience is there the critical mechanism supplementing the market. And all three examples explain why it is misleading to describe capitalism as 'the market system'. For elucidation as to why markets can never be comprehensive, see Stiglitz (1994) and Molho (1997). See also Eichengreen (2007), who explains why specific types of non-market institutions and state interventions are needed for rapid 'catch-up' growth.
9. Smith (1776), Book IV, Chapter 9. The neoclassical definition of a pure public good is a good that is non-rivalrous in utilisation and not subject to exclusion in provision.
10. Pierson (1999); Wetherly (2005).
11. States foster both individualism and nationalism via the organisations under their jurisdiction, such as schools, universities, the military and the mass media.
12. Crone (2003); Gellner (1988); Tawney (1926). The importance of religion in capitalist societies may be disputed. This is particularly so for modern America, where over 80% of the population declare themselves to be religious, and nearly 40% are evangelical Christians evincing a belief in the infallibility of the Bible. But, for the issues of concern to historical materialism, all that we have said applies to the United States as much as other advanced capitalisms. The brute facts are that Christian fundamentalists have usually not sought to change relations of production, superstructures or social consciousness in ways that impeded the development of the productive forces, and where they have tried to change them in a dysfunctional way they have been largely unsuccessful.
13. See Chapter 1, Section 1.1.
14. Howard and King (2001a); Geuss (2001); MacPherson (1962).
15. MacHardy (2003); Mann (1986), (1993); Marshall (1950).

16. Gellner (1983); Mann (2005).
17. Mann (2005), pp.59–60.
18. Collins (1982); Macfarlane (2000).
19. Schumpeter (1942).
20. Moore (1966); Sen (1995).
21. Olson (1982).
22. Wilensky (2002), pp.61–2, 234–41, argues that Christian Democracy has been as important as Social Democracy in creating and sustaining Western European welfare states.
23. Acemoglu and Robinson (2006); Sunstain 2003.
24. Gellner (1983).
25. Mills (1948); Przeworski (1985).
26. See Cohen (1978), pp.329–38, for a discussion of 'use fettering'.
27. This was a central point of Lenin's *Imperialism* (1916) and the fact that this work can be legitimately criticised on other arguments it makes does not detract from the accuracy with which it specified this particular problem.
28. Fischer (1967); Fromkin (2004); Mearsheimer (2001); Stevenson (2004).
29. See Chapter 7, Section 7.3, for further analysis on the nature of war.
30. Of course, this may have improved the lives of many people, but that does not bear upon the point we are making.
31. This is also a problem for neoclassical growth theory, which predicts a general convergence towards the productivity levels of advanced capitalism.
32. See Chapter 1, Section 1.5.
33. See Chapter 1, Section 1.4.
34. Collier (2007).
35. Cohen *et al.* (1981); Rose-Ackerman (1999); Chua (2003).
36. See Chomsky (1991); Chang (2002) and Sørensen (2001). The disadvantage that poor countries experience as a result of protectionism in advanced capitalist economies is widely recognised by neoclassical economists. See, for example, Wolf (2004). But the international economic regime also includes other features that are damaging, such as the possibility of holding foreign bank accounts and marketing raw materials with 'no questions asked'. Both contribute to corruption and violence in the periphery.
37. Howard and King (1992), part III, and Howard and King (1999), cited in Chilcote (1999).
38. This has occurred in the past; see Diamond (2005).
39. See, for example, Ferguson (2004), (2005); Mann (2003) and Section 8.7 of Chapter 8.
40. Williamson (1985).
41. Baudrillard (1970), pp.viif and 93f; Moore (1998), pp.71–81; Runciman (2006).
42. On average about half of government expenditure is on redistributive transfers and about half on government consumption and investment. See Tanzi and Schuknecht (2000), p.31.
43. Vogel (1996).
44. Tanzi and Schuknect (2000), pp.6–7.
45. Moore (1966); Gerschenkron (1966); Greenfeld (2001); Mann (1993); Streeck and Yamamura (2001); Wilensky (2002), pp.116–25.
46. For a good review of this literature, see Howell (2003).

47. Dore (2000); Milgrom and Roberts (1992).
48. The Japanese firm thus sacrifices *numerical* flexibility in exchange for *functional* flexibility, securing *wage* flexibility through the annual bonus component of the employees' pay. US firms, by contrast, tend to sacrifice wage flexibility (through an implicit contract preventing them from cutting money wages in adverse business conditions) in exchange for functional flexibility and a higher degree of numerical flexibility than the typical large Japanese firm is able to obtain. See Bewley (1999); Bray *et al.* (2005), Chapter 2; Dore (2000); Milgrom and Roberts (1992); Kalleberg (2001); Olson (1982) and Wilensky (2002).
49. Chang (1994), (2002); Evans (1995); Johnson (1982), (1984).
50. Anon. (2004); Eichengreen (2007), pp.18–19, 381, 398–406.
51. Chang (2002); Weiss and Hobson (1995).
52. Dore (2000); Krugman (1997); Yamamura and Streeck (2003). Likewise in France; see Eichengreen (2007).
53. Chang (1994).
54. Scott (1997).
55. Acheson (1969); Harrop (1992).
56. See Chapter 6, Section 6.3.
57. Gordon *et al.* (1982).
58. Dunning and Boyd (2003); Rugman and Boyd (2003).
59. Grahl (2001); Howell (2003); Pain and Welsum (2003); Spong (2003); Vogel (1996); Yamamura and Streeck (2003). We return to discuss this matter in Chapter 7. What is now called the European Union took this name only in 1993. Between 1967 and 1993 it was known as the European Community (EC) and before that, from 1958 to 1967, as the European Economic Community (EEC) or Common Market. In this book, we ignore these changes and always use the term EU.
60. Siebert (2005); Howell (2003).
61. This is admitted even by Wilensky (2002). See also Dore (2000).
62. Suleiman (2003), chapter 5.
63. Dore (2000); Evans (1995); Eichengreen (2007).
64. Rosenberg (2000).
65. Ostry (1997).
66. The neoliberal effects of globalisation actually cut both ways. Not only does integration into the world market set up pressures to harmonise institutions, but those institutions that have been specific to European and Asian capitalisms in the postwar years have rested upon bargains and practices between national groups, and been secured by national states, so they are not easily duplicated elsewhere. By contrast, the institutions and practices promoting markets are relatively easily duplicatable in all advanced capitalist economies. See, for example, Grahl (2001); Przeworski (1985); Streeck and Yamamura (2001) and Yamamura and Streeck (2003).
67. See especially Chapter 6.
68. Gellner (1994) is very good in describing this.
69. Bourdieu (1984); Baudrillard (1970).
70. Wilensky (2002), Chapter 1.
71. It is often difficult to assess the exact degree of change, since it may occur in substance but not in form. For example, Yamamura and Streeck (2003)

write of German codetermination as follows. 'German codetermination ... is highly unlikely to disappear as an institution in any foreseeable future. But ... it may be undergoing a transformation from a general legal right of industrial citizenship into an economically expedient device to improve a firm's competitiveness, differently organised in different work places to fit specific technological and market requirements and based more on contractual arrangements than on the traditional, public constitution of the workplace' (p.43).

72. See, for example, Emmott (2005).

3 Marx and the marxists on the decline of the market

1. Friedman (2005).
2. Hobsbawm (1998).
3. Howard and King (1989), chapters 4, 5, 13, 16; (1992), chapters 1, 4.
4. Brenner (1989), p.285.
5. Brenner (1989), p.292; see also Brenner (1978).
6. Marx and Engels (1845), p.57.
7. Marx and Engels (1845), p.60.
8. Marx and Engels (1845), p.81.
9. Marx and Engels (1845), p.82.
10. Marx and Engels (1848), pp.109–10, cited in Marx and Engels (1973a).
11. Marx and Engels (1848), pp.110,112.
12. Marx and Engels (1848), p.112.
13. Marx and Engels (1848), p.114.
14. Marx and Engels (1848), p.119.
15. Hobsbawm (1998), pp.16, 18.
16. Oakley (1984), p.128; original emphasis.
17. Hobsbawm (1998), p.13; 'communist Smithian' would be a much better description.
18. Hobsbawn (1998), p.22.
19. Marx (1844), p.83.
20. Marx (1844), pp.84–5.
21. Marx (1844), p.85.
22. Engels (1844), p.213.
23. Engels (1844), p.223.
24. Oakley (1984), p.33.
25. Marx (1859), p.21. See also Chapter 1, Section 1.2, for another quotation from this Preface.
26. Dobb (1971), pp.5–6.
27. Marx (1894), pp.332–3.
28. Sweezy (1968).
29. Marx (1867), p.349; cf. Babbage (1832), pp.172–3.
30. Marx (1867), pp.625–6. Marx's concepts of constant and variable capital derive from his value theory, which is not logically related to his argument about the nature of technical progress. In this context, there is no distortion of meaning in translating 'constant capital' into 'capital' and 'variable capital' into 'labour'. A rising constant capital relative to variable capital, then, refers to a process of capital deepening. Marx also sometimes refers to the ratio

of constant capital to variable capital as the 'organic composition of capital' but, again, it can be translated without distortion into 'capital per worker'. Thus a rising 'organic composition of capital' would be synonymous with capital deepening.

31. Marx and Engels (1848), p.126.
32. Marx (1872), p.290.
33. Marx (1867), p.626.
34. Marx (1894), pp.79–80.
35. Marx (1894), p.241. Also see note 30 above.
36. Marx (1894), p.246.
37. Marx (1867), pp.626–7.
38. Marx (1885), p.110.
39. Marx (1885), p.239.
40. Marx (1894), pp.439–40.
41. Marx (1894), p.607. In this context, the term 'associated labour' can be understood to mean 'socialism'.
42. Marx (1894), p.386.
43. Marx (1894), pp.387–8.
44. Marx (1894), p.437.
45. Marx (1894), p.440.
46. Marx to Engels 29 March 1858, cited by Oakley (1983), p.67.
47. Marx and Engels (1973c), pp.431–2; original emphasis.
48. Marx (1894), p.120.
49. Marx (1894), p.120n.
50. Marx (1894), p.438.
51. Marx and Engels (1973c), pp.143, 151; original stress.
52. Marx and Engels (1973c), p.144.
53. Marx and Engels (1973c), p.145.
54. Marx (1867), pp.264–5.
55. Marx (1867), p.265.
56. Marx (1867), p.270.
57. Marx (1867), p.266.
58. Marx (1867), p.299.
59. Marx and Engels (1973b), p.16.
60. Marx and Engels (1973c), p.441.
61. Marx and Engels (1973c), p.441.
62. Marx (1867), p.490.
63. Marx (1867), p.503.
64. Marx (1857), pp.157–8.
65. Marx and Engels (1973b), p.52.
66. Marx (1857), p.158; stress added.
67. Marx (1894), p.104.
68. Cited by Draper (1978), pp.496–8.
69. Marx (1863), p.343.
70. See, for example, Webb (1916), pp.34–9.
71. Howard and King (1992, chapter 4).
72. Gay (1952), pp.107–9.
73. Bernstein (1898), p.69.
74. Bernstein (1898), p.71; original stress.

75. Bernstein (1898), p.101.
76. Bernstein (1898), p.91.
77. Bernstein (1898), p.94.
78. Bernstein (1898), pp.58, 61–2.
79. Bernstein (1898), p.86.
80. Bernstein (1898), p.87; Bernstein is quoting here from volume III of *Capital.*
81. Bernstein (1898), p.137.
82. Bernstein (1898), p.139.
83. Kautsky (1892), p.68.
84. Kautsky (1892), p.109.
85. Kautsky (1898), p.295.
86. Kautsky (1899), p.63.
87. Kautsky (1899), p.65.
88. Kautsky (1899), p.80.
89. Luxemburg (1898), p.257.
90. Luxemburg (1898), p.254.
91. Luxemburg (1898), p.259.
92. Luxemburg (1898), p.258.
93. Luxemburg (1898), p.261.
94. Luxemburg (1898), p.260.
95. Luxemburg (1898), p.262.
96. Luxemburg (1913).
97. Hilferding (1910), p.234.
98. Hilferding (1910), p.297.
99. Hilferding (1910), p.164.
100. Hilferding (1910), pp.297–8.
101. Hilferding (1910), pp.307–9.
102. Hilferding (1910), p.335.
103. Hilferding (1910), p.180.
104. Hilferding (1910), p.180.
105. Hilferding (1910), p.196.
106. Hilferding (1910), p.235.
107. Hilferding (1910), pp.367–8.
108. Bukharin (1915), p.27.
109. Bukharin (1915), p.54.
110. Bukharin (1915), p.61.
111. Bukharin (1915), p.65.
112. Bukharin (1915), p.70.
113. Bukharin (1915), pp.73–4; original stress removed.
114. Bukharin (1915), p.74.
115. Bukharin (1915), p.80.
116. Bukharin (1915), p.103.
117. Bukharin (1915), p.115.
118. Bukharin (1915), p.145.
119. Bukharin (1915), p.148.
120. Bukharin (1915), p.155.
121. Bukharin (1915), p.155.
122. Hilferding (1915), p.22.
123. Harding (1983), chapters 1–4; Howard and King (1989), chapters 11 and 13.

124. Howard and King (2003).
125. Cohen (1974).
126. Howard and King (1989), chapter 16.
127. Kautsky (1919), p.146.
128. Howard and King (1989), chapters 12 and 13.
129. Howard and King (2001b).
130. Dunayevskaya (1941), unpaginated; original stress.
131. Dunayevskaya (1944), (1945); Baran (1944); Lange (1945).
132. Mattick (1939), p.81; original stress deleted.
133. Pollock (1932).
134. Pollock (1933), p.347.
135. Pollock (1933), p.351.
136. Pollock (1933), p.350.
137. Baumann (1936), pp.402–3.
138. Schefold (1980).
139. Hilferding (1940), p.266.
140. Djilas (1957), p.122.
141. Marcuse (1942). See also Marcuse (1958).
142. Burnham (1941), p.237.
143. Burnham (1941), p.232.
144. Burnham (1941), p.166.
145. Burnham (1941), p.17.
146. Burnham (1941), p.18.
147. Burnham (1941), p.200.
148. Burnham (1941), p.198.
149. Burnham (1941), p.64.
150. Burnham (1941), pp.93–4.
151. Burnham (1941), p.94.
152. Burnham (1941), p.217.
153. Burnham (1941), p.72.
154. Burnham (1941), p.114.
155. Burnham (1941), p.108.
156. Pollock (1941), p.72.
157. Pollock (1941), pp.72–3.
158. Pollock (1941), p.73.
159. Pollock (1941), p.73.
160. Pollock (1941), p.78.
161. Pollock (1941), pp.86–7.
162. Burnham (1941), pp.146–7.
163. Pollock (1941), pp.89–90.
164. Baran and Sweezy (1966); cf. Howard and King (1992, chapter 6).
165. Aglietta (1979), p.385.

4 Neoclassicals, Keynesians and Heterodox economists on the decline of the market

1. Grundman and Stehr (2004).
2. Fischer (1989), p.47.

3. Hayek (1944), p.135.
4. Hayek (1944), pp.144–6.
5. Hayek (1944), pp.151–3.
6. Hayek (1944), p.148.
7. Hayek (1944), p.32.
8. Hayek (1944), p.34.
9. Hayek (1944), pp.40–1. Hayek nowhere explains how the wars then currently raging between the great powers could be fought on the basis of market coordination. See Chapter 7, Section 7.3, below.
10. Hayek (1944), p.3.
11. Hayek (1944), p.35.
12. Schumpeter (1942), p.61.
13. Bottomore (1992), p.9.
14. Swedberg (1991), pp.169–70.
15. Rothschild (1981), p.114.
16. Bottomore (1992), pp.33–4 points to similar prognostications in Schumpeter's writing as early as 1911. But see also Heertje (2006).
17. Schumpeter (1928), p.384.
18. Schumpeter (1928), p.385.
19. Schumpeter (1928), pp.385–6.
20. Schumpeter (1942), p.131.
21. Schumpeter (1942), p.132.
22. Schumpeter (1942), p.133.
23. Schumpeter (1942), p.134.
24. Schumpeter (1942), p.139.
25. Schumpeter (1942), pp.141–2.
26. Schumpeter (1942), p.142.
27. Schumpeter (1942), p.121; original stress.
28. Schumpeter (1942), p.123.
29. Schumpeter (1942), p.127.
30. Schumpeter (1942), pp.143, 153. A very similar argument was made by Selig Perlman (1928) in his book *A Theory of the Labor Movement*, suggesting an – unacknowledged institutionalist influence on Schumpeter, at least on this issue.
31. Schumpeter (1942), p.143.
32. Schumpeter (1942), pp.156–7.
33. Schumpeter (1942), p.161; original stress. See also Bell (1976).
34. Schumpeter (1942), p.162; original stress.
35. For a comprehensive historical account of institutionalism, see Rutherford (1994).
36. Veblen (1904). See also Veblen (1921) and (1923).
37. See note 88 below.
38. Berle and Means (1932), p.xli.
39. Berle and Means (1932), p.7.
40. Berle and Means (1932), p.8.
41. Berle and Means (1932), p.10.
42. Berle and Means (1932), pp.45–6. It is a substantial hand, since a figure of 2000 powerful directors is cited in a footnote on p.46, n.34.
43. Berle and Means (1932), p.46.

44. Berle and Means (1932), pp.312–13.
45. Lee and Samuels (1992).
46. Means (1935a); Means (1968).
47. Solow (1997).
48. Berle (1968), p.viii.
49. Berle and Means (1968), p.xxvi.
50. Means (1968), p.xxxiii.
51. See Shultz and Aliber (1966).
52. Means (1968), p.xxxviii.
53. Dorfman (1959), pp.97–100.
54. Reagan (1999).
55. Burns (1936), p.3.
56. Burns (1936), p.245.
57. Burns (1936), p.265.
58. Burns (1936), p.266.
59. Gordon (1945), p.145.
60. Gordon (1945), p.305.
61. Gordon (1945), pp.214–21.
62. Gordon (1960).
63. Galbraith (1952), p.141; original stress.
64. Galbraith (1952), pp.214–15.
65. Galbraith (1967).
66. Galbraith (1967), p.25.
67. Galbraith (1967), pp.32–3.
68. Galbraith (1967), p.33.
69. Galbraith (1967), p.58.
70. Galbraith (1967), p.89.
71. Galbraith (1967), pp.89–90.
72. Galbraith (1967), p.104.
73. Galbraith (1967), p.111.
74. Galbraith (1967), p.158.
75. Here Galbraith endorses the 'managerial' models of the firm proposed by William Baumol and Robin Marris, which we discuss in Section 4.8 below (Galbraith 1967, p.171n.).
76. Galbraith (1967), p.190.
77. Galbraith (1967), p.197.
78. Galbraith (1967), p.251.
79. Galbraith (1967), p.260.
80. Galbraith (1967), p.315.
81. Galbraith (1967), p.316.
82. Galbraith (1967), p.394.
83. Galbraith (1967), p.397.
84. Allen (1967).
85. Meade (1968).
86. Averitt (1968).
87. Galbraith (1973).
88. Galbraith (1978), p.8. There is some controversy as to whether Galbraith's 'technostructure' resembles the 'new order' proclaimed half a century earlier

by Thorstein Veblen, who identified a profound social conflict between technicians and financiers that could well be settled in favour of the former (Leathers and Evans 1973; Evans and Leathers 1980). But Veblen's writings on this topic were confused and inconsistent (Rutherford 1980, 1981).

89. Chandler (1977), p.1.
90. Chandler (1977), p.6.
91. Chandler (1977), p.11.
92. Chandler (1977), p.493.
93. Chandler (1990), p.610.
94. Eichner (1976).
95. Marshall (1919).
96. Whitaker (2003), p.147.
97. Whitaker (2003), pp.150–1.
98. Keynes (1926), pp.288–9.
99. Keynes (1926), p.289.
100. Keynes (1926), p.289.
101. Keynes (1926), p.290.
102. Keynes (1926), p.290.
103. Keynes (1925), p.305.
104. Keynes (1936), p.378.
105. Keynes (1936), p.128.
106. Keynes (1936), p.376.
107. Kregel (1985).
108. Keynes (1936), p.164
109. Keynes (1936), p.320.
110. Keynes (1936), p.377.
111. Henry (2001).
112. Skidelsky (2000), p.273.
113. Keynes to Hayek 28 June 1944, cited by Skidelsky (2000), p.285.
114. Brady (1943), p.181.
115. Howard and King (1992), pp.94–5.
116. Kaldor *et al.* (1943); Meade (1948); Robinson (1943a).
117. Compare Wootton (1934), (1945).
118. Robinson (1943b).
119. Robinson (1942), pp.404–5; King (2004).
120. Copland (1937), p.1.
121. Macmillan (1938), p.116.
122. Macmillan (1938), pp.119–20.
123. Macmillan (1938), p.172.
124. Macmillan (1938), p.260.
125. Macmillan (1938), p.293.
126. Lekachman (1969).
127. Crosland (1956).
128. Skidelsky (1977a), p.lx.
129. Winkler (1977), p.86.
130. Keynes (1936), pp.378–9.
131. Papandreou (1972), pp. 28, 30; original stress.
132. Sraffa (1926), p.542.

133. Wootton (1938), p.129.
134. Robinson (1933), chapter 23.
135. Fellner (1949).
136. Sweezy (1939).
137. Robinson (1954), p.254.
138. Dobb (1946).
139. Robinson (1933), p.xii.
140. Pigou (1937), p.21; original emphasis.
141. This is an implication of 'The Second Theorem of Welfare Economics'. For an elementary exposition see Varian (2006), pp.583–4.
142. On this see Wicksell (1934), p. 109 and Samuelson (1957).
143. Richardson (1960).
144. See Richardson (1960), pp.25–8, for a critical contemporary assessment of the adequacy of cobweb models.
145. Henderson (1954), p.533.
146. Pigou (1937), chapter 4.
147. Buchanan (1997). See also Section I.5 of the Introduction.
148. Samuelson (1966b), p.1410n.
149. Samuelson (1966c), p.1423.
150. Samuelson (1966d), p.1442.
151. Samuelson (1966b), p.1423.
152. Arrow (1976), p.16.
153. Arrow (1974), p.23.
154. Arrow (1978), p.478.
155. Arrow (1959), p.47.
156. Arrow (1986), p.S392.
157. Coase (1960).
158. Samuelson (1966b), p.1411n.
159. Samuelson (1966c), p.1423.
160. Leontief (1976), p.3.
161. Leontief (1976), p.4.
162. Dickinson (1933), pp.246–7.
163. Taylor (1929).
164. Lange (1936–1937), p.142.
165. Lange (1967), p.158.
166. Johansen (1976).
167. Samuelson (1966a), p.497; stress added.
168. Baumol (1959).
169. Williamson (1964).
170. Simon (1956).
171. Cyert and March (2001), p.15.
172. Marris (1967), p.2.
173. Marris (1967), p.99.
174. Marris (1967), p.105.
175. Burns (1974), p.129.
176. Marris (1974), pp.398–9.
177. Meade (1968).
178. Williamson (1970).

5 Market elimination in modern capitalism: where the theorists were right

1. Remember that Marx rather confusingly used the term 'concentration' to denote the rise in the average size of a unit of capital, and 'centralisation' to refer to what is today universally described as increasing concentration, that is, the growth in the proportion of output or employment controlled by a given number of large enterprises (see Chapter 3). In this chapter, we follow the normal conventions.
2. Prais (1976), pp.4–7.
3. Prais (1976), pp.140–1.
4. Micklethwait and Wooldridge (2003), p.116.
5. Dormois (2004), Table 8.2, p.115.
6. Hart and Clarke (1980), p.95.
7. Supple (1992).
8. Mitchell (1998a), p.934.
9. Mitchell (1998a), p.930.
10. Flora *et al.* (1987), pp.524, 512.
11. Berle and Means (1932).
12. Bain (1956).
13. Baran and Sweezy (1966).
14. Aaronovitch and Sawyer (1975).
15. Fellner (1960); Galambos (1994).
16. Means (1935a).
17. Eichner (1969). See Chapter 4, Section 4.5.
18. Rosenberg and Birdzell (1986), pp.242–3.
19. Mokyr (1990), pp.77, 98–100.
20. Baumol (2002), p.2.
21. Baumol (2002), p.13.
22. Gabor (2000).
23. Dutton (1984).
24. Bernal (1939), p.146.
25. Hobsbawm (1994), pp.289–93.
26. Flora *et al.* (1987), pp.494, 512, 524.
27. Glyn (2006), p.3.
28. Flora *et al.* (1987), pp.637–9.
29. Perkin (1989).
30. Hilferding (1910), p.350; cf. Mills (1951), pp.297, 351–4.
31. Przeworski and Sprague (1987).
32. Veblen (1921).
33. Dorfman (1959), pp.97–100. See Chapter 3, Section 3.8 and Chapter 4, Section 4.4.
34. Bienefeld (1972), Table 1, p.77 and Table 4, p.111.
35. Burnett (1969), pp.263, 264.
36. Burnett (1969), pp.266–7.
37. Burnett (1969), pp.268–9.
38. Schneider (2004), pp.20–1.
39. Schneider (2004), p.29.

40. Schneider (2004), p.34.
41. Burnett (1986), pp.94–5.
42. Burnett (1986), p.147.
43. Burnett (1986), pp.253, 282.
44. Webb (1894), (1897); see also Hobsbawm 1964.
45. The classic reference is Braverman (1974).
46. Stone (1974).
47. Kerr (1954).
48. Ross (1958).
49. Doeringer and Piore (1971); Fine (1998).
50. See Table 2.2 in Section 2.5 of Chapter 2.
51. Australia, Austria, Canada, France, Germany, Italy, Ireland, Japan, New Zealand, Norway, Sweden, Switzerland, UK and USA.
52. Tanzi and Schuknecht (2000), Table I.1, p.6; cf. O'Hara (2004a).
53. Lindbeck (1998), pp.7, 9, 15.
54. Tanzi and Schuknecht (2000), Table II.2, p.26.
55. Lee (2000).
56. Pigou (1914), pp.62–3, cited by Lee (2000), p.13.
57. Chase (1997).
58. Dicey (1914); Atiyah (1979).
59. Curthoys (2004), p.239.
60. Wedderburn (1965), p.252, original stress deleted.
61. Wedderburn (1965), p.23.
62. Wedderburn (1965), p.24.
63. Rickard (1984).
64. Cited by Evans (1985), p.38.
65. Cited by Evans (1985), p.37.
66. Brown (1983).
67. Howell (2005) argues that the state's encouragement of collective bargaining was important also in Britain between 1890 and 1945.
68. Kerr *et al.* (1960); Lester (1958).
69. Cockett (1994), chapter 4.
70. Glyn (2006), Table 1.1, p.3.
71. Steedman (1995), p.4.
72. Pigou (1920).
73. Rawls (1971).
74. Papandreou (1972).
75. Lange (1936–7).
76. Dickinson (1933).
77. Meade (1945), (1948).
78. Meade (1970).
79. Keynes (1936), p.378. See Chapter 4, Section 4.6.
80. Dobb (1969).

6 The return of the market: where they all went wrong

1. Sawyer (2000), p.67.
2. Baumol *et al.* (2003).

3. Dormois (2004), Table 8.2, p.115.
4. Robinson (1958), p.156.
5. Prais (1976), pp.58–9.
6. Martin (2004), p.50.
7. Prais (1976), pp.85–6, 167–8.
8. Micklethwait and Wooldridge (2003), p.166.
9. Micklethwait and Wooldridge (2003), p.169.
10. Micklethwait and Wooldridge (2003), p.175.
11. Stigler (1951), p.192.
12. Micklethwait and Wooldridge (2003), pp.175–6. These authors conclude, however, that 'the idea that the company will retreat to the periphery of the economy looks farfetched' (p.176), as indeed it is.
13. Lichtenstein, 2006.
14. Palley (2006), p.3
15. Audretsch (2004), p.109.
16. Steindl (1945), pp.60, 61.
17. Andrews (1944), p.67.
18. Russell (1949), p.86.
19. Levinson (2006).
20. Quiggin (2001), p.25. Somewhat perversely, however, Quiggin goes on to dispute the significance of these changes as a factor contributing to the growth of international financial transactions (Quiggin (2001), pp.25–6).
21. Wigand and Benjamin (1995), p.3.
22. Malone, Yates and Benjamin (1987), p.496.
23. Davis (2004), p.138.
24. We are grateful to Christina Fader for these examples.
25. Cornes and Sandler (1996).
26. Meade (1968), p.391.
27. Again we are grateful to Christina Fader for these examples.
28. Mincer (1962); Ironmonger (1989); Greenwood *et al.* (2005).
29. Milgrom and Roberts (1992); Molho (1997); Tirole (2006).
30. Wigand and Benjamin (1995), p.2.
31. Winter and Taylor (2001), pp.20–1.
32. Shapiro and Varian (1999), Chapter 7.
33. Castells (1996), p.164; stress removed.
34. Castells (1996), pp.168–9.
35. See also Thompson (2003).
36. Castells (1996), pp.162–3.
37. Piore and Sabel (1984).
38. Pakulski and Waters (1996), p.74.
39. Porter (1985).
40. Compare Mathews (1989) with Gahan (1991); and Hodgson (1999) with Bell and Henry (2001).
41. Winter and Taylor (2001), p.25; cf. Marx (1867), chapter XIV.
42. Sabel and Zeitlin (1997).
43. Anon. (2002).
44. Howard and King (2000); cf. Fukuyama (1993).
45. Gershuny (1978).
46. Blackaby (1979).

47. Mitchell (1998a), pp. 934, 930; Mitchell (1998b), p.788.
48. Calculated from Mitchell (1998a), p.150; Mitchell (1998b), p.107.
49. Bell (1973) was among the earliest.
50. See also Anon. (2005).
51. Kealey (1996).
52. Lydall (1998), p.37; original stress.
53. Webster (1999).
54. Weiss, Thurborn and Mathews (2004).
55. Perelman (1998), p.81.
56. Perelman (1998), p.81.
57. cf. Arrow (1999), pp.24–5.
58. Baumol (2002), chapters 6 and 13.
59. Etzkowitz (2002); Bok (2003); Washburn (2004).
60. See Chapter 3, Section 3.3.
61. Berger and Piore (1980).
62. Minford, Mahambare and Nowell (2005), pp.71–9.
63. Flora *et al.* (1987), pp.524, 637–9.
64. Glyn (2006), p.203 n 18.
65. Atkinson (1987).
66. Blair and Lafontaine (2005).
67. Martinelli (1994).
68. Frank (2004), p.11.
69. Perkin (1996), p.xiii.
70. Perkin (1996), p.xiv.
71. Williamson (1970), p.ix.
72. See Chapter 2, Section 2.6.
73. Williamson (1970), p.175.
74. Gordon, Edwards and Reich (1982).
75. Polanyi (1944); Calhoun (1982).
76. Baudrillard (1970); Hirsch (1976); Bowman (1996); Ger and Belk (1996); Glyn (2006), pp.121–2.
77. Bain and Price (1980), Table 3.1, pp.88–9.
78. Bray *et al.* (2005), Table 6.1, p.6.4.
79. Harbridge (2006), Table 2, p.5.
80. Fernie (2005), p.2.
81. Bain and Price (1980), Table 6.1, pp.133–4; Schnabel (2005), cited in Fernie and Metcalf (2005), Table 11.1, p.218; figures are for the Western *Länder* only.
82. Brown and Ryan (2003), pp.405–6.
83. Peetz (2006).
84. Harrison and Bluestone (1988); Pollin (2003); Appelbaum, Bernhardt and Murnane (2003).
85. Pollin (2003), p.42.
86. Norris, Kelly and Giles (2005), Table 4.7, p.91.
87. Dalziel and Lattimore (2001), pp.30–1.
88. Pontusson (2005).
89. Godard (2004), p.232.
90. Yamamura and Streeck (2003).
91. Greenwood *et al.*, (2005).

92. Baudrillard (1970); Pakulski and Waters (1996).
93. Ritzer (2004).
94. Bryman (2004).
95. Sassen (1998), p.161.
96. Howells (1999); Glyn (2006), pp.52–4. However, see Friedman (1957) for an alternative view.
97. Burnett (1986), p.282.
98. Matheson and Babb (2002), p.166; cf. Glyn (2006), p.172.
99. Blackburn (2002), chapter 1; Esping-Andersen (1990), chapter 4.
100. Hannah (1986), pp. 40, 67, 145.
101. Matheson and Babb (2002), p.147.
102. Blackburn (2002).
103. Suleiman (2003), pp.93, 95.
104. O'Hara (2004a), Figure 16.3, p.331.
105. Tanzi and Schulknecht (2000), Table II.2, p.26; Suleiman (2003), pp.118–19.
106. Le Grand and Bartlett (1993); Osborne and Gaebler (1992).
107. Moe (1984), p.759.
108. Moe (1984), p.760.
109. Singer (2003).
110. Cavallaro (2004); Klein (2007).
111. State Services Commission (2002), pp.10, 13; original stress.
112. State Services Commission (2002), p.18.
113. State Services Commission (2002), p.24.
114. Lindbeck 1998; Suleiman (2003), pp.116–19.
115. Vogel (1996).
116. Murray (1994).
117. Wacquant (1999); Garland (2001).
118. Edsall (1971); Arblaster (1984); Kanth (1986).
119. Wedderburn (1965), pp.261–75.
120. Petzall *et al.* (2003), pp.244–5.
121. Bray *et al.* (2005), pp.133–4.
122. Freeman, Hersch and Mishel (2005).
123. Kaysen (1996), p.106.
124. Mason (1959).
125. Kaysen (1957).
126. Kaysen (1996), pp.3–20.
127. Glyn (2001); Grieve Smith (2005). See also Przeworski and Sprague (1987) for a longer term historical analysis.
128. Friedman (1968), p.8. For a devastating critique of this concept from a neoclassical perspective, see Hahn (1980).
129. Lerner (1943); cf. Arestis and Sawyer (2004b).
130. Blinder (2004); Forder (2004) cited in Arestis and Sawyer (2004c); Arestis, McCombie and Baddeley (2005).
131. Carlin and Soskice (2006).
132. Cornwall (1994). See also Chapter 7, Sections 7.5 and 7.6.
133. Smithin (1990); Arestis and Sawyer (2001); Arestis and Sawyer (2004a); Henderson (1998).
134. Glyn (2006); Iversen (2005); Södersten (2004).

135. There is some dispute as to the strength of this pressure; for a contrary view, see Kite (2004).
136. Esping-Andersen (1996); Pontusson (2005).
137. Przeworski (1985), p.219.
138. See Chapter 7 for a discussion of postwar economic policies in the 'golden age'.
139. Jomo and Fine (2006); Priewe and Herr (2005).
140. George and Sabelli (1994).
141. Gowan (2005).
142. Anon. (1999).
143. Backhouse (2005).
144. Morgan and Rutherford (1998).
145. Smithin (1990).
146. Mueller (1997).
147. Medema (1994).
148. Chase (1997).
149. Cockett (1994); Henderson (1998).
150. George (1999), pp. 2–3.
151. Bourdieu (1998) and Therborn (2001).

7 Why was neoliberalism delayed?

1. Lipsey *et al.* (2005).
2. This is a common mistake in discussions of neoliberalism; see, for example, Frieden (2006) and Harvey (2005).
3. The phrase 'age of catastrophe' originates in Hobsbawm (1994) and describes the period 1914–45.
4. James (2002).
5. Eichengreen (2007).
6. Maddison (2003), pp.50–3, 85–6, 174–5, 261.
7. Johnson (2004). The limitations of US military power are discussed in Chapter 8.
8. See Chapter 2, Section 2.2.
9. Nonetheless, there are a host of problems introduced by the liberalisation of finance, and we deal with some of these in Chapter 8.
10. See Gowan (1999) and (2001) for an excellent description of the new regime. However, not everything has changed and there have been important continuities, as Rosenberg (1994) explains.
11. Howard and King (2002).
12. Maddison (2003), p.85.
13. Goldin (2000), pp.590–1; Walton and Rockoff (2005), p.452.
14. Maddison (2003), pp.50–1, 172.
15. Stiglitz (1989).
16. Bernanke (2000); Bordo *et al.* (1998); Hobsbawm (1994); James (2002); Kindleberger (1987); Mazower (1999).
17. Barzel (1989); Milgrom and Roberts (1992); Williamson (1996).
18. Higgs (1987); Mann (1988); Porter (1994).
19. Eley (2002); Halperin (1997); Williamson and Lindert (1981).

20. Mann (2004); Mazower (1999).
21. However, Halperin (1997) and Mann (1993) raise some serious doubts about this.
22. Skidelsky (2000).
23. Skidelsky (2000).
24. Of course, it is easy to argue that the most radical consequences occurred in Germany and Japan. But these consequences were far less important for the problem with which we are concerned. Germany and Japan were unambiguously defeated in the Second World War and then fell prey to American social engineering.
25. Maier (1987).
26. Maddison (2003), pp.49, 55.
27. Kindleberger (1987), Chapter 14.
28. Gowan (2004).
29. Vatter (1985).
30. Quoted in Kennedy (1989), p.447.
31. Goldin (2000), pp.580–5; Freeman (1998); Piven and Cloward (1971); Tomlins (2000); Vietor (2000), pp.977–98.
32. Goldin (2000), pp. 599–602; Plotnick *et al.* (2000).
33. Bordo *et al.* (1998); Calomiris (2004); Temin (2000), pp.318–21; Vietor (2000), pp.978–81; White (2000), pp.743–73.
34. Galbraith (1954); Kindleberger (1987).
35. Bernanke (2000); Friedman and Schwartz (1963); Temin (2000), pp.311–13.
36. Levy (1989), pp.210–14. See also Skocpol (1979); Hobsbawm (1994), pp.13, 43–4, 48–53 and Tilly (1993), pp.197–8.
37. Hubbard (1991); Kindleberger (1996); Sherman (1991).
38. This had been defined as an American national interest long before the Second World War made its realisation feasible. See Gowan (2002) and (2004); as well as Skidelsky (2000), pp.94, 98, 126, 137, 237 and 322. The weakening of European imperial states as a result of the war also meant that they had less power to preserve their colonies and especially in the face of US hostility to the maintenance of traditional empires.
39. This system may be sensibly regarded as an 'empire', but not in the traditional sense. See Ferguson (2005); Johnson (2004); Mann (2003) and, above all, Rosenberg (1994).
40. See Chapter 2, Section 2.6 and Eichengreen (2007).
41. Armstrong *et al.* (1991); Kunz (1997); Skidelsky (2000).
42. See Section 7.3 above.
43. Sent and Mirowski (2002).
44. Eichengreen (2007); Judt (2005).
45. Maier (1987), Chapters 3 and 4.
46. Marglin and Schor (1990).
47. There were the GI Bill of Rights in the 1940s, and the Great Society programmes during the 1960s, including Medicard, Medicare, the Food Stamp programme, Supplemental Security Income, the Elementary and Secondary Education Act and Head Start.
48. China, North Korea, Cuba and Vietnam were the principal failures in the containment policy.
49. Held *et al.* (1999).

50. Skidelsky (2000).
51. See Brenner (1998); Duménil and Lévy (2004); Eichengreen (2007), pp.199, 216–24, 238–42; Glyn (2006) and Glyn and Sutcliffe (1972).
52. Lipsey *et al.* (2005).
53. Friedman and Friedman (1996); Sloan (2002).
54. Lipsey *et al.* (2005).
55. White (2000), pp.775–8.
56. Euro–dollar deposits met the needs of countries, like the Soviet Union, and later OPEC nations, as well as individuals, who wished to hold dollar balances beyond the control of the US government. Britain facilitated the development of the euro–dollar system in order to aid the City of London in remaining a major financial centre. See Helleiner (1994).
57. Eatwell *et al.* (1992a), pp.36, 238, 635–6, 641; (1992b), pp.54f., 72f., 88, 94–5, 104–5, 243f., 434f., 491f.; (1992c), pp.326–7, 526f.
58. White (2000), pp.790–2.
59. Eatwell *et al.* (1992a), pp.638, 683; (1992b), pp.51f.; (1992c), pp.326.
60. Vogel (1996), pp.98–9.
61. Eatwell *et al.* (1992a), pp.138–40, 186, 202f., 463–70, 475, 537–8, 637–8, 683–4, 780f.; (1992b), pp.33, 36–9, 41–3, 45–6, 56f., 68–75, 94, 187, 422f., 553f., 577f., 635f., 657f., 672, 812; (1992c), pp.127f., 206f., 432f., 435f.
62. Eatwell *et al.* (1992a), pp.137–8, 157, 813; (1992b), pp.56, 88–90, 94.
63. Cottrell (2006); Eatwell *et al.* (1992c), pp.36–7, 157f., 238–9; White (2000), pp.792–802.
64. Lipsey *et al.* (2005).
65. David (1989), (1997).
66. Kalecki (1943).
67. Duménil and Lévy (2004); Gamble (1988); Glyn (2006).
68. Brittan (2005), p.68. See also Eatwell *et al.* (1992a), pp.238, 523, 687, 780f., 813–5; (1992b), pp.51–4, 105, 189; (1992c), pp.63f.
69. Krugman and Obstfeld (2005), p.506. The reference is to Triffin (1960). See also Eichengreen (2007), pp.244–5.
70. Gilpin (1981); Kennedy (1989); Mearsheimer (2001).
71. Johnson (1982); Thurow (1992).
72. Friedman and Lebard (1991).
73. Ostry (1997).
74. Walton and Rockoff (2005), p.570.
75. Bernstein and Munro (1997); Carpenter (2005).
76. See Chapters 1 and 2.
77. Walton and Rockoff (2005), pp.426, 431, 508–9, 580–3; Porter (1994), pp.284–5.
78. Gowan (1999); Lindert (2000), pp.408, 434–9, 446–9, 451–2.
79. See Krugman (1997), chapters 1 and 5, for an alternative view.
80. The United States and Britain were partial exceptions because of the international role played by Wall Street and the City of London. See also Gerschenkron (1966) and Streeck and Yamamura (2001).
81. Grahl (2001). The distinction between 'exit' and 'voice' comes from Hirschman (1970).
82. See Chapter 2, Section 2.6.
83. Vietor (2000).

84. Suleiman (2003).
85. Eichengreen (2007); Gowan (2005).
86. Eichengreen (2007).
87. Vogel (1996), p.27.
88. Vogel (1996), pp.26–31, 137–66, 218–23, 244–50.
89. Schlosser (2002); Victor (2000); Vogel (1996).

8 What might reverse neoliberalism?

1. See Chapters 3 and 4.
2. See Chapter 1.
3. See Chapters 1 and 2.
4. Popper (1957).
5. Olson (1982); Parkin (1979); Polanyi (1944).
6. Howard and King (2001a), pp.787–92.
7. Agliardi (1998); Baumol and Benhabib (1989); Fearon and Laitin (2000); Schelling (1978).
8. Friedman and Friedman (1996); Mandelbaum (2003); Nye (2004); Rosenberg (1994); Spulber (1995); Wade (2003).
9. Ferguson (2005); Kennedy (1989); Mann (2003); Wallerstein (2003).
10. Baumol and Benhabib (1989).
11. For reasons of space and style, we do not always spell out the 'ifs' as fully as the argument logically requires, but the conditional structure should always be taken as characterising our argument.
12. Pierson (1996).
13. In the United States, the involvement of the 50 state governments in the provision of health care is actually likely to expand. American 'exceptionalism' in retaining a large sector of private health insurance, and providing much of the coverage through employment, is anachronistic in the neoliberal age. Many US states are implementing policies aimed at universal coverage for their residents. See Anon (2007).
14. Ostry (1997); Williamson (1996).
15. See Chapter 6; Mair (2006); and Suleiman (2003).
16. Monbiot (2001); Krugman (2006b); Singer (2003).
17. Washburn (2004).
18. See Section 6.6 below, and Chapter 6.
19. Though not, perhaps, to Hobson (1902), who correctly identified the importance of powerful business lobbies.
20. See Section 8.5 below.
21. Smith (1776), pp.264–5; Tirole (2006).
22. Advani (2006); Carr (2007); Froud (2006); Levitt (2002); MacAvoy and Millstern (2003).
23. By 'normal circumstances' we mean the conditions in which the transformative influences discussed in Sections 8.3–8.7 are absent.
24. Chapter 2, Section 2.2.
25. Hirschman (1970).
26. Carr (2007).
27. Lipsey *et al.* (2005).

28. 'Design' characteristics occur when it is known in advance how different elements in an organisation have to be integrated and where the lack of full integration can be very disruptive and costly. See Milgrom and Roberts (1992), pp.91–2, 108, 115–8.
29. Diamond (1997), (2005).
30. Blinder (1987); Schelling (2006).
31. Duncan (2006), p.4.
32. Flannery (2006); Kolbert (2006); McKibben (2007); Speth (2004), and Stern (2006).
33. Olson (1965).
34. Duncan (2006), p.11.
35. Duncan (2006), p.8.
36. Duncan (2006), pp.6, 8, and 9; and Jorgenson *et al.* (2004). However, forecasts of specific climate changes in particular regions of the world involve more uncertainty and controversy than is the case for the warming of the globe as a whole; see for example, Kerr (2002) and Seager (2006).
37. See Chapter 1, Section 1.3.
38. Chapter 7, Section 7.3.
39. Bogle (2005); Levitt (2002); Kindleberger (1996).
40. Koshimura (1977).
41. Ingham (2004).
42. Galbraith (1954); James (2002); Kindleberger (1987) and (1996).
43. Minsky (1982).
44. See Chapters 6 and 7.
45. Snowdon and Vane (2005).
46. Blinder (1997).
47. Minsky (1982).
48. Baumol and Benhabib (1989); Mandelbrot and Hudson (2004).
49. Glyn (2006), pp.51f, 131f, 152f; Pollin (2003).
50. Gilpin (2000), (2001); Kapstein (1994)
51. Glyn (2006), pp.70–3; Krugman and Obstfeld (2005), pp.589–91.
52. Brittan (2005), pp.169–74; Ingham (2004), pp.159–64; Krugman (1999).
53. Frieden (2006), pp.109f and 457f, and chapter 20.
54. Klein (2002).
55. Hardt and Negi (2000), (2004).
56. Arrow (1951); Beetham (1985); Rosenberg (1994), (1996), (2000).
57. Gowan (2005).
58. Baudrillard (1970); Garland (2001); Geuss (2001); Mair (2006); Runciman (2006); Sassoon (1997). See also Chapter 6.
59. Fukuyama (1992); Pakulski and Waters (1996).
60. Baker (2006); Brandolini and Smeeding (2006); Engerman and Gallman (2000); Glyn (2006), pp.157f and 156f; Krugman (2006a). See also Chapter 6, Section 6.3.
61. Carr (2007); Duménil and Lévy (2004b).
62. See Chapter 6.
63. Woodall (2006).
64. Acemoglu (1998); Autor, Katz and Krueger (1998); Berman, Bourd and Machin (1998); Kahn and Lim (1998); Machin and Reenen (1998).

65. Ohlin (1933); Samuelson (1948), (1949); Stolper and Samuelson (1941). See also Wood (1994).
66. But see Rogowski (1989).
67. Sen (1995); Stubbs (2005).
68. Guinnane *et al.* (2004); Luce (2007).
69. See Chapter 6, Section 6.2. This book itself is one example of new types of outsourcing. The main offices of Palgrave Macmillan are located in Basingstoke in the UK, but the copy-editing of the manuscript, and other related tasks, were undertaken in India, and communications with the authors was via email.
70. See Chapter 7.
71. Bernstein and Munro (1997); Brzezinski (2005); Gilpin (1981); Kennedy (1989); Wallerstein (2003). A US–EU war may sound absurd and it is, of course, at present very unlikely. But a persuasive scenario for such an occurrence can be constructed, in which American unilateralist militarism threatens EU interests, bringing on deeper integration and the taking of direct responsibility for European security, so increasingly coming into conflict with the United States.
72. Dyer (2005).
73. Dyer (2005).
74. Thatcher (2002), pp.53–4. See also Ceadal (2003)
75. Gray (2005); Mearsheimer (2001).
76. Fukuyama (2006); Mann (2003).
77. Chomsky (1991) and (1994).
78. Ferguson (2005), and Mann (2003) discuss the huge difficulties in attempting this.
79. Dyer (2005), chapter 10. See also Mann (2005) for an indication of how unpleasant the erosion might be.

References

Aaronovitch, S. and Sawyer, M.C. 1975. *Big Business: Theoretical and Empirical Aspects of Concentration and Mergers in the United Kingdom*. London: Macmillan and New York: Holmes & Meier.

Acemoglu, D. 1998. 'Why do new technologies complement skills? Directed technical change and wage inequality', *Quarterly Journal of Economics* 113(4), November, pp.1055–89.

Acemoglu, D. and Robinson, J.A. 2006. *Economic Origins of Dictatorship and Democracy*. Cambridge: Cambridge University Press.

Acheson, D. 1969. *Present at the Creation: My Years at the State Department*. New York: Norton.

Advani, R. 2006. *The Wall Street MBA: Your Personal Crash Course in Corporate Finance*. New York: McGraw Hill.

Agliardi, E. 1998. *Positive Feedback Economics*. New York: St. Martin's Press.

Aglietta, M. 1979. *A Theory of Capitalist Regulation: The US Experience*. London: New Left Books.

Allen, G.C. 1967. *Economic Fact and Fantasy: A Rejoinder to Galbraith's Reith Lectures*. London: Institute of Economic Affairs.

Anderson, P. 2000. 'Renewals', *New Left Review* 1, January–February Second Series, pp.5–24.

Andrews, P.W.S. 1944. 'Report from the "accountancy" side of the inquiry into the relative efficiency of small- and large-scale business', in F.S. Lee and P.E. Earl (eds). *The Economics of Competitive Enterprise: Selected Essays of P. W. S. Andrews*. Aldershot: Edward Elgar, 1993, pp.35–72.

Anon. [J.-L.M.]. 1999. 'Der interessierte Blick der Wall Street', *Le Monde Diplomatique*, 16 April, http://www.taz.de/tpl/1999/04/16.nf [accessed 21 April 1999].

Anon. 2002. *Economist*, 21 February, pp.71–3.

Anon. 2004. *Economist*, 19 June, pp.65–7.

Anon. 2005. *Economist*, 29 September, pp.69–70.

Anon. 2007. *Economist*, 13 January, pp.15, 27–8.

Appelbaum, E., Bernhardt, A. and Murnane, R.J. 2003. *Low-Wage America: How Employers are Reshaping Opportunity in the Workplace*. New York: Russell Sage Foundation.

Arblaster, A.A. 1984. *The Rise and Decline of Western Liberalism*. Oxford: Blackwell.

Arestis, P. and Sawyer, M. (eds). 2001. *The Economics of the Third Way: Experiences from Around the World*. Cheltenham: Edward Elgar.

Arestis, P. and Sawyer, M. (eds). 2004a. *Neo-liberal Economic Policy: Critical Essays*. Cheltenham: Edward Elgar.

Arestis, P. and Sawyer, M. (eds). 2004b. *Re-examining Monetary and Fiscal Policy for the 21st Century*. Cheltenham: Edward Elgar.

Arestis, P. and Sawyer, M. (eds). 2004c. *The Rise of the Market: Critical Essays on the Political Economy of Neo-Liberalism*. Cheltenham: Edward Elgar.

Arestis, P., McCombie, J. and Baddeley, M. (eds). 2005. *The New Monetary Policy: Implications and Relevance*. Cheltenham: Edward Elgar.

Armstrong, P., Glyn, A. and Harrison, J. 1991. *Capitalism since 1945*. Oxford: Blackwell.

Arrow, K.J. 1951. *Social Choice and Individual Values*. New York: Wiley.

Arrow, K.J. 1959. 'Toward a theory of price adjustment', in M. Abramovitz *et al.*, *The Allocation of Economic Resources: Essays in Honor of Bernard Francis Haley*. Stanford: Stanford University Press, pp.41–51.

Arrow, K.J. 1974. *The Limits of Organization*. New York: Norton.

Arrow, K.J. 1976. *The Viability and Equity of Capitalism*. Vancouver: University of British Columbia, Department of Economics (E.S. Woodward Lectures in Economics).

Arrow, K.J. 1978. 'A cautious case for socialism', *Dissent* 25(4), Fall, pp.472–80.

Arrow, K.J. 1986. 'Rationality of self and others in an economic system', *Journal of Business* 59(4:2), October, pp.S385–S399.

Arrow, K.J. 1999. 'Information and the organization of industry', in G. Chichilnisky (ed.). *Markets, Information, and Uncertainty: Essays in Economic Theory in Honor of Kenneth J. Arrow*. Cambridge: Cambridge University Press, pp.19–25.

Arrow, K.J. and Hahn, F.H. 1971. *General Competitive Analysis*. Edinburgh: Oliver & Boyd.

Aston, T.H. and Philpin, C.H.E. (eds). 1985. *The Brenner Debate: Agrarian Class Structure and Economic Development in Pre-Industrial Europe*. Cambridge: Cambridge University Press.

Atiyah, P.S. 1979. *The Rise and Fall of Freedom of Contract*. Oxford: Clarendon Press and New York: Oxford University Press.

Atkinson, J. 1987. 'Flexibility or fragmentation: the UK labour market in the 1980s', *Labour and Society* 12(1), pp.87–105.

Audretsch, D.B. 2004. 'Small firms, innovation and competition', in Neumann and Weigand (2004), pp.88–114.

Author, D.H., Katz, L.F. and Krueger, A.B. 1998. 'Computing inequality: have computers changed the labor market?', *Quarterly Journal of Economics* 113(4), November, pp.1169–213.

Averitt, R.T. 1968. *The Dual Economy: The Dynamics of American Industry Structure*. New York: Norton.

Babbage, C. 1832. *On the Economy of Machinery and Manufactures*. London: Charles Knight.

Backhouse, R.E. 2005. 'The rise of free market economics: economists and the role of the state since 1970', in S.G. Medema and P. Boettke (eds). *The Role of Government in the History of Economic Thought: Annual Supplement to Volume 37 History of Political Economy*. Durham, NC: Duke University Press, pp.355–92.

Bain, G.S. and Price, R. 1980. *Profiles of Union Growth: A Comparative Statistical Portrait of Eight Countries*. Oxford: Blackwell.

Bain, J.S. 1956. *Barriers to New Competition: Their Character and Consequences in Manufacturing Industries*. Cambridge, MA: Harvard University Press.

Baker, D. 2006. 'Increasing inequality in the United States', *Post-Autistic Economics Review* 40, December, pp.18–22.

Ball, T. and Bellamy, R. (eds). 2003. *The Cambridge History of Twentieth-Century Political Thought*. Cambridge: Cambridge University Press.

Baran, P. 1944. 'New trends in Russian thinking', *American Economic Review* 34(4), December, pp.862–71.

Baran, P.A. and Sweezy, P.M. 1966. *Monopoly Capital: An Essay on the American Economic and Social Order*. New York: Monthly Review Press.
Bardhan, P.K. and Roemer, J.E. (eds). 1993. *Market Socialism: The Current Debate*. Oxford: Oxford University Press.
Barzel, Y. 1989. *Economic Analysis of Property Rights*. Cambridge: Cambridge University Press.
Baudrillard, J. 1970. *The Consumer Society: Myths and Structures*. Thousand Oaks, CA: Sage, 1998.
Baumann, E. [K. Mandelbaum and F. Pollock] 1936. 'Keynes's revision der liberalistischen nationalöknomie', *Zeitschrift für Sozialforschung* 5, pp.384–403.
Baumol, W.J. 1959. *Business Behavior, Value and Growth*. New York: Harcourt, Brace & World, 1967.
Baumol, W.J. 2002. *The Free-Market Innovation Machine: Analyzing the Growth Miracle of Capitalism*. Princeton: Princeton University Press.
Baumol, W.J. and Benhabib, J. 1989. 'Chaos: significance, mechanism, and economic applications', *Journal of Economic Perspectives* 3(1), Winter, pp.77–105.
Baumol, W.J., Blinder, A.S. and Wolff, E.N. 2003. *Downsizing in America: Reality, Causes, and Consequences*. New York: Russell Sage Foundation.
Beetham, D. 1985. *Max Weber on the Theory of Modern Politics*. Cambridge: Polity Press.
Bell, D. 1968. *The Cultural Contradictions of Capitalism*. New York: Basic Books, 1976.
Bell, D. 1973. *The Coming of Post-industrial Society: A Venture in Social Forecasting*. London: Heinemann, 1974.
Bell, S.A. and Henry, J.F. 2001. 'Are employment relations undergoing a fundamental change that threatens the future of capitalism? A critique of Hodgson's view of the labour contract', *Journal of Economic Issues* 35(2), June, pp.335–43.
Berger, S. and Piore, M.J. 1980. *Dualism and Discontinuity in Industrial Societies*. Cambridge: Cambridge University Press.
Berle, A. 1968. 'Preface', in Berle and Means (1932), pp.vii–xxvii.
Berle, A.A. and Means, G.C. 1932. *The Modern Corporation and Private Property*. New York: Harcourt, Brace & World, revised edition, 1968.
Berman, E., Bound, J. and Machin, S. 1998. 'Implications of skill-biased technological change: international evidence', *Quarterly Journal of Economics* 113(4), November, pp.1245–79.
Bernal, J.D. 1939. *The Social Function of Science*. New York: Macmillan and London: Routledge.
Bernanke, B.S. 2000. *Essays on the Great Depression*. Princeton: Princeton University Press.
Bernstein, E. 1898. *The Preconditions of Socialism*, H. Tudor (ed.). Cambridge: Cambridge University Press, 1993.
Bernstein, R. and Munro, R.H. 1997. *The Coming Conflict with China*. New York: Knopf.
Bertram, C. 1990. 'International competition in historical materialism', *New Left Review* 183, September/October, First Series, pp.116–28.
Bertram, C. and Chitty, A. (eds). 1994. *Has History Ended?: Fukuyama, Marx, Modernity*. Aldershot: Avebury.
Bewley, T.F., 1999. *Why Wages Don't Fall During a Recession*. Cambridge, MA: Harvard University Press.

Bhagwati, J. 1991. *Political Economy and International Economics*. Cambridge, MA: MIT Press.

Bienefeld, M.A. 1972. *Working Hours in British Industry: An Economic History*. London: Weidenfeld & Nicolson.

Blackaby, F. (ed.). 1979. *De-industrialization*. London: Heinemann Educational Books.

Blackburn, R. 2002. *Banking on Death. Or, Investing in Life: The History and Future of Pensions*. London: Verso.

Blackburn, R.J. 1990. *The Vampire of Reason: An Essay in the Philosophy of History*. London: Verso.

Blackledge, P. and Kirkpatrick, G. (eds). 2002. *Historical Materialism and Social Evolution*. London: Palgrave.

Blair, R.D. and Lafontaine, F. 2005. *The Economics of Franchising*. Cambridge: Cambridge University Press.

Blinder, A.S. 1987. *Hard Heads and Soft Hearts: Tough-Minded Economics for a Just Society*. Reading, MA: Addison Wesley.

Blinder, A.S. 1997. 'A core of macroeconomic beliefs?', *Challenge* 40(4), pp.36–44.

Blinder, A.S. 2004. *The Quiet Revolution: Central Banking Goes Modern*. New Haven, CT: Yale University Press.

Bogle, J.C. 2005. *The Battle for the Soul of Capitalism*. New Haven, CT: Yale University Press.

Bok, D.C. 2003. *Universities in the Marketplace: The Commercialisation of Higher Education*. Princeton: Princeton University Press.

Bordo, M.D., Goldin, C.D. and White, E.N. (eds). 1998. *The Defining Moment: The Great Depression and the American Economy in the Twentieth Century*. Chicago: University of Chicago Press.

Bottomore, T.B. 1992. *Between Marginalism and Marxism: The Economic Sociology of J. A. Schumpeter*. London: Harvester Wheatsheaf.

Bourdieu, P. 1984. *Distinction: A Social Critique of the Judgement of Taste*. Cambridge, MA: Harvard University Press.

Bourdieu, P. 1998. 'A reasoned utopia and economic fatalism', *New Left Review* 227, January–February, First Series, pp.11–24.

Bowman, K.H. 1996. 'A reaffirmation of self-reliance?, A new ethic of self-sufficiency?', *The Public Perspective* 7(2), February–March, pp.5–9.

Brady, R.A. 1943. *Business as a System of Power*. New York: Columbia University Press, 1947.

Brandolini, A. and Smeeding, T.M. 2006. 'Patterns of economic inequality in western democracies: some facts on levels and trends', *PS: Political Science and Politics*, 39, pp.21–6.

Braudel, F. 1981. *The Structures of Everyday Life: Civilization and Capitalism, 15th–18th Centuries, Volume 1*. New York: Harper & Row.

Braudel, F. 1982. *The Wheels of Commerce: Civilization and Capitalism, 15th–18th Centuries, Volume 2*. New York: Harper & Row.

Braudel, F. 1984. *The Perspective of the World: Civilization and Capitalism, 15th–18th Centuries, Volume 3*. New York: Harper & Row.

Braverman, H. 1974. *Labor and Monopoly Capital: The Degradation of Work in the Twentieth Century*. New York: Monthly Review Press.

Bray, M., Deery, S., Walsh, J. and Waring, P. 2005. *Industrial Relations: A Contemporary Approach*. Sydney: McGraw-Hill, third edition.

Brenner, R. 1978. 'Dobb on the transition from feudalism to capitalism', *Cambridge Journal of Economics* 2(2), June, pp.121–40.

Brenner, R. 1986. 'The social basis of economic development', in J. Roemer (ed.). *Analytical Marxism*. Cambridge: Cambridge University Press, pp.23–53.

Brenner, R. 1989. 'Bourgeois revolution and transition to capitalism', in A.L. Beier, D. Cannadine and J.M. Rosenheim (eds). *The First Modern Society: Essays in English History in Honour of Lawrence Stone*. Cambridge: Cambridge University Press, pp.271–304.

Brenner, R. 1998. 'The economics of global turbulence', *New Left Review* 229, May–June, First Series, pp.1–265.

Brittan, S. 2005. *Against the Flow: Reflections of an Individualist*. London: Atlantic Books.

Broadie, A. 1997. *The Scottish Enlightenment: An Anthology*. Edinburgh: Canongate Books.

Brown, E.H. Phelps. 1983. *The Origins of Trade Union Power*. Oxford: Clarendon Press and New York: Oxford University Press.

Brown, W. and Ryan, P. 2003. 'The irrelevance of trade union recognition? A comparison of two matched companies', *Australian Journal of Labour Economics* 6(3), September, pp.383–408.

Bryman, A. 2004. *The Disneyization of Society*. London: Sage.

Brzezinski, Z. 2005. *The Choice: Global Domination or Global Leadership*. New York: Basic Books.

Buchanan, J.M. 1997. *Post-Socialist Political Economy: Selected Essays*. Cheltenham: Edward Elgar.

Bukharin, N.I. 1915. *Imperialism and World Economy*. London: Merlin Press, 1972.

Burnett, J. 1969. *A History of the Cost of Living*. Harmondsworth: Penguin.

Burnett, J. 1986. *A Social History of Housing, 1815–1985*. London: Methuen, second edition.

Burnham, J. 1941. *The Managerial Revolution*. London: Penguin, 1945.

Burns, A.R. 1936. *The Decline of Competition: A Study of the Evolution of American Industry*. New York: McGraw-Hill.

Burns, T. 1974. 'On the rationale of the corporate system', in Marris (1974), pp.121–77.

Calhoun, C. 1982. *The Question of Class Struggle: Social Foundations of Popular Radicalism During the Industrial Revolution*. Chicago: Chicago University Press.

Calomiris, C.W. 2004. 'Financial history and the long reach of the thirty-years war', in T.W. Guinnane *et al.* (eds). *History Matters: Essays on Economic Growth, Technology, and Demographic Change*. Stanford: Stanford University Press, pp.115–41.

Carlin, W. and Soskice, D. 2006. *Macroeconomics: Imperfections, Institutions and Policies*. Oxford: Oxford University Press.

Carling, A.H. 1991. *Social Division*. London: Verso.

Carling, A.H. 1993. 'Analytical Marxism and historical materialism: the debate on social evolution', *Science and Society* 57(1), Spring, pp.31–65.

Carling, A.H. 2004. 'The Darwinian Weberian: W.G. Runciman and the microfoundations of historical materialism', *Historical Materialism* 12, March, pp.71–105.

Carling, A. 2006. 'Karl Marx's theory of history and the recovery of the Marxian tradition', *Science and Society* 70(2), April, pp.275–97.

Carling, A.H. and Nolan, P. 2000. 'Historical materialism, natural selection and world history', *Historical Materialism* 6, pp.216–64.
Carpenter, T.G. 2005. *America's Coming War With China: A Collision Course Over Taiwan*. Basingstoke: Palgrave Macmillan.
Carr, E. 2007. 'Survey: in the money', *Economist*, 20 January 2007.
Casal, P. 1994. 'On societal and global historical materialism', in Bertram and Chitty (1994), pp.87–111.
Castells, M. 1996. *The Rise of the Network Society*. Cambridge, MA: Blackwell.
Cavallaro, L. 2004. *Il modello mafioso e la società globale*. Rome: Manifestolibri.
Ceadal, M. 2003. 'Pacifism and *Pacifism*', in Ball and Bellamy (2003), pp.473–92.
Chamberlin, E.H. (ed.). 1954. *Monopoly and Competition and Their Regulation: Papers and Proceedings of a Conference Held By the International Economic Association*. London: Macmillan.
Chandler, A.D. 1977. *The Visible Hand: The Managerial Revolution in American Business*. Cambridge, MA: Harvard University Press.
Chandler, A.D. 1990. *Scale and Scope: The Dynamics of Industrial Capitalism*. Cambridge, MA: Harvard University Press.
Chang, H.-J. 1994. *The Political Economy of Industrial Policy*. Basingstoke: Macmillan.
Chang, H.-J. 2002. *Kicking Away the Ladder: Development Strategy in Historical Perspective*. London: Anthem Press.
Chase, A. 1997. *Law and History: The Evolution of the American Legal System*. New York: The New Press.
Chilcote, R.H. (ed.). 1999. *The Political Economy of Imperialism: Critical Appraisals*. Boston: Klumer, 1999 and New York: Rowman & Littlefield, 2000.
Chomsky, N. 1991. *Deterring Democracy*. London: Verso.
Chomsky, N. 1994. *World Orders Old and New*. New York: Columbia University Press.
Chua, A. 2003. *World on Fire: How Exporting Free-Market Democracy Breeds Ethnic Hatred and Global Instability*. New York: Anchor Books.
Clower, R.W. 1965. 'The Keynesian counter-revolution: a theoretical appraisal', in F.H. Hahn and R. Brechling, *The Theory of Interest Rates*. London: Macmillan, pp.103–25.
Coase, R. 1960. 'The problem of social cost', *Journal of Law and Economics* 3(1), October, pp.1–44.
Cockett, R. 1994. *Thinking the Unthinkable: Think-Tanks and the Economic Counter-Revolution, 1931–1983*. London: Harper Collins.
Cohen, G., Brown, B. and Organski, A. 1981. 'The paradoxical nature of state making: the violent creation of order', *American Political Science Review* 75(4), December, pp.901–10.
Cohen, G.A. 1978. *Karl Marx's Theory of History: A Defence*. Princeton: Princeton University Press, second edition, 2000.
Cohen, G.A. 1988. *History, Labour and Freedom: Themes from Marx*. Oxford: Clarendon Press.
Cohen, G.A. 1995. *Self-Ownership, Freedom, and Equality*. Cambridge: Cambridge University Press.
Cohen, G.A. 2000. *If You're an Egalitarian, How Come You're So Rich*? Cambridge, MA: Harvard University Press.
Cohen, S. 1974. *Bukharin and the Bolshevik Revolution*. Oxford: Oxford University Press.

Collier, P. 2007. *The Bottom Billion: Why the Poorest Countries are Failing and What Can be Done About It*. Oxford: Oxford University Press.
Collins, H. 1982. *Marxism and Law*. Oxford: Oxford University Press.
Conway, D. 1995. *Classical Liberalism: The Unvanquished Ideal*. Houndmills: Macmillan.
Copland, D.B. 1937. 'The experience of the war and pre-war trends', in D.B. Copland, *The Road to High Employment: Administrative Controls in a Free Economy*. Sydney: Angus & Robertson, 1945, pp.1–17.
Cornes, R. and Sandler, T. 1996. *The Theory of Externalities, Public Goods and Club Goods*. Cambridge: Cambridge University Press, second edition.
Cornwall, J. 1994. *Economic Breakdown and Recovery: Theory and Policy*. Armonk, NY: M. E. Sharpe.
Cottrell, R. 2006. 'Thinking big: a survey of international banking', *Economist*, 20 May 2006.
Crone, P. 2003. *Pre-Industrial Societies*. Oxford: One World Publications.
Crosland, C.A.R. 1956. *The Future of Socialism*. London: Cape.
Curthoys, M. 2004. *Governments, Labour, and the Law in Mid-Victorian Britain: The Trade Union Legislation of the 1870s*. Oxford: Clarendon Press and New York: Oxford University Press.
Cyert, R.M. and March, J.G. 1963. *A Behavioral Theory of the Firm*. Cambridge, MA: Blackwell, second edition, 2001.
Dalziel, P. and Lattimore, R. 2001. *The New Zealand Macroeconomy: A Briefing on the Reforms and Their Legacy*. South Melbourne: Oxford University Press, fourth edition.
David, P.A. 1989. 'Computer and dynamo: the modern productivity paradox in a not too distant mirror', in *Technology and Productivity: The Challenge for Economic Policy*. Paris: OECD, 1991, pp.315–45.
David, P.A. 1997. 'Path dependence and the quest for historical economics: one more chorus of ballad of QWERTY', *Discussion Papers in Economic and Social History*, No. 20, November, Oxford University.
Davis, D.B. 2003. *Challenging the Boundaries of Slavery*. Cambridge, MA: Harvard University Press.
Davis, J.B. 2004. 'Transnational corporations: dynamic structures, strategies, and processes', in O'Hara (2004), pp.129–46.
Diamond, J. 1997. *Guns, Germs and Steel: The Fates of Human Societies*. New York: Norton.
Diamond, J. 2005. *Collapse: How Societies Choose to Fail or Succeed*. New York: Viking.
Dicey, A.V. 1914. *Lectures on the Relation between Law and Public Opinion in England During the Nineteenth Century*. London: Macmillan, second edition.
Dickinson, H.D. 1933. 'Price formation in a socialist economy', *Economic Journal* 43(170), June, pp.237–50.
Djilas, M. 1957. *The New Class: An Analysis of the Communist System*. London: Thames & Hudson.
Dobb, M.H. 1946. 'Bernard Shaw and economics', in M. Dobb, *On Economic Theory and Socialism: Collected Papers*, London: Routledge & Kegan Paul, 1955, pp.205–14.
Dobb, M.H. 1964. *Studies in the Development of Capitalism*. London: Routledge.
Dobb, M.H. 1969. *Welfare Economics and the Economics of Socialism: Towards a Commonsense Critique*. Cambridge: Cambridge University Press.

Dobb, M.H. 1971. 'Introduction' to Marx (1859), pp.5–16.
Doeringer, P.B. and Piore, M.J. 1971. *Internal Labor Markets and Manpower Analysis*. Lexington, MA: D. C. Heath.
Dore, R. 2000. *Stock Market Capitalism: Welfare Capitalism. Japan and Germany Versus the Anglo-Saxons*. Oxford: Oxford University Press.
Dorfman, J. 1959. *The Economic Mind in American Civilization: Volumes IV and V, 1918–1933*. New York: Kelley.
Dormois, J.-P. 2004. *The French Economy in the Twentieth Century*. Cambridge: Cambridge University Press.
Douglas, R. 1993. *Unfinished Business*. New Zealand: Random House.
Draper, H. 1978. *Karl Marx's Theory of Revolution. Volume II: The Politics of Social Classes*. New York: Monthly Review Press.
Duménil, G. and Lévy D. 2004a. *Capital Resurgent: Roots of the Neoliberal Revolution*. Cambridge, MA: Harvard University Press.
Duménil, G. and Lévy, D. 2004b. 'Neoliberal income trends: wealth, class and ownership in the USA', *New Left Review*, 30, November–December, Second Series, pp.105–130.
Dunayevskaya, R. 1941. 'The Union of Soviet Socialist republics is a state capitalist society', unpaginated, in a pocket at the back of R. Dunayevskaya, *The Marxist-Humanist Theory of State Capitalism*, Chicago: News and Letters, 1992.
Dunayevskaya, R. 1944. 'A new revision of Marxian economics', *American Economic Review* 34(3), September, pp.531–7.
Dunayevskaya, R. 1945. 'Revision or reaffirmation of Marxism? A rejoinder', *American Economic Review* 35(3), September, pp.660–4.
Duncan, E. 2006. 'Survey: the heat is on', *Economist*, 9 September 2006.
Dunning, J.H. and Boyd, E. (eds). 2003. *Alliance Capitalism and Corporate Management: Entrepreneurial Cooperation in Knowledge Based Economies*. Cheltenham: Edward Elgar.
Dutton, H.I. 1984. *The Patent System and Inventive Activity During the Industrial Revolution, 1750–1852*. Manchester: Manchester University Press.
Dyer, G. 2005. *War: The New Edition*. Toronto: Vintage Canada.
Eagleton, T. 1996. *The Illusions of Postmodernism*. Oxford: Blackwell.
Earl, P. (ed.). 2001. *The Legacy of Herbert Simon in Economic Analysis*. Cheltenham: Edward Elgar.
Eatwell, J. Milgate, M. and Newman, P. (eds). 1992a. *The New Palgrave Dictionary of Money and Finance, Volume I*. London: Macmillan.
Eatwell, J. Milgate, M. and Newman, P. (eds). 1992b. *The New Palgrave Dictionary of Money and Finance, Volume II*. London: Macmillan.
Eatwell, J. Milgate, M. and Newman, P. (eds). 1992c. *The New Palgrave Dictionary of Money and Finance, Volume III*. London: Macmillan.
Edsall, N.C. 1971. *The Anti-Poor Law Movement 1834–44*. Manchester: Manchester University Press.
Eichengreen, B. 2007. *The European Economy since 1945: Coordinated Capitalism and Beyond*. Princeton: Princeton University Press.
Eichner, A.S. 1969. *The Emergence of Oligopoly: Sugar Refining as a Case Study*. Baltimore: Johns Hopkins Press.
Eichner, A.S. 1976. *The Megacorp and Oligopoly: Micro Foundations of Macro Dynamics*. Cambridge: Cambridge University Press.
Eley, G. 2002. *Forging Democracy: The History of the Left in Europe, 1850–2000*. Oxford: Oxford University Press.

Elster, J. 1985. 'The nature and scope of rational-choice explanation', in E. Le Pore and B.P. McLaughlin (eds). *Actions and Events: Perspectives on the Philosophy of Donald Davidson*. Oxford: Blackwell, pp.311–22.

Emmott, B. 2005. 'The sun also rises: a survey of Japan', *Economist*, 8 October 2005.

Engels, F. 1844. 'Outlines of a critique of political economy', in Marx (1844), pp.197–216.

Engels, F. 1891. 'A critique of the draft social-democratic programme of 1891', in Marx and Engels (1973c), pp.429–39.

Engerman S.L. and Gallman, R.E. (eds). 2000. *The Cambridge Economic History of the United States, Volume III, the Twentieth Century*. Cambridge: Cambridge University Press.

Esping-Andersen, G. 1990. *The Three Worlds of Welfare Capitalism*. Princeton: Princeton University Press.

Esping-Andersen, G. 1996. 'After the golden age? Welfare state dilemmas in a global economy', in G. Esping-Andersen (ed.). *Welfare States in Transition: National Adaptations in Global Economies*, London: Sage, pp.1–30.

Etzkowitz, H. 2002. *MIT and the Rise of Entrepreneurial Science*. London: Routledge.

Evans, J.S. and Leathers, C.G. 1980. 'Veblen on owners, managers, and the control of industry: a reply', *History of Political Economy* 12(3), Fall, pp.441–8.

Evans, P. 1995. *Embedded Autonomy: States and Industrial Transformation*. Princeton: Princeton University Press.

Evans, P., Rueschemeyer, D. and Skocpol, T. (eds). 1985. *Bringing the State Back In*. Cambridge: Cambridge University Press.

Evans, R. 1985. 'Justice Higgins: architect and builder of an Australian folly', in J. Hyde and J. Nurick (eds). *Wages Wasteland: A Radical Examination of the Australian Wage Fixing System*. Sydney: Hale & Ironmonger, pp.29–40.

Fearon, J.D. and Laitin, D.D. 2000. 'Violence and the social construction of ethnic identity,' *International Organisation* 54(4), Autumn, pp.845–77.

Fellner, W.J. 1949. *Competition Among the Few: Oligopoly and Similar Market Structures*. New York: Alfred Knopf.

Fellner, W.J. 1960. *Competition Among the Few: Oligopoly and Similar Market Structures*. New York: Kelley.

Ferguson, N. 2004. *Empire: How Britain Made the Modern World*. Harmondsworth: Penguin.

Ferguson, N. 2005. *Colossus: The Rise and Fall of the American Empire*. Harmondsworth: Penguin.

Fernie, S. 2005. 'The future of British unions: introduction and conclusions', in Fernie and Metcalf (2005), pp.1–18.

Fernie, S. and Metcalf, D. (eds). 2005. *Trade Unions: Resurgence or Demise?* London: Routledge.

Fine, B. 1998. *Labour Market Theory: A Constructive Reassessment*. London: Routledge.

Fischer, F. 1967. *Germany's Aims in the First World War*. New York: Norton.

Fischer, K.P. 1989. *History and Prophecy: Oswald Spengler and the Decline of the West*. New York: Peter Lang.

Flannery, T. 2006. *The Weather Makers: How Man Is Changing the Climate and What it Means for Life on Earth*. New York: Atlantic Monthly Press.

Flora, P., Klaus, F. and Pfenning, W. 1987. *State, Economy and Society in Western Europe, 1815–1975: A Data Handbook in Two Volumes, Volume II*. London:

Macmillan and Frankfurt am Main: Campus Verlag and Chicago: St. James Press.
Fogel, R.W. 2004. *The Escape from Hunger and Premature Death, 1700–2100: Europe, America and the Third World.* Cambridge: Cambridge University Press.
Forder, J. 2004. 'Central bank independence: economic theory, evidence and political legitimacy', in Arestis and Sawyer (2004c), pp.145–80.
Foucault, M. 1980. *Power / Knowledge: Selected Interviews and Other Writings, 1972–1977.* New York: Pantheon.
Frank, R.H. 2004. *Are Positional Externalities Different From Other Externalities?* Ithaca, NY: Cornell University, mimeo.
Freeman, R.B. 1998. 'Spurts in union growth: defining moments and social processes', in Bordo *et al.* (1998), pp.265–95.
Freeman, R.B., Hersch, J. and Mishel, L. 2005. *Emerging Labor Market Institutions for the Twenty-first Century.* Chicago: Chicago University Press.
Frieden, J.A. 2006. *Global Capitalism: Its Fall and Rise in the Twentieth Century.* New York: Norton.
Friedman, G. and Friedman, M. 1996. *The Future of War: Power, Technology and American World Dominance in the 21st Century.* New York: Crown.
Friedman, G. and Lebard, M. 1991. *The Coming War with Japan.* New York: St. Martin's Press.
Friedman, M. 1957. *A Theory of the Consumption Function: A Study by the National Bureau of Economic Research, New York.* Princeton: Princeton University Press.
Friedman, M. 1968. 'The role of monetary policy', *American Economic Review* 58(1), March, pp.1–17.
Friedman, M. and Schwartz, A.J. 1963. *A Monetary History of the United States, 1867–1960.* Princeton: Princeton University Press.
Friedman, T. 2005. *The World is Flat: A Brief History of the Twenty-First Century.* New York: Farrar, Straus & Giroux.
Fromkin, D. 2004. *Europe's Last Summer. Who Started the Great War in 1914?* London: Heineman.
Froud, J., Leaver, A., Williams, K. and Johal, S. 2006. *Financialisation and Strategy: Narrative and Numbers.* London: Routledge.
Fukuyama, F. 1992. *The End of History and the Last Man.* New York: Free Press.
Fukuyama, F. 1993. 'Capitalism & democracy: the missing link', in L. Diamond and M.F. Plattner (eds). *Capitalism, Socialism, and Democracy Revisited.* Baltimore: Johns Hopkins University Press, pp.94–104.
Fukuyama, F. 2002. *Our Posthuman Future: Consequences of the Biotechnology Revolution.* New York: Farrar, Straus & Giroux.
Fukuyama, F. 2006. *After the Neocons: America at the Crossroads.* New Haven, CT: Yale University Press.
Gabor, A. 2000. *The Capitalist Philosophers: The Geniuses of Modern Business – Their Lives, Times, and Ideas.* New York: Three Rivers Press.
Gahan, P. 1991. 'Forward to the past? The case of "new production concepts" ', *Journal of Industrial Relations* 33(2), June, pp.155–77.
Galambos, L. 1994. 'The triumph of oligopoly', in T. Weiss and D. Schaefer (eds). *American Economic Development in Historical Perspective.* Stanford: Stanford University Press, pp.241–53.
Galbraith, J.K. 1952. *American Capitalism: The Concept of Countervailing Power.* Harmonsworth: Penguin, 1963.

Galbraith, J.K. 1954. *The Great Crash: 1929*. Harmondsworth: Penguin.
Galbraith, J.K. 1967. *The New Industrial State*. London: Deutsch, 1972.
Galbraith, J.K. 1973. *Economics and the Public Purpose*. Boston: Houghton Mifflin.
Galbraith, J.K. 1978. 'On post Keynesian economics', *Journal of Post Keynesian Economics* 1(1), Fall, pp.8–11.
Gamble, A. 1988. *The Free Economy and the Strong State: The Politics of Thatcherism*. London: Macmillan.
Gamble, A., Marsh, D. and Tant, T. (eds). 1999. *Marxism and Social Science*. London: Macmillan.
Garland, D. 2001. *The Culture of Control: Crime and Social Order in Contemporary Society*. Chicago: University of Chicago Press.
Gay, P. 1952. *The Dilemmas of Democratic Socialism: Edward Bernstein's Challenge to Marx*. London: Collier Macmillan, 1970.
Gellner, E. 1980a. 'A Russian Marxist philosophy of history', in Gellner (1980b), pp.59–82.
Gellner, E. (ed.). 1980b. *Soviet and Western Anthropology*. London: Duckworth.
Gellner, E. 1983. *Nations and Nationalism*. Ithaca, NY: Cornell University Press.
Gellner, E. 1988. *Plough, Sword and Book: The Structure of Human History*. London: Paladin.
Gellner, E. 1994. *Conditions of Liberty: Civil Society and Its Rivals*. Harmondsworth: Penguin.
George, S. 1999. 'A short history of neo-liberalism: twenty years of elite economics and emerging opportunities for structural change', from a conference on Economic Sovereignty in a Globalising World, Bangkok, 24–26 March 1999. http://www.globalexchange.org/economy/econ101/neoliberalism.html [accessed 13 February 2003].
George, S. and Sabelli, F. 1994. *Faith and Credit: The World Bank's Secular Empire*. Boulder, CO: Westview Press.
Ger, G. and Belk, R.W. 1996. 'Cross-cultural differences in materialism', *Journal of Economic Psychology* 17(1), April, pp.55–77.
Gerschenkron, A. 1966. *Economic Backwardness in Historical Perspective: A Book of Essays*. Cambridge, MA: Harvard University Press, 1966.
Gershuny, J. 1978. *After Industrial Society? The Emerging Self-Service Economy*. London: Macmillan.
Geuss, R. 2001. *History and Illusion in Politics*. Cambridge: Cambridge University Press.
Giddens, A. 1994. *Beyond Left and Right: The Future of Radical Politics*. Cambridge: Polity Press.
Giddens, A. 2000. *The Third Way and Its Critics*. Cambridge: Polity Press.
Gilmour, I. 1992. *Dancing with Dogma: Britain Under Thatcherism*. London: Simon & Schuster.
Gilpin, R. 1981. *War and Change in World Politics*. Cambridge: Cambridge University Press.
Gilpin, R. 2000. *The Challenge of Global Capitalism: The World Economy in the 21st Century*. Princeton: Princeton University Press.
Gilpin, R. 2001. *Global Political Economy: Understanding the International Economic Order*. Princeton: Princeton University Press.
Glyn, A. (ed.). 2001. *Social Democracy in Neoliberal Times: The Left and Economic Policy since 1980*. Oxford: Oxford University Press.

Glyn, A. 2006. *Capitalism Unleashed: Finance, Globalization and Welfare*. Oxford: Oxford University Press.
Glyn, A. and Sutcliffe, R. 1972. *British Capitalism, Workers and the Profit Squeeze*. Harmondsworth: Penguin.
Godard, J. 2004. 'The new institutionalism, capitalist diversity, and industrial relations', in B.E. Kaufman (ed.). *Theoretical Perspectives on Work and the Employment Relationship*. Champaign-Urbana, IL: Industrial Relations Research Association, pp.229–64.
Goldin, G. 2000. 'Labor markets in the twentieth century', in Engerman and Gallman (2000), pp.549–623.
Gordon, D., Edwards, R. and Reich, M. 1982. *Segmented Work, Divided Workers; The Historical Transformation of Labor in the United States*. Cambridge: Cambridge University Press.
Gordon, R.A. 1945. *Business Leadership in the Large Corporation*. Berkeley: University of California Press, second edition, 1962.
Gordon, R.A. 1960. 'Preface and postscript' to R.A. Gordon, *Business Leadership in the Large Corporation*. Berkeley: University of California Press, 1962, pp.v–xvii.
Gowan, P. 1999. *The Global Gamble: Washington's Faustian Bid for World Dominance*. London: Verso.
Gowan, P. 2001. 'Neoliberal cosmopolitanism', *New Left Review* 11, September–October, Second Series, pp.79–93.
Gowan, P. 2002. 'A calculus of power', *New Left Review* 16, July–August, Second Series, pp.47–67.
Gowan, P. 2004. 'American lebensraum', *New Left Review* 30, November–December, Second Series, pp.155–64.
Gowan, P. 2005. 'A salutary shock for bien pensant Europe', *Radical Philosophy* 133, September–October, pp.7–12.
Grahl, J. 2001. 'Globalized finance: the challenge to the euro', *New Left Review* 8, March–April, Second Series, pp.23–47.
Gray, C.S. 2005. *Another Bloody Century: Future Warfare*. London: Weidenfeld & Nicolson.
Greenfeld, L. 2001. *The Spirit of Capitalism: Nationalism and Economic Growth*. Cambridge, MA: Harvard University Press.
Greenwood, J., Seshadri, A. and Yorukoglu, M. 2005. 'Engines of liberation', *Review of Economic Studies* 72(1), January, pp.109–33.
Grieve Smith, J. 2001. *There is a Better Way: A New Economic Agenda for Labour*. London: Anthem Press, 2005, revised edition.
Grundmann, R. and Stehr, N. 2004. 'Sombart, Werner', in G. Ritzer (ed.). *Encyclopedia of Social Theory, Volume II*. Thousand Oaks, CA: Sage, pp.775–7.
Guinnane, T.W., Sundstrom, W. and Whatley, W. (eds). 2004. *History Matters: Essays on Economic Growth, Technology, and Demographic Change*. Stanford: Stanford University Press.
Hahn, F.H. 1980. 'Monetarism and economic theory', *Economica* 47(185), February, pp.1–17.
Hahn, F.H. and Brechling, R. (eds). 1965. *The Theory of Interest Rates*. London: Macmillan.
Halperin, S. 1997. *In the Mirror of the Third World: Capitalist Development in Modern Europe*. Ithaca, NY: Cornell University Press.
Hannah, L. 1986. *Inventing Retirement. The Development of Occupational Pensions in Britain*. Cambridge: Cambridge University Press.

Harbridge, R. 2006. *Case Study on Industrial Relations: Reforms in New Zealand*, La Trobe University, mimeo.
Harding, N. 1983. *Lenin's Political Thought: Theory and Practice in the Democratic and Socialist Revolutions*. London: Macmillan.
Hardt, M. and Negri, A. 2000. *Empire*. Cambridge, MA: Harvard University Press.
Hardt, M. and Negri, A. 2004. *Multitude: War and Democracy in the Age of Empire*. Harmondsworth: Penguin.
Hargreaves Heap, S., Hollis, M., Lyons, B., Sugden, R. and Weale, A. 1992. *The Theory of Choice: A Critical Guide*. Oxford: Blackwell.
Hargreaves Heap, S. and Varoufakis, Y. 1995. *Game Theory: A Critical Analysis*. London: Routledge.
Harrison, B. and Bluestone, B. 1988. *The Great U-Turn: Corporate Restructuring and the Polarizing of America*. New York: Basic Books.
Harrop, M. (ed.). 1992. *Power and Policy in Liberal Democracies*. Cambridge: Cambridge University Press.
Hart, P.E. and Clarke, R. 1980. *Concentration in British Industry 1935–75. A Study of the Growth, Causes and Effects of Concentration in British Manufacturing Industries*. Cambridge: Cambridge University Press.
Harvey, D. 2005. *A Brief History of Neoliberalism*. Oxford: Oxford University Press.
Hayek, F. von. 1944. *The Road to Serfdom*. London: Routledge.
Heertje, A. 2006. *Schumpeter on the Economics of Innovation and the Development of Capitalism*. Cheltenham: Edward Elgar.
Held, D., McGrew, A., Goldblatt, D. and Perraton, J. 1999. *Global Transformations: Politics, Economics and Culture*. Stanford: Stanford University Press.
Helleiner, E. 1994. *States and the Reemergence of Global Finance: From Bretton Woods to the 1990s*. Ithaca, NY: Cornell University Press.
Henderson, D. 1998. *The Changing Fortunes of Economic Liberalism: Yesterday, Today and Tomorrow*. London: Institute of Economic Affairs.
Henderson, E. 1954. 'Summary record of the debate', in Chamberlin (1954), pp.493–540.
Henry, J.F. 2001. 'Keynes' economic program, social institutions, ideology, and property rights', *Journal of Economic Issues* 35(3), September, pp.633–55.
Hicks, J.R. 1969. *A Theory of Economic History*. Oxford: Oxford University Press.
Higgs, R. 1987. *Crisis and Leviathan: Critical Episodes in the Growth of American Government*. Oxford: Oxford University Press.
Hilferding, R. 1910. *Finance Capital: A Study of the Latest Phase of Capitalist Development*. London: Routledge & Kegan Paul, 1981.
Hilferding, R. 1915. 'Arbeitsgemeinschaft der Klassen?', *Der Kampf* 8(10), October, pp.321–9.
Hilferding, R. 1940. 'State capitalism or totalitarian state economy', *Modern Review*, June, pp.266–71.
Hilton, R.H. (ed.). 1976. *The Transition from Feudalism to Capitalism*. London: New Left Books.
Hirsch, F. 1976. *Social Limits to Growth*. Cambridge, MA: Harvard University Press.
Hirschman, A.O. 1970. *Exit, Voice and Loyalty: Responses to Decline in Firms, Organisations and States*. Cambridge, MA: Harvard University Press.
Hirschman, A.O. 1991. *The Rhetoric of Reaction: Perversity, Futility, Jeopardy*. Cambridge, MA: Harvard University Press.
Hobsbawm, E.J. 1964. *Labouring Men: Studies in the History of Labour*. London: Weidenfeld & Nicolson.

Hobsbawm, E. 1994. *Age of Extremes: The Short Twentieth Century 1914–1991*. London: Michael Joseph and New York: Pantheon Books.

Hobsbawm, E. 1998. 'Introduction' to Karl Marx and Friedrich Engels, *The Communist Manifesto: A Modern Edition*. London: Verso, pp.1–31.

Hobson, J.A. 1902. *Imperialism: A Study*. London: James Nisbet.

Hodgson, G.M. 1999. *Economics and Utopia: Why the Learning Community is not the End of History*. London: Routledge.

Holmes, S. 1993. *The Anatomy of Antiliberalism*. Cambridge, MA: Harvard University Press.

Howard, M.C. and King, J.E. 1985. *The Political Economy of Marx*. Harlow: Longmans.

Howard, M.C. and King, J.E. 1989. *A History of Marxian Economics: Volume I, 1883–1929*. London: Macmillan and Princeton: Princeton University Press.

Howard, M.C. and King, J.E. 1992. *A History of Marxian Economics: Volume II, 1929–1990*. London: Macmillan and Princeton: Princeton University Press.

Howard, M.C. and King, J.E. 1994. 'Is socialism economically feasible? An analysis in terms of historical materialism', *Review of Political Economy* 6(2), pp.133–51.

Howard, M.C. and King, J.E. 1999. 'Whatever happened to imperialism?', in Chilcote (1999), pp.19–40.

Howard, M.C. and King, J.E. 2000. 'The Stalinists' counter-revolutions', in Pollin (2000), pp.279–99.

Howard, M.C. and King, J.E. 2001a. 'Where Marx was right: toward a more secure foundation for heterodox economics', *Cambridge Journal of Economics* 25(6), November, pp.785–807.

Howard, M.C. and King, J.E. 2001b. ' "State capitalism" in the Soviet Union', *History of Economics Review* 34, Summer, pp.110–26.

Howard, M.C. and King J.E. 2002. 'Crises in Marx's analysis of the market', *International Journal of Applied Economics and Econometrics* 10(3), July–September, pp.319–50.

Howard, M.C. and King, J.E. 2003. 'Rudolf Hilferding', in W.J. Samuels (ed.). *European Economists of the Early 20th Century: Studies of Neglected Thinkers of Belgium, France, the Netherlands, and Scandinavia, Volume 2*. Cheltenham: Edward Elgar, pp.119–36.

Howard, M.C. and King, J.E. 2004. 'The rise of neoliberalism in advanced capitalist economies', in Arestis and Sawyer (2004c), pp.107–44. This article was originally published in *International Papers in Political Economy* in 2002.

Howell, C. 2003. 'Varieties of capitalism: and then there was one?', *Comparative Politics* 36(1), October, pp.103–24.

Howell, C. 2005. *Trade Unions and the State: The Construction of Industrial Relations Institutions in Britain, 1890–2000*. Princeton: Princeton University Press.

Howells, P.G.A. 1999. 'The source of endogenous money', *Economic Issues* 4(1), March, pp.101–12.

Hubbard, R.G. (ed.). 1991. *Financial Markets and Financial Crises*. Chicago: University of Chicago Press.

Ingham, G. 2004. *The Nature of Money*. Cambridge: Polity Press.

Ironmonger, D. 1989. *Households Work: Productive Activities, Women and Income in the Household Economy*. Sydney: Allen & Unwin.

Iversen, T. 2005. *Capitalism, Democracy, and Welfare*. Cambridge: Cambridge University Press.
James, H. 2002. *The End of Globalization: Lessons from the Great Depression*. Cambridge, MA: Harvard University Press.
Johansen, L. 1976. 'L.V. Kantorovich's contribution to economics', *Scandinavian Journal of Economics* 78(1), March, pp.61–80.
Johnson, C. 1982. *MITI and the Japanese Miracle: The Growth of Industrial Policy, 1925–1975*. Stanford, CA: Stanford University Press.
Johnson, C. (ed.). 1984. *The Industrial Policy Debate*. San Francisco: ICS Press.
Johnson, C. 2004. *The Sorrows of Empire: Militarism, Secrecy and the End of the Republic*. New York: Henry Holt and Company.
Jomo, K.S. and Fine, B. (eds). 2006. *The New Development Economics: After the Washington Consensus*. London: Zed Books.
Jorgenson, D.W., Goettle, R.J., Hurd, B.H. and Smith, J.B. 2004. *US Market Consequences of Global Climate Change*. Arlington: Pew Center on Global Climate Change.
Judt, T. 2005. *Postwar: A History of Europe since 1945*. New York: Penguin.
Kahn, J.A. and Lim, J-S. 1998. 'Skilled labor-augmenting technical progress in US manufacturing', *Quarterly Journal of Economics*, 113(4), November, pp.1281–308.
Kaldor, N. 1996. *Causes of Growth and Stagnation in the World Economy*. Cambridge: Cambridge University Press.
Kaldor, N., Robinson, J., Evans, A.A., Schumacher, E.F. and Yates, P.L. 1943. *Planning For Abundance*. London: National Peace Council, Peace Aims Pamphlet No. 21.
Kalecki, M. 1943. 'Political aspects of full employment', *Political Quarterly* 14(4), October, pp.322–31.
Kalleberg, A.L. 2001. 'Organising flexibility: the flexible firm in a new century', *British Journal of Industrial Relations*, 39(4), December, pp.479–504.
Kanth, R.K. 1986. *Political Economy and Laissez-faire: Economics and Ideology in the Ricardian Era*. Totowa, NJ: Rowman & Littlefield.
Kapstein, E.B. 1994. *Governing the Global Economy: International Finance and the State*. Cambridge, MA: Harvard University Press.
Kautsky, K. 1892. *The Class Struggle*. New York: Norton, 1971.
Kautsky, K. 1898. 'Speech at the party conference at Stuttgart', in Tudor and Tudor (1988), pp.293–8.
Kautsky, K. 1899. *Bernstein und das Sozialdemokratische Program: eine Antikritik*. Stuttgart: Dietz.
Kautsky, K. 1919. 'Terrorism and communism', in P. Goode (ed.). *Karl Kautsky: Selected Political Writings*. London: Macmillan, 1983.
Kaysen, C. 1957. 'The social significance of the modern corporation', *American Economic Review* 47(2), May, Papers and Proceedings of the Sixty-eighth Annual Meeting of the American Economic Association, pp.311–19.
Kaysen, C. (ed.). 1996. *The American Corporation Today*. New York: Oxford University Press.
Kealey, T. 1996. *The Economic Laws of Scientific Research*. Basingstoke: Macmillan.
Kennedy, P. 1989. *The Rise and Fall of the Great Powers: Economic Change and Military Conflict from 1500 to 2000*. London: Fontana.
Kerr, C. 1954. 'The balkanization of labor markets', in E. Wight Bakke (ed.). *Labor Mobility and Economic Opportunity*. New York: Wiley and MIT Press, pp.92–110.

Kerr, C., Dunlop, J.T., Harbison, F.H. and Myers, C.A. 1960. *Industrialism and Industrial Man: Problems of Labor and Management in Economic Growth*. Cambridge, MA: Harvard University Press.

Kerr, R.A. 2002. 'European winters: mild winters mostly hot air, not gulf stream, *Science* 297, September, number 5590, p.2202.

Keynes, J.M. 1925. 'Am I a liberal?', in Keynes (1972), pp.295–306.

Keynes, J.M. 1926. 'The end of laissez-faire', in Keynes (1972), pp.273–94.

Keynes, J.M. 1936. *The General Theory of Employment, Interest and Money*, reprinted as volume VII of *The Collected Writings of John Maynard Keynes*. London: Macmillan for the Royal Economic Society, 1972.

Keynes, J.M. 1972. *The Collected Writings of John Maynard Keynes, Volume IX: Essays in Persuasion*. London: Macmillan for the Royal Economic Society, 1973.

Kindleberger, C.P. 1987. *The World in Depression 1929–1939*. Harmondsworth: Penguin.

Kindleberger, C.P. 1996. *Manias, Panics and Crashes: A History of Financial Crises*. New York: Wiley, third edition.

King, J.E. 2002. *A History of Post Keynesian Economics since 1936*. Cheltenham: Edward Elgar.

King, J.E. 2004. 'Planning for abundance: Nicholas Kaldor and Joan Robinson on the socialist reconstruction of Britain, 1942–45', in I. Barens, V. Caspari and B. Schefold (eds). *Political Events and Economic Ideas*. Cheltenham: Edward Elgar, pp.306–24.

Kite, C. 2004. 'The stability of the globalized welfare state', in Södersten (2004), pp.213–38.

Klein, N. 2002. *No Logo: Taking Aim at the Brand Bullies*. New York: Picador.

Klein, N. 2007. *The Shock Doctrine: The Rise of Disaster Capitalism*. Toronto: Alfred A. Knopf.

Kolbert, E. 2006. *Field Notes from a Catastrophe: Man, Nature, and Climate Change*. New York: Bloomsbury.

Koshimura, S. 1977. 'Equations of chain bankruptcy: from sectoral to general crises', in J. Schwartz (ed.). *The Subtle Anatomy of Capitalism*. Santa Monica: Goodyear Publishing Company, pp.255–82.

Kotz, D.M. 2003. 'Neoliberalism and the social structure of accumulation theory of long-run capital accumulation', *Review of Radical Political Economics* 35(3), pp.263–70.

Kregel, J.A. 1985. 'Budget deficits, stabilization policy and liquidity preference: Keynes's postwar policy proposals', in F. Vicarelli (ed.). *Keynes's Relevance Today*. London: Macmillan, pp.28–50.

Krugman, P.R. 1997. *Pop Internationalism*. Cambridge, MA: MIT Press.

Krugman, P.R. 1999. *The Return of Depression Economics*. New York: Norton.

Krugman, P.R. 2006a. 'The great wealth transfer', *Rolling Stone*, 30 November 2006.

Krugman, P.R. 2006b. 'Outsourcer in chief', *New York Times*, 11 December 2006.

Krugman, P.R. and Obstfeld M. 2005. *International Economics: Theory and Policy*. New York: Addison Wesley, seventh edition.

Kunz, D.B. 1997. *Butter and Guns: America's Cold War Economic Diplomacy*. New York: Free Press.

Lange, O. 1936–7. 'On the economic theory of socialism', in O. Lange and F.M. Taylor, *On the Economic Theory of Socialism*, B.E. Lippincott (ed.). New York: McGraw-Hill, 1964, pp.57–142.

Lange, O. 1945. 'Marxian economics in the Soviet Union', *American Economic Review* 35(1), March, pp.127–33.

Lange, O. 1967. 'The computer and the market', in C.H. Feinstein (ed.). *Socialism, Capitalism and Economic Growth: Essays Presented to Maurice Dobb*. Cambridge: Cambridge University Press, pp.158–61.

Le Grand, J. and Bartlett, W. 1993. *Quasi-markets and Social Policy*. London: Macmillan.

Leathers, C.G. and Evans, J.S. 1973. 'Thorstein Veblen and the new industrial state', *History of Political Economy* 5(2), Fall, pp.420–37.

Lee, C.H. 2000. *The Origins of Leviathan: The Growth of Public Expenditure and Taxation in the United Kingdom 1880–1938*. University of Aberdeen, mimeo.

Lee, F.S. and Samuels, W.J. (eds). 1992. *The Heterodox Economics of Gardiner C. Means: A Collection*. Armonk, NY: M. E. Sharpe.

Leijonhufvud, A. 1968. *On Keynesian Economics and the Economics of Keynes*. Oxford: Oxford University Press.

Lekachman, R. 1969. *The Age of Keynes: A Biographical Study*. Harmondsworth: Penguin.

Lenin, V.I. 1916. *Imperialism: The Highest Stage of Capitalism: A Popular Outline*, in *Collected Works, Volume XXII*. Moscow: Progress Publishers, 1960–70, pp.185–304.

Leontief, W. 1976. *National Economic Planning: Methods and Problems*. St. Louis, Missouri: School of Business and Administration, St. Louis University, Second Annual Distinguished Guest Lecture Program, April 23, 1976.

Lerner, A.P. 1943. 'Functional finance and the federal debt', *Social Research* 10(1), February, pp.38–51.

Lester, R.A. 1958. *As Unions Mature: An Analysis of the Evolution of American Unionism*. Princeton: Princeton University Press.

Levinson, M. 2006. *The Box: How the Shipping Container Made the World Smaller and the World Economy Bigger*. Princeton: Princeton University Press.

Levitt, A. 2002. *Take on the Street: What Wall Street and Corporate American Don't Want You to Know. What You Can Do to Fight Back*. New York: Pantheon.

Levy, J. 1989. 'The causes of war: a review of theories and evidence', in P. Tetlock *et al.* (eds). *Behavior, Society and Nuclear War, Volume I*. Oxford: Oxford University Press, pp.209–333.

Lichtenstein, N. (ed.). 2006. *Wal-Mart: The Face of Twenty-First Century Capitalism*. New York: The New Press.

Lindbeck, A. 1998. *Swedish Lessons for Post-Socialist Countries*. Stockholm: Institute for International Economic Studies, mimeo.

Lindert, P.H. 2000. 'US foreign trade and trade policy in the twentieth century', in Engerman and Gallman (2000), pp.407–62.

Lipsey, R.G., Carlaw, K.I. and Bekar, C. 2005. *Economic Transformations: General Purpose Technologies and Long Term Economic Growth*. Oxford: Oxford University Press.

Lopson, P. 2001. *Theories of Human Nature*. Peterborough, Ontario: Broadview Press.

Löwry, M. 1996. 'Figures in Weberian Marxism', *Theory and Society* 25(3), June, pp.431–46.

Luce, E. 2007. *In Spite of the Gods: The Strange Rise of Modern India*. New York: Doubleday.

Lukes, S. 2003. 'The grand dichotomy of the twentieth century', in Ball and Bellamy (2003), pp.602–26.

Luxemburg, R. 1898. 'Social reform or revolution?', in Tudor and Tudor (1988), pp.249–75.

Luxemburg, R. 1913. *The Accumulation of Capital*. London: Routledge & Kegan Paul, 1951.

Lydall, H. 1998. *A Critique of Orthodox Economics: An Alternative Model*. Basingstoke: Macmillan and New York: St. Martin's Press.

MacAvoy, P.W. and Millstein, I.M. 2003. *The Recurrent Crisis in Corporate Governance*. Houndmills: Palgrave Macmillan.

Macfarlane, A. 2000. *The Riddle of the Modern World: Of Liberty, Wealth, and Equality*. London: Palgrave.

MacHardy, K.J. 2003. *War, Religion and Court Patronage in Habsburg Austria: The Social and Cultural Dimensions of Political Interaction, 1521–1622*. London: Palgrave Macmillan.

Machin, S. and van Reenan, J. 1998. 'Technology and changes in skill structure: evidence from seven OECD countries', *Quarterly Journal of Economics* 113(4), November, pp.1215–44.

MacIntyre, A. 1985. *After Virtue: A Study in Moral Theory*. London: Duckworth.

Macmillan, H. 1938. *The Middle Way: A Study of the Problem of Economic and Social Progress in a Free and Democratic Society*. London: Macmillan.

Macpherson, C.B. 1962. *The Political Theory of Possessive Individualism: Hobbes to Locke*. Oxford: Oxford University Press.

Maddison, A. 2001. *The World Economy: A Millennial Perspective*. Paris: OECD.

Maddison, A. 2003. *The World Economy: Historical Statistics*. Paris: OECD.

Maier, C.S. 1987. *In Search of Stability: Explorations in Historical Political Economy*. Cambridge: Cambridge University Press.

Mair, P. 2006. 'Ruling the void? The hollowing of western democracy', *New Left Review* 42, November–December, Second Series, pp.25–51.

Malone, T.W., Yates, J. and Benjamin, R.I. 1987. 'Electronic markets and electronic hierarchies', *Communications of the Association for Computing Machinery* 30(6), June, pp.484–97.

Mandelbaum, M. 2003. *The Ideas that Conquered the World: Peace, Democracy and Free Markets in the Twenty-First Century*. New York: Public Affairs.

Mandelbrot, B. and Hudson, R.L. 2004. *The (Mis)Behaviour of Markets: A Fractal View of Risk, Ruin and Reward*. New York: Basic Books.

Mann, M. 1986. *The Sources of Social Power, Volume I: A History of Power from the Beginning to A.D. 1760*. Cambridge: Cambridge University Press.

Mann, M. 1988. *States, War and Capitalism*. Oxford: Blackwell.

Mann, M. 1993. *The Sources of Social Power, Volume II: The Rise of Classes and Nation-States, 1760–1914*. Cambridge: Cambridge University Press.

Mann, M. 2003. *Incoherent Empire*. London: Verso.

Mann, M. 2004. *Fascists*. Cambridge: Cambridge University Press.

Mann, M. 2005. *The Dark Side of Democracy. Explaining Ethnic Cleansing*. Cambridge: Cambridge University Press.

Marcuse, H. 1942. 'Staat und individuum im nationalsozialismus', *Tageszeitung* [Berlin], 13 October 2000.

Marcuse, H. 1958. *Soviet Marxism: A Critical Analysis*. London: Routledge & Kegan Paul.

Marglin, S. and Schor, J. (eds). 1990. *The Golden Age of Capitalism: Lessons for the 1990s*. Oxford: Oxford University Press.

Marris, R.L. 1967. *The Economic Theory of 'Managerial' Capitalism*. London: Macmillan.

Marris, R.L. (ed.). 1974. *The Corporate Society*. London: Macmillan.

Marshall, A. 1919. *Industry and Trade: A Study of Industrial Technique and Business Organisation*. London: Macmillan.

Marshall, T.H. 1950. *Citizenship and Social Class and Other Essays*. Cambridge: Cambridge University Press.

Martin, S. 2004. 'Globalization and the natural limits of competition', in Neumann and Weigand (2004), pp.16–64.

Martinelli, A. 1994. 'Entrepreneurship and management', in N.J. Smelser and R. Swedberg (eds). *The Handbook of Economic Sociology*. Princeton: Princeton University Press and New York: Russell Sage Foundation, pp.476–503.

Marx, K. 1844. *Economic and Philosophical Manuscripts of 1844*, D.J. Struik (ed.). London: Lawrence and Wishart, 1970.

Marx, K. 1857. *The Grundrisse*, D. McLellan (ed.). London: Paladin, 1973.

Marx, K. 1859. *A Contribution to a Critique of Political Economy*, with introduction by Maurice Dobb. London: Lawrence & Wishart, 1971.

Marx, K. 1863. *Theories of Surplus Value, Volume I*. London: Lawrence & Wishart, 1969.

Marx, K. 1867. *Capital: A Critique of Political Economy, Volume I, Capitalist Production*. London: Lawrence & Wishart, 1970.

Marx, K. 1872. 'The nationalisation of the land', in Marx and Engels (1973b), pp.288–90.

Marx, K. 1885. *Capital: A Critique of Political Economy, Volume II, The Process of Circulation of Capital*. Moscow: Progress Publishers, 1967.

Marx, K. 1894. *Capital: A Critique of Political Economy, Volume III, The Process of Capitalist Production as a Whole*. London: Lawrence & Wishart, 1972.

Marx, K. and Engels, F. 1845. *'The German Ideology'* in *The German Ideology: Including Theses on Feuerbach and Introduction to The Critique of Political Economy*. Amherst, NY: Prometheus Books, 1998.

Marx, K. and Engels, F. 1848. *Manifesto of the Communist Party*, in Marx and Engels (1973a), pp.108–37.

Marx, K. and Engels, F. 1973a. *Selected Works in Three Volumes: Volume One*. Moscow: Progress Publishers.

Marx, K. and Engels, F. 1973b. *Selected Works in Three Volumes: Volume Two*. Moscow: Progress Publishers.

Marx, K. and Engels, F. 1973c. *Selected Works in Three Volumes: Volume Three*. Moscow: Progress Publishers.

Mason, E.S. (ed.). 1959. *The Corporation in Modern Society*. Cambridge, MA: Harvard University Press.

Matheson, J. and Babb, P. (eds). 2002. *Social Trends 32, 2002*. London: Stationary Office.

Mathews, J.A. 1989. *Tools of Change: New Technology and the Democratisation of Work*. Sydney: Pluto.

Mattick, P. 1939. 'Council Communism', in P. Mattick (ed.). *Anti-Bolshevik Communism*. White Plains, NY: M. E. Sharpe, 1978, pp.73–86.

Mazower, M. 1999. *Dark Continent: Europe's Twentieth Century*. New York: Knopf.

McKibben, B. 2007. 'Warning on Warming', *New York Review*, 15 March 2007, pp.44–5.

McNeill, W.H. 1982. *The Pursuit of Power: Technology, Armed Force, and Society since A.D. 1000*. Chicago: University of Chicago Press.
Meade, J.E. 1945. 'Economic planning', in S. Howson (ed.). *The Collected Papers of James Meade, Volume I*. London: Unwin Hyman, 1988, pp.265–74.
Meade, J.E. 1948. *Planning and the Price Mechanism: The Liberal-Socialist Solution*, London: Allen & Unwin.
Meade, J.E. 1968. 'Is "The New Industrial State" inevitable?', *Economic Journal* 78(310), June, pp.372–92.
Meade, J.E. 1970. 'The theory of indicative planning', in S. Howson (ed.). *The Collected Papers of James Meade, Volume 2*. London: Unwin Hyman, 1988, pp.109–57.
Means, G.C. 1935a. 'Industrial prices and their relative inflexibility', in Lee and Samuels (1992), pp.32–72.
Means, G.C. 1935b. 'The major causes of the depression', in Lee and Samuels (1992), pp.73–92.
Means, G.C. 1968. 'Implications of the corporate revolution in economic theory', in Berle and Means (1932), pp.xxix–xxxviii.
Mearsheimer, J.J. 2001. *The Tragedy of Great Power Politics*. New York: Norton.
Medema, S.G. 1994. *Ronald H. Coase*. Basingstoke: Macmillan and New York: St. Martin's Press.
Meek, R.L. 1973. (ed.). *Turgot on Progress, Sociology and Economics: A Philosophical Review of the Successive Advances of the Human Mind, On Universal History [and] Reflections on the Formation and the Distribution of Wealth*. Cambridge: Cambridge University Press.
Meek, R.L. 1976. *Social Science and the Ignoble Savage*. Cambridge: Cambridge University Press.
Micklethwait, J. and Wooldridge, A. 2003. *The Company: A Short History of a Revolutionary Idea*. London: Weidenfeld & Nicolson and New York: Modern Library.
Milgrom, P. and Roberts, J. 1992. *Economics, Organization and Management*. Englewood Cliffs, NJ: Prentice-Hall.
Mills, C.W. 1948. *The New Men of Power: American's Labor Leaders*. Chicago: University of Illinois Press, 2001.
Mills, C.W. 1951. *White Collar: The American Middle Class*. New York: Oxford University Press.
Mills, C.W. 1959. *The Power Elite*. Oxford: Oxford University Press.
Mills, C.W. 1962. *The Marxists*. Harmondsworth: Penguin.
Mills, C.W. 1989. 'Determination and consciousness in Marx', *Canadian Journal of Philosophy* 19, pp.421–46.
Mincer, J. 1962. 'Labor force participation of married women: a study in labor supply', in National Bureau for Economic Research, *Aspects of Labor Economics*. Princeton: Princeton University Press, pp.63–97.
Minford, P., Mahambare, V. and Nowell, E. 2005. *Should Britain Leave the EU? An Economic Analysis of a Troubled Relationship*. Cheltenham: Edward Elgar.
Minsky, H.P. 1982. *Can 'It' Happen Again? Essays on Instability and Finance*. Armonk, NY: M. E. Sharpe.
Mitchell, B.R. 1998a. *International Historical Statistics: Europe 1750–1993*. Basingstoke: Macmillan and New York: Stockton Press, fourth edition.
Mitchell, B.R. 1998b. *International Historical Statistics: The Americas 1750–1993*. Basingstoke: Macmillan and New York: Stockton Press, fourth edition.

Moe, T.M. 1984. 'The new economics of organisation', *American Journal of Political Science* 28(4), November, pp.739–77.
Mokyr, J. 1990. *Twenty-Five Centuries of Technological Change: An Historical Survey*. Chur, Switzerland: Harwood Academic Publishers.
Molho, I. 1997. *The Economics of Information: Lying and Cheating in Markets and Organizations*. Oxford: Blackwell.
Monbiot, G. 2001. *Captive State: The Corporate Takeover of Britain*. Basingstoke: Pan Books.
Moore, B. 1966. *Social Origins of Dictatorship and Democracy: Lord and Peasant in the Making of the Modern World*. Harmondsworth: Penguin.
Moore, B. 1998. *Moral Aspects of Economic Growth and Other Essays*. Ithaca: NY: Cornell University Press.
Morgan, M.S. and Rutherford, M. 1998. 'American economics: the character of the transformation', in M.S. Morgan and M. Rutherford (eds). *From Interwar Pluralism to Postwar Neoclassicism*. Durham, NC: Duke University Press, pp.1–26.
Mueller, D.C. (ed.). 1997. *Perspectives on Public Choice: A Handbook*. Cambridge: Cambridge University Press.
Muller, J.Z. 1997. *Conservatism: An Anthology of Social and Political Thought from David Hume to the Present*. Princeton: Princeton University Press.
Muller, J.Z. 2002. *The Mind and the Market: Capitalism in Modern European Thought*. New York: Knoft.
Murray, C.A. 1994. *Underclass: The Crisis Deepens*. London: Institute of Economic Affairs Health and Welfare Unit.
Myrdal, G. 1957. *Economic Theory and Under-Developed Regions*. London: Duckworth.
Neumann, M. and Weigand, J. (eds). 2004. *The International Handbook of Competition*. Cheltenham: Edward Elgar.
Norris, K., Kelly, R. and Giles, M. 2005. *Economics of Australian Labour Markets*, French's Forest, NSW: Pearson, sixth edition.
Nye, J.S. 2004. *Soft Power: The Means to Success in World Politics*. New York: Public Affairs.
O'Hara, P.A. 2004a. 'Viability of national government policies in a global political economy', in O'Hara (2004b), pp.327–46.
O'Hara, P.A. (ed.). 2004b. *Global Political Economy and the Wealth of Nations: Performance, Institutions, Problems and Policies*. London: Routledge.
Oakley, A. 1983. *The Making of Marx's Critical Theory: A Bibliographical Analysis*. London: Routledge & Kegan Paul.
Oakley, A. 1984. *Marx's Critique of Political Economy. Intellectual Sources and Evolution. Volume I: 1844 to 1860*. London: Routledge & Kegan Paul.
Ohlin, B. 1933. *Interregional and International Trade*. Cambridge, MA: Harvard University Press.
Olson, M. 1965. *The Logic of Collective Action: Public Goods and the Theory of Groups*. Cambridge, MA: Harvard University Press.
Olson, M. 1982. *The Rise and Decline of Nations: Economic Growth, Stagflation, and Social Rigidities*. New Haven, CT: Yale University Press.
Olson, M. 2000. *Power and Prosperity: Outgrowing Communist and Capitalist Dictatorships*. New York: Basic Books.
Osborne, D. and Gaebler, T. 1992. *Reinventing Government: How the Entrepreneurial Spirit Is Transforming the Public Sector*. New York: Plume and Reading, MA: Addison Wesley.

Ostry, S. 1997. *The Post-Cold War Trading System: Who's On First?*. Chicago: University of Chicago Press.

Overbeek, H. (ed.). 1993. *Restructuring Hegemony in the Global Political Economy: The Rise of Transnational Neoliberalism in the 1980s*. London: Routledge.

Pain, N. and van Welsum, D. 2003. 'Financial liberalism, alliance capitalism and the changing structure of financial markets', in Dunning and Boyd (2003), pp.92–128.

Pakulski, J. and Waters, M. 1996. *The Death of Class*. Thousand Oaks: Sage.

Palley, T. 2006. 'The economics of outsourcing: how should policy respond?', Foreign Policy in Focus *Report*, 2 March, http://www.fpif.org/fpiftxt/3134 [accessed 10 March 2006].

Papandreou, A. 1972. *Paternalistic Capitalism*. Minneapolis: University of Minnesota Press.

Parkin, F. 1979. *Marxism and Class Theory: A Bourgeois Critique* . London: Tavistock.

Peetz, D. 2006. *Brave New Workplace: How Individual Contracts are Changing Our Jobs*. Crows Nest, NSW: Allen & Unwin.

Perelman, M. 1998. *Class Warfare in the Information Age*. New York: St. Martin's Press.

Perkin, H.J. 1989. *The Rise of Professional Society: England since 1880*. London: Routledge.

Perkin, H.J. 1996. *The Third Revolution. Professional Elites in the Modern World*. London: Routledge.

Perlman, S. 1928. *A Theory of the Labor Movement*. New York: Kelley, 1966.

Petzall, S., Abbott, K. and Timo, N. 2003. *Australian Industrial Relations in an Asian Context*. Melbourne: Eruditions Publishing, second edition.

Pierson, C. 1999. 'Marxism and the welfare state', in Gamble *et al.* (1999), pp.175–94.

Pierson, P. 1996. 'The new politics of the welfare state', *World Politics*, 48(2), January, pp.143–79.

Pigou, A.C. 1912. *Wealth and Welfare*. London: Macmillan.

Pigou, A.C. 1914. *Some Aspects of the Housing Problem* in *Lectures on Housing: The Warburton Lectures for 1914*. Manchester: The University Press.

Pigou, A.C. 1920. *The Economics of Welfare*. London: Macmillan.

Pigou, A.C. 1937. *Socialism Versus Capitalism*. London: Macmillan.

Pinker, S. 2002. *The Blank Slate: The Modern Denial of Human Nature*. New York: Viking Penguin.

Piore, M.J. and Sabel, C.F. 1984. *The Second Industrial Divide: Possibilities for Prosperity*. New York: Basic Books.

Piven, F.F. and Cloward, R. 1971. *Regulating the Poor: The Functions of Public Welfare*. New York: Pantheon Books.

Plotnick, R.D., Smolensky, E., Evenhouse, E. and Reilly, S. 2000. 'The twentieth-century record of inequality and poverty in the United States', in Engerman and Gallman (2000), pp.249–99.

Polanyi, K. 1944. *The Great Transformation*. Boston: Beacon Press.

Pollin, R. (ed.). 2000. *Capitalism, Socialism and Radical Political Economy: Essays in Honor Of Howard J. Sherman*. Cheltenham: Edward Elgar.

Pollin, R. 2003. *Contours of Descent: U.S. Economic Fractures and the Landscape of Global Austerity*. London: Verso.

Pollock, F. 1932. 'Die gegenwärtige lage des kapitalismus und die aussichten einer planwirtschaftliche neuordnung', *Zeitschrift für Sozialforschung* 1, pp.8–27.

Pollock, F. 1933. 'Bemerkungen zur wirtschaftskrise', *Zeitschrift für Sozialforschung* 2, pp.321–53.

Pollock, F. 1941. 'State capitalism: its possibilities and limitations', in A. Amato and E. Gebhardt (eds). *The Essential Frankfurt School Reader.* Oxford: Blackwell, 1978, pp.71–94.

Pontusson, J. 2005. *Inequality and Prosperity: Social Europe versus Liberal America.* Ithaca, NY: Cornell University Press.

Popper, K.R. 1957. *The Poverty of Historicism.* London: Routledge & Kegan Paul.

Porter, B.D. 1994. *War and the Rise of the State: The Military Foundations of Modern Politics.* New York: Free Press.

Porter, M. 1985. *Competitive Advantage: Creating and Sustaining Superior Performance.* New York: Free Press, 2004.

Prais, S.J. 1976. *The Evolution of Giant Firms in Britain: A Study of the Growth of Concentration in Manufacturing Industry in Britain, 1909–70.* Cambridge: Cambridge University Press.

Priewe, J. and Herr, H. 2005. *The Macroeconomics of Development and Poverty Reduction: Strategies Beyond the Washington Consensus.* Baden-Baden: Nomos.

Przeworski, A. 1985. *Capitalism and Social Democracy.* Cambridge: Cambridge University Press.

Przeworski, A. and Sprague J. 1987. *Paper Stones: A History of Electoral Socialism.* Chicago: Chicago University Press.

Quiggin, J. 2001. 'The fall and rise of the global economy: finance', in C. Sheil (ed.). *Globalisation: Australian Impacts.* Sydney: University of New South Wales Press, pp.19–34.

Rawls, J. 1971. *A Theory of Justice.* Cambridge, MA: Harvard University Press.

Readings, B. 1997. *The University in Ruins.* Cambridge, MA: Harvard University Press.

Reagan, P.D. 1999. *Designing a New America: The Origins of New Deal Planning, 1890–1943.* Amherst, MA: University of Massachusetts Press.

Richardson, G.B. 1960. *Information and Investment: A Study in the Working of the Competitive Economy.* Oxford: Oxford University Press.

Rickard, J.D. 1984. *H. B. Higgins: The Rebel as Judge.* London: Allen & Unwin.

Ritzer, G. 2004. *The McDonaldization of Society.* Thousand Oaks, CA: Pine Forge, new century edition.

Robinson, E.A.G. 1958. *The Structure of Competitive Industry,* revised edition. London: Nisbet.

Robinson, J. 1933. *The Economics of Imperfect Competition.* London: Macmillan, second edition, 1969.

Robinson, J. 1942. 'Industry and the state', *Political Quarterly* 13(4), October, pp.400–6.

Robinson, J. 1943a. *The Problem of Full Employment: An Outline for Study Circles.* London: Workers' Educational Association for Workers Educational Trade Union Committee.

Robinson, J. 1943b. 'Planning', *Fabian Quarterly* 36, January, pp.4–8.

Robinson, J. 1954. 'The impossibility of competition', in Chamberlin (1954), pp.245–54.

Rogowski, R. 1989. *Commerce and Coalitions: How Trade Affects Domestic Political Alignments.* Princeton: Princeton University Press.

Rose-Ackerman, S. 1999. *Corruption and Government: Causes, Consequences, and Reform.* Cambridge: Cambridge University Press.

Rosenberg, J. 1994. *The Empire of Civil Society: A Critique of the Realist Theory of International Relations*. London: Verso.
Rosenberg, J.P. 1996. 'Isaac Deutscher and the lost history of international relations', *New Left Review*, 215, January–February, First Series, pp.3–15.
Rosenberg, J.P. 2000. *The Follies of Globalisation Theory: Polemical Essays*. London, Verso.
Rosenberg, N. and Birdzell, Jr. L.E. 1986. *How the West Grew Rich: The Economic Transformation of the Industrial World*. New York: Basic Books.
Ross, A.M. 1958. 'Do we have a new industrial feudalism?', *American Economic Review* 48(5), December, pp.903–20.
Rothschild, K.W. 1981. 'Schumpeter and socialism', in H. Frisch (ed.). *Schumpeterian Economics*. New York: Praeger, pp.113–25.
Rubinstein, A. 1998. *Modeling Bounded Rationality*. Cambridge, MA: MIT Press.
Rugman, A.M. and Boyd, G. (eds). 2003. *Alliance Capitalism for the New American Economy*. Cheltenham: Edward Elgar.
Runciman, W.G. 2006. 'What happened to the labour party?', *London Review of Books* 28(12), 22 June, 2006, pp.17–21.
Russell, B. 1949. *Authority and the Individual*. London: Allen & Unwin.
Rutherford, M. 1980. 'Veblen on owners, managers, and the control of industry', *History of Political Economy* 12(3), Fall, pp.434–40.
Rutherford, M. 1981. 'Veblen on owners, managers, and the control of industry: a rejoinder', *History of Political Economy* 13(1), Spring, pp.156–8.
Rutherford, M. 1994. *Institutions in Economics: The Old and the New Institutionalism*. Cambridge: Cambridge University Press.
Sabel, C.F. and Zeitlin, J. 1997. 'Stories, strategies, structures: rethinking historical alternatives to mass production', in C.F. Sabel and T. Zeitlin (eds). *World of Possibilities: Flexibility and Mass Production in Western Industrialization*. Cambridge: Cambridge University Press, pp.1–33.
Sahlins, M. 1995. *How 'Natives' Think: About Captain Cook, For Example*. Chicago: University of Chicago Press.
Samuelson, P.A. 1948. 'International trade and the equalisation of factor prices', *Economic Journal* 58 (230), June, pp.163–84.
Samuelson, P.A. 1949. 'International factor price equalisation once again', *Economic Journal* 59 (234), June, pp.181–97.
Samuelson, P.A. 1957. 'Wages and interest. A modern dissection of Marxian economic models', *American Economic Review* 47(6), December, pp.884–912.
Samuelson, P.A. 1966a. 'Linear programming and economic theory', in Stiglitz (1966a), pp.493–504.
Samuelson, P.A. 1966b. 'Modern economic realities and individualism', in Stiglitz (1966b), pp.1407–18.
Samuelson, P.A. 1966c. 'The economic role of private activity', in Stiglitz (1966b), pp.1419–25.
Samuelson, P.A. 1966d. 'Full employment after the war', in Stiglitz (1966b), pp.1429–55.
Sassen, S. 1998. *Globalization and its Discontents: Essays on the New Mobility of People and Money*. New York: The New Press.
Sassoon, D. 1996. *One Hundred Years of Socialism: The West European Left in the Twentieth Century*. London: Fontana.
Sassoon, D. (ed.). 1997. *Looking Left: Socialism in Europe After the Cold War*. London: I.B. Tauris.

Sawyer, M. 2000. ' "Big business" (almost) twenty-five years on', in J. Toporowski (ed.). *Political Economy and the New Capitalism: Essays in Honour of Sam Aaronovitch*. London: Routledge, pp.65–75.

Sayer, D. 1991. *Capitalism and Modernity: An Excursus on Marx and Weber*. London: Routledge.

Schefold, B. 1980. 'The *General Theory* for a totalitarian state? A note on Keynes's preface to the German edition of 1936', *Cambridge Journal of Economics* 4(2), June, pp.175–6.

Schelling, T. 1978. *Micromotives and Macrobehavior*. New York: Norton.

Schelling, T.C. 2006. *Strategies of Commitment and Other Essays*. Cambridge, MA: Harvard University Press.

Schlosser, E. 2002. *Fast Food Nation: The Dark Side of the All-American Meal*. New York: Perennial.

Schnabel, C. 2005. 'Trade unions in Germany: on the road to perdition?', in Fernie and Metcalf (2005), pp.213–30.

Schneider, M.P. 2004. *The Distribution of Wealth*. Cheltenham: Edward Elgar.

Schumpeter, J.A. 1928. 'The instability of capitalism', *Economic Journal* 38(151), September, pp.361–86.

Schumpeter, J.A. 1934. *The Theory of Economic Development: An Inquiry into Profits, Capital, Credit, Interest, and the Business Cycle*. Oxford: Oxford University Press.

Schumpeter, J.A. 1942. *Capitalism, Socialism and Democracy*. London: Allen & Unwin, 1970.

Scott, J. 1997. *Corporate Business and Capitalist Classes*. Oxford: Oxford University Press.

Screpani, E. 2001. *The Fundamental Institutions of Capitalism*. London: Routledge.

Scruton, R. 1990. *The Philosopher on Dover Beach*. New York: St. Martin's Press.

Scruton, R. (ed.). 1991. *Conservative Texts*. London: Macmillan.

Seager, R. 2006. 'The source of Europe's mild climate', *American Scientist* 94, July–August, pp.334–41.

Searle, G.R. 1999. *Morality and the Market in Victorian Britain*. Oxford: Oxford University Press.

Searle, J. 1995. *The Construction of Social Reality*. Harmondsworth: Penguin.

Semenov, Y.I. 1980. 'The theory of socio-economic formations and world history', in Gellner (1980b), pp.29–58.

Sen, G. 1995. *The Military Origins of Industrialisation and International Trade Rivalry*. London: Pinter.

Sent, E.-M. and Mirowski, P. (eds). 2002. *Science Bought and Sold*. Chicago: University of Chicago Press.

Shapiro, C. and Varian, H.R. 1999. *Information Rules: A Strategic Guide to the Network Economy*. Cambridge, MA: Harvard Business School Press.

Sherman, H.J. 1991. *The Business Cycle: Growth and Crisis Under Capitalism*. Princeton: Princeton University Press.

Shultz, G.P. and Aliber, R.Z. (eds). 1966. *Guidelines, Informal Controls and the Marketplace*. Chicago: Chicago University Press.

Siebert, H. 2005. *The German Economy. Beyond the Social Market*. Princeton: Princeton University Press.

Simon, H. 1951. 'A formal theory of the employment relationship', *Econometrica* 19(3), July, pp.293–305.

Simon, H.A. 1956. *Models of Man: Social and Rational. Mathematical Essays on Rational Human Behavior in a Social Setting*. New York: Wiley.

Singer, P.W. 2003. *Corporate Warriors: The Rise of the Privatized Military Industry*. Ithaca: Cornell University Press.

Skidelsky, R. 1977a. 'Introduction', in Skidelsky (1977b), pp.vii–xii.

Skidelsky, R. 1977b. (ed.). *The End of the Keynesian Era: Essays on the Disintegration of the Keynesian Political Economy*. London: Macmillan.

Skidelsky, R. 2000. *John Maynard Keynes: Fighting for Britain 1937–1946*. Basingstoke: Palgrave Macmillan.

Skocpol, T. 1979. *States and Social Revolutions: A Comparative Analysis of France, Russia, and China*. Cambridge: Cambridge University Press.

Sloan, E.C. 2002. *The Revolution in Military Affairs: Implications for Canada and NATO*. Montreal: McGill–Queens University Press.

Smith, A. 1776. *An Inquiry into the Nature and Causes of the Wealth of Nations*. London: Methuen, 1904.

Smithin, J.N. 1990. *Macroeconomics after Thatcher and Reagan: The Conservative Policy Revolution in Retrospect*. Aldershot: Edward Elgar.

Snowdon, B. and Vane, H.R. 2005. *Modern Macroeconomics: Its Origins, Development and Current State*. Cheltenham: Edward Elgar.

Södersten, B. (ed.). 2004. *Globalization and the Welfare State*. Basingstoke: Palgrave Macmillan.

Solow, R.M. 1997. 'Is there a core of usable macroeconomic theory we should all believe in?', *American Economic Review* 87(2), May, Papers and Proceedings, pp.230–2.

Sørensen, G. 2001. 'War and state-making. Why doesn't it work in the third world?', *Security Dialogue* 32(3), September, pp.341–54.

Speth, J.G. 2004. *Red Sky at Morning: America and the Crisis of the Global Environment*. New Haven: Yale University Press.

Spong, K. 2003. 'The US financial sector: regulatory issues', in Rugman and Boyd (2003), pp.82–103.

Spulber, N. 1995. *The American Economy: The Struggle for Supremacy in the 21st Century*. Cambridge: Cambridge University Press.

Sraffa, P. 1926. 'The laws of returns under competitive conditions', *Economic Journal* 36(144), December, pp.535–50.

State Services Commission. 2002. *New Zealand's State Sector Reform: A Decade of Change*, http://www.ssc.govt.nz/decade-of-change [accessed 21 July 2004].

Steedman, I. (ed.). 1995. *Socialism and Marginalism in Economics, 1870–1930*. London: Routledge.

Steindl, J. 1945. *Small and Big Business: Economic Problems of the Size of Firms*. Oxford: Blackwell.

Stern, N. 2006. 'What is the economics of climate change?', *World Economics* 7(2), April–June, pp.1–10, 153–7.

Stevenson, D. 2004. *Cataclysm: The First World War as Political Tragedy*. New York: Basic Books.

Stevenson, L. (ed.). 2000. *The Study of Human Nature: Readings*. Oxford: Oxford University Press.

Stevenson, L. and Haberman D.L. 1998. *Ten Theories of Human Nature*. Oxford: Oxford University Press.

Stigler, G.J. 1951. 'The division of labour is limited by the extent of the market', *Journal of Political Economy* 59(3), June, pp.185–93.

Stiglitz, J.E. (ed.). 1966a. *The Collected Scientific Papers of Paul A. Samuelson, Volume I*. Cambridge, MA: MIT Press.
Stiglitz, J.E. (ed.). 1966b. *The Collected Scientific Papers of Paul A. Samuelson, Volume II*. Cambridge, MA: MIT Press.
Stiglitz, J.E. 1989. *The Economic Role of the State*. Oxford: Basil Blackwell.
Stiglitz, J.E. 1994. *Whither Socialism*. Cambridge, MA: MIT Press.
Stolper, W. and Samuelson, P.A. 1941. 'Protection and real wages', *Review of Economic Studies* 9, November, pp.58–73.
Stone, K. 1974. 'The origins of job structures in the steel industry', *Review of Radical Political Economics* 6(2), Summer, pp.113–73.
Streeck, W. and Yamamura, K. (eds). 2001. *The Origins of Nonliberal Capitalism: Germany, and Japan in Comparison*. Ithaca, NY: Cornell University Press.
Stubbs, R. 2005. *Rethinking Asia's Economic Miracle: The Political Economy of War, Prosperity and Crisis*. Basingstoke: Palgrave Macmillan.
Suleiman, E. 2003. *Dismantling Democratic States*. Princeton: Princeton University Press.
Sunstein, C. 2003. *Why Societies Need Dissent*. Cambridge, MA: Harvard University Press.
Supple, B.E. (ed.). 1992. *The Rise of Big Business*. Aldershot: Edward Elgar.
Swedberg, R. 1991. *Schumpeter: A Biography*. Princeton: Princeton University Press.
Sweezy, P.M. 1939. 'Demand under conditions of oligopoly', *Journal of Political Economy* 47(3), August, pp.568–73.
Sweezy, P.M. 1968. 'Karl Marx and the industrial revolution', in R.V. Eagly (ed.). *Events, Ideology, and Economic Theory: The Determinants of Progress in the Development Economic Analysis*. Detroit: Wayne State University Press, pp.107–19, 124–6.
Takács, K. 2002. *Social Networks and Intergroup Conflict*. Groningen: Interuniversity Center for Social Science Theory and Methodology.
Tanzi, V. and Schuknecht, L. 2000. *Public Spending in the 20th Century: A Global Perspective*. Cambridge: Cambridge University Press.
Tawney, R.H. 1926. *Religion and the Rise of Capitalism: A Historical Study*. New York: Harcourt, Brace & Company.
Taylor, C. 1966. 'Marxism and empiricism', in B. Williams and A. Montefiore (eds). *British Analytical Philosophy*. New York: Humanities Press, pp.227–46.
Taylor, F.M. 1929. 'The guidance of production in a socialist state', *American Economic Review* 19(1), March, pp.1–8.
Temin, P. 2000. 'The great depression', in Engerman and Gallmann (2000), pp.301–28.
Tetlock, P., Husbands, J.L. and Stern, P.C. (eds). 1989. *Behavior, Society and Nuclear War, Volume I*. Oxford: Oxford University Press.
Thatcher, M. 2002. *Statecraft: Strategies for a Changing World*. New York: Harper Collins.
Therborn, G. 2001. 'Into the 21st century', *New Left Review* 10, July–August, Second Series, pp.87–110.
Thompson, G.F. 2003. *Between Hierarchies and Markets: The Logic and Limits of Network Forms of Organization*. Oxford: Oxford University Press.
Thurow, L.C. 1992. *Head to Head: The Coming Economic Battle Among Japan, Europe and America*. New York: Morrow.

Tilly, C. 1984. *Big Structures, Large Processes, Huge Comparisons*. New York: Russell Sage Foundation.
Tilly, C. 1985. 'War making and state making as organised crime', in Evans, Rueschemeyer, and Skocpol (1985), pp.169–91.
Tilly, C. 1990. *Coercion, Capital and European States, AD 990–1990*. Oxford: Blackwell.
Tilly, C. 1993. *European Revolutions, 1492–1992*. Oxford: Blackwell.
Tirole, J. 2006. *The Theory of Corporate Finance*. Princeton: Princeton University Press.
Tomlins, C.L. 2000. 'Labor law', in Engerman and Gallman (2000), pp.625–91.
Torrance, J. 1995. *Karl Marx's Theory of Ideas*. Cambridge: Cambridge University Press.
Tressall, R. 1940. *The Ragged Trousered Philanthropists*. Harmondsworth: Penguin.
Triffin, R. 1960. *Gold and the Dollar Crisis: The Future of Convertibility*. New Haven, CT: Yale University Press.
Trigg, R. 1999. *Ideas of Human Nature: An Historical Introduction*. Oxford: Blackwell.
Tudor, H. and Tudor, J.M. (eds). 1988. *Marxism and Social Democracy: The Revisionist Debate 1896–1898*. Cambridge: Cambridge University Press.
Varian, H.R. 2006. *Intermediate Microeconomics: A Modern Approach*. New York: Norton, seventh edition.
Vatter, H.G. 1985. *The U.S. Economy in World War II*. New York: Columbia University Press.
Veblen, T. 1904. *The Theory of Business Enterprise*. New Brunswick, NJ: Transactions Press, 1978.
Veblen, T. 1921. *The Engineers and the Price System*. New York: Kelley, 1965.
Veblen, T. 1923. *Absentee Ownership and Business Enterprise in Recent Times: The Case of America*. New York: Kelley, 1964.
Vietor, R.H.K. 2000. 'Government regulation of business', in Engerman and Gallman (2000), pp.969–1012.
Vogel, S.K. 1996. *Freer Markets, More Rules: Regulatory Reform in Advanced Industrial Countries*. Ithaca, NY: Cornell University Press.
Wacquant, L. 1999. 'Die Armen bekãmpfen', *Le Monde Diplomatique*, April, http://www.taz.de/tpl/1999/04/16.nf/mondeText?Tname=a0008&idx=0 [accessed 21 April 1999].
Wade, R.H. 2003. 'The invisible hand of the American empire', *Ethics and International Affairs* 17(2), September (Fall 2003), pp.77–88.
Wallerstein, I. 2003. *The Decline of American Power: The US in a Chaotic World*. New York: The New Press.
Walton, G.M. and Rockoff, H. 2005. *History of the American Economy*. Mason, OH: Thomson, tenth edition.
Warsh D. 2006. *Knowledge and the Wealth of Nations: A Story of Economic Discovery*. New York: Norton.
Washburn, J. 2004. *University Inc.: The Corporate Corruption of Higher Education*. New York: Basic Books.
Webb, S. 1916. *Towards Social Democracy? A Study of Social Evolution During the Past Three-Quarters of a Century*. London: Fabian Society.
Webb, S. and B. 1894. *The History of Trade Unionism*. London: Longmans.
Webb, S. and B. 1897. *Industrial Democracy*. London: Longmans, Green.

Weber, M. 1946. *From Max Weber*, H. Gerth and C. Wright Mills (eds). London: Routledge.
Weber, M. 1978. *Economy and Society*. Berkeley: University of California Press.
Weber, M. 1981. *General Economic History*. New Brunswick, NJ: Transaction Publishers.
Webster, E. 1999. *The Economics of Intangible Investment*. Cheltenham: Edward Elgar.
Wedderburn, K.W. 1965. *The Worker and the Law*. Harmondsworth: Penguin.
Weiss L. and Hobson, J.M. 1995. *States and Economic Development*. Cambridge: Polity Press.
Weiss, L., Thurborn, E. and Mathews, J. 2004. *How to Kill a Country: Australia's Devastating Trade Deal with the United States*. Sydney: Allen & Unwin.
Wetherly, P. 2005. *Marxism and the State: An Analytical Approach*. London: Palgrave Macmillan.
Whitaker, J.W. 2003. 'Alfred Marshall's *Principles of Economics* and *Industry and Trade*: two books or one? Marshall and the joint stock company', in R. Arena and M. Quéré (eds). *The Economics of Alfred Marshall: Revisiting Marshall's Legacy*. Basingstoke: Palgrave Macmillan, pp.137–57.
White, E.N. 2000. 'Banking and finance in the twentieth century', in Engerman and Gallman (2000), pp.743–802.
Wicksell, K. 1934. *Lectures on Political Economy, Volume I*. London: Routledge & Kegan Paul.
Wigand, R.T. and Benjamin, R.I. 1995 'Electronic commerce: effects on electronic markets', *Journal of Computer-Mediated Communication* 1(3), December, http://www.ascusc.org/jcmc/vol11/issue3/wigand.html [accessed 19 August 2004].
Wilensky, H.L. 2002. *Rich Democracies: Political Economy, Public Policy and Performance*. Berkeley: University of California Press.
Williamson, J. and Lindert, P. 1981. *American Inequality: A Macroeconomic History*. New York: Academic Press.
Williamson, O.E. 1964. *The Economics of Discretionary Behavior: Managerial Objectives in a Theory of the Firm*. Englewood Cliffs, NJ: Prentice-Hall.
Williamson, O.E. 1970. *Corporate Control and Business Behavior: An Inquiry into the Effects of Organizational Form on Enterprise Behavior*. Englewood Cliffs, NJ: Prentice-Hall.
Williamson, O.E. 1985. *The Economic Institutions of Capitalism*. New York: The Free Press.
Williamson, O.E. 1996. *The Mechanisms of Governance*. Oxford: Oxford University Press.
Winch, P. 1958. *The Idea of a Social Science and Its Relation to Philosophy*. London: Routledge & Kegan Paul.
Winkler, J.T. 1977. 'The coming corporatism', in Skidelsky (1977b), pp.78–87.
Winter, S.J. and Taylor, S.L. 2001. 'The role of information technology in the transformation of work: a comparison of post-industrial, industrial, and proto-industrial organization', in J. Yates and J.V. Maanen (eds). *Information Technology and Organizational Transformation. History, Rhetoric, and Practice*. Thousand Oaks, CA: Sage, pp.7–34.
Wolf, M. 2004. *Why Globalisation Works*. New Haven, CT: Yale University Press.
Wood, A. 1994. *North-South Trade, Employment and Inequality: Changing Fortunes in a Skill-Driven World*. Oxford: Clarendon Press.

Woodall, P. 2006. 'The new titans: a survey of the world economy', *Economist*, 16 September 2006.
Wootton, B. 1934. *Plan Or No Plan*. London: Gollancz.
Wootton, B. 1938. *Lament for Economics*. London: Allen & Unwin.
Wootton, B. 1945. *Freedom Under Planning*. London: Allen & Unwin.
Yamamura, K. and Streeck, W. 2003. (eds). *The End of Diversity: Prospects for German and Japanese Capitalism*. Ithaca, NY: Cornell University Press.

Name Index

Subject Index